ACCA

PAPER F7

FINANCIAL REPORTING
(UNITED KINGDOM)

In this June 2007 new edition

- We discuss the **best strategies** for revising and taking your ACCA exams

- We show you how to be well prepared for the **December 2007 exam**

- We give you **lots of great guidance** on tackling questions

- We show you how you can **build your own exams**

- We provide you with **three** mock exams including the **Pilot paper**

- We provide the **ACCA examiner's answers** as well as our own to key exam questions and the Pilot Paper as an additional revision aid

Our **i-Pass** product also supports this paper.

PRACTICE & REVISION KIT

FOR EXAMS IN DECEMBER 2007

D1438358

BPP LEARNING MEDIA

First edition June 2007

ISBN 9780 7517 3360 0

British Library Cataloguing-in-Publication Data
A catalogue record for this book
is available from the British Library

Published by

BPP Learning Media Ltd
Aldine House, Aldine Place
London W12 8AW

www.bpp.com/learningmedia

Printed in Great Britain by
Ashford Colour Press Ltd
Unit 600
Fareham Reach, Fareham Road
Gosport
PO13 0FW

Your learning materials, published by BPP Learning
Media Ltd, are printed on paper sourced from
sustainable, managed forests.

We are grateful to the Association of Chartered
Certified Accountants for permission to reproduce past
examination questions. The answers to past
examination questions have been prepared by BPP
Learning Media Ltd.

Contents

Review form & free prize draw

Question index

The headings in this checklist/index indicate the topics of questions. Most questions are marked 2.5, which means they were examination questions under the previous Financial Reporting syllabus. Some have since been amended or split into shorter questions on different topics.

Preparation questions, listed in italics, provide you with a firm foundation for attempts at exam-standard questions.

Examiners answers. For any 2006 questions (6/06 or 12/06) the examiners answers can be found at the end of this kit.

BPP
LEARNING MEDIA

Mock exam 1

Mock exam 2

Mock exam 3 (Pilot paper)

Planning your question practice

Our guidance from page 23 shows you how to organise your question practice, either by attempting questions from each syllabus area or **by building your own exams** – tackling questions as a series of practice exams.

Using your BPP Practice and Revision Kit

Tackling revision and the exam

You can significantly improve your chances of passing by tackling revision and the exam in the right ways. Our advice is based on recent feedback from ACCA examiners.

- We look at the dos and don'ts of revising for, and taking, ACCA exams

- We focus on Paper F7; we discuss revising the syllabus, what to do (and what not to do) in the exam, how to approach different types of question and ways of obtaining easy marks

Selecting questions

We provide signposts to help you plan your revision.

- A full **question index**

- **BPP's question plan** highlighting the most important questions and explaining why you should attempt them

- **Build your own exams**, showing how you can practise questions in a series of exams

Making the most of question practice

At BPP we realise that you need more than just questions and model answers to get the most from your question practice.

- Our **Top tips** provide essential advice on tackling questions, presenting answers and the key points that answers need to include

- We show you how you can pick up **Easy marks** on questions, as we know that picking up all readily available marks often can make the difference between passing and failing

- We summarise **Examiner's comments** to show you how students who sat the exam coped with the questions

- We include ACCA's **marking guides** to show you what the examiner rewards

- We refer to the **BPP 2007 Study Text** for detailed coverage of the topics covered in each question

- A number of questions include **Analysis** and **Helping hands** attached to show you how to approach them if you are struggling

- In a bank at the end of this Kit we include the **examiner's answers** to the Pilot paper and other questions. Used in conjunction with our answers they provide an indication of all possible points that could be made, issues that could be covered and approaches to adopt.

Attempting mock exams

There are three mock exams that provide practice at coping with the pressures of the exam day. We strongly recommend that you attempt them under exam conditions. **Mock exams 1 and 2** reflect the question styles and syllabus coverage of the exam; **Mock exam 3** is the Pilot paper. To help you get the most out of doing these exams, we not only provide help with each answer, but also guidance on how you should have approached the whole exam.

Passing ACCA exams

Revising and taking ACCA exams

To maximise your chances of passing your ACCA exams, you must make best use of your time, both before the exam during your revision, and when you are actually doing the exam.

- Making the most of your revision time can make a big, big difference to how well-prepared you are for the exam

- Time management is a core skill in the exam hall; all the work you've done can be wasted if you don't make the most of the three hours you have to attempt the exam

In this section we simply show you what to do and what not to do during your revision, and how to increase and decrease your prospects of passing your exams when you take them. Our advice is grounded in feedback we've had from ACCA examiners. You may be surprised to know that much examiner advice is the same whatever the exam, and the reasons why many students fail don't vary much between subjects and exam levels. So if you follow the advice we give you over the next few pages, you will **significantly** enhance your chances of passing **all** your ACCA exams.

How to revise

☑ Plan your revision

At the start of your revision period, you should draw up a **timetable** to plan how long you will spend on each subject and how you will revise each area. You need to consider the total time you have available and also the time that will be required to revise for other exams you're taking.

☑ Practise Practise Practise

The **more exam-standard questions** you do, the **more likely you are to pass** the exam. Practising full questions will mean that you'll get used to the time pressure of the exam. When the time is up, you should note where you've got to and then try to complete the question, giving yourself practice at everything the question tests.

☑ Revise enough

Make sure that your revision covers the breadth of the syllabus, as in most papers most topics could be examined in a compulsory question. However it is true that some topics are **key** – they often appear in compulsory questions or are a particular interest of the examiner – and you need to spend sufficient time revising these. Make sure you also know the **basics** – the fundamental calculations, proformas and report layouts.

☑ Deal with your difficulties

Difficult areas are topics you find dull and pointless, or subjects that you found problematic when you were studying them. You mustn't become negative about these topics; instead you should build up your knowledge by reading the **Passcards** and using the **Quick quiz** questions in the Study Text to test yourself. When practising questions in the Kit, go back to the Text if you're struggling.

☑ Learn from your mistakes

Having completed a question you must try to look at your answer critically. Always read the **Top tips guidance** in the answers; it's there to help you. Look at **Easy marks** to see how you could have quickly gained credit on the questions that you've done. As you go through the Kit, it's worth noting any traps you've fallen into, and key points in the **Top tips** or **Examiner's comments** sections, and referring to these notes in the days before the exam. Aim to learn at least one new point from each question you attempt, a technical point perhaps or a point on style or approach.

☑ Read the examiners' guidance

We refer throughout this Kit to **Examiner's comments**; these are available on ACCA's website. As well as highlighting weaknesses, examiners' reports as often provide clues to future questions, as many examiners will quickly test again areas where problems have arisen. ACCA's website also contains articles by examiners which you **must** read, as they may form the basis of questions on any paper after they've been published.

Read through the examiner's answers to key exam questions and the Pilot paper included at the back of the Kit. In general these are far longer and more comprehensive than any answer you could hope to produce in the exam, but used in conjunction with our more realistic solutions, they provide a useful revision tool, covering all possible points and approaches.

☑ Complete all three mock exams

You should attempt the **Mock exams** at the end of the Kit under **strict exam conditions**, to gain experience of selecting questions, managing your time and producing answers.

How NOT to revise

☒ Revise selectively

Examiners are well aware that some students try to forecast the contents of exams, and only revise those areas that they think will be examined. Examiners try to prevent this by doing the unexpected, for example setting the same topic in successive sittings or setting topics in compulsory questions that have previously only been examined in optional questions.

☒ Spend all the revision period reading

You cannot pass the exam just by learning the contents of Passcards, Course Notes or Study Texts. You have to develop your **application skills** by practising questions.

☒ Audit the answers

This means reading the answers and guidance without having attempted the questions. Auditing the answers gives you **false reassurance** that you would have tackled the questions in the best way and made the points that our answers do. The feedback we give in our answers will mean more to you if you've attempted the questions and thought through the issues.

☒ Practise some types of question, but not others

Although you may find the numerical parts of certain papers challenging, you shouldn't just practise calculations. These papers will also contain written elements, and you therefore need to spend time practising written question parts.

☒ Get bogged down

Don't spend a lot of time worrying about all the minute detail of certain topic areas, and leave yourself insufficient time to cover the rest of the syllabus. Remember that a key skill in the exam is the ability to **concentrate on what's important** and this applies to your revision as well.

☒ Overdo studying

Studying for too long without interruption will mean your studying becomes less effective. A five minute break each hour will help. You should also make sure that you are leading a **healthy lifestyle** (proper meals, good sleep and some times when you're not studying).

How to PASS your exams

☑ Prepare for the day

Make sure you set at least one alarm (or get an alarm call), and allow plenty of time to get to the exam hall. You should have your route planned in advance and should listen on the radio for potential travel problems. You should check the night before to see that you have pens, pencils, erasers, watch, calculator with spare batteries, also exam documentation and evidence of identity.

☑ Select the right questions

You should select the optional questions you feel you can answer **best**, basing your selection on the topics covered, the requirements of the question, how easy it will be to apply the requirements and the availability of easy marks.

☑ Plan your three hours

You need to make sure that you will be answering the correct number of questions, and that you spend the right length of time on each question – this will be determined by the number of marks available. Each mark carries with it a **time allocation** of **1.8 minutes**. A 25 mark question therefore should be selected, completed and checked in 45 minutes. With some papers, it's better to do certain types of question first or last.

☑ Read the questions carefully

To score well, you must follow the requirements of the question, understanding what aspects of the subject area are being covered, and the tasks you will have to carry out. The requirements will also determine what information and examples you should provide. Reading the question scenarios carefully will help you decide what **issues** to discuss, **techniques** to use, **information** and **examples** to include and how to **organise** your answer.

☑ Plan your answers

Five minutes of planning plus twenty-five minutes of writing is certain to earn you more marks than thirty minutes of writing. Consider when you're planning how your answer should be **structured,** what the **format** should be and **how long** each part should take.

Confirm before you start writing that your plan makes **sense,** covers **all relevant points** and does not include **irrelevant material.**

☑ Show evidence of judgement

Remember that examiners aren't just looking for a display of knowledge; they want to see how well you can **apply** the knowledge you have. Evidence of application and judgement will include writing answers that only contain **relevant** material, using the material in scenarios to **support** what you say, **criticising** the **limitations** and **assumptions** of the techniques you use and making **reasonable recommendations** that follow from your discussion.

☑ Stay until the end of the exam

Use any spare time to **check and recheck** your script. This includes checking you have filled out the candidate details correctly, you have labelled question parts and workings clearly, you have used headers and underlining effectively and spelling, grammar and arithmetic are correct.

How to FAIL your exams

☒ Don't do enough questions

If you don't attempt sufficient questions on the paper, you are making it harder for yourself to pass the questions that you do attempt. If for example you don't do a 20 mark question, then you will have to score 50 marks out of 80 marks on the rest of the paper, and therefore have to obtain 63% of the marks on the questions you do attempt. Failing to attempt all of the paper is symptomatic of poor time management or poor question selection.

☒ Include irrelevant material

Markers are given detailed mark guides and will not give credit for irrelevant content. Therefore you should **NOT** braindump all you know about a broad subject area; the markers will only give credit for what is **relevant**, and you will also be showing that you lack the ability to **judge what's important.**

☒ Fail to use the details in the scenario

General answers or reproductions of old answers that don't refer to what is in the scenario in **this** question won't score enough marks to pass.

☒ Copy out the scenario details

Examiners see **selective** use of the right information as a key skill. If you copy out chunks of the scenario which aren't relevant to the question, or don't use the information to support your own judgements, you won't achieve good marks.

☒ Don't do what the question asks

Failing to provide all the examiner asks for will limit the marks you score. You will also decrease your chances by not providing an answer with enough **depth** – producing a single line bullet point list when the examiner asks for a discussion.

☒ Present your work poorly

Markers will only be able to give you credit if they can read your writing. There are also plenty of other things that will make it more difficult for markers to reward you. Examples include:

- Not using black or blue ink
- Not showing clearly which question you're attempting
- Scattering question parts from the same question throughout your answer booklet
- Not showing clearly workings or the results of your calculations

Paragraphs that are too long or which lack headers also won't help markers and hence won't help you.

Using your BPP products

This Kit gives you the question practice and guidance you need in the exam. Our other products can also help you pass:

- **Learning to Learn Accountancy** gives further valuable advice on revision

- **Passcards** provide you with clear topic summaries and exam tips

- **Success CDs** help you revise on the move

- **i-Pass CDs** offer tests of knowledge against the clock

- **Learn Online** is an e-learning resource delivered via the Internet, offering comprehensive tutor support and featuring areas such as study, practice, email service, revision and useful resources

You can purchase these products by visiting www.bpp.com/mybpp.

Visit our website www.bpp.com/acca/learnonline to sample aspects of Learn Online free of charge. Learn Online is hosted by BPP Professional Education.

Passing F7

Revising F7

F7 is a demanding and time-pressured paper. However, you can pass by learning the basics really well and then keeping your head and producing sensible, readable answers. This does not mean that you only revise certain topics. The examiner warns against 'question spotting' and he will produce questions which cover a wide range of the syllabus. You are very unlikely to pass this paper on three questions.

Topics to revise

What we do know about F7 is that there will be a compulsory consolidation question. This can be a balance sheet or profit and loss account or both, and it will probably include an associate, so be prepared for all of this. Therefore you must revise all the consolidation workings, and you must know how to account for an associate.

Question 2 will be a single company accounts preparation question. This allows the examiner to bring in more complex issues that he would not test in the consolidation question. Make sure you can deal with finance leases, deferred tax, calculating finance costs using the effective interest rate, prior period adjustments, discontinued operations and construction contracts.

Question 3 will be on cash flow statements or interpretation of accounts. You have studied both of these at 1.1, so make sure you can do them well. Other recent questions have involved fixed assets and impairment, intangible assets, EPS, provisions and regulatory issues. These are all likely topics for questions 4 and 5.

There will be a certain amount of discussion in some of the questions, so be prepared to write about financial reporting topics, such as the *Statement* or specific accounting standards.

Question practice

This is the most important thing to do if you want to get through. All of the most up- to-date exam questions from the previous syllabus are in this kit. Practice doing them under timed conditions, then go through the answers and go back to the study text for any topic you are really having trouble with. Come back to a question week later and try it again – you will be surprised at how much better you are getting. Be very ruthless with yourself at this stage – you have to do the question in the time, without looking at the answer. This will really sharpen your wits and make the exam experience less worrying. Just keep doing this and you will get better at doing questions and you will really find out what you know and what you don't know.

Passing the F7 exam

If you have honestly done your revision then you can pass this exam. What you must do is remain calm and tackle it in a professional manner. The examiner stresses a number of points which you should bear in mind.

- You must read the question properly. Students often fail to read the question properly and miss some of the information. Time spent reading the question a second time would be time well spent. Make yourself do this, don't just rush into it in a panic.

- Workings must be clear and cross-referenced. If the marker can read and understand your workings they can give you credit for using the right method, even if your answer is wrong. If your answer is wrong and there are no workings, or they are illegible and incomprehensible, you will get no marks for that part of the question.

- Stick to the timings and answer all questions. Do not spend too long on one question at the expense of others. The number of extra marks you will gain on that question will be minimal, and you could have at least obtained the easy marks on the next question.

- Do not neglect the short parts of the question. If you get a 20-mark consolidation with a 5-mark discussion topic at the end, leave time for that last part. You can't afford to throw away 5 marks.

- Make sure you get the easy marks. If an accounts preparation question contains something that you are unable to do, just ignore it and do the rest. You will probably only lose a few marks and if you start trying to puzzle it out you might waste a lot of minutes.

- Answer the question. In a discussion-type question you may be tempted to just write down everything you know about the topic. This will do you no good. The marking parameters for these questions are quite precise. You will only get marks for making points that answer the question exactly as it has been set. So don't waste your time waffling – you could be scoring marks somewhere else.

Gaining the easy marks

The first point to make is that you do not get any marks for just writing down the formats for a financial statement. But, once you have put the formats down, you are then in a position to start filling in the numbers and getting the easy marks. Also, correct formats will give you a guide so that you don't miss things. For instance, it's easy to forget about the minority interest in a group profit and loss account. So that's a good place to start.

Having put down the formats, then go through the workings and slot in the figures. Make sure you get in all the ones you can do easily. Complicated parts are well worth doing if you are able to do them – there will be marks for those. Complicated parts which you don't know how to do are best left alone.

If you have an interpretation question, you will not get many marks for just producing lots of ratios or restating information you have already been given in the question. You have to be able to evaluate the information and see what judgements can be made. So go through the information critically and see which ratios are actually relevant. Then calculate them and say something sensible about them.

Exam information

Format of the exam

All questions are compulsory.

	Number of marks
Questions 1-3; 25 marks each	75
Question 4	15
Question 5	10
	100

Time allowed: 3 hours

Additional information

The Study Guide provides more detailed guidance on the syllabus.

Pilot paper

		Marks
1	Consolidated balance sheet including associate	25
2	Single company accounts preparation question	25
3	Performance appraisal including calculation of ratios	25
4	Discursive question on qualitative characteristics of financial information including short scenario	15
5	Construction contract	10
		100

Useful websites

The websites below provide additional sources of information of relevance to your studies for *Financial Reporting.*

- www.ft.com

    This website provides information about current international business. You can search for information and articles on specific industry groups as well as individual companies.

- www.bpp.com

    Our website provides information about BPP products and services, with a link to the ACCA website.

- www.accaglobal.com

    ACCA's website. Includes student section.

Planning your question practice

Planning your question practice

We have already stressed that question practice should be right at the centre of your revision. Whilst you will spend some time looking at your notes and Paper F7 Passcards, you should spend the majority of your revision time practising questions.

We recommend two ways in which you can practise questions.

- Use **BPP's question plan** to work systematically through the syllabus and attempt key and other questions on a section-by-section basis

- **Build your own exams** – attempt questions as a series of practice exams

These ways are suggestions and simply following them is no guarantee of success. You or your college may prefer an alternative but equally valid approach.

BPP's question plan

The BPP plan below requires you to devote a **minimum of 45 hours** to revision of Paper F7. Any time you can spend over and above this should only increase your chances of success.

Step 1   **Review your notes** and the chapter summaries in the Paper F7 **Passcards** for each section of the syllabus.

Step 2   **Answer the key questions** for that section. These questions have boxes round the question number in the table below and you should answer them in full. Even if you are short of time you must attempt these questions if you want to pass the exam. You should complete your answers without referring to our solutions.

Step 3   **Attempt the other questions** in that section.

Step 4   Attempt **Mock exams 1, 2 and 3** under strict exam conditions.

Syllabus section	2007 Passcards chapters	Questions in this Kit	Comments	Done ☑
The conceptual framework	1	1, 2	Peterlee is a straightforward question on the *Statement* and Derringdo gets you to apply the *Statement* to the issue of revenue recognition.	☐
The regulatory framework	2	3	This question covers a lot of material and is good revision.	☐
Presentation of published financial statements	3	4	All of these questions are good. Do as many as you can. Winger is a good all-round example.	☐
Fixed assets	4	10	Broadoak is a full question on FRS 15, so make sure you do it. The other questions reflect what you may see for a 10 or 15-mark question.	☐
Intangible assets	5	15	Dexterity is a 25-mark on goodwill and intangible assets, so it covers a lot of ground.	
Impairment of assets	6	17	Wilderness is an excellent question on impairment. See if you can do it in the time.	☐
Reporting financial performance	7	19, 23	Research Ltd is a good preparation question and Partway is a recent question on discontinued operations.	☐
Introduction to groups	8	24, 25	Question 24 is a good preparation question on the basics. Question 25 looks at the effect of related parties on group accounts. This is the context within which the examiner will examine related parties.	☐
The consolidated balance sheet	9	27, 28	Hample is a straightforward consolidated balance sheet. Highveldt does not require the whole balance sheet, but gets you to produce the key workings.	☐
The consolidated profit and loss account	10	29, 30, 32, 32	Start with the preparation question, and then Hydan, which is the most recent question.	☐
Accounting for associates	11	33, 34, 39	Do the two preparation questions first and then question 39, which is the latest exam question.	☐
Stock and long-term contracts	12	40, 41	Start with the preparation question and make sure you also do Merryview.	☐
Provisions, contingent liabilities and contingent assets	13	44	Make sure you do Bodyline, which is a full question on provisions.	☐
Financial assets and financial liabilities	14	46, 47	Both of these questions cover calculation of interest costs. Make sure you can do them.	☐
The legal versus the commercial view of accounting	16	50, 51	These are good questions on the application of substance over form. Do both of them.	☐
Leasing	16	52, 53, 54	These are all short questions. Do them all.	☐

Syllabus section	2007 Passcards chapters	Questions in this Kit	Comments	Done ☑
Accounting for taxation	17	56 , 57	Do the preparation question. Question 57 is good practice for a discursive question on deferred tax.	☐
Earnings per share	18	59, 60	Question 60 is part of a recent exam question, so good practice.	☐
Analysing and interpreting financial statements	19	62	Rytetrend is a good question on ratio analysis.	☐
Limitations of financial statements and interpretation techniques	20	64 , 65	Breadline is a good question on these issues.	☐
Cash flow statements	21	66, 71	Do the preparation question and Minster, which is the most recent question.	☐
Alternative models and practices	22	73	Update is a typical question on this area.	☐
Specialised, not-for-profit and public sector entities	23	Pilot paper 3(c)	You will not get a full question on this. The examiner has stated that this part-question in the pilot paper is typical of how it will be examined.	☐

Build your own exams

Having revised your notes and the BPP Passcards, you can attempt the questions in the Kit as a series of practice exams. This is our suggestion:

	Practice exams					
	1	2	3	4	5	6
1	26	29	30	34	35	36
2	5	6	7	21	22	23
3	68	69	70	71	62	63
4	10	15	17	49	48	44

We have selected these question on the following basis:

- Question 1 will be a consolidation
- Question 2 will be an accounts preparation question
- Question 3 will be a cash flow statement or an interpretation of account question
- Questions 4 and 5 will test other areas of the syllabus

In your exam Question 4 will be 15 marks and Question 5 will be 10 marks. In our selections we have given you a 25-mark Question 4 instead.

Questions

1 Peterlee (2.5 6/06)   23 mins

(a)   The ASB's *Statement of principles for financial reporting* (Statement) sets out the concepts that underlie the preparation and presentation of financial statements that external users are likely to rely on when making economic decisions about a reporting entity.

Required

Explain the purpose and authoritative status of the *Statement of principles for financial reporting*. **(5 marks)**

(b)   Of particular importance within the Statement are the definitions and recognition criteria for assets and liabilities.

Required

Define assets and liabilities and explain the important aspects of their definitions. Explain why these definitions are of particular importance to the preparation of an entity's balance sheet and profit and loss account.   **(8 marks)**

(Total = 13 marks)

2 Derringdo (2.5 6/03)   20 mins

Revenue recognition is the process by which companies decide when and how much income should be included in the profit and loss account. It is a topical area of great debate in the accounting profession. The ASB looks at revenue recognition from conceptual and substance points of view. There are occasions where a more traditional approach to revenue recognition does not entirely conform to the ASB guidance; indeed neither do some accounting standards.

Required

(a)   Explain the implications that the ASB's Statement of Principles and the application of substance over form have on the recognition of income. Give examples of how this may conflict with traditional practice and some accounting standards.   **(6 marks)**

(b)   Derringdo plc sells goods supplied by Gungho plc. The goods are classed as A grade (perfect quality) or B grade, having slight faults. Derringdo plc sells the A grade goods acting as an agent for Gungho plc at a fixed price calculated to yield a gross profit margin of 50%. Derringdo plc receives a commission of 12·5% of the sales it achieves for these goods. The arrangement for B grade goods is that they are sold by Gungho plc to Derringdo plc and Derringdo plc sells them at a gross profit margin of 25%. The following information has been obtained from Derringdo plc's financial records:

		£'000
Stock held on premises 1 April 20X2	– A grade	2,400
	– B grade	1,000
Goods from Gungho plc year to 31 March 20X3	– A grade	18,000
	– B grade	8,800
Stock held on premises 31 March 20X3	– A grade	2,000
	– B grade	1,250

Required

Prepare the profit and loss account extracts for Derringdo plc for the year to 31 March 20X3 reflecting the above information.   **(5 marks)**

(Total = 11 marks)

3 Regulatory framework (2.5 12/04)   45 mins

Financial reporting in the UK is regulated through a formal structure involving both statutory and institutional bodies. The European Union and the International Accounting Standards Board also contribute to what is described as the UK Regulatory Framework.

Required

(a)   Describe the various bodies and institutions that make up the UK Regulatory Framework.   **(10 marks)**

(b)   Describe the UK standard setting process including how standards are produced, enforced and occasionally supplemented.   **(10 marks)**

(c)   Comment on whether you feel the structure in (a) and the processes in (b) above have been successful.

(5 marks)

(Total = 25 marks)

4 Winger (2.5 Pilot paper amended)   45 mins

The following trial balance relates to Winger plc at 31 March 20X1:

	£'000	£'000
Turnover (note i)		358,450
Cost of sales	185,050	
Distribution costs	28,700	
Administration expenses	15,000	
Lease rentals (note ii)	20,000	
Debenture interest paid	2,000	
Interim dividends	12,000	
Land and buildings - cost (note iii)	200,000	
Plant and equipment - cost	154,800	
Depreciation 1 April 20X0 - plant and equipment		34,800
Development expenditure (note iv)	30,000	
Profit on disposal of fixed assets		45,000
Trade debtors	55,000	
Stocks - 31 March 20X1	28,240	
Cash and bank	10,660	
Trade creditors		29,400
Taxation - over provision in year to 31 March 20X0		2,200
Ordinary shares of 25p each		150,000
8% Debenture (issued in 20W8)		50,000
Profit and loss reserve 1 April 20X0		71,600
	741,450	741,450

The following notes are relevant:

(i)   Included in the turnover is £27 million, which relates to sales made to customers under sale or return agreements. The expiry date for the return of these goods is 30 April 20X1. Winger plc has charged a mark-up of 20% on cost for these sales.

(ii)   A lease rental of £20 million was paid on 1 April 20X0. It is the first of five annual payments in advance for the rental of an item of equipment that has a cash purchase price of £80 million. The auditors have advised that this is a finance lease and have calculated the implicit interest rate in the lease as 12% per annum. Leased assets should be depreciated on a straight-line basis over the life of the lease.

(iii)   On 1 April 20X0 Winger plc acquired new land and building at a cost of £200 million. For the purpose of calculating depreciation only, the asset has been separated into the following elements:

Separate asset	Cost	Life
	£'000	
Land	50,000	Freehold
Heating system	20,000	10 years
Lifts	30,000	15 years
Building	100,000	50 years

The depreciation of the elements of the building should be calculated on a straight-line basis. The new building replaced an existing building that was sold on the same date for £95 million. It had cost £50 million and had a carrying value of £80 million at the date of sale. The profit on this building has been calculated on the original cost. It had not been depreciated on the basis that the depreciation charge would not be material.

Plant and machinery is depreciated at 20% on the reducing balance basis.

(iv) The figure for development expenditure in the trial balance represents the amounts capitalised in previous years in respect of the development of a new product. Unfortunately, during the current year, the Government has introduced legislation which effectively bans this type of product. As a consequence of this the project has been abandoned. The directors of Winger plc are of the opinion that writing off the development expenditure, as opposed to its previous capitalisation, represents a change of accounting policy and therefore wish to treat the write off as a prior period adjustment.

(v) A provision for corporation tax for the year to 31 March 20X1 of £15 million is required.

Required

(a) Prepare the profit and loss account of Winger plc for the year to 31 March 20X1. **(9 marks)**

(b) Prepare a balance sheet as at 31 March 20X1 in accordance with the Companies Acts and current accounting standards so far as the information permits. **(11 marks)**

Notes to the financial statements are not required.

(c) Discuss the current acceptability of the company's previous policy in respect of non-depreciation of buildings. **(5 marks)**

(Total = 25 marks)

5 Harrington (2.5 6/05) 45 mins

Reproduced below are the draft financial statements of Harrington, a private limited company, for the year to 31 March 20X5:

PROFIT AND LOSS ACCOUNT – YEAR TO 31 MARCH 20X5

	£'000
Turnover (note (i))	13,700
Cost of sales (note (ii))	(9,200)
Gross profit	4,500
Operating expenses	(2,400)
Profit on ordinary activities before interest	2,100
Loan note interest paid (refer to balance sheet)	(25)
Profit on ordinary activities before tax	2,075
Taxation (note (vi))	(55)
Profit on ordinary activities for the period	2,020

BALANCE SHEET AS AT 31 MARCH 20X5

	£'000	£'000
Tangible fixed assets (note (iii))		6,270
Investments (note (iv))		1,200
		7,470
Current assets		
Stock	1,750	
Trade debtors	2,450	
Bank	350	
	4,550	
Creditors: amounts falling due within one year		
Trade creditors	(4,130)	
Net current assets		420
Creditors: amounts falling due after more than one year		
10% loan note (issued 2002)		(500)
Provisions for liabilities		
Deferred tax (note (vi))		(280)
Net Assets		7,110
Capital and reserves:		
Ordinary shares of 25p each (note (v))		2,000
Share premium		600
Capital reserves		
Ordinary shares of 25p each (note (v))		2,000
Share premium		600
Profit and loss account – 1 April 20X4	2,990	
– Year to 31 March 20X5	1,520	
		4,510
		7,110

The company policy for ALL depreciation is that it is charged to cost of sales and a full year's charge is made in the year of acquisition or completion and none in the year of disposal.

The following matters are relevant:

(i)   Included in turnover is £300,000 being the sale proceeds of an item of plant that was sold in January 20X5. The plant had originally cost £900,000 and had been depreciated by £630,000 at the date of its sale. Other than recording the proceeds in sales and cash, no other accounting entries for the disposal of the plant have been made. All plant is depreciated at 25% per annum on the reducing balance basis.

(ii)   On 31 December 20X4 the company completed the construction of a new warehouse. The construction was achieved using the company's own resources as follows:

	£'000
purchased materials	150
direct labour	800
supervision	65
design and planning costs	20

Included in the above figures are £10,000 for materials and £25,000 for labour costs that were effectively lost due to the foundations being too close to a neighbouring property. All the above costs are included in cost of sales. The building was brought into immediate use on completion and has an estimated life of 20 years (straightline depreciation).

(iii) Details of the other tangible fixed assets at 31 March 20X5 are:

	£'000	£'000
Land at cost		1,000
Buildings at cost	4,000	
Less accumulated depreciation at 31 March 20X4	(800)	
		3,200
Plant at cost	5,200	
Less accumulated depreciation at 31 March 20X4	(3,130)	
		2,070
		6,270

At the beginning of the current year (1 April 20X4), Harrington had an open market basis valuation of its properties (excluding the warehouse in note (ii) above). Land was valued at £1·2 million and the property at £4·8 million. The directors wish these values to be incorporated into the financial statements. The properties had an estimated remaining life of 20 years at the date of the valuation (straight-line depreciation is used). Harrington makes a transfer to realised profits in respect of the excess depreciation on revalued assets.

Note: depreciation for the year to 31 March 20X5 has not yet been accounted for in the draft financial statements.

(iv) The investments are in quoted companies that are carried at their stock market values with any gains and losses recorded in the profit and loss account. The value shown in the balance sheet is that at 31 March 20X4 and during the year to 31 March 20X5 the investments have risen in value by an average of 10%. Harrington has not reflected this increase in its financial statements.

(v) On 1 October 20X4 there had been a fully subscribed rights issue of 1 for 4 at 60p. This has been recorded in the above balance sheet. Dividends of £500,000 were paid during the year.

(vi) Corporation tax on the profits for the year to 31 March 20X5 is estimated at £260,000. The figure in the profit and loss account is the underprovision for the year to 31 March 20X4. There are net accelerated timing differences of £1·4 million at 31 March 20X5. The corporation tax rate is 25%.

Required

(a) Prepare a restated profit and loss account for the year to 31 March 20X5 reflecting the information in notes (i) to (vi) above. **(9 marks)**

(b) Prepare a statement showing the movement of share capital and reserves for the year to 31 March 20X5. **(6 marks)**

(c) Prepare a restated balance sheet at 31 March 20X5 reflecting the information in notes (i) to (vi) above. **(10 marks)**

(Total = 25 marks)

6 Petra (2.5 12/05)   45 mins

The following trial balance relates to Petra, a public listed company, at 30 September 20X5:

	£'000	£'000
Turnover (note (i))		197,800
Cost of sales (note (i))	114,000	
Distribution costs	17,000	
Administration costs	18,000	
Loan interest paid	1,500	
Ordinary shares of 25p each fully paid		40,000
Share premium		12,000
Profit and loss reserve 1 October 20X4		34,000
6% Redeemable loan note (issued in 20X3)		50,000
Land and buildings at cost ((land element £40 million) note (ii))	100,000	
Plant and equipment at cost (note (iii))	66,000	
Deferred development expenditure (note (iv))	40,000	
Accumulated depreciation 1 October 20X4 – buildings		16,000
– plant and equipment		26,000
Accumulated amortisation of development expenditure at 1 October 20X4		8,000
Corporation tax (note (v))	1,000	
Deferred tax (note (v))		15,000
Trade debtors	24,000	
Stocks – 30 September 20X5	21,300	
Bank	11,000	
Trade creditors		15,000
	413,800	413,800

The following notes are relevant:

(i)   Included in turnover is £12 million for receipts that the company's auditors have advised are commission sales. The costs of these sales, paid for by Petra, were £8 million. £3 million of the profit of £4 million was attributable to and remitted to Sharma (the auditors have advised that Sharma is the principal for these transactions). Both the £8 million cost of sales and the £3 million paid to Sharma have been included in cost of sales.

(ii)   The buildings had an estimated life of 30 years when they were acquired and are being depreciated on the straight-line basis.

(iii)   Following a review of the company's operations in September 20X5, Petra sold some surplus plant that had cost £16 million and had accumulated depreciation of £6 million to Haden. Petra has not accounted for the sale of the plant, because of the difficulty in negotiating a selling price. The two companies agreed that a broker specialising in the sale of used plant should determine a fair price for the sale. In October 20X5 the broker concluded that the selling price of this plant should be £7·5 million. The broker is entitled to a commission of 8% of the selling price for his services.

The company policy is to depreciate at 20% per annum using the reducing balance method all plant held at the year end. Depreciation of buildings and plant is charged to cost of sales.

(iv)   The development expenditure relates to the capitalised cost of developing a product called the Topaz. It had an original estimated life of five years. Production and sales of the Topaz started in October 20X3. A review of the sales of the Topaz in late September 20X5, showed them to be below forecast and an impairment test concluded that the fair value of the development costs at 30 September 20X5 was only £18 million and the expected period of future sales (from this date) was only a further two years.

(v)   The balance on the corporation tax account in the trial balance is the under-provision in respect of the tax liability for the year ended 30 September 20X4. The directors have estimated the provision for corporation tax for the year ended 30 September 20X5 to be £4 million and the required balance sheet provision for deferred tax at 30 September 20X5 is £17·6 million.

Required

Applying UK GAAP, prepare for Petra:

(a)   A profit and loss account for the year ended 30 September 20X5; and   **(10 marks)**

(b)   A balance sheet as at 30 September 20X5.   **(10 marks)**

Note: A statement of total recognised gains and losses is NOT required. Disclosure notes are NOT required.

The directors hold options to purchase 24 million shares for a total of £7·2 million. The options were granted two years ago and have been correctly accounted for. The options do not affect your answer to (a) and (b) above. The average stock market value of Petra's shares for the year ended 30 September 20X5 can be taken as 90p per share.

Required

(c)   A calculation of the basic and diluted earnings per share for the year ended 30 September 20X5 (comparatives are not required).   **(5 marks)**

(Total = 25 marks)

7 Allgone (2.5 6/03 amended)   45 mins

The following trial balance relates to Allgone plc at 31 March 20X3:

	£'000	£'000
Turnover (note (i))		236,200
Purchases	127,850	
Operating expenses	12,400	
Loan interest paid	2,400	
Preference dividend	1,000	
Land and buildings – at valuation (note (ii))	130,000	
Plant and equipment – cost	84,300	
Software – cost 1 April 20X0	10,000	
Stock market investments – valuation 1 April 20X2 (note (iii))	12,000	
Depreciation 1 April 20X2 – plant and equipment		24,300
Depreciation 1 April 20X2 – software		6,000
Extraordinary item (note (iv))	32,000	
Trade debtors	23,000	
Stocks – 1 April 20X2	19,450	
Bank		350
Trade creditors		15,200
Ordinary shares of 25p each		60,000
10% Preference shares redeemable 20Z8		20,000
12% Loan note (issued 1 July 20X2)		40,000
Deferred tax		3,000
Revaluation reserve (relating to land and buildings and the investments)		45,000
Profit and loss reserve – 1 April 20X2		4,350
	454,400	454,400

The following notes are relevant:

(i)   Turnover includes £8 million for goods sold in March 20X3 for cash to Funders plc, a merchant bank. The cost of these goods was £6 million. Funders plc has the option to require Allgone plc to repurchase these goods within one month of the year-end at their original selling price plus a facilitating fee of £250,000.

The stock at 31 March 20X3 was counted at a cost value of £8·5 million. This includes £500,000 of slow moving stock that is expected to be sold for a net £300,000.

(ii) Fixed assets:

On 1 April 20X2 Allgone plc revalued its land and buildings. The details are:

	cost 1 April 20W7	valuation 1 April 20X2
	£'000	£'000
Land	20,000	25,000
Building	80,000	105,000

The building had an estimated life of 40 years when it was acquired and this has not changed as a result of the revaluation. Depreciation is on a straight-line basis. The surplus on the revaluation has been added to the revaluation reserve, but no other movements on the revaluation reserve have been recorded.

Plant and equipment is depreciated at 20% per annum on the reducing balance basis.

Software is depreciated by the sum of the digits method over a 5-year life.

(iii) The investment represents 7·5% of the ordinary share capital of Wondaworld plc. These are 'available for sale' investments and are carried at fair value in accordance with FRS 26. Changes in value are taken to the revaluation reserve which at 1 April 20X2 contained a surplus of £5 million for previous revaluations of the investments. The stock market price of Wondaworld plc's ordinary shares was £2·50 each on 1 April 20X2 and by 31 March 20X3 this had fallen to £2·25.

(iv) The extraordinary item is a loss incurred due to a fraud relating to the company's investments. A senior employee of the company, who left in January 20X2, had diverted investment funds into his private bank account. The fraud was discovered by the employee's replacement in April 20X2. It is unlikely that any of the funds will be recovered. Allgone plc has now implemented tighter procedures to prevent such a fraud recurring. The company has been advised that this loss will not qualify for any tax relief.

(v) The directors have estimated the provision for corporation tax for the year to 31 March 20X3 at £11·3 million. The deferred tax provision at 31 March 20X3 is to be adjusted to reflect net accelerated capital allowances of £16 million. The rate of corporation tax is 30%. The revaluation of the company's fixed assets will not affect the deferred tax balance.

(vi) The finance charge relating to the preference shares is £2,000,000 per annum. This is equivalent to the dividend payable.

Required

In accordance with the Companies Acts and current Accounting Standards as far as the information permits, prepare:

(a)	the Profit and Loss Account of Allgone plc for the year to 31 March 20X3; and	**(9 marks)**
(b)	the Statement of Total Recognised Gains and Losses for the year to 31 March 20X3; and	**(3 marks)**
(c)	a Balance Sheet as at 31 March 20X3.	**(13 marks)**

Notes to the financial statements are not required. **(Total = 25 marks)**

8 Tadeon (2.5 12/06)   45 mins

The following trial balance related to Tadeon, a publicly listed company, at 30 September 2006:

	£'000	£'000
Turnover		277,800
Cost of sales	118,000	
Operating expenses	40,000	
Loan interest paid (note (i))	1,000	
Rental of vehicles (note (ii))	6,200	
Investment income		2,000
25 year leasehold property at cost (note (iii))	225,000	
Plant and equipment at cost	181,000	
Investments at amortised cost	42,000	
Accumulated depreciation at 1 October 2005 – leasehold property		36,000
– plant and equipment		85,000
Equity shares of 20 pence each fully paid		150,000
Profit and loss account at 1 October 2005		18,600
2% loan note (note (i))		50,000
Deferred tax 1 October 2005 (note (iv))		12,000
Trade debtors	53,500	
Stock at 30 September 2006	33,300	
Bank		1,900
Trade creditors		18,700
Suspense account (note (v))		48,000
	700,000	700,000

The following notes are relevant:

(i)   The loan note was issued on 1 October 2005. it is redeemable on 30 September 2010 at a large premium (in order to compensate for the low interest rate). The finance department has calculated that the effective interest rate on the loan is 5.5% per annum.

(ii)   The rental of the vehicles related to two separate contracts. These have been scrutinised by the finance department and they have come to the conclusion that £5 million of the rentals relate to a finance lease. The finance lease was entered into on 1 October 2005 (the date £5 million was paid) for a four year period. The vehicles had a fair value of £20 million (straight-line depreciation should be used) at 1 October 2005 and the lease agreement requires three further annual payments of £6 million each on the anniversary of the lease. The interest rate implicit in the lease is to be taken as 10% per annum. The other contract is an operating lease and should be charged to operating expenses.

Other plant and equipment is depreciate at $12\frac{1}{2}\%$ per annum on the reducing balance basis.

All depreciation of property, plant and equipment is charged to cost of sales.

(iii)   On 30 September 2006 the leasehold property was revalued to £200 million. The directors wish to incorporate this valuation into the financial statements as the sale of the property is likely to take place in the near future and it will be replaced by a rented property. Tadeon has been advised that a tax charge will arise on the sale of the leasehold (see (iv) below).

(iv)   The directors have estimated the provision for corporation tax for the year ended 30 September 2006 at £38 million. At 30 September 2006 there were £74 million of timing differences which would lead to a deferred tax liability. £20 million of the timing differences related to the revaluation of the leasehold property (see (iii) above). The corporation tax rate is 20%.

(v)   The suspense account balance can be reconciled from the following transactions:

The payment of a dividend on October 2005. this was calculated to give a 5% yield on the company's share price of 80 pence as at 30 September 2005.

The net receipt in March 2006 of a fully subscribed rights issue of one new share for every three held at a price of 32 pence each. The expenses of the share issue were £2 million and should be charged to share premium.

Note: the cash entries for these transactions have been correctly accounted for.

Required

Prepare for Tadeon:

(a)   A profit and loss account for the year ended 30 September 2006; and   **(8 marks)**

(b)   A balance sheet as at 30 September 2006.   **(17 marks)**

Note: A statement of total recognised gains and losses is not required. Disclosure notes are not required.

(Total = 25 marks)

9 Derringdo II (2.5 6/03)   16 mins

Derringdo plc acquired an item of plant at a gross cost of £800,000 on 1 October 20X2. The plant has an estimated life of 10 years with a residual value equal to 15% of its gross cost. Derringdo plc uses straight-line depreciation on a time apportioned basis. The company received a government grant of 30% of its cost price at the time of its purchase. The terms of the grant are that if the company retains the asset for four years or more, then no repayment liability will be incurred. If the plant is sold within four years a repayment on a sliding scale would be applicable. The repayment is 75% if sold within the first year of purchase and this amount decreases by 25% per annum. Derringdo plc has no intention to sell the plant within the first four years. Derringdo plc's accounting policy for capital based government grants is to treat them as deferred credits and release them to income over the life of the asset to which they relate.

Required

(a)   Discuss whether the company's policy for the treatment of government grants meets the definition of a liability in the ASB's Statement of Principles; and   **(3 marks)**

(b)   Prepare extracts of Derringdo plc's financial statements for the year to 31 March 20X3 in respect of the plant and the related grant:

   –   applying the company's policy;

   –   in compliance with the definition of a liability in the Statement of Principles. Your answer should consider whether the sliding scale repayment should be used in determining the deferred credit for the grant.   **(6 marks)**

(Total = 9 marks)

10 Question with answer plan: Broadoak (2.5 12/01)   45 mins

The broad principles of accounting for tangible fixed assets involve distinguishing between capital and revenue expenditure, measuring the cost of assets, determining how they should be depreciated and dealing with the problems of subsequent measurement and subsequent expenditure. FRS 15 'Tangible Fixed Assets' was issued in February 1999 with the intention of improving consistency in these areas.

Required

(a)   Explain:

   (i)   how the initial cost of tangible fixed assets should be measured; and   **(4 marks)**
   (ii)   the circumstances in which subsequent expenditure on those assets should be capitalised. **(3 marks)**

(b)   Explain FRS 15's requirements regarding the revaluation of fixed assets and the accounting treatment of gains and losses on both the revaluation and the disposal of fixed assets.   **(8 marks)**

(c)   (i)   Broadoak plc has recently purchased an item of plant from Plantco plc, the details of this are:

	£	£
Basic list price of plant		240,000
trade discount applicable to Broadoak plc		12.5% on list price
Ancillary costs:		
shipping and handling costs		2,750
estimated pre-production testing		12,500
maintenance contract for three years		24,000
site preparation costs:		
electrical cable installation	14,000	
concrete reinforcement	4,500	
own labour costs	7,500	26,000

Broadoak plc paid for the plant (excluding the ancillary costs) within four weeks of order, thereby obtaining an early settlement discount of 3%.

Broadoak plc had incorrectly specified the power loading of the original electrical cable to be installed by the contractor. The cost of correcting this error of £6,000 is included in the above figure of £14,000.

The plant is expected to last for 10 years. At the end of this period there will be compulsory costs of £15,000 to dismantle the plant and £3,000 to restore the site to its original use condition.

Required

Calculate the amount at which the initial cost of the plant should be measured. (Ignore discounting).

(5 marks)

(ii)   Broadoak acquired a 12 year lease on a property on 1 October 20X0 at a cost of £240,000. The company policy is to revalue its properties on an existing use value (EUV) at the end of each year, and calculate annual amortisation on the carrying value at the beginning of the year. The valuations (EUV) of the property on 30 September 20X1 and 20X2 were £231,000 and £175,000 respectively.

Required

Prepare extracts of the profit and loss account, the Statement of Total Recognised Gains and Losses and the balance sheet of Broadoak plc for the years to 30 September 20X1 and 20X2 in respect of the leasehold properties.   **(5 marks)**

(Total = 25 marks)

11 Elite Leisure (2.5 12/05)   22 mins

Elite Leisure is a private limited company that operates a single cruise ship. The ship was acquired on 1 October 20W6. Details of the cost of the ship's components and their estimated useful lives are:

component	original cost (£million)	depreciation basis
ship's fabric (hull, decks etc)	300	25 years straight-line
cabins and entertainment area fittings	150	12 years straight-line
propulsion system	100	useful life of 40,000 hours

At 30 September 20X4 no further capital expenditure had been incurred on the ship.

In the year ended 30 September 20X4 the ship had experienced a high level of engine trouble which had cost the company considerable lost revenue and compensation costs. The measured expired life of the propulsion system at 30 September 20X4 was 30,000 hours. Due to the unreliability of the engines, a decision was taken in early October 20X4 to replace the whole of the propulsion system at a cost of £140 million. The expected life of the new propulsion system was 50,000 hours and in the year ended 30 September 20X5 the ship had used its engines for 5,000 hours.

At the same time as the propulsion system replacement, the company took the opportunity to do a limited upgrade to the cabin and entertainment facilities at a cost of £60 million and repaint the ship's fabric at a cost of £20 million. After the upgrade of the cabin and entertainment area fittings it was estimated that their remaining life was five years (from the date of the upgrade). For the purpose of calculating depreciation, all the work on the ship can be assumed to have been completed on 1 October 20X4. All residual values can be taken as nil.

Required

Calculate the carrying value of Elite Leisure's cruise ship at 30 September 20X5 and its related profit and loss account expenditure for the year ended 30 September 20X5. Your answer should explain the treatment of each item. **(12 marks)**

12 Myriad (2.5 12/01)   16 mins

Myriad plc owns several properties which are revalued each year. Three of its properties are rented out under annually renewable operating leases. Details of these properties and their valuations are:

Property	Type	Cost	Value 30 September 20X0	Value 30 September 20X1
		£'000	£'000	£'000
A	50 year lease	150	240	200
B	50 year lease	120	180	145
C	15 year lease	120	140	150

All three properties were acquired on 1 October 20W9. The valuations of the properties are based on their age at the date of the valuation. Myriad plc's policy is to carry all non-investment properties at cost. Annual amortisation, where appropriate, is based on the carrying value of assets at the beginning of the relevant period.

Property A is let to a subsidiary of Myriad plc on normal commercial terms. The other properties are let on normal commercial terms to companies not related to Myriad plc.

Required

(a) Explain why investment properties require a different accounting treatment to owner-occupied properties; and **(3 marks)**

(b) Prepare extracts of the financial statements of Myriad plc for the year to 30 September 20X1 reflecting the appropriate treatment of the above properties. **(6 marks)**

(Total = 9 marks)

13 Merryview (2.5 6/02)   18 mins

Merryview plc conducts its activities from two properties, a head office in the city centre and a property in the countryside where staff training is conducted. Both properties were acquired on 1 April 20W9 and had estimated lives of 25 years with no residual value. The company has a policy of carrying its land and buildings at current values. However, until recently property prices had not changed for some years. On 1 October 20X1 the properties were revalued by a firm of surveyors. Details of this and the original costs are:

		Land	Buildings
		£	£
Head office	- cost 1 April 20W9	500,000	1,200,000
	- revalued 1 October 20X1	700,000	1,350,000
Training premises	- cost 1 April 20W9	300,000	900,000
	- revalued 1 October 20X1	350,000	600,000

The fall in value of the training premises is due mainly to damage done by the use of heavy equipment during training. the surveyors have also reported that the expected life of the training property in its current use will only be a further 10 years from the date of the valuation. The estimated life of the head office remained unaltered.

Note. Merryview plc treats its land and its buildings as separate assets. Depreciation is based on the straight line method from the date of purchase or subsequent revaluation.

Required

Prepare extracts of the financial statements of Merryview plc in respect of the above properties for the year to 31 March 20X2. **(10 marks)**

14 Myriad II (2.5 12/01)   18 mins

You have been asked to assist the financial accountant of Myriad plc in preparing the company's financial statements for the year to 30 September 20X1. The financial accountant has asked for your advice in the following matters:

A review of the company policy on the treatment of deferred development expenditure has come to the conclusion that it would be preferable for the company to change its current accounting policy of immediate write off of all development costs. The new policy, to be first applied for the financial statements to 30 September 20X1, is to recognise development costs as an intangible asset where they meet the recognition criteria in SSAP 13 'Accounting for Research and Development'. Amortisation of all 'qualifying' development expenditure is on a straight-line basis over a four-year period (assuming a nil residual value). Recognised development expenditure 'qualifies' for amortisation when the project starts commercial production of the related product.

The amount of recognised development expenditure, and the amount qualifying for amortisation each year is as follows:

	£'000 amount recognised as an asset	£'000 amount qualifying for amortisation
In the year to 30 September 20W9	420	300
In the year to 30 September 20X0	250	360
In the year to 30 September 20X1	560	400
	1,230	1,060

No development costs were incurred by Myriad plc prior to 20W9.

Required

(a) Explain the circumstances when a company should change its accounting policies; and **(4 marks)**

(b) Prepare extracts of Myriad plc's financial statements for the year to 30 September 20X1 including the comparative figures to reflect the change in accounting policy. **(6 marks)**

     Note: Ignore taxation.

                                                               (Total = 10 marks)

15 Dexterity (2.5 6/04)   45 mins

(a) During the last decade it has not been unusual for the premium paid to acquire control of a business to be greater than the fair value of its tangible net assets. This increase in the relative balance sheet proportions of intangible assets has made the accounting practices for them all the more important. During the same period many companies have spent a great deal of money internally developing new intangible assets such as software and brands. FRS 10 'Goodwill and Intangible Assets' was issued by the ASB in December 1997 and prescribes the accounting treatment for goodwill and intangible assets.

Required

In accordance with FRS 10, discuss whether intangible assets should be recognised, and if so how they should be initially recorded and subsequently amortised in the following circumstances:

- when they are purchased separately from other assets;
- when they are obtained as part of acquiring the whole of a business; and
- when they are developed internally. **(10 marks)**

Note. Your answer should consider goodwill separately from other intangibles.

(b) Dexterity is a public listed company. It has been considering the accounting treatment of its intangible assets and has asked for your opinion on how the matters below should be treated in its financial statements for the year to 31 March 20X4.

(i) On 1 October 20X3 Dexterity acquired Temerity, a small company that specialises in pharmaceutical drug research and development. The purchase consideration was by way of a share exchange and valued at £35 million. The fair value of Temerity's net assets was £15 million (excluding any items referred to below). Temerity owns a patent for an established successful drug that has a remaining life of eight years. A firm of specialist advisors, Leadbrand, have estimated the current value of this patent to be £10 million, however the company is awaiting the outcome of clinical trials where the drug has been tested to treat a different illness. If the trials are successful, the value of the drug is then estimated to be £15 million. Also included in the company's balance sheet is £2 million for medical research that has been conducted on behalf of a client. **(4 marks)**

(ii) Dexterity has developed and patented a new drug which has been approved for clinical use. The costs of developing the drug were £12 million. Based on early assessments of its sales success, Leadbrand have estimated its market value at £20 million. **(3 marks)**

(iii) Dexterity's manufacturing facilities have recently received a favourable inspection by government medical scientists. As a result of this the company has been granted an exclusive five-year licence to manufacture and distribute a new vaccine. Although the licence had no direct cost to Dexterity, its directors feel its granting is a reflection of the company's standing and have asked Leadbrand to value the licence. Accordingly they have placed a value of £10 million on it. **(3 marks)**

(iv) In the current accounting period, Dexterity has spent £3 million sending its staff on specialist training courses. Whilst these courses have been expensive, they have led to a marked improvement in production quality and staff now need less supervision. This in turn has led to an increase in revenue and cost reductions. The directors of Dexterity believe these benefits will continue for at least three years and wish to treat the training costs as an asset. **(2 marks)**

(v) In December 20X3, Dexterity paid £5 million for a television advertising campaign for its products that will run for six months from 1 January 20X4 to 30 June 20X4. The directors believe that increased sales as a result of the publicity will continue for two years from the start of the advertisements. **(3 marks)**

Required

Explain how the directors of Dexterity should treat the above items in the financial statements for the year to 31 March 20X4. **(15 marks as indicated)**

Note. The values given by Leadbrand can be taken as being reliable measurements. You are not required to consider depreciation aspects. **(Total = 25 marks)**

16 Derwent (2.5 12/04 amended)

23 mins

Advent is a publicly listed company.

Details of Advent's fixed assets at 1 October 20X3 were:

	Land and building	Plant	Telecommunications licence	Total
	£m	£m	£m	£m
Cost/valuation	280	150	300	730
Accumulated depreciation/amortisation	(40)	(105)	(30)	(175)
Net book value	240	45	270	555

The following information is relevant:

(i) The land and building were revalued on 1 October 20W8 with £80 million attributable to the land and £200 million to the building. At that date the estimated remaining life of the building was 25 years. A further revaluation was not needed until 1 October 20X3 when the land and building were valued at £85 million and £180 million respectively. The remaining estimated life of the building at this date was 20 years.

(ii) Plant is depreciated at 20% per annum on cost with time apportionment where appropriate. On 1 April 20X4 new plant costing £45 million was acquired. In addition, this plant cost £5 million to install and commission. No plant is more than four years old.

(iii) The telecommunications licence was bought from the government on 1 October 20X2 and has a 10 year life. It is amortised on a straight line basis. In September 20X4, a review of the sales of the products related to the licence showed them to be very disappointing. As a result of this review the estimated recoverable amount of the licence at 30 September 20X4 was estimated at only £100 million.

There were no disposals of fixed assets during the year to 30 September 20X4.

Required

(a) Prepare balance sheet extracts of Advent's fixed assets as at 30 September 20X4 (including comparative figures), together with any disclosures (other than those of the accounting policies) required under current Accounting Standards and the Companies Acts as far as the information permits. **(9 marks)**

(b) Explain the usefulness of the above disclosures to the users of the financial statements. **(4 marks)**

(Total = 13 marks)

17 Wilderness (2.5 12/05)

45 mins

(a) FRS 11 *Impairment of fixed assets and goodwill* was issued in July 1998. Its main objective is to prescribe the procedures that should ensure that an entity's assets are included in its balance sheet at no more than their recoverable amounts. Where an asset is carried at an amount in excess of its recoverable amount, it is said to be impaired and FRS 11 requires an impairment loss to be recognised.

Required

(i) Define an impairment loss explaining the relevance of net realisable value and value in use; and state how frequently assets should be tested for impairment. **(6 marks)**

Note. Your answer should NOT describe the possible indicators of an impairment.

(ii) Explain how an impairment loss is accounted for after it has been calculated. **(5 marks)**

(b) The assistant financial controller of the Wilderness group has identified the matters below which she believes may indicate an impairment to one or more assets:

(i)   Wilderness owns and operates an item of plant that cost £640,000 and had accumulated depreciation of £400,000 at 1 October 20X4. It is being depreciated at 12½% on cost. On 1 April 20X5 (exactly half way through the year) the plant was damaged when a factory vehicle collided into it. Due to the unavailability of replacement parts, it is not possible to repair the plant, but it still operates, albeit at a reduced capacity. Also it is expected that as a result of the damage the remaining life of the plant from the date of the damage will be only two years. Based on its reduced capacity, the estimated present value of the plant in use is £150,000. The plant has a current disposal value of £20,000 (which will be nil in two years' time), but Wilderness has been offered a trade-in value of £180,000 against a replacement machine which has a cost of £1 million (there would be no disposal costs for the replaced plant). Wilderness is reluctant to replace the plant as it is worried about the long-term demand for the product produced by the plant. The trade-in value is only available if the plant is replaced.

Required

Prepare extracts from the balance sheet and profit and loss account of Wilderness in respect of the plant for the year ended 30 September 20X5. Your answer should explain how you arrived at your figures. **(7 marks)**

(ii)   On 1 April 20X4 Wilderness acquired 100% of the share capital of Mossel, whose only activity is the extraction and sale of spa water. Mossel had been profitable since its acquisition, but bad publicity resulting from several consumers becoming ill due to a contamination of the spa water supply in April 20X5 has led to unexpected losses in the last six months. The carrying amounts of Mossel's assets at 30 September 20X5 are:

	£'000
Brand (Quencher – see below)	7,000
Land containing spa	12,000
Purifying and bottling plant	8,000
Stocks	5,000
	32,000

The source of the contamination was found and it has now ceased.

The company originally sold the bottled water under the brand name of 'Quencher', but because of the contamination it has rebranded its bottled water as 'Phoenix'. After a large advertising campaign, sales are now starting to recover and are approaching previous levels. The value of the brand in the balance sheet is the depreciated amount of the original brand name of 'Quencher'.

The directors have acknowledged that £1·5 million will have to be spent in the first three months of the next accounting period to upgrade the purifying and bottling plant.

The stocks contain some old 'Quencher' bottled water at a cost of £2 million; the remaining stock is labeled with the new brand 'Phoenix'. Samples of all the bottled water have been tested by the health authority and have been passed as fit to sell. The old bottled water will have to be relabelled at a cost of £250,000, but is then expected to be sold at the normal selling price of (normal) cost plus 50%.

Based on the estimated future cash flows, the directors have estimated that the value in use of Mossel at 30 September 20X5, calculated according to the guidance in FRS 11, is £20 million. There is no reliable estimate of the net realisable value of Mossel.

Required

Applying UK GAAP, calculate the amounts at which the assets of Mossel should appear in the consolidated balance sheet of Wilderness at 30 September 20X5. Your answer should explain how you arrived at your figures. **(7 marks)**

(Total = 25 marks)

18 Multiplex (2.5 Pilot paper)   20 mins

(a) On 1 January 20X1 Multiplex plc acquired Steamdays Ltd, a company that operates a scenic railway along the coast of a popular tourist area. The summarised balance sheet at fair values of Steamdays Ltd on 1 January 20X1, reflecting the terms of the acquisition was:

	£'000
Goodwill	200
Operating licence	1,000
Property - train stations and land	250
Rail track and coaches	250
Two steam engines	1,000
Other net assets	300
Purchase consideration	3,000

The operating licence is for ten years. It was renewed on 1 January 20X1 by the transport authority and is stated at the cost of its renewal. The carrying values of the property and rail track and coaches are based on their value in use. The engines, and other net assets are valued at their net selling prices.

On 1 February 20X1 the boiler of one of the steam engines exploded, completely destroying the whole engine. Fortunately no one was injured, but the engine was beyond repair. Due to its age a replacement could not be obtained. Because of the reduced passenger capacity the estimated value in use of the whole of the business after the accident was assessed at £2 million.

Passenger numbers after the accident were below expectations even after allowing for the reduced capacity. A market research report concluded that tourists were not using the railway because of their fear of a similar accident occurring to the remaining engine. In the light of this the value in use of the business was re-assessed on 31 March 20X1 at £1.8 million. On this date Multiplex plc received an offer of £600,000 in respect of the operating licence (it is transferable). The realisable value of the other net assets has not changed significantly.

Required

Calculate the carrying value of the assets of Steamdays Ltd (in Multiplex plc's consolidated balance sheet) at 1 February 20X1 and 31 March 20X1 after recognising the impairment losses.   **(6 marks)**

(b) On 1 January 20X1 the Board of Multiplex plc approved a resolution to close the whole of its loss-making engineering operation. A binding agreement to dispose of the assets was signed shortly afterwards. The sale will be completed on 10 July 20X1 at an agreed value of £30 million. The costs of the closure are estimated at:

(i)   £2 million for redundancy
(ii)   £3 million in penalty costs for non-completion of contracted orders
(iii) £1.5 million for associated professional costs
(iv)   Losses on the sale of the net assets whose book value at 31 March 20X1 was £46 million
(v)   Operating losses for the period from 1 April 20X1 to the date of sale are estimated at £4.5 million.

Multiplex plc accounts for its various operations on a divisional basis.

Required

Advise the directors on the correct accounting treatment of the closure of the engineering division.

(5 marks)

(Total = 11 marks)

19 Preparation question: Research Ltd

Research Ltd for many years capitalised all expenditure on development projects. It was decided that on the grounds of prudence it would be fairer to write such costs off to the profit and loss account in the year incurred.

Balance sheet extracts are as follows:

	20X1	20X0
	£'000	£'000
Development costs	680	460
Amortisation	(150)	(100)
	530	360
Other net assets	2,270	1,600
	2,800	1,960
Share capital	550	500
Revaluation reserve (re properties)	120	–
Profit and loss reserve	2,130	1,460
	2,800	1,960

During 20X0 the company made a profit of £410,000 after charging £50,000 for amortisation of development costs and incurring development costs of £180,000.

No dividends were paid in either year.

Required

Prepare revised extracts for the following:

(a) balance sheet;
(b) statement of recognised gains and losses;
(c) reconciliation of movement in shareholders' funds;
(d) statement of movement in reserves.

20 Derringdo III (2.5 6/03)   9 mins

Derringdo plc sells carpets from several retail outlets. In previous years the company has undertaken responsibility for fitting the carpets in customers' premises. Customers pay for the carpets at the time they are ordered. The average length of time from a customer ordering a carpet to its fitting is 14 days. In previous years, Derringdo plc had not recognised a sale in income until the carpet had been successfully fitted as the rectification costs of any fitting error would be expensive. From 1 April 20X2 Derringdo plc changed its method of trading by sub-contracting the fitting to approved contractors. Under this policy the sub-contractors are paid by Derringdo plc and they (the sub-contractors) are liable for any errors made in the fitting. Because of this Derringdo plc is proposing to recognise sales when customers order and pay for the goods, rather than when they have been fitted. Details of the relevant sales figures are:

	£'000
Sales made in retail outlets for the year to 31 March 20X3	23,000
Sales value of carpets fitted in the 14 days to 14 April 20X2	1,200
Sales value of carpets fitted in the 14 days to 14 April 20X3	1,600

Note: the sales value of carpets fitted in the 14 days to 14 April 20X2 are not included in the annual sales figure of £23 million, but those for the 14 days to 14 April 20X3 are included.

Required

Discuss whether the above represents a change of accounting policy, and, based on your discussion, calculate the amount that you would include in sales revenue for carpets in the year to 31 March 20X3.   **(5 marks)**

21 Telenorth (2.5 12/01)   **45 mins**

The following trial balance relates to Telenorth plc at 30 September 20X1:

	£'000	£'000
Turnover		283,460
Stock 1 October 20X0	12,400	
Purchases	147,200	
Distribution expenses	22,300	
Administration expenses	34,440	
Debenture interest paid	300	
Interim dividends - ordinary	2,000	
- preference	480	
Investment income - UK dividends received		1,080
- interest received (net)		420
25 year leasehold building – cost	56,250	
Plant and equipment – cost	55,000	
Computer system – cost	35,000	
Investments – at valuation	34,500	
Depreciation 1 October 20X0 (note (ii)) - leasehold		18,000
- plant and equipment		12,800
- computer system		9,600
Trade debtors (note (iii))	35,700	
Bank overdraft		1,680
Trade creditors		17,770
Deferred tax (note (iv))		5,200
Ordinary shares of £1 each		20,000
Suspense account (note (v))		26,000
6% Debentures (issued 1 October 20X0)		10,000
8% Preference shares (redeemable)		12,000
Revaluation reserve (note (iv))		3,400
Profit and loss reserve 1 October 20X0		14,160
	435,570	435,570

The following notes are relevant.

(i)   Stocktaking could not be conducted by Telenorth plc until 4 October 20X1 due to operational reasons. The value of the stock on the premises at this date was £16 million at cost. Between the year end and the stock take the following transactions have been identified:

Normal sales at a mark up on cost of 40%	£1,400,000
Sales on a sale or return basis at a mark up on cost of 30%	£650,000
Goods received at cost	£820,000

All sales and purchases had been correctly recorded in the period in which they occurred.

(ii)   Telenorth plc has the following depreciation policy:

–   leasehold – straight-line;
–   plant and equipment – five years straight line with residual values estimated at £5,000,000'
–   computer system – 40% per annum reducing balance.

Depreciation of the leasehold and plant is treated as cost of sales; depreciation of the computer system is an administration expense.

(iii)   The outstanding balance (debtor) of a major customer amounting to £12 million was factored to Kwickfinance on 1 September 20X1. The terms of the factoring were:

–   Kwickfinance will pay 80% of the gross debtor outstanding account to Telenorth plc immediately;

      –   the balance will be paid (less the charges below) when the debtor is collected in full. Any amount of the debt outstanding after four months will be transferred back to Telenorth plc at its full book value.

      –   Kwickfinance will charge 1.0% per month to the net amount owing from Telenorth plc at the beginning of each month. Kwickfinance had not collected any of the factored debtor by the year end.

Telenorth plc debited the cash from Kwickfinance to its bank account and removed the debtor from its sales ledger. It has prudently charged the difference as an administration cost.

(iv)   A provision for corporation tax of £23.4 million for the year to 30 September 20X1 is required. The deferred tax liability is to be increased by £2.2 million, of which £1 million is to be charged direct to the revaluation reserve.

(v)   The suspense account contains the proceeds of two share issues:

      –   the exercise of all the outstanding directors' share options of four million shares on 1 October 20X0 at £2 each;

      –   a fully subscribed rights issue on 1 July 20X1 of 1 for 4 held at a price of £3 each. The stock market price of Telenorth plc's shares immediately before the rights issue was £4.

(vi)   The finance charge relating to the preference shares is equivalent to the dividend payable.

Required

Prepare:

(a)   (i)   The profit and loss account of Telenorth plc for the year to 30 September 20X1; and   **(9 marks)**

    (ii)   A balance sheet as at 30 September 20X1 in accordance with the Companies Acts and current Accounting Standards as far as the information permits.   **(11 marks)**

Notes to the financial statements are not required.

(b)   Calculate the Earnings per Share in accordance with FRS 22 for the year to 30 September 20X1 (ignore comparatives).   **(5 marks)**

(Total = 25 marks)

22 Tourmalet (2.5 12/03 amended)

45 mins

The following extracted balances relate to Tourmalet at 30 September 20X3:

	£'000	£'000
Ordinary shares of 20p each		50,000
Profit and loss reserve 1 October 20X2		64,200
Revaluation reserves (including investment property revaluations)		2,100
6% Redeemable preference shares		30,000
Trade creditors		35,300
Corporation tax		2,100
Land and buildings – at valuation (note (iii))	150,000	
Plant and equipment – cost (note (v))	98,600	
Investment property – valuation at 1 October 20X2 (note (iv))	10,000	
Depreciation 1 October 20X2 – land and buildings		9,000
Depreciation 1 October 20X2 – plant and equipment		24,600
Trade debtors	31,200	
Stock – 1 October 20X2	26,550	
Bank	3,700	
Turnover (note (i))		313,000
Investment income (from properties)		1,200
Purchases	158,450	
Distribution expenses	26,400	
Administration expenses	23,200	
Interim preference dividend	900	
Ordinary dividend paid	2,500	
	531,500	531,500

The following notes are relevant:

(i)   Turnover includes £50 million for an item of plant sold on 1 June 20X3. The plant had a book value of £40 million at the date of its sale, which was charged to cost of sales. On the same date, Tourmalet entered into an agreement to lease back the plant for the next five years (being the estimated remaining life of the plant) at a cost of £14 million per annum payable annually in arrears. An arrangement of this type is deemed to have a financing cost of 12% per annum. No depreciation has been charged on the item of plant in the current year.

(ii)   The stock at 30 September 20X3 was valued at cost of £28·5 million. This includes £4·5 million of slow moving goods. Tourmalet is trying to sell these to another retailer but has not been successful in obtaining a reasonable offer. The best price it has been offered is £2 million.

(iii) On 1 October 20W9 Tourmalet had its land and buildings revalued by a firm of surveyors at £150 million, with £30 million of this attributed to the land. At that date the remaining life of the building was estimated to be 40 years. These figures were incorporated into the company's books. There has been no significant change in property values since the revaluation.

(iv)   Details of the investment property are:

Valuation – 1 October 20X2   £10 million
Valuation – 30 September 20X3   £9·8 million

The company policy is to revalue its investment property at the end of each financial year.

(v)   Plant and equipment (other than that referred to in note (i) above) is depreciated at 20% per annum on the reducing balance basis. All depreciation is to be charged to cost of sales.

(vi)   The above balances contain the results of Tourmalet's car retailing operations which ceased on 31 December 20X2 due to mounting losses. The results of the car retailing operation, which is to be treated as a discontinued operation, for the year to 30 September 20X3 are:

	£'000
Sales	15,200
Cost of sales	16,000
Operating expenses	3,200

The operating expenses are included in the figure for administration expenses in the trial balance. Tourmalet is still paying rentals for the lease of its car showrooms. The rentals are included in operating expenses. Tourmalet is hoping to use the premises as an expansion of its administration offices. This is dependent on obtaining planning permission from the local authority for the change of use, however this is very difficult to obtain. Failing this, the best option would be early termination of the lease which will cost £1·5 million in penalties. This amount has not been provided for.

(vii) The balance on the corporation tax account in the trial balance is the result of the settlement of the previous year's tax charge. The directors have estimated the provision for corporation tax for the year to 30 September 20X3 at £9·2 million.

(viii) The preference dividend is equal to the annual finance cost.

Required

(a) Comment on the substance of the sale of the plant and the directors' treatment of it.   **(5 marks)**

(b) Prepare the Profit and Loss Account; and   **(18 marks)**

(c) The Statement of Total Recognised Gains and Losses of Tourmalet for the year to 30 September 20X3 in accordance with current accounting standards.   **(2 marks)**

Note. A balance sheet is NOT required. Disclosure notes are NOT required.   **(Total = 25 marks)**

23 Partway (2.5 12/06)   45 mins

(a) (i) State the definition of discontinued operations and explain the usefulness of information for discontinued operations and why a robust definition of them is needed.   **(4 marks)**

Partway is in the process of preparing its financial statements for the year ended 31 October 2006. the company's main activity is in the travel industry mainly selling package holidays (flights and accommodation) to the general public through the internet and retail travel agencies. During the current year the number of holidays sold by travel agencies has declined dramatically and the directors decided at a board meeting on 15 November 2006 to close down its chain of travel agents. Immediately after the meeting the travel agencies' staff and suppliers were notified of the situation and an announcement was made in the press. The directors wish to show the travel agencies' results as a discontinued operation in the financial statements, to 31 October 2006. due to the declining business of the travel agents, on 1 August 2006 Partway expended its internet operations to offer car hire facilities to purchasers of its internet holidays.

The following are Partway's summarised profit and loss account results – years ended.

		31 October 2006		31 October 2005	
	Internet	Travel agencies	Car hire	Total	Total
Turnover	23,000	14,000	2,000	39,000	40,000
Cost of sales	(18,000)	(16,500)	(1,500)	(36,000)	(32,000)
Gross profit/(loss)	5,000	(2,500)	500	3,000	8,000
Operating costs	(1,000)	(1,500)	(100)	(2,600)	(2,000)
Profit/(loss) before tax	4,000	(4,000)	400	400	6,000

The results for the travel agencies for the year ended 31 October 2005 were: turnover £18 million, cost of sales £15 million and operating costs of £1.5 million.

Required

(ii)   Discuss whether the directors' wish to show the travel agencies' results as a discounted operation is justifiable.   **(4 marks)**

(iii)   Assuming the closure of the travel agencies is a discontinued operation, prepare the (summarised) profit and loss account of Partway for the year ended 31 October 2006 together with its comparatives.   **(6 marks)**

(b)   (i)   Describe the circumstances in which an entity may change its accounting policies and how a change should be applied.   **(5 marks)**

The terms under which Partway sells its holidays are that a 10% deposit is required on booking and the balance of the holiday must be paid six weeks before the travel date. In previous years, Partway has recognised revenue (and profit) from the sale of its holidays at the holiday is actually taken. From the beginning of November 2005, Partway has made it a condition, of booking that all customers must have holiday cancellation insurance and as a result it is unlikely that the outstanding balance of any holidays will be unpaid due to cancellation. In preparing its financial statements to 31 October 2006, the directors are proposing to change to recognising revenue (and related estimated costs) at the date when a booking is made. The directors also feel that this change will help to negate the adverse effect of comparison with last year's results (year ended 31 October 2005) which were better than the current year's.

Required

(ii)   Comment on whether Partway's proposal to change the timing of its recognition of its revenue is acceptable and whether this would be a change of accounting policy.   **(6 marks)**

(Total = 25 marks)

24 Preparation question with helping hands: Simple consolidation

Boo plc has owned 80% of Goose Ltd's equity since its incorporation. On 31 December 20X8 it despatched goods which cost £80,000 to Goose, at an invoiced cost of £100,000. Goose received the goods on 2 January 20X9 and recorded the transaction then. The two companies' draft accounts as at 31 December 20X8 are shown below.

PROFIT AND LOSS ACCOUNTS FOR THE YEAR ENDED 31 DECEMBER 20X8

	Boo	Goose
	£'000	£'000
Sales	5,000	1,000
Cost of sales	2,900	600
Gross profit	2,100	400
Other expenses	1,700	320
Net profit	400	80
Tax	130	25
Profit after tax	270	55

BALANCE SHEETS AT 31 DECEMBER 20X8

	£'000	£'000
Fixed assets	2,000	200
Current assets		
Stock	500	120
Trade debtors	650	40
Bank and cash	390	35
	1,540	195
Current liabilities		
Trade creditors	910	30
Tax	130	25
	1,040	55
Net current assets	500	140
Total assets less current liabilities	2,500	340
Capital and reserves		
Share capital	2,000	100
Profit and loss account	500	240
	2,500	340

Required

Prepare draft consolidated financial statements.

Helping hands

1   This is a very easy example to ease you into the technique of preparing consolidated accounts. There are a number of points to note.

2   Stock in transit should be included in the balance sheet and deducted from cost of sales at cost to the group.

3   Similarly, the intra-group debtor and sale should be eliminated as a consolidation adjustment.

4   Boo plc must have included its intercompany account in trade debtors as it is not specifically mentioned elsewhere in the accounts.

5   Remember that only the parent company's shares are shown in the group accounts.

6   The minority interest in the P&L account is easily calculated as 20% of post-tax profit for the year as shown in Goose's accounts. However, in the balance sheet, the minority interest represents the minority interest in retained profits and share capital only.

7   Don't forget that Boo's accounts must somewhere contain a balance for its investment in Goose Ltd (its holding of shares in Goose, issued at par value, since no share premium is shown in Goose's books). Fixed assets must therefore be reduced by this amount to correspond to the cancellation of Goose's share capital.

---

25 Hideaway (2.5 12/05 amended)   23 mins

Related party relationships are a common feature of commercial life. The objective of FRS 8 *Related party disclosures* is to ensure that financial statements contain the necessary disclosures to make users aware of the possibility that financial statements may have been affected by the existence of related parties.

Required

(a)   Describe the main circumstances that give rise to related parties.   **(4 marks)**

(b)   Explain why the disclosure of related party relationships and transactions may be important.   **(3 marks)**

(c) Hideaway is a public listed company that owns two subsidiary company investments. It owns 100% of the equity shares of Benedict and 55% of the equity shares of Depret. During the year ended 30 September 20X5 Depret made several sales of goods to Benedict. These sales totalled £15 million and had cost Depret £14 million to manufacture. Depret made these sales on the instruction of the Board of Hideaway. It is known that one of the directors of Depret, who is not a director of Hideaway, is unhappy with the parent company's instruction as he believes the goods could have been sold to other companies outside the group at the far higher price of £20 million. All directors within the group benefit from a profit sharing scheme.

Required

Describe the financial effect that Hideaway's instruction may have on the financial statements of the companies within the group and the implications this may have for other interested parties. **(6 marks)**

(Total = 13 marks)

26 Highveldt (2.5 6/05)   **45 mins**

Highveldt, a private company, acquired 75% of Samson's ordinary shares on 1 April 20X4. Highveldt paid an immediate £3·50 per share in cash and agreed to pay a further amount of £108 million on 1 April 20X5. Highveldt's cost of capital is 8% per annum. Highveldt has only recorded the cash consideration of £3·50 per share.

The summarised balance sheets of the two companies at 31 March 20X5 are shown below:

	Highveldt		Samson	
	£million	£million	£million	£million
Tangible fixed assets (note (i))		420		320
Investments (note (ii))		300		20
Development costs (note (iv))		nil		40
		720		380
Current assets	133		91	
Creditors: amounts falling due within one year	(108)		(81)	
Net current assets		25		10
Creditors: amounts falling due after more than one year				
10% inter company loan (note (ii))		nil		(60)
Net assets		745		330
Share capital and reserves:				
Ordinary shares of £1 each		270		80
Reserves:				
Share premium		80		40
Revaluation reserve		45		nil
Profit and loss account at 1 April 20X4	160		134	
Profit for year to 31 March 20X5	190		76	
		350		210
		745		330

The following information is relevant:

(i) Highveldt has a policy of revaluing land and buildings to fair value. At the date of acquisition Samson's land and buildings had a fair value £20 million higher than their book value and at 31 March 20X5 this had increased by a further £4 million (ignore any additional depreciation).

(ii) Included in Highveldt's investments is a loan of £60 million made to Samson at the date of acquisition. Interest is payable annually in arrears. Samson paid the interest due for the year on 31 March 20X5, but Highveldt did not receive this until after the year end. Highveldt has not accounted for the accrued interest from Samson.

(iii)   Samson had established a line of products under the brand name of Titanware. Acting on behalf of Highveldt, a firm of specialists, had valued the brand name at a value of £40 million with an estimated life of 10 years as at 1 April 20X4. The brand is not included in Samson's balance sheet.

(iv)   Samson's development project was completed on 30 September 20X4 at a cost of £50 million. £10 million of this had been amortised by 31 March 20X5. Development costs capitalised by Samson at the date of acquisition were £18 million. Highveldt's policy for development costs is that they should be written off as incurred.

(v)   Samson sold goods to Highveldt during the year at a profit of £6 million, one third of these goods were still in the stock of Highveldt at 31 March 20X5.

(vi)   Goodwill is amortised over a four year life.

Required

(a)   Calculate the following figures as they would appear using UK GAAP in the consolidated balance sheet of Highveldt at 31 March 20X5:

(i)   goodwill;   **(8 marks)**

(ii)   minority interest;   **(4 marks)**

(iii)   the following consolidated reserves: share premium, revaluation reserve and the profit and loss reserve.   **(8 marks)**

Note: show your workings

(b)   Explain why consolidated financial statements are useful to the users of financial statements (as opposed to just the parent company's separate (entity) financial statements).   **(5 marks)**

(Total = 25 marks)

27 Hample (2.5 6/99 amended)   36 mins

On 1 April 20X8 Hample plc acquired 90% of the equity shares in Sopel Ltd. On the same day Hample plc accepted a 10% loan note from Sopel Ltd for £200,000 which was repayable at £40,000 per annum (on 31 March each year) over the next five years. Sopel Ltd's retained profits at the date of acquisition were £2,200,000.

BALANCE SHEETS AS AT 31 MARCH 20X9

	Hample plc £'000	Hample plc £'000	Sopel Ltd £'000	Sopel Ltd £'000
Fixed assets				
Intangible – Software		–		1,800
Tangible:				
Property		600		900
Plant and equipment		1,520		1,090
Investments - equity in Sopel Ltd		4,110		–
- 10% loan note from Sopel Ltd		200		–
- others		65		210
		6,495		4,000
Current assets				
Stock	719		560	
Debtors	524		328	
Sopel Ltd current account	75		–	
Cash	20		–	
	1,338		888	
Creditors: amounts falling due within one year				
Trade creditors	475		472	
Hample plc current account	–		60	
Taxation	228		174	
Operating overdraft	–		27	
	(703)		(733)	
Net current assets		635		155
Creditors: amounts falling due after more than one year				
10% Loan note		–		(160)
Government grants		(230)		(40)
Net assets		6,900		3,955
Share capital and reserves				
Ordinary shares of £1 each		2,000		1,500
Share premium	2,000		500	
Retained earnings	2,900		1,955	
		4,900		2,455
		6,900		3,955

The following information is relevant:

(i)   Included in Sopel Ltd's property at the date of acquisition was a leasehold property recorded at its depreciated historic cost of £400,000. The leasehold had been sublet for its remaining life of only four years at an annual rental of £80,000 payable in advance on 1 April each year. The directors of Hample plc are of the opinion that the fair value of this leasehold is best reflected by the present value of its future cash flows. An appropriate cost of capital for the group is 10% per annum.

The present value of a £1 annuity received at the end of each year where interest rates are 10% can be taken as:

3 year annuity	£2.50
4 year annuity	£3.20

(ii)   The software of Sopel Ltd represents the depreciated cost of the development of an integrated business accounting package. It was completed at a capitalised cost of £2,400,000 and went on sale on 1 April 20X7. Sopel Ltd's directors are depreciating the software on a straight-line basis over an eight-year life (ie £300,000 per annum). However, the directors of Hample plc are of the opinion that a five-year life would be more appropriate as sales of business software rarely exceed this period.

(iii)   The stock of Hample plc on 31 March 20X9 contains goods at a transfer price of £25,000 that were supplied by Sopel Ltd who had marked them up with a profit of 25% on cost.

(iv)   On 31 March 20X9 Sopel Ltd remitted to Hample plc a cash payment of £55,000. This was not received by Hample plc until early April. It was made up of an annual repayment of the 10% loan note of £40,000 (the interest had already been paid) and £15,000 off the current account balance.

(v)   Consolidated goodwill is amortised over a five-year life.

Required

Prepare the consolidated balance sheet of Hample plc at 31 March 20X9.   **(20 marks)**

28 Preparation question: Acquisition during the year

Port has many investments, but before 20X4 none of these investments met the criteria for consolidation as a subsidiary. One of these older investments was a £2.3m 12% loan to Alfred Ltd which was made in 20W1 and is not due to be repaid until 20Y6.

On 1st November 20X4 Port purchased 75% of the equity of Alfred for £650,000. The consideration was 35,000 £1 equity shares in Port with a fair value of £650,000.

Noted below are the draft profit and loss accounts and movement in retained earnings for Port and its subsidiary Alfred for the year ending 31st December 20X4 along with the draft balance sheets as at 31st December 20X4.

PROFIT AND LOSS ACCOUNTS FOR THE YEAR ENDING 31 DECEMBER 20X4

	Port	Alfred
	£'000	£'000
Turnover	100	996
Cost of sales	(36)	(258)
Gross profit	64	738
Interest on loan to Alfred	276	-
Other investment income	158	-
Operating expenses	(56)	(330)
Finance costs	-	(276)
Profit before tax	442	132
Tax	(112)	(36)
Profit after tax	330	96

CHANGES IN RETAINED EARNINGS FOR THE YEAR ENDING 31 DECEMBER 20X4

	Port	Alfred
	£'000	£'000
Opening retained earnings	2,640	235
Profit for the year	330	96
Dividends paid	(70)	–
Closing retained earnings	2,900	331

BPP
LEARNING MEDIA

BALANCE SHEETS AS AT 31 DECEMBER 20X4

	Port £'000	Alfred £'000
Assets		
Fixed assets		
Tangible assets	100	3,000
Investments		
Loan to Alfred	2,300	–
Other investments	600	
	3,000	3,000
Current assets	800	139
Current liabilities	(200)	(323)
Net current assets	600	(184)
Total assets less current liabilities	3,600	2,816
Long-term liabilities		
Loan from Port	–	(2,300)
	3,600	516
Capital and reserves		
Share capital	200	100
Share premium	500	85
Retained earnings	2,900	331
	3,600	516

Notes

(a)   Port has not accounted for the issue of its own shares or for the acquisition of the investment in Alfred.

(b)   Amortisation of goodwill is to commence in 20X5.

Required

Prepare the consolidated profit and loss account for the Port Group for the year ending 31 December 20X4, along with a consolidated balance sheet at that date.

Approaching the question

1   Establish the **group structure**, noting for how long Alfred was a subsidiary.

2   Adjust Port's balance sheet for the issue of its own shares and the cost of the investment in Alfred.

3   Sketch out the **format** of the group profit and loss account and balance sheet, and then fill in the amounts for each company directly from the question. (Note, sub-totals are not normally needed when you do this.)

4   **Time apportion** the income, expenditure and taxation for the subsidiary acquired.

5   Calculate the **goodwill**.

6   Remember to time apportion the minority interest in Alfred.

29 Hillusion (2.5 6/03)   45 mins

In recent years Hillusion plc has acquired a reputation for buying modestly performing businesses and selling them at a substantial profit within a period of two to three years of their acquisition. On 1 July 20X2 Hillusion plc acquired 80% of the ordinary share capital of Skeptik plc at a cost of £10,280,000. On the same date it also acquired 50% of Skeptik plc's 10% loan notes at par. The summarised draft financial statements of both companies are:

PROFIT AND LOSS ACCOUNTS: YEAR TO 31 MARCH 20X3

	Hillusion plc	Skeptik plc
	£'000	£'000
Turnover	60,000	24,000
Cost of sales	(42,000)	(20,000)
Gross profit	18,000	4,000
Operating expenses	(6,000)	(200)
Loan interest received (paid)	75	(200)
Operating profit	12,075	3,600
Taxation	(3,000)	(600)
Profit after tax for the year	9,075	3,000
Profit brought forward	16,525	5,400
Retained profit per balance sheet	25,600	8,400

BALANCE SHEETS: AS AT 31 MARCH 20X3

	£'000	£'000	£'000	£'000
Tangible Fixed Assets		19,320		8,000
Investments		11,280		nil
		30,600		8,000
Current Assets	15,000		8,000	
Creditors: amounts falling due within one year	(10,000)		(3,600)	
Net Current Assets		5,000		4,400
		35,600		12,400
Creditors: amounts falling due after more than one year				
10% Loan notes		nil		(2,000)
Net Assets		35,600		10,400
Capital and Reserves				
Ordinary shares of £1 each		10,000		2,000
Profit and loss account		25,600		8,400
		35,600		10,400

The following information is relevant:

(i)   The fair values of Skeptik plc's assets were equal to their book values with the exception of its plant, which had a fair value of £3·2 million in excess of its book value at the date of acquisition. The remaining life of all of Skeptik plc's plant at the date of its acquisition was four years and this period has not changed as a result of the acquisition. Depreciation of plant is on a straight-line basis and charged to cost of sales. Skeptik plc has not adjusted the value of its plant as a result of the fair value exercise.

(ii)   In the post acquisition period Hillusion plc sold goods to Skeptik plc at a price of £12 million. These goods had cost Hillusion plc £9 million. During the year Skeptik plc had sold £10 million (at cost to Skeptik plc) of these goods for £15 million.

(iii)   Hillusion plc bears almost all of the administration costs incurred on behalf of the group (invoicing, credit control etc). It does not charge Skeptik plc for this service as to do so would not have a material effect on the group profit.

(iv)   Revenues and profits should be deemed to accrue evenly throughout the year.

(v)   The current accounts of the two companies were reconciled at the year-end with Skeptik plc owing Hillusion plc £750,000.

(vi)   Consolidated goodwill is to be written off as an operating expense over a three-year life. Time apportionment should be used in the year of acquisition.

Required

(a)   Prepare a consolidated profit and loss account and balance sheet for Hillusion plc for the year to 31 March 20X3

(20 marks)

(b)   Explain why it is necessary to eliminate unrealised profits when preparing group financial statements; and how reliance on the entity financial statements of Skeptik plc may mislead a potential purchaser of the company.   **(5 marks)**

(Total = 25 marks)

Note. Your answer should refer to the circumstances described in the question.

30 Hydan (2.5 6/06)   **45 mins**

On 1 October 20X5 Hydan, a publicly listed company, acquired a 60% controlling interest in Systan paying £9 per share in cash. Prior to the acquisition Hydan had been experiencing difficulties with the supply of components that it used in its manufacturing process. Systan is one of Hydan's main suppliers and the acquisition was motivated by the need to secure supplies. In order to finance an increase in the production capacity of Systan, Hydan made a non-dated loan at the date of acquisition of £4 million to Systan that carried an actual and effective interest rate of 10% per annum. The interest to 31 March 20X6 on this loan has been paid by Systan and accounted for by both companies. The summarised draft financial statements of the companies are:

Profit and loss accounts for the year ended 31 March 20X6

	Hydan	Systan Pre-acquisition	Systan Post-acquisition
	£'000	£'000	£'000
Turnover	98,000	24,000	35,200
Cost of sales	(76,000)	(18,000)	(31,000)
Gross profit	22,000	6,000	4,200
Operating expenses	(11,800)	(1,200)	(8,000)
Interest income	350	nil	Nil
Interest payable	(420)	nil	(200)
Profit/(loss) before tax	10,130	4,800	(4,000)
Taxation (expense)/relief	(4,200)	(1,200)	1,000
Profit/(loss) for the financial year	5,930	3,600	(3,000)

Balance sheets as at 31 March 20X6

	Hydan		Systan	
	£'000	£'000	£'000	£'000
Tangible fixed assets		18,400		9,500
Investments (including loan to Systan)		16,000		nil
		34,400		9,500
Current assets	18,000		7,200	
Creditors: amounts falling due within one year	(11,400)		(3,900)	
Net current assets		6,600		3,300
Total assets less current liabilities		41,000		12,800
Creditors: amounts falling due after more than one year				
7% Bank loan		(6,000)		nil
10% loan from Hydan		nil		(4,000)
		35,000		8,800
Capital and reserves				
Ordinary shares of £1 each		10,000		2,000
Share premium		5,000		500
Profit and loss account		20,000		6,300
		35,000		8,800

The following information is relevant:

(i)   At the date of acquisition, the fair values of Systan's tangible fixed assets were £1·2 million in excess of their carrying amounts. This will have the effect of creating an additional depreciation charge (to cost of sales) of £300,000 in the consolidated financial statements for the year ended 31 March 20X6. Systan has not adjusted its assets to fair value.

(ii)   In the post acquisition period Systan's sales to Hydan were £30 million on which Systan had made a consistent profit of 5% of the selling price. Of these goods, £4 million (at selling price to Hydan) were still in the stock of Hydan at 31 March 20X6. Prior to its acquisition Systan made all its sales at a uniform gross profit margin.

(iii)   Included in Hydan's creditors falling due within one year is £1 million owing to Systan. This agreed with Systan's sales ledger balance for Hydan at the year end.

(iv)   Consolidated goodwill is to be written off as an operating expense over a four-year life using time apportionment where appropriate.

(v)   Neither company paid a dividend in the year to 31 March 20X6.

Required

(a)   Prepare the consolidated profit and loss account for the year ended 31 March 20X6 and the consolidated balance sheet at that date.   **(20 marks)**

(b)   Discuss the effect that the acquisition of Systan appears to have had on Systan's operating performance.
                                                                                                              (5 marks)

                                                                                                    (Total = 25 marks)

31 Hydrate (2.5 12/02 amended)   36 mins

Hydrate plc is a public company operating in the industrial chemical sector. In order to achieve economies of scale, it has been advised to enter into business combinations with compatible partner companies. As a first step in this strategy Hydrate plc acquired all of the ordinary share capital of Sulphate plc by way of a share exchange on 1 April 20X2. Hydrate plc issued five of its own shares for every four shares in Sulphate plc. The market value of Hydrate plc's shares on 1 April 20X2 was £6 each. The share issue has not yet been recorded in Hydrate plc's books. The summarised financial statements of both companies for the year to 30 September 20X2 are:

PROFIT AND LOSS ACCOUNTS FOR THE YEAR TO 30 SEPTEMBER 20X2

	Hydrate plc £'000	Sulphate plc £'000
Turnover	24,000	20,000
Cost of sales	(16,600)	(11,800)
Gross profit	7,400	8,200
Operating expenses	(1,600)	(1,000)
Operating profit	5,800	7,200
Taxation	(2,000)	(3,000)
Profit after tax	3,800	4,200

BALANCE SHEETS AS AT 30 SEPTEMBER 20X2

	Hydrate plc		Sulphate plc	
	£'000	£'000	£'000	£'000
Fixed assets				
Land and Buildings		20,000		15,000
Plant		44,000		20,000
Investment		nil		12,800
		64,000		47,800
Current assets				
Stock	22,800		23,600	
Debtors	16,400		24,200	
Bank	500		200	
	39,700		48,000	
Creditors: amounts falling due within one year				
Trade creditors	15,300		17,700	
Taxation	2,200		3,000	
	(17,500)		(20,700)	
Net current assets		22,200		27,300
Creditors: amounts falling after more than one year				
8% Loan note		(5,000)		(18,000)
Net assets		81,200		57,100
Capital and reserves				
Ordinary shares of £1 each		20,000		12,000
Reserves:				
Share premium	4,000		2,400	
Profit and loss account	57,200	61,200	42,700	45,100
		81,200		57,100

The following information is relevant.

(i)   The fair value of Sulphate plc's investment was £5 million in excess of its book value at the date of acquisition. The fair values of Sulphate plc's other net assets were equal to their book value.

(ii)   Consolidated goodwill is deemed to have a five year life, with time apportioned charges (treated as operating expense) in the year of acquisition.

(iii)   No dividends have been paid or proposed by either company.

Required

Prepare the consolidated profit and loss account and balance sheet of Hydrate plc for the year to 30 September 20X2. **(20 marks)**

32 Preparation question: Laurel Ltd

Laurel Ltd acquired 80% of the ordinary share capital of Hardy Ltd for £160,000 and 40% of the ordinary share capital of Comic Ltd for £70,000 on 1 January 20X7 when the profit and loss reserve balances were £64,000 in Hardy Ltd and £24,000 in Comic Ltd.

The balance sheets of the three companies at 31 December 20X9 are set out below:

	Laurel Ltd £'000	Hardy Ltd £'000	Comic Ltd £'000
Fixed assets			
Tangible	220	160	78
Investment	230		
	450	160	78
Current assets			
Stocks	384	234	122
Debtors	275	166	67
Cash at bank	42	10	34
	701	410	223
Creditors: amounts falling due within one year			
Trade creditors	(457)	(343)	(124)
Net current assets	244	67	99
	694	227	177
Capital and reserves			
£1 ordinary shares	400	96	80
Share premium account	16	3	–
Profit and loss reserve	278	128	97
	694	227	177

You are also given the following information:

(i) On 30 November 20X9 Laurel Ltd sold some goods to Hardy Ltd for cash for £32,000. These goods had originally cost £22,000 and none had been sold by the year-end. On the same date Laurel Ltd also sold goods to Comic Ltd for cash for £22,000. These goods originally cost £10,000 and Comic had sold half by the year end.

(ii) On 1 January 20X7 Hardy Ltd owned fixed assets with a book value of £45,000 that had a fair value of £57,000. These assets were originally purchased by Hardy on 1 January 20X5 and are being depreciated over 6 years.

(iii) Goodwill is capitalised and is being amortised over four years

Required

Prepare a consolidated balance sheet for Laurel Ltd and its subsidiary company, incorporating its associate in accordance with FRS 9.

33 Preparation question: Tyson plc

Below are the profit and loss accounts of Tyson plc, its subsidiary and associate at 31 December 20X8.

	Tyson plc £'000	Douglas Ltd £'000	Frank Ltd £'000
Turnover	500	150	70
Cost of sales	(270)	(80)	(30)
Gross profit	230	70	40
Operating expenses	(150)	(20)	(15)
Operating profit	80	50	25
Interest receivable	15	10	-
Interest payable	(20)	–	(10)
Profit before tax	75	60	15
Taxation	(25)	(15)	(5)
Profit after tax	50	45	10

You are also given the following information:

(i) Tyson plc acquired 80,000 shares in Douglas Ltd for £188,000 3 years ago when Douglas Ltd had a credit balance on the profit and loss reserve of £40,000. Douglas Ltd has 100,000 £1 ordinary shares.

(ii) Tyson plc acquired 40,000 shares in Frank Ltd for £60,000 2 years ago when that company had a credit balance on its profit and loss reserve of £20,000. Frank Ltd has 100,000 £1 ordinary shares.

(iii) During the year Douglas Ltd sold some goods to Tyson plc for £66,000 (cost £48,000). None of the goods had been sold by the year end.

(iv) Any goodwill is to be amortised over 5 years.

Required

Prepare the consolidated profit and loss account for the year ended 31 December 20X8 for Tyson plc, incorporating its associate.

34 Question with analysis: Hepburn (2.5 Pilot Paper)   45 mins

(a) On 1 October 20X0 Hepburn plc acquired 80% of the ordinary share capital of Salter Ltd by way of a share exchange. Hepburn plc issued five of its own shares for every two shares it acquired in Salter Ltd. The market value of Hepburn plc's shares on 1 October 20X0 was £3 each. The share issue has not yet been recorded in Hepburn plc's books. The summarised financial statements of both companies are:

PROFIT AND LOSS ACCOUNTS FOR THE YEAR TO 31 MARCH 20X1

	Hepburn plc £'000	Salter Ltd £'000
Turnover	1,200	1,000
Cost of sales	(650)	(660)
Gross profit	550	340
Operating expenses	(120)	(88)
Finance charge on debentures	nil	(12)
Operating profit	430	240
Taxation	(100)	(40)
Profit after tax	330	200

BALANCE SHEETS AS AT 31 MARCH 20X1

	Hepburn plc		Salter Ltd	
	£'000	£'000	£'000	£'000
Fixed assets				
Land and Buildings		400		150
Plant and Machinery		220		510
Investments		20		10
		640		670
Current assets				
Stock	240		280	
Debtors	170		210	
Bank	20		40	
	430		530	
Creditors: amounts falling due within one year				
Trade creditors	170		155	
Taxation	50		45	
	(220)		(200)	
Net current assets		210		330
Creditors: amounts falling due after more than one year				
8% Debentures		nil		(150)
Net assets		850		850
Capital and reserves				
Ordinary shares of £1 each		400		150
Profit and loss account		450		700
		850		850

The following information is relevant.

(i) The fair values of Salter Ltd's assets were equal to their book values with the exception of its land, which had fair value of £125,000 in excess of its book value at the date of acquisition.

(ii) In the post acquisition period Hepburn plc sold goods to Salter Ltd at a price of £100,000, this was calculated to give a mark-up on cost of 25% to Hepburn plc. Salter Ltd had half of these goods in stock at the year end.

(iii) Consolidated goodwill is to be written off as an operating expense over a five-year life. Time apportionment should be used in the year of acquisition.

(iv) The current accounts of the two companies disagreed due to a cash remittance of £20,000 to Hepburn plc on 26 March 20X1 not being received until after the year end. Before adjusting for this, Salter Ltd's debtor balance in Hepburn plc's books was £56,000.

Required

Prepare a consolidated profit and loss account and balance sheet for Hepburn plc for the year to 31 March 20X1. **(20 marks)**

(b) At the same date as Hepburn plc made the share exchange for Salter Ltd's shares, it also acquired 6,000 'A' shares in Woodbridge Ltd for a cash payment of £20,000. The share capital of Woodbridge Ltd is made up of:

Ordinary voting A shares 10,000

Ordinary non-voting B shares 14,000

All of Woodbridge Ltd's equity shares are entitled to the same dividend rights; however during the year to 31 March 20X1 Woodbridge Ltd made substantial losses and did not pay any dividends.

Hepburn plc has treated its investment in Woodbridge Ltd as an ordinary fixed asset investment on the basis that:

(i) It is only entitled to 25% of any dividends that Woodbridge Ltd may pay

(ii)   It does not have any directors on the board of Woodbridge Ltd

(iii)   It does not exert any influence over the operating policies or management of Woodbridge Ltd.

Required

Comment on the accounting treatment of Woodbridge Ltd by Hepburn plc's directors and state how you believe the investment should be accounted for. **(5 marks)**

Note. You are not required to amend your answer to part (a) in respect of the information in part (b).

(Total = 25 marks)

Approaching the answer

(a)   On 1 October 20X0 Hepburn plc acquired 80% of the equity share capital of Salter Ltd by way of a share exchange. Hepburn issued five of its own shares for every two shares in Salter. The market value of Hepburn's shares on 1 October 20X0 was £3 each. The share issue has not yet been recorded in Hepburn's books. The summarised financial statements of both companies are:

You can work out the cost of the investment or the goodwill calculation

PROFIT AND LOSS ACCOUNTS
YEAR TO 31 MARCH 20X1

	Hepburn plc	Salter Ltd
	£'000	£'000
Turnover	1,200	1,000
Cost of sales	(650)	(660)
Gross profit	550	340
Operating expenses	(120)	(88)
Debenture interest	Nil	(12)
Operating profit	430	240
Taxation	(100)	(40)
Profit after tax	330	200

BALANCE SHEETS AS AT 31 MARCH 20X1

	Hepburn plc		Salter Ltd	
	£'000	£'000	£'000	£'000
Fixed assets				
Land and Buildings		400		150
Plant and Machinery		220		510
Investments		20		10
		640		670
Current assets				
Stock	240		280	
Debtors	170		210	
Bank	20		40	
	430		530	
Creditors: amounts falling due within one year				
Trade creditors	170		155	
Taxation	50		45	
	(220)		(200)	
Net current assets		210		330
Creditors: amounts falling after more than one year				
8% Debentures		nil		(150)
Net assets		850		850
Capital and reserves				
Ordinary shares of £1 each		400		150
Profit and loss account		450		700
		850		850

The following information is relevant:

You will use this to calculate goodwill

(i) The fair values of Salter Ltd's assets were equal to their book values with the exception of its land, which had fair value of £125,000 in excess of its book value at the date of acquisition.

(ii) In the post acquisition period Hepburn plc sold goods to Salter Ltd at a price of £100,000, this was calculated to give a mark-up on cost of 25% to Hepburn plc. Salter Ltd had half of these goods in stock at the year end.

There will be an unrealised profit

(iii) Consolidated goodwill is to be written off as an operating expense over a five-year life. Time apportionment should be used in the year of acquisition.

Agree current accounts before eliminating inter-company items

(iv) The current accounts of the two companies disagreed due to a cash remittance of £20,000 to Hepburn plc on 26 March 20X1 not being received until after the year end. Before adjusting for this, Salter Ltd's debtor balance in Hepburn plc's books was £56,000.

Required

Prepare a consolidated profit and loss account and balance sheet for Hepburn plc for the year to 31 March 20X1. **(20 marks)**

(b) At the same date as Hepburn plc made the share exchange for Salter Ltd's shares, it also acquired 6,000 'A' shares in Woodbridge for a cash payment of £20,000. The share capital of Woodbridge Ltd is made up of:

The % age of shares with voting rights is important

| Ordinary voting A shares | 10,000 |
| Ordinary non-voting B shares | 14,000 |

All of Woodbridge Ltd's equity shares are entitled to the same dividend rights; however during the year to 31 March 20X1. Woodbridge Ltd made substantial losses and did not pay any dividends.

Hepburn plc has treated its investment in Woodbridge Ltd as an ordinary fixed asset investment on the basis that:

(i) It is only entitled to 25% of any dividends that Woodbridge Ltd may pay
(ii) It does not any have directors on the board of Woodbridge Ltd
(iii) It does not exert any influence over the operating policies or management of Woodbridge Ltd

Required

This is a big hint that the treatment may be wrong

Comment on the accounting treatment of Woodbridge Ltd by Hepburn plc's directors and state how you believe the investment should be accounted for. **(5 marks)**

Note. You are not required to amend your answer to part (a) in respect of the information in part (b).
(Total = 25 marks)

35 Holdrite (2.5 12/04) **45 mins**

Holdrite purchased 75% of the issued share capital of Staybrite and 40% of the issued share capital of Allbrite on 1 April 20X4.

Details of the purchase consideration given at the date of purchase are:

Staybrite: a share exchange of 2 shares in Holdrite for every 3 shares in Staybrite plus an issue to the shareholders of Staybrite 8% loan notes redeemable at par on 30 June 20X6 on the basis of £100 loan note for every 250 shares held in Staybrite.

Allbrite: a share exchange of 3 shares in Holdrite for every 4 shares in Allbrite plus £1 per share acquired in cash.

The market price of Holdrite's shares at 1 April 20X4 was £6 per share.

The summarised profit and loss accounts for the three companies for the year to 30 September 20X4 are:

LEARNING MEDIA

	Holdrite	Staybrite	Allbrite
	£'000	£'000	£'000
Turnover	75,000	40,700	31,000
Cost of Sales	(47,400)	(19,700)	(15,300)
Gross Profit	27,600	21,000	15,700
Operating expenses	(10,480)	(9,000)	(9,700)
Operating Profit	17,120	12,000	6,000
Interest expense	(170)	nil	nil
Profit before tax	16,950	12,000	6,000
Taxation	(4,800)	(3,000)	(2,000)
Profit after tax	12,150	9,000	4,000

The following information is relevant:

(i)   A fair value exercise was carried out for Staybrite at the date of its acquisition with the following results:

	Book Value	Fair Value
	£'000	£'000
Land	20,000	23,000
Plant	25,000	30,000

The fair values have not been reflected in Staybrite's financial statements. The increase in the fair value of the plant would create additional depreciation of £500,000 in the post acquisition period in the consolidated financial statements to 30 September 20X4.

Depreciation of plant is charged to cost of sales.

(ii)   The details of each company's share capital and reserves at 1 October 20X3 are:

	Holdrite	Staybrite	Allbrite
	£'000	£'000	£'000
Equity shares of £1 each	20,000	10,000	5,000
Share premium	5,000	4,000	2,000
Profit and loss reserve	18,000	7,500	6,000

(iii)   In the post acquisition period Holdrite sold goods to Staybrite for £10 million. Holdrite made a profit of £4 million on these sales. One-quarter of these goods were still in the stock of Staybrite at 30 September 20X4.

(iv)   Goodwill is to be amortised over a five-year life, time apportioned where appropriate.

(v)   Holdrite paid a dividend of £5 million on 20 September 20X4.

Required

(a)   Calculate the goodwill arising on the purchase of the shares in both Staybrite and Allbrite at 1 April 20X4.

(8 marks)

(b)   Prepare a consolidated profit and loss account for the Holdrite Group for the year to 30 September 20X4.

(15 marks)

(c)   Show the movement on the consolidated profit and loss reserve for the year to 30 September 20X4.

(2 marks)

(Total = 25 marks)

36 Hapsburg (2.5 6/04)   45 mins

(a)   Hapsburg, a public listed company, acquired the following investments:

   –   On 1 April 20X3, 24 million shares in Sundial. This was by way of an immediate share exchange of 2 shares in Hapsburg for every 3 shares in Sundial plus a cash payment of £1 per Sundial share payable on 1 April 20X6. The market price of Hapsburg's shares on 1 April 20X3 was £2 each.

   –   On 1 October 20X3, 6 million shares in Aspen paying an immediate £2·50 in cash for each share.

Based on Hapsburg's cost of capital (taken as 10% per annum), £1 receivable in three years' time can be taken to have a present value of £0·75.

Hapsburg has not yet recorded the acquisition of Sundial but it has recorded the investment in Aspen.

The summarised balance sheets at 31 March 20X4 are:

	Hapsburg		Sundial		Aspen	
	£'000	£'000	£'000	£'000	£'000	£'000
Fixed assets						
Land and buildings		16,600		9,700		17,500
Plant		24,400		25,100		20,200
Investments		15,000		3,000		nil
		56,000		37,800		37,700
Current assets						
Stock	9,900		4,800		7,900	
Debtors	13,600		8,600		14,400	
Cash	1,200		3,800		nil	
	24,700		17,200		22,300	
Creditors: amounts falling due within one year						
Trade creditors	16,500		6,900		13,600	
Bank overdraft	nil		nil		4,500	
Taxation	9,600		3,400		1,900	
	(26,100)		(10,300)		(20,000)	
Net current (liabilities)/assets		(1,400)		6,900		2,300
Creditors: amounts falling due after more than one year						
10% loan note		(16,000)		(4,200)		(12,000)
Net assets		38,600		40,500		28,000
Share capital and reserves						
Ordinary shares £1 each		20,000		30,000		20,000
Reserves:						
Share premium	8,000		2,000		nil	
Profit and loss reserve	10,600		8,500		8,000	
		18,600		10,500		8,000
		38,600		40,500		28,000

The following information is relevant:

(i)   Below is a summary of the results of a fair value exercise for Sundial carried out at the date of acquisition:

Asset	Carrying value at acquisition £'000	Fair value at acquisition £'000	Notes
Plant	10,000	15,000	remaining life at acquisition four years
Investments	3,000	4,500	no change in value since acquisition

The book values of the net assets of Aspen at the date of acquisition were considered to be a reasonable approximation to their fair values.

(ii)   The profits of Sundial and Aspen for the year to 31 March 20X4, as reported in their entity financial statements, were £4·5 million and £6 million respectively. No dividends have been paid by any of the companies during the year. All profits are deemed to accrue evenly throughout the year.

(iii)   In January 20X4 Aspen sold goods to Hapsburg at a selling price of £4 million. These goods had cost Aspen £2·4 million. Hapsburg had £2·5 million (at cost to Hapsburg) of these goods still in stock at 31 March 20X4.

(iv) Goodwill is to be written off over a five-year life with a proportionate charge in the year of acquisition.

(v) All depreciation/amortisation is charged on a straight-line basis.

Required

Prepare the consolidated balance sheet of Hapsburg as at 31 March 20X4. **(20 marks)**

Note. The additional disclosures relating to material associates are not required.

(b) Some commentators have criticised the use of equity accounting on the basis that it can be used as a form of off balance sheet financing.

Required

Explain the reasoning behind the use of equity accounting and discuss the above comment. **(5 marks)**

(Total = 25 marks)

37 Hedra (2.5 12/05)   **45 mins**

Hedra, a public listed company, acquired the following investments:

(i) On 1 October 20X4, 72 million shares in Salvador for an immediate cash payment of £195 million. Hedra agreed to pay further consideration on 30 September 20X5 of £49 million if the post acquisition profits of Salvador exceeded an agreed figure at that date. Hedra has not accounted for this deferred payment as it did not believe it would be payable, however Salvador's profits have now exceeded the agreed amount (ignore discounting). Salvador also accepted a £50 million 8% loan from Hedra at the date of its acquisition.

(ii) On 1 April 20X5, 40 million shares in Aragon by way of a share exchange of two shares in Hedra for each acquired share in Aragon. The stock market value of Hedra's shares at the date of this share exchange was £2.50. Hedra has not yet recorded the acquisition of the investment in Aragon.

The summarised balance sheets of the three companies as at 30 September 20X5 are:

	Hedra £m	Hedra £m	Salvador £m	Salvador £m	Aragon £m	Aragon £m
Fixed assets						
Land and buildings		208		105		100
Plant		150		135		170
Investments – in Salvador		245		nil		nil
– other		45		nil		nil
		648		240		270
Current assets						
Stocks	130		80		110	
Debtors	142		97		70	
Cash	nil		4		20	
	272		181		200	
Creditors: amounts falling due within one year						
Trade creditors	118		141		40	
Operating overdraft	12		nil		nil	
Taxation	50		nil		30	
	(180)		(141)		(70)	
Net current assets		92		40		130
Creditors: amounts falling due after more than one year						
8% loan note		nil		(50)		nil
Provisions for liabilities						
Deferred tax		(45)		nil		nil
		695		230		400

	Hedra		Salvador		Aragon	
	£m	£m	£m	£m	£m	£m
Capital and reserves						
Ordinary shares (£1 each)		400		120		100
Reserves:						
Share premium	40		50		nil	
Revaluation	15		nil		nil	
Profit and loss reserve	240		60		300	
		295		110		300
		695		230		400

The following information is relevant:

(a) Fair value adjustments and revaluations:

　　(i) Hedra's accounting policy for land and buildings is that they should be carried at their fair values. The fair value of Salvador's land at the date of acquisition was £20 million in excess of its carrying value. By 30 September 20X5 this excess had increased by a further £5 million. Salvador's buildings did not require any fair value adjustments. The fair value of Hedra's own land and buildings at 30 September 20X5 was £12 million in excess of its carrying value in the above balance sheet.

　　(ii) The fair value of some of Salvador's plant at the date of acquisition was £20 million in excess of its carrying value and had a remaining life of four years (straight-line depreciation is used).

　　(iii) At the date of acquisition Salvador had unrelieved tax losses of £40 million from previous years. Salvador had not accounted for these as a deferred tax asset as its directors did not believe the company would be sufficiently profitable in the near future. However, the directors of Hedra were confident that these losses would be utilised and accordingly they should be recognised as a deferred tax asset. By 30 September 20X5 the group had not yet utilised any of these losses. The corporation tax rate is 25%.

(b) The profit and loss reserves of Salvador and Aragon at 1 October 20X4, as reported in their separate financial statements, were £20 million and £200 million respectively. All profits are deemed to accrue evenly throughout the year.

(c) All goodwill is amortised over a five year life with a proportionate charge in the year of acquisition where appropriate.

Required

Prepare, under UK GAAP, the consolidated balance sheet of Hedra as at 30 September 20X5.　　**(25 marks)**

38 Hosterling (2.5 12/06)　　　　　　　　　　　　　　　　　**45 mins**

Hosterling purchased the following equity investments.

On 1 October 2005: 8% of the issued share capital of Sunlee. The acquisition was through a share exchange of three shares in Hosterling for every five shares in Sunlee. The market price of Hosterling's shares at 1 October 2005 was £5 per share.

On 1 July 2006: 6 million shares in Amber paying £4 per share in cash.

The summarised profit and loss account for the three companies for the year ended 30 September 2006 are:

	Hosterling £'000	Sunlee £'000	Amber £'000
Turnover	105,000	62,000	50,000
Cost of sales	(68,000)	(36,500)	(61,000)
Gross profit/(loss)	37,000	25,500	(11,000)
Distribution costs	(4,000)	(2,000)	(4,500)
Administrative expenses	(7,500)	(7,000)	(8,500)
Other income (note (i))	400	Nil	nil
Finance costs	(1,200)	(900)	nil
Profit/(loss) before tax	24,700	15,600	(24,000)
Tax (change)/credit	(8,700)	(2,600)	4,000
Profit/(loss) for the financial year	16,000	13,000	(20,000)

The following information is relevant;

(i)   The other income is a dividend received from Sunlee on 31 March 2006.

(ii)   The details of Sunlee's and Amber's share capital and reserves at 1 October 2005 were:

	Sunlee £'000	Amber £'000
Equity shares of £1 each	20,000	15,000
Profit and loss account	18,000	35,000

(iii)   The details of Sunlee's and Amber's share capital of acquisition of Sunlee with the following results:

	Carrying amount £'000	Fair value £'000	Remaining life (straight line)
Intellectual property	18,000	22,000	Still in development
Land	17,000	20,000	Not applicable
plant	30,000	35,000	Five years

The fair values have not been reflected in Sunlee's financial statements.

Plant depreciation is included in cost of sales.

No fair value adjustments were required on the acquisition of Amber.

(iv)   In the year ended 30 September 2006 Hosterling sold goods to Sunlee at a selling price of £18 million. Hosterling made a profit of cost plus 25% on these sales. £7.5 million (at cost to Sunlee) of these goods were still in the stock of Sunlee at 30 September 2006.

(v)   All goodwill is amortised on a straight-line basis with time apportionment where appropriate. The estimated life of all goodwill is five years.

(vi)   All trading profit and losses are deemed to accrue evenly though out the year.

Required

(a)   Calculate the goodwill arising on the acquisition of Sunlee at 1 October 2005.   **(5 marks)**

(b)   Calculate the carrying amount of the investment in Amber at 30 September 2006 under the equity method.
        (4 marks)

(c)   Prepare the consolidated profit and loss account for the Hosterling Group for the year ended 30 September 2006.   **(16 marks)**

(Total = 25 marks)

39 Preparation question: Contract

The following details are as at the 31 December 20X5.

	Contract 1	Contract 2	Contract 3	Contract 4
Contract value	£120,000	£72,000	£240,000	£500,000
Costs to date	£48,000	£6,000	£103,200	£299,600
Estimated costs to completion	£48,000	£54,000	£160,800	£120,400
Progress payments received and receivable	£50,400	–	£76,800	£345,200
Date started	1.3.20X5	15.10.20X5	1.7.20X5	1.6.20X4
Estimated completion date	30.6.20X6	15.9.20X6	30.11.20X6	30.7.20X6
% complete	45%	10%	35%	70%

You are to assume that profit accrues evenly over the contract.

The profit and loss account for the previous year showed turnover of £225,000 and cost of sales of £189,000 in relation to contract 4.

The company considers it imprudent to recognise any profit until a contract is 25% complete.

Required

Calculate the amounts to be included in the profit and loss account for the year ended 31 December 20X5 and the balance sheet as at that date.

40 Merryview (2.5 6/02)   27 mins

Merryview plc specialises in construction contracts. One of its contracts, with Better Homes plc, is to build a complex of luxury flats. The price agreed for the contract is £40 million and its scheduled date of completion is 31 December 20X2. Details of the contract to 31 March 20X1 are:

Commencement date	1 July 20X0

Contract costs:	£'000
Architects' and surveyors' fees	500
Materials delivered to site	3,100
Direct labour costs	3,500
Overheads are apportioned at 40% of direct labour costs	
Estimated cost to complete (excluding depreciation – see below)	14,800

Plant and machinery used exclusively on the contract cost £3,600,000 on July 20X0. At the end of the contract it is expected to be transferred to a different contract at a value of £600,000. Depreciation is to be based on a time apportioned basis.

Stock of materials on site at 31 March 20X1 is £300,000.

Better Homes plc paid a progress payment of £12,800,000 to Merryview plc on 31 March 20X1.

At 31 March 20X2 the details for the construction contract have been summarised as:

Contract costs to date (ie since the start of the contract) excluding all depreciation	20,400
Estimated cost to complete (excluding depreciation)	6,600

A further progress payment of £16,200,000 was received on 31 March 20X2.

Merryview plc accrues profit on its long-term contracts using the percentage of completion basis as measured by the percentage of the cost to date compared to the total estimated contract cost.

Required

Prepare extracts of the financial statements of Merryview plc for the contract with Better Homes plc for:

(a) the year to 31 March 20X1   **(8 marks)**
(b) the year to 31 March 20X2   **(7 marks)**

(Total = 15 marks)

41 Linnet (2.5 6/04)   23 mins

(a) Linnet is a large public listed company involved in the construction industry. Accounting standards normally require long term contracts to be accounted for using the percentage (stage) of completion basis. However under certain circumstances they should be accounted for using the completed contracts basis.

Required

Discuss the principles that underlie each of the two methods and describe the circumstances in which their use is appropriate.   **(5 marks)**

(b) Linnet is part way through a contract to build a new football stadium at a contracted price of £300 million.

Details of the progress of this contract at 1 April 20X3 are shown below:

	£ million
Cumulative turnover invoiced	150
Cumulative cost of sales to date	112
Profit to date	38

The following information has been extracted from the accounting records at 31 March 20X4:

	£ million
Total progress payment received for work certified at 29 February 20X4	180
Total costs incurred to date (excluding rectification costs below)	195
Rectification costs	17

Linnet has received progress payments of 90% of the work certified at 29 February 20X4. Linnet's surveyor has estimated the sales value of the further work completed during March 20X4 was £20 million.

At 31 March 20X4 the estimated remaining costs to complete the contract were £45 million.

The rectification costs are the costs incurred in widening access roads to the stadium. This was the result of an error by Linnet's architect when he made his initial drawings.

Linnet calculates the percentage of completion of its contracts as the proportion of sales value earned to date compared to the contract price.

All estimates can be taken as being reliable.

Required

Prepare extracts of the financial statements for Linnet for the above contract for the year to 31 March 20X4.

(8 marks)

(Total = 13 marks)

42 Torrent (2.5 6/06)

22 mins

Torrent is a large publicly listed company whose main activity involves long-term construction projects. Details of three of its contracts for the year ended 31 March 20X6 are:

Contract	Alfa	Beta	Ceta
Date commenced	1 April 2004	1 October 20X5	1 October 20X5
Estimated duration	3 years	18 months	2 years
	£m	£m	£m
Fixed contract price	20	6	12
Estimated costs at start of contract	15	7·5 (note (iii))	10
Cost to date:			
at 31 March 20X5	5	nil	nil
at 31 March 20X6	12.5 (note (ii))	2	4
Estimated costs at 31 March 20X6 to complete	3.5	5.5 (note (iii))	6
Progress payments received at 31 March 20X5 (note (i))	5.4	nil	nil
Progress payments received at 31 March 20X6 (note (i))	12.6	1.8	nil

Notes

(i)   The company's normal policy for determining the percentage completion of contracts is based on the value of work invoiced to date compared to the contract price. Progress payments received represent 90% of the work invoiced. However, no progress payments will be invoiced or received from contract Ceta until it is completed, so the percentage completion of this contract is to be based on the cost to date compared to the estimated total contract costs.

(ii)   The cost to date of £12·5 million at 31 March 20X6 for contract Alfa includes £1 million relating to unplanned rectification costs incurred during the current year (ended 31 March 20X6) due to subsidence occurring on site.

(iii)   Since negotiating the price of contract Beta, Torrent has discovered the land that it purchased for the project is contaminated by toxic pollutants. The estimated cost at the start of the contract and the estimated costs to complete the contract include the unexpected costs of decontaminating the site before construction could commence.

Required

Prepare extracts of the profit and loss account and balance sheet for Torrent in respect of the above contracts for the year ended 31 March 20X6.   **(12 marks)**

43 Multiplex II (2.5 Pilot paper amended)

16 mins

Multiplex plc is in the intermediate stage of a long-term, construction contract for the building of a new privately owned road bridge over a river estuary. The original details of the contract are:

Approximate duration of contract:	3 years
Date of commencement:	1 October 20W9
Total contract price:	£40 million
Estimated total cost:	£28 million

An independent surveyor certified the value of the work in progress as follows.

- On 31 March 20X0   £12 million
- On 31 March 20X1   £30 million (including the £12 million in 20X0)

Costs incurred at:

- 31 March 20X0   £9 million
- 31 March 20X1   £28.5 million (including the £9 million in 20X0)

Payments received on account by 31 March 20X1 were £25 million

On 1 April 20X0 Multiplex plc agreed to a contract variation that would involve an additional fee of £5 million with associated additional estimated costs of £2 million.

The costs incurred during the year to 31 March 20X1 include £2.5 million relating to the replacement of some bolts which had been made from material that had been incorrectly specified by the firm of civil engineers who were contracted by Multiplex plc to design the bridge. These costs were not included in the original estimates, but Multiplex plc is hopeful that they can be recovered from the firm of civil engineers.

Multiplex plc calculates profit on long-term contracts using the percentage of completion method. The percentage of completion of the contract is based on the value of the work certified to date compared to the total contract price.

Required

Prepare the profit and loss account and balance sheet extracts in respect of the contract for the year to 31 March 20X1 only.   **(9 marks)**

44 Bodyline (2.5 12/03)   **45 mins**

FRS 12 'Provisions, Contingent Liabilities and Contingent Assets' was issued in 1998. The Standard sets out the principles of accounting for these items and clarifies when provisions should and should not be made. The inappropriate use of provisions is a practice that could allow companies to manipulate their financial statements.

Required

(a)   Describe the nature of provisions and the accounting requirements of FRS 12 for them.   **(6 marks)**

(b)   Explain why there is a need for an accounting standard in this area. Illustrate your answer with three practical examples of how the standard addresses controversial issues.   **(6 marks)**

(c)   Bodyline sells sports goods and clothing through a chain of retail outlets. It offers customers a full refund facility for any goods returned within 28 days of their purchase provided they are unused and in their original packaging. In addition, all goods carry a warranty against manufacturing defects for 12 months from their date of purchase. For most goods the manufacturer underwrites this warranty such that Bodyline is credited with the cost of the goods that are returned as faulty. Goods purchased from one manufacturer, Header, are sold to Bodyline at a higher negotiated discount which is designed to compensate Bodyline for any manufacturing defects. No refunds are given by Header, thus Bodyline has to bear the costs of any manufacturing faults of these goods.

Bodyline makes a uniform mark up on cost of 25% on all goods it sells, except for those supplied from Header on which it makes a mark up on cost of 40%. Sales of goods manufactured by Header consistently account for 20% of all Bodyline's sales.

Sales in the last 28 days of the trading year to 30 September 20X3 were £1,750,000. Past trends reliably indicate that 10% of all goods are returned under the 28-day return facility. These are not faulty goods. Of these 70% are later resold at the normal selling price and the remaining 30% are sold as 'sale' items at half the normal retail price.

In addition to the above expected returns an estimated £160,000 (at selling price) of the goods sold during the year are likely to have manufacturing defects and have yet to be returned by customers. Goods returned as faulty have no resale value.

Required

Describe the nature of the above warranty/return facilities and calculate the provision Bodyline is required to make at 30 September 20X3:

(i)   for goods subject to the 28 day returns policy; and

(ii)   for goods that are likely to be faulty.   **(8 marks)**

(d)   Rockbuster has recently purchased an item of earth moving plant at a total cost of £24 million. The plant has an estimated life of 10 years with no residual value, however its engine will need replacing after every 5,000 hours of use at an estimated cost of £7·5 million. The directors of Rockbuster intend to depreciate the plant at £2·4 million (£24 million/10 years) per annum and make a provision of £1,500 (£7·5 million/5,000 hours) per hour of use for the replacement of the engine.

Required

Explain how the plant should be treated in accordance with Accounting Standards and comment on the Directors' proposed treatment.   **(5 marks)**

(Total = 25 marks)

45 Myriad III (2.5 12/01)   11 mins

Myriad plc manufactures and sells high quality printing paper. The auditor has drawn the company's attention to the sale of some packs of paper on 20 October 20X1 at a price of £45 each. These items were included in closing stock on 30 September 20X1 at their manufactured cost of £48 each. Further investigations revealed that during stocktaking on 30 September 20X1 a quantity of packs of A3 size paper had been damaged by a water leak. The following week the company removed the damage by cutting the paper down to A4 size (A4 size is smaller than A3). The paper was then repackaged and put back into stock. The cost of cutting and repackaging was £4 per pack. The normal selling price of the paper is £75 per pack for the A3 and £50 per pack for the A4, however on 12 October 20X1 the company reduced the selling price of all its paper by 10% in response to similar price cuts by its competitors.

Securiprint plc, one of the customers that bought some of the 'damaged' paper had used it to print some share certificates for a customer. Securiprint plc informed Myriad plc that these share certificates had been returned by the customer because they contained marks that were not part of the design. Securiprint plc believes the marks were part of a manufacturing flaw on the part of Myriad plc and is seeking appropriate compensation.

Required

Discuss the impact the above information may have on the draft financial statements of Myriad plc for the year to 30 September 20X1.   **(6 marks)**

46 Peterlee II (2.5 6/06 part)   22 mins

Peterlee is preparing its financial statements for the year ended 31 March 20X6. The following items have been brought to your attention:

(i)   Peterlee acquired the entire share capital of Trantor during the year. The acquisition was achieved through a share exchange. The terms of the exchange were based on the relative values of the two companies obtained by capitalising the companies' estimated future cash flows. When the fair value of Trantor's identifiable net assets was deducted from the value of the company as a whole, its goodwill was calculated at £2·5 million. A similar exercise valued the goodwill of Peterlee at £4 million. The directors wish to incorporate both the goodwill values in the companies' consolidated financial statements.   **(4 marks)**

(ii)   During the year Peterlee acquired an iron ore mine at a cost of £6 million. In addition, when all the ore has been extracted (estimated in 10 years time) the company will face estimated costs for landscaping the area affected by the mining that have a present value of £2 million. These costs would still have to be incurred even if no further ore was extracted. The directors have proposed that an accrual of £200,000 per year for the next ten years should be made for the landscaping. **(4 marks)**

(iii) On 1 April 20X5 Peterlee issued an 8% £5 million convertible loan at par. The loan is convertible in three years time to ordinary shares or redeemable at par in cash. The directors decided to issue a convertible loan because a non-convertible loan would have required an interest rate of 10%. The directors intend to show the liability for the loan at £5 million. The following discount rates are available for £1 receivable at the end of the year:

	8%	10%
Year 1	0.93	0.91
Year 2	0.86	0.83
Year 3	0.79	0.75

(4 marks)

Required

Describe (and quantify where possible) how Peterlee should treat the items in (i) to (iii) in its financial statements for the year ended 31 March 20X6 commenting on the directors' views where appropriate.

The mark allocation is shown against each of the three items above.

(Total = 12 marks)

47 Jedders (2.5 12/00 amended) 27 mins

Your assistant at Jedders, a small listed company, has been preparing the financial statements for the year ended 31 December 20X0 and has raised the following queries.

(a) The company has three long leasehold properties in different parts of the region. The leases were acquired at different times, and the lease terms are all for fifty years. As at 1 January 20X0, their original cost, accumulated depreciation to date and carrying (book) values were as follows.

	Cost	Depreciation	Carrying value 1.1.20X0
	£'000	£'000	£'000
Property in North	3,000	1,800	1,200
Property in Central	6,000	1,200	4,800
Property in South	3,750	1,500	2,250

On 1 January an independent surveyor provided valuation information to suggest that the value of the South property was the same as book value, the North property had fallen against carrying value by 20% and the Central property had risen by 40% in value against the carrying value.

The directors of the company wish to include the revaluation of the Central property in the accounts to 31 December 20X0, whilst leaving the other properties at their depreciated historical cost.

The directors believe that this treatment of the North property is prudent and can be justified because property prices are expected to recover within the next few years so that this fall in value will be entirely reversed.

Required

(i) Advise the directors whether their proposal is acceptable, assuming they are committed to the use of current value for the Central property. **(2 marks)**

(ii) Assuming that all of the properties are revalued, calculate the income statement charges and the non-current asset balance sheet extracts for all the properties for the year ended 31 December 20X0. **(3 marks)**

(b) On 1 October 20X0, Jedders signed a debt factoring agreement with a company Fab Factors. Jedders' trade debtors are to be split into three groups, as follows.

- *Group A* debtors will not be factored or administered by Fab Factors under the agreement, but instead will be collected as usual by Jedders.

- *Group B* debtors are to be factored and collected by Fab Factors on a 'with recourse' basis. Fab Factors will charge a 1% per month finance charge on the balance outstanding at the beginning of the month. Jedders will reimburse in full any individual balance outstanding after three months.

- *Group C* debtors will be factored and collected by Fab Factors 'without recourse'; Fab Factors will pay Jedders 95% of the book value of the debtors.

Jedders has a policy of making a debtors' allowance (doubtful debt provision) of 20% of a trade debtor balance when it becomes three months old.

The debtor groups have been analysed as follows.

		% of 1 October 20X0 balance collected in:		
	Balance at 1 Oct 20X0	October	November	December
	£'000			
Group A	1,250	30%	30%	20%
Group B	1,500	40%	30%	20%
Group C	2,000	50%	25%	22%

Required

For the accounts of Jedders, calculate the finance costs and charge for debtors' allowance for each group of trade debtors for the period 1 October - 31 December 20X0 and show the balance sheet values for those trade debtors as at 31 December 20X0. **(5 marks)**

(c) On 1 January 20X0, Jedders issued £15m of 7% convertible debentures at par. The debentures are convertible into equity shares in the company, at the option of the debenture holders, five years after the date of issue (31 December 20X4) on the basis of 25 shares for each £100 of debenture stock. Alternatively, the debentures will be redeemed at par.

Jedders has been advised by Fab Factors that, had the company issued similar debentures without the conversion rights, then it would have had to pay interest of 10%; the rate is thus lower because the conversion rights are favourable.

Fab Factors also suggest that, as some of the debenture holders will choose to convert, the debentures are, in substance, equity and should be treated as such on Jedders' balance sheet. Thus, as well as a reduced finance cost being achieved to boost profitability, Jedders' gearing has been improved compared to a straight issue of debt.

The present value of £1 receivable at the end of each year, based on discount rates of 7% and 10% can be taken as:

End of year	7%	10%
1	0.93	0.91
2	0.87	0.83
3	0.82	0.75
4	0.76	0.68
5	0.71	0.62

Required

In relation to the 7% convertible debentures, calculate the finance cost to be shown in the profit and loss account and the balance sheet extracts for the year to 31 December 20X0 for Jedders and comment on the advice from Fab Factors. **(5 marks)**

(Total = 15 marks)

48 Triangle (2.5 6/05)

45 mins

Triangle, a private company, is in the process of preparing its draft financial statements for the year to 31 March 20X5. The following matters have been brought to your attention:

(i) On 1 April 20X4 the company brought into use a new processing plant that had cost £15 million to construct and had an estimated life of ten years. The plant uses hazardous chemicals which are put in containers and shipped abroad for safe disposal after processing. The chemicals have also contaminated the plant itself which occurred as soon as the plant was used. It is a legal requirement that the plant is decontaminated at the end of its life. The estimated present value of this decontamination, using a discount rate of 8% per annum, is £5 million. The financial statements have been charged with £1·5 million (£15 million/10 years) for plant depreciation and a provision of £500,000 (£5 million/10 years) has been made towards the cost of the decontamination.

(8 marks)

(ii) On 15 May 20X5 the company's auditors discovered a fraud in the material requisitions department. A senior member of staff who took up employment with Triangle in August 20X4 had been authorising payments for goods that had never been received. The payments were made to a fictitious company that cannot be traced. The member of staff was immediately dismissed. Calculations show that the total amount of the fraud to the date of its discovery was £240,000 of which £210,000 related to the year to 31 March 20X5. (Assume the fraud is material).

(5 marks)

(iii) The company has contacted its insurers in respect of the above fraud. Triangle is insured for theft, but the insurance company maintains that this is a commercial fraud and is not covered by the theft clause in the insurance policy. Triangle has not yet had an opinion from its lawyers.

(4 marks)

(iv) On 1 April 20X4 Triangle sold maturing stock that had a carrying value of £3 million (at cost) to Factorall, a finance house, for £5 million. Its estimated market value at this date was in excess of £5 million. The stock will not be ready for sale until 31 March 20X8 and will remain on Triangle's premises until this date. The sale contract includes a clause allowing Triangle to repurchase the stock at any time up to 31 March 20X8 at a price of £5 million plus interest at 10% per annum compounded from 1 April 20X4. The stock will incur storage costs until maturity. The cost of storage for the current year of £300,000 has been included in debtors (in the name of Factorall). If Triangle chooses not to repurchase the stock, Factorall will pay the accumulated storage costs on 31 March 20X8. The proceeds of the sale have been debited to the bank and the sale has been included in Triangle's turnover.

(8 marks)

Required

Explain how the items in (i) to (iv) above should be treated in Triangle's financial statements for the year to 31 March 20X5 in accordance with UK GAAP's current accounting standards. Your answer should quantify the amounts where possible.

The mark allocation is shown against each of the four matters above.

(Total = 25 marks)

49 Forest

45 mins

The overriding requirement of a company's financial statements is that they should represent faithfully the underlying transactions and other events that have occurred. To achieve this, transactions have to be accounted for in terms of their 'substance' or economic reality rather than their legal form. This principle is set out in FRS 5 *Reporting the substance of transactions*.

Required

(a) Describe why it is important that substance rather than legal form is used to account for transactions, and describe how financial statements can be adversely affected if the substance of transactions is not recorded.

(5 marks)

(b) Describe, using examples, how the following features may indicate that the substance of a transaction is different from its legal form.

  (i) Separation of ownership from beneficial use
  (ii) The linking of transactions including the use of option clauses
  (iii) When an asset is sold at a price that differs from its fair value **(9 marks)**

(c) On 1 April 20X1 Forest had a stock of cut seasoning timber which had cost £12 million two years ago. Due to shortages of this quality of timber its value at 1 April 20X1 had risen to £20 million. It will be a further three years before this timber is sold to a manufacturer of high-class furniture. On 1 April 20X1 Forest entered into an arrangement to sell Barret Bank the timber for £15 million. Forest has an option to buy back the timber at any time within the next three years at a cost of £15 million plus accumulated interest at 2% per annum above the base rate. This will be charged from the date of the original sale. The base rate for the period of the transaction is expected to be 8%. Forest intends to buy back the timber on 31 March 20X4 and sell it the same day for an expected price of £25 million.

Note. Ignore any storage costs and capitalisation of interest that may relate to stocks.

Required

Assuming the above transactions take place as expected, prepare extracts to reflect the transactions in the profit and loss accounts for the years to 31 March 20X2, 20X3 and 20X4 and the balance sheets (ignore cash) at those year ends:

  (i) If Forest treated the transactions in their legal form
  (ii) If the substance of the transactions is recorded

Comment briefly on your answer to (c) above. **(11 marks)**

(Total = 25 marks)

50 Atkins (2.5 12/02) 27 mins

FRS 5 *'Reporting the Substance of Transactions'* was issued partly in reaction to a minority of public companies entering into certain complex transactions. These transactions sometimes led to accusations that company directors were involved in creative accounting.

Required

(a) Atkins plc's operations involve selling cars to the public through a chain of retain car showrooms. It buys most of its new vehicles directly from the manufacturer on the following terms.

  • Atkins plc with pay the manufacturer for the cars on the date they are sold to the customer or six months after they are delivered to its showrooms whichever is the sooner.

  • The price paid will be 80% of the retail price list as set by the manufacturer at the date that the goods are delivered.

  • Atkins plc will pay the manufacturer 1.5% per month (of the cost price to Atkins plc) as 'display charge' until the goods are paid for.

  • Atkins plc may return the cars to the manufacturer any time up until the date the cars are due to be paid for. Atkins plc will incur the freight cost of any such returns. Atkins plc has never taken advantage of this right of return.

  • The manufacturer can recall the cars or request them to be transferred to another retailer any tie up until the time they are paid for by Atkins plc.

Required

Discuss which party bears the risks and rewards in the above arrangement and come to a conclusion on how the transactions should be treated by each party **(6 marks)**

(b)   Atkins plc bought five identical plots of development land for £2 million in 20W9. On 1 October 20X1 Atkins plc sold three of the plots of land to an investment company, Landbank plc, for a total of £2.4 million. This price was based on 75% of the fair market value of £3.2 million as determined by an independent surveyor at the date of sale. The terms of the sale contained two clauses:

- Atkins plc can re-purchase the plots of land for the full fair value of £3.2 million (the value determined at the date of sale) any time until 30 September 20X4; and

- On 1 October 20X4, Landbank plc has the option to require Atkins plc to re-purchase the properties for £3.2 million. You may assume that Landbank plc seeks a return on its investments of 10% per annum

Required

Discuss the substance of the above transactions; and **(3 marks)**

Prepare extracts of the profit and loss account and balance sheet (ignore cash) of Atkins plc for the year to 30 September 20X2:

- if the plots of land are considered as sold to Landbank plc; and **(2 marks)**
- reflecting the substance of the above transactions. **(4 marks)**

(Total = 15 marks)

51 Angelino (2.5 12/06)   45 mins

(a)   Recording the substance of transactions, rather then their legal form is an important principle in financial accounting. Abuse of this principle can lead to profit manipulation, non-recognition of assets and substantial debt not being recorded on the balance sheet.

Required

Describe how the use of off balance sheet financing can mislead users of financial statements.

Note: your answer should refer to specific user groups, and include examples were recording the legal form of transactions may mislead them. **(9 marks)**

(b)   Angelino has entered into the following transactions during the year ended 30 September 2006:

(i)   In September 2006 Angelino sold (factored) some of its trade debtors to Omar, a financial house. On selected account balances Omar paid Angelino 80% of their book value. The agreement was that Omar would administer the collection of the debtors and remit a residual amount to Angelino depending upon how quickly individual customers paid. Any balance uncollected by Omar after six months will be refunded to Omar by Angelino. **(5 marks)**

(ii)   On 1 October 2005 Angelino owned a freehold building that had a carrying amount of £7.5 million and had an estimated remaining life of 20 years. On this date it sold the building to Finaid for a price of £12 million and entered into an agreement with Finaid to rent back the building for an annual rental of £1.3 million for a period of five years. The auditors of Angelino have commented that in their opinion the building had a market value of only £10 million at the date of its sale and to rent an equivalent building under similar terms to the agreement between Angelino and Finaid would only cost £800,000 per annum. Assume any finance costs are 10% per annum. **(6 marks)**

(iii)   Angelino is a motor car dealer selling vehicles to the public. Most of its vehicles are supplied on consignment by two manufacturers. Monza and Capri, who trade on different terms.

Monza supplies cars on terms that allow Angelino to display the vehicles for a period of three months from the date of delivery or when Angelino sells the cars on to a retail customer if this is less than three months. Within this period Angelino can return the cars to Monza or can be asked by Monza to transfer the cards to another dealership (both at no cost to Angelino). Angelino pays the manufacturer's list price at the end of the three month period (or at the date of sale if sooner). In recent years Angelino has returned several cars to Monza that were not selling very well and has also been required to transfer cars to other dealerships at Monza's request.

Capri's terms of supply are that Angelino pays 10% of the manufacturer's price at the date of delivery and 1% of the outstanding balance per month as a display charge. After six months (or sooner if Angelino chooses), Angelino must pay the balance of the purchase price or return the cars to Capri. If the cars are returned to the manufacturer, Angelino has to pay for the transportation costs and forfeits the 10% deposit. Because of this Angelino has only returned vehicles to Capri once in the last three years. **(5 marks)**

Required

Describe how the above transitions and events should be treated in the financial statements of Angelino for the year ended 30 September 2006. Your answer should explain, where relevant, the difference between the legal form of the transactions and their substance.

Note: the mark allocation is shown against each of the three transactions above.

(Total = 25 marks)

52 Preparation question: Branch Ltd

Branch Ltd acquired an item of plant and machinery on a finance lease on 1 January 20X1. The terms of the agreement were as follows:

Deposit	:	£1,150
Instalments	:	£4,000 pa for seven years payable in arrears
Cash price	:	£20,000

The asset has useful life of four years and the interest rate implicit in the lease is 11%.

Required

Prepare extracts of the profit and loss account and balance sheet for the year ending 31 December 20X1.

(Notes to the accounts are not required.)

53 Evans   22 mins

On 1 October 20X3 Evans plc entered into a non-cancellable agreement whereby Evans plc would lease a new rocket booster. The terms of the agreement were that Evans plc would pay 26 rentals of £3,000 quarterly in advance commencing on 1 October 20X3, and that after this initial period Evans plc could continue, at its option, to use the rocket booster for a nominal rental which is not material.

The cash price of this asset would have been £61,570 and the asset has a useful life of 10 years.

Evans plc considers this lease to be a finance lease and charges a full year's depreciation in the year of purchase of an asset. The rate of interest implicit in the lease is 2% per quarter.

On 1 July 20X2 Evans plc entered into another non-cancellable agreement to lease a Zarkov rocket for a period of 10 years at a rental of £5,000 half-yearly to be paid in advance, commencing on 1 July 20X2. Evans plc considers this lease to be an operating lease.

Required

Show how these transactions would be reflected in the financial statements for the year ended 31 December 20X3.

(12 marks)

54 Bowtock (2.5 12/03 amended)
9 mins

Bowtock has leased an item of plant under the following terms:

Commencement of the lease was 1 January 20X2

Term of lease 5 years

Annual payments in advance £12,000

Cash price and fair value of the asset – £52,000 at 1 January 20X2

Implicit interest rate within the lease (as supplied by the lessor) 8% per annum (to be apportioned on a time basis where relevant).

The company's depreciation policy for this type of plant is 20% per annum on cost (apportioned on a time basis where relevant).

Required

Prepare extracts of the profit and loss account and balance sheet for Bowtock for the year to 30 September 20X3 for the above lease.

(5 marks)

55 Preparation question: Julian Co

The following information has been provided by the directors of Fuller plc as at 31 December 20X1:

(i)   At 31 December 20X1 there is an excess of capital allowances over depreciation of £120 million. It is anticipated that the timing differences will reverse according to the following schedule:

	30 Dec 20X2	30 Dec 20X3	30 Dec 20X4
	£m	£m	£m
Depreciation	560	560	560
Capital allowances	530	520	510
	30	40	50

(ii)   The directors wish to revalue a property by £20 million as at 31 December 20X1.

(iii)   Corporation tax is 30% and the company wishes to discount any deferred tax liabilities at a rate of 4%

Required

Explain the deferred tax implications of the above and calculate the deferred tax provision as at 31 December 20X1.

Note: Present Value Table (extract)

Present value of £1 i.e. $(1+r)-n$ where r = interest rate, n = number of periods until payment or receipt.

Periods (n)	4%
1	0.962
2	0.925
3	0.889

56 Deferred taxation

18 mins

Explain, with examples, the nature and purpose of deferred taxation.

(10 marks)

57 Bowtock II (2.5 12/03 part)

20 mins

(a)   FRS 19 'Deferred Tax' was issued in December 2000. It details the requirements relating to the accounting treatment of deferred tax.

Required

Explain why it is considered necessary to provide for deferred tax and briefly outline the principles of accounting for deferred tax contained in FRS 19 'Deferred Tax'.   **(5 marks)**

(b)   Bowtock purchased a fixed asset for £2,000,000 on 1 October 20X0. It had an estimated life of eight years and an estimated residual value of £400,000. The plant is depreciated on a straight-line basis. The Inland Revenue allow 40% of the cost of this type of asset to be claimed against corporation tax in the year of purchase and 20% per annum (on a reducing balance basis) of its tax written down value thereafter. The rate of corporation tax can be taken as 25%.

Required

In respect of the above item of plant, calculate the deferred tax charge/credit in Bowtock's profit and loss account for the year to 30 September 20X3 and the deferred tax balance in the balance sheet at that date.

(6 marks)

Note. Work to the nearest £'000.

(Total = 11 marks)

58 Preparation question: Fenton plc

(a)   Fenton plc had 5,000,000 ordinary shares in issue on 1 January 20X1.

On 31 January 20X1, the company made a rights issue of 1 for 4 at £1.75. The cum rights price was £2 per share.

On 30 June 20X1, the company made an issue at full market price of 125,000 shares.

Finally, on 30 November 20X1, the company made a 1 for 10 bonus issue.

Profit for the year was £2,900,000.

The reported EPS for year ended 31 December 20X0 was 46.4p.

Required

What was the earnings per share figure for year ended 31 December 20X1 and the restated EPS for year ended 31 December 20X0?

(b)   Sinbad plc had the same 10 million ordinary shares in issue on both 1 January 20X1 and 31 December 20X1. On 1 January 20X1 the company issued 1,200,000 £1 units of 5% convertible loan stock. Each unit of stock is convertible into 4 ordinary shares on 1 January 20X9 at the option of the holder. The following is an extract from Sinbad plc's profit and loss account for the year ended 31 December 20X1:

	£'000
Operating profit	980
Interest payable on 5% convertible loan stock	(60)
Profit on ordinary activities before taxation	920
Taxation: Corporation tax at 30%	(276)
Profit after tax	644

Required

What was the basic and diluted earnings per share for the year ended 31 December 20X1?

(c)   Talbot plc has in issue 5,000,000 50p ordinary shares throughout 20X3.

During 20X1 the company had given certain senior executives options over 400,000 shares exercisable at £1.10 at any time after 31 May 20X4. None were exercised during 20X3. The average fair value of one ordinary share during the period was £1.60.

Talbot plc had made a profit after tax of £540,000 in 20X3.

Required

What is the basic and diluted earnings per share for the year ended 31 December 20X3?

59 Savoir (2.5 6/06 part)   23 mins

(a)   The issued share capital of Savoir, a publicly listed company, at 31 March 20X3 was £10 million. Its shares are denominated at 25p each. Savoir's earnings attributable to its ordinary shareholders for the year ended 31 March 20X3 were also £10 million, giving an earnings per share of 25p.

Year ended 31 March 20X4

On 1 July 20X3 Savoir issued eight million ordinary shares at full market value. On 1 January 20X4 a bonus issue of one new ordinary share for every four ordinary shares held was made. Earnings attributable to ordinary shareholders for the year ended 31 March 20X4 were £13,800,000.

Year ended 31 March 20X5

On 1 October 20X4 Savoir made a rights issue of shares of two new ordinary shares at a price of £1·00 each for every five ordinary shares held. The offer was fully subscribed. The market price of Savoir's ordinary shares immediately prior to the offer was £2·40 each. Earnings attributable to ordinary shareholders for the year ended 31 March 20X5 were £19,500,000.

Required

Calculate Savoir's earnings per share for the years ended 31 March 20X4 and 20X5 including comparative figures.   **(9 marks)**

(b)   On 1 April 20X5 Savoir issued £20 million 8% convertible loan stock at par. The terms of conversion (on 1 April 20X8) are that for every £100 of loan stock, 50 ordinary shares will be issued at the option of loan stockholders. Alternatively the loan stock will be redeemed at par for cash. Also on 1 April 20X5 the directors of Savoir were awarded share options on 12 million ordinary shares exercisable from 1 April 20X8 at £1·50 per share. The average market value of Savoir's ordinary shares for the year ended 31 March 20X6 was £2·50 each. The corporation tax rate is 25%. Earnings attributable to ordinary shareholders for the year ended 31 March 20X6 were £25,200,000. The share options have been correctly recorded in the profit and loss account.

Required

Calculate Savoir's basic and diluted earnings per share for the year ended 31 March 20X6 (comparative figures are not required).

You may assume that both the convertible loan stock and the directors' options are dilutive.   **(4 marks)**

(Total = 13 marks)

60 Niagara (2.5 6/03 part)

23 mins

Extracts of Niagara plc's consolidated profit and loss account for the year to 31 March 20X3 are:

	£'000
Sales	36,000
Cost of sales	(21,000)
Gross profit	15,000
Other operating expenses	(6,200)
Operating profit	8,800
Income from associated companies	1,500
Interest payable	(800)
Profit before exceptional item	9,500
Exceptional item – fixed asset impairment	(4,000)
Profit before tax	5,500
Taxation	(2,800)
Profit after tax	2,700
Minority interest	(115)
Profit for financial year	2,585

The exceptional item attracted tax relief of £1 million which has been included in the tax charge.

Niagara plc paid an interim ordinary dividend of 3p per share in June 20X2 and declared a final dividend at the year end of 6p per share.

The issued share capital of Niagara plc on 1 April 20X2 was:

Ordinary shares of 25p each	£3 million
8% Preference shares (irredeemable)	£1 million

The company also had in issue £2 million 7% convertible loan stock dated 20X5. The loan stock will be redeemed at par in 20X5 or converted to ordinary shares on the basis of 40 new shares for each £100 of loan stock at the option of the stockholders. Niagara plc's corporation tax rate is 30%.

There are also in existence directors' share warrants (issued in 20X1) which entitle the directors to receive 750,000 new shares in total in 20X5 at no cost to the directors.

The following share issues took place during the year to 31 March 20X3:

(i)   1 July 20X2; a rights issue of 1 new share at £1.50 for every 5 shares held. The market price of Niagara plc's shares the day before the rights issue was £2.40.

(ii)   1 October 20X2; an issue of £1 million 6% preference shares at par.

Both issues were fully subscribed.

Niagara plc's basic earnings per share in the year to 31 March 20X2 was correctly disclosed as 24p.

Required

Calculate for Niagara plc for the year to 31 March 20X3:

(a)   the dividend cover and explain its significance **(3 marks)**

(b)   the basic earnings per share including the comparative **(4 marks)**

(c)   the fully diluted earnings per share (ignore comparative); and advise a prospective investor of the significance of the diluted earnings per share figure **(6 marks)**

(Total = 13 marks)

61 Preparation question: Analytical review

As internal auditor of Signomi plc you are conducting an investigation of the company's trading results. Your directors believe a further issue of debenture stock is needed to fund both the repayment of the 10% stock due for repayment in 20X9 and for investment in new plant and machinery. The industry in which Signomi plc operates is, and is likely to remain, highly competitive.

Note. 'Now' is November 20X8.

The following financial information has been provided.

BALANCE SHEETS AS AT 31 DECEMBER

	20X7	20X6	20X5	20X4	20X3
Net fixed assets	£m	£m	£m	£m	£m
Land and buildings	3.0	2.5	2.4	1.6	1.5
Plant and machinery	3.2	2.0	1.2	0.8	0.6
	6.2	4.5	3.6	2.4	2.1
Current assets					
Stocks	5.0	4.7	3.0	2.4	1.9
Debtors	2.6	2.0	1.9	1.5	1.4
Total assets	13.8	11.2	8.5	6.3	5.4
Creditors: amounts falling due within one year	4.3	4.0	3.5	2.2	2.0
Total assets less current liabilities*	9.5	7.2	5.0	4.1	3.4
Creditors: amounts falling due after more than one year					
10% debenture stock 20X9	1.5	1.5	1.5	1.5	1.5
12% debenture stock 20Y5	2.0	2.0	-	-	-
Net capital employed	6.0	3.7	3.5	2.6	1.9
Capital and reserves					
Authorised and issued £1 shares fully paid	1.5	1.5	1.5	1.5	1.0
Retained profit	4.5	2.2	2.0	1.1	0.9
Shareholders' interest	6.0	3.7	3.5	2.6	1.9
*Includes bank overdraft	1.9	1.3	0.6	0.8	0.9

EXTRACTS FROM PROFIT AND LOSS ACCOUNT

	20X7	20X6	20X5	20X4	20X3
Net sales	16.4	13.5	10.0	8.5	7.3
Cost of sales	8.9	7.1	6.1	5.5	4.8
Net profit before tax	3.0	1.5	1.4	0.8	0.5

Some average statistics for the industry as a whole in 20X7 are given as follows.

Net profit before tax: sales	14%
Net profit before tax: total assets less current liabilities	18%
Working capital (current) ratio	2.2:1
Liquidity ratio	0.75:1
Sales: fixed assets	3.0
Turnover of stock	2.8
Debtors collection period (based on average debtors)	45 days
Age of stock	120 days

Required

(a)   Present a schedule of data derived from the financial information provided for AB plc which would be used as the basis of an analytical review.

(b)   Use the data from (a) above:

(i)   To analyse the financing proposals
(ii)   To assess the reasonableness of the figures in the five-year statement of results

Approaching the question

1   Do not calculate too many ratios: the question itself gives you a big hint as to those you should provide.
2   Your analysis must be as good as your calculations, as well as being supported by them.
3   Make sensible points and do not be afraid to state the obvious.

62 Rytetrend (2.5 6/03)   45 mins

Rytetrend plc is a retailer of electrical goods. Extracts from the company's financial statements are set out below:

PROFIT AND LOSS ACCOUNT FOR THE YEAR ENDED 31 MARCH

	20X3		20X2	
	£'000	£'000	£'000	£'000
Turnover		31,800		23,500
Cost of sales		(22,500)		(16,000)
Gross profit		9,300		7,500
Other operating expenses		(5,440)		(4,600)
Operating profit		3,860		2,900
Interest payable – loan notes	(260)		(500)	
– overdraft	(200)		nil	
		(460)		(500)
Profit before taxation		3,400		2,400
Taxation		(1,000)		(800)
Profit after taxation		2,400		1,600

BALANCE SHEETS AS AT 31 MARCH

	20X3		20X2	
	£'000	£'000	£'000	£'000
Fixed assets (note (i))		24,500		17,300
Current assets				
Stock	2,650		3,270	
Debtors	1,100		1,950	
Bank	nil		400	
	3,750		5,620	
Creditors: amounts falling due within one year				
Bank overdraft	1,050		nil	
Trade creditors	2,850		1,980	
Taxation	720		630	
Warranty provision (note (ii))	500		150	
	(5,120)		(2,760)	
Net current assets		(1,370)		2,860
Creditors: amounts falling due after more than one year				
10% loan notes		(nil)		(4,000)
6% loan notes		(2,000)		(nil)
		21,130		16,160
Share capital and reserves				
Ordinary capital (£1 shares)		11,500		10,000
Share premium		1,500		nil
Profit and loss reserve		8,130		6,160
		21,130		16,160

BPP
LEARNING MEDIA

Notes.

(i)   The details of the fixed assets are:

	Cost	Accumulated depreciation	Net book value
	£'000	£'000	£'000
At 31 March 20X2	27,500	10,200	17,300
At 31 March 20X3	37,250	12,750	24,500

During the year there was a major refurbishment of display equipment. Old equipment that had cost £6 million in September 20W8 was replaced with new equipment at a gross cost of £8 million. The equipment manufacturer had allowed Rytetrend plc a trade in allowance of £500,000 on the old display equipment. In addition to this Rytetrend plc used its own staff to install the new equipment. The value of staff time spent on the installation has been costed at £300,000, but this has not been included in the cost of the asset. All staff costs have been included in operating expenses. All display equipment held at the end of the financial year is depreciated at 20% on its cost. No equipment is more than five years old.

(ii)   Operating expenses contain a charge of £580,000 for the cost of warranties on the goods sold by Rytetrend plc. The company makes a warranty provision when it sells its products and cash payments for warranty claims are deducted from the provision as they are settled.

(iii)   Dividends paid were £430,000 in the year to 31 March 20X3.

Required

(a)   Prepare a cash flow statement for Rytetrend plc for the year ended 31 March 20X3.   **(12 marks)**

(b)   Write a report briefly analysing the operating performance and financial position of Rytetrend plc for the years ended 31 March 20X2 and 20X3.   **(13 marks)**

Your report should be supported by appropriate ratios.   **(Total = 25 marks)**

63 Harper (2.5 12/02)   45 mins

You are a partner in a small audit and accounting practice. You have just completed the audit and finalised the financial statements of a small family owned company in discussion with its managing director, Mrs Harper. After the meeting Mrs Harper has asked you for your help. She has obtained the published financial statements of several quoted companies in which she is considering buying some shares as a personal investment. She presents you with the following information.

(a)   In the year to 30 September 20X2, two companies, Gamma plc and Toga plc, reporting identical profits before tax of £100 million. Information in the Chairman's reports said both companies also expected profits from their core activities (to be interpreted as from continuing operations) to grow by 10% in the following year. Mrs Harper has extracted information from the profit and loss accounts and made the following summary.

	Gamma plc	Toga plc
	£m	£m
Operating profit:		
Continuing activities	70	90
Acquisitions	nil	50
Discontinued activities	30	(40)
	100	100

A note to the financial statements of Toga plc said that both the discontinuation and acquisition occurred on 1 April 20X2 and were part of an overall plan to focus on it traditional core activities after incurring large losses on a new foreign venture.

Required

(i)   Briefly explain to Mrs Harper why information on discontinued operations is useful   **(3 marks)**

(ii) Calculate the expected operating profit for both companies for the year to 30 September 20X3 (assuming the Chairmen's growth forecasts are correct):

– in the absence of information of the discontinued operations; and
– based on the information provided above. **(4 marks)**

(b) Taylor plc is another company about which Mrs Harper has obtained the following information from its published financial statements.

Earnings per share

Year to 30 September	20X2	20X1
Basic earnings per share	25p	20p

The earnings per share is based on attributable earnings of £50 million (£30 million in 20X1) and 200 million ordinary shares in issue throughout the year (150 million weighted average number of ordinary shares in 20X1).

Balance sheet extracts	£ million	£ million
8% Convertible loan stock	200	200

The loan stock is convertible to ordinary shares in 20X4 on the basis of 79 new shares for each £100 of loan stock

Note to the financial statements

There are directors' share options (in issue since 19X9) that allow Taylor plc's directors to subscribe for at total of 50 million new ordinary shares at a price of £1.50 each.

(Assume the current rate of corporation tax for Taylor plc is 25% and the market price of its ordinary shares throughout the year had been £2.50.)

Mrs Harper has read that the trend of the earnings per share is a reliable measure of a company's profit trend. She cannot understand why the increase in profits is 67% (£30 million to £50 million), but the increase in the earnings per share is only 25% (20p to 25p). She is also confused by the company also quoting a fully diluted earnings per share figure, which is lower than the basic earnings per share.

Required

(i) Explain why the trend of earnings per share may be different from the trend of the reported profit, and which is the more useful measure of performance. **(3 marks)**

(ii) Calculate the diluted earnings per share for Taylor plc based on the effect of the convertible loan stock and the director's share options for the year to 30 September 20X2 (ignore comparatives); and **(5 marks)**

(iii) Explain the relevance of the diluted earnings per share measure. **(4 marks)**

(c) Mrs Harper has noticed that the tax charge for a company called Stepper plc is £5 million on profits before tax of £35 million. This is an effective rate of tax of 14.3%. Another company Jenni plc has a tax charge of £10 million on profit before tax of £30 million. This is an effective rate of tax of 33.3% yet both companies state the rate of corporation tax applicable to them is 25%. Mrs Harper has also noticed that in the cash flow statements each company has paid the same amount of tax of £8 million.

Required

Advise Mrs Harper of the possible reasons why the tax charge in the financial statements as a percentage of the operating profit may not be the same as the applicable corporation tax rate, and why the tax paid in the cash flow statement may not be the same as the tax charge in the profit and loss account. **(6 marks)**

(Total = 25 marks)

64 Comparator (2.5 12/03)

45 mins

Comparator assembles computer equipment from bought in components and distributes them to various wholesalers and retailers. It has recently subscribed to an interfirm comparison service. Members submit accounting ratios as specified by the operator of the service, and in return, members receive the average figures for each of the specified ratios taken from all of the companies in the same sector that subscribe to the service. The specified ratios and the average figures for Comparator's sector are shown below.

Ratios of companies reporting a full year's results for periods ending between 1 July 20X3 and 30 September 20X3

Return on capital employed	22·1%
Net assets turnover	1·8 times
Gross profit margin	30%
Net profit (before tax) margin	12·5%
Current ratio	1·6:1
Quick ratio	0·9:1
Stock holding period	46 days
Debtors' collection period	45 days
Creditors' payment period	55 days
Debt to equity	40%
Dividend yield	6%
Dividend cover	3 times

Comparator's financial statements for the year to 30 September 20X3 are set out below:

PROFIT AND LOSS ACCOUNT

	£'000
Turnover	2,425
Cost of sales	(1,870)
Gross profit	555
Other operating expenses	(215)
Operating profit	340
Interest payable	(34)
Exceptional item (note (ii))	(120)
Profit before taxation	186
Taxation	(90)
Profit after taxation	96

BALANCE SHEET

	£'000	£'000
Fixed assets (note (i))		540
Current assets		
Stock	275	
Debtors	320	
Bank	nil	
	595	
Creditors: amounts falling due within one year		
Bank overdraft	35	
Trade creditors	350	
Taxation	85	
	(470)	
Net current assets		125
Creditors: amounts falling due after more than one year		
8% loan notes		(300)
		365

	£'000	£'000
Share capital and reserves		
Ordinary shares (25p each)		150
Profit and loss account		215
		365

Notes.

(i)   The details of the fixed assets are:

	Cost	Accumulated depreciation	Net book value
	£'000	£'000	£'000
At 30 September 20X3	3,600	3,060	540

(ii)   The exceptional item relates to losses on the sale of a batch of computers that had become worthless due to improvements in microchip design.

(iii)   The market price of Comparator's shares throughout the year averaged £6·00 each.

(iv)   Dividends paid during the year were £60,000.

Required

(a)   Explain the problems that are inherent when ratios are used to assess a company's financial performance. Your answer should consider any additional problems that may be encountered when using interfirm comparison services such as that used by Comparator.   **(7 marks)**

(b)   Calculate the ratios for Comparator equivalent to those provided by the interfirm comparison service.
                                                                                                                        (6 marks)

(c)   Write a report analysing the financial performance of Comparator based on a comparison with the sector averages.   **(12 marks)**

                                                                                                       (Total = 25 marks)

65 Breadline (2.5 6/02)   45 mins

You are the assistant financial controller of Judicious plc. One of your company's credit controllers has asked you to consider the account balance of one of your customers, Breadline Ltd. He is concerned at the pattern of payments and increasing size and age of the debtor. As part of company policy he has obtained the most recently filed financial statements of Breadline Ltd from Companies House and these are summarised below. A note to the financial statements of Breadline Ltd states that it is a wholly owned subsidiary of Wheatmaster plc, and its main activities are the production and distribution of bakery products to wholesalers. By coincidence your company's Chief Executive has been made aware that Breadline Ltd may be available for sale. She has asked you for your opinion on whether Breadline Ltd would make a suitable addition to the group's portfolio.

BREADLINE LTD
PROFIT AND LOSS ACCOUNT

Year to	31 December 20X1		31 December 20X0	
	£'000	£'000	£'000	£'000
Sales		8,500		6,500
Cost of sales		(5,950)		(4,810)
Gross profit		2,550		1,690
Operating expenses		(560)		(660)
Finance costs - loan note	10		nil	
- overdraft	10		5	
		(20)		(5)
Profit before tax		1,970		1,025
Taxation		(470)		(175)
Profit after tax		1,500		850

BALANCE SHEETS AS AT

	31 December 20X1		31 December 20X0	
	£'000	£'000	£'000	£'000
Fixed assets				
Freehold premises at valuation		nil		1,250
Leasehold premises		2,500		nil
Plant		1,620		750
		4,120		2,000
Current assets				
Stock	370		240	
Debtors	960		600	
Bank	nil		250	
	1,330		1,090	
Creditors: amounts falling due within one year				
Creditors	1,030		590	
Overdraft	220		nil	
	(1,250)		(590)	
Net current assets		80		500
Creditors: amounts falling due after more than one year				
2% Loan note		(500)		nil
Net assets		3,700		2,500
Share capital and reserves				
Ordinary shares of £1 each		500		100
Reserves:				
Share premium	200		nil	
Revaluation reserve (re freehold premises)	nil		700	
Profit and loss reserve	3,000		1,700	
		3,200		2,400
		3,700		2,500

From your company's own records you have ascertained that sales to Breadline Ltd for the year 20X1 and 20X0 were £1,200,000 and £800,000 respectively and the year-end debtor balances were £340,000 and £100,000 respectively. Normal credit terms, which should apply to Breadline Ltd, are that payment is due 30 days after the end of the month of sale. You are aware that the company has not changed its address and is trading from the same premises. A note to Breadline Ltd's financial statements says that the profit on the disposal of its freehold premises has been included in cost of sales as this is where the depreciation on the freehold has been charged. Dividends of £900,000 were paid in 20X1. No dividends were paid in 20X0.

Note. A commercial rate of interest on the loan note of Breadline Ltd would be 8% per annum.

Required

(a) Describe the matters that may be relevant when entity financial statements are used to assess the performance of a company that is a wholly owned subsidiary. **(5 marks)**

Note. Your answer should give attention to related party issues.

(b) From the information above and with the aid of suitable ratios, prepare a report for your Chief Executive on the overall financial position of Breadline Ltd. Your answer should include reference to matters in the financial statements of Breadline Ltd that may give you cause for concern or require further investigation. **(20 marks)**

(Total = 25 marks)

66 Preparation question: Dickson Ltd

Below are the balance sheets of Dickson Ltd as at 31 March 20X8 and 31 March 20X7, together with the profit and loss account for the year ended 31 March 20X8.

	20X8		20X7	
	£'000	£'000	£'000	£'000
Fixed assets				
Intangible		390		260
Tangible		825		637
		1,215		897
Current assets				
Stocks	360		227	
Debtors	274		324	
Investments	143		46	
Cash	29		117	
	806		714	
Creditors: amounts falling due within one year				
Trade creditors	(291)		(364)	
Bank overdraft	(137)		(54)	
Taxation	(104)		(198)	
	(532)		(616)	
Net current assets		274		98
		1,489		995
Creditors: amounts falling due in more than one year				
6% debentures		(250)		(200)
		1,239		795
Share capital and reserves				
£1 ordinary shares		500		400
Share premium		300		100
Revaluation reserve		160		60
Profit and loss reserve		279		235
		1,239		795

Profit and loss account

	£'000
Turnover	1,476
Cost of sales	(962)
Gross profit	514
Expenses	(172)
Profit before tax	342
Tax	(162)
Profit after tax	180
Dividends paid during the period	136

LEARNING MEDIA

Notes

(1) Intangible assets represent goodwill arising on the acquisition of unincorporated businesses and development expenditure, as follows:

	20X8	20X7
	£'000	£'000
Goodwill	100	100
Development expenditure	290	160
	390	260

During 20X8 expenditure on development projects totalled £190,000.

(2) During 20X8 tangible fixed assets with a net book value of £103,000 were sold for £110,000. Depreciation charged in the year on tangible fixed assets totalled £57,000.

(3) The current asset investments are government bonds and fall within the definition of liquid resources.

(4) Interest on the 6% debentures of £15,000 has been paid and is included in expenses in the profit and loss account.

(5) Staff costs of £20,000 have been paid and are included in expenses in the profit and loss account.

Required

Prepare a cash flow statement using the direct method for Dickson Ltd in accordance with FRS 1 (Revised).

67 Planter (2.5 6/04 amended)   45 mins

The following information relates to Planter, a small private company. It consists of an opening balance sheet as at 1 April 20X3 and a listing of the company's ledger accounts at 31 March 20X4 after the draft operating profit before interest and taxation (of £17,900) had been calculated.

PLANTER – BALANCE SHEET AS AT 1 APRIL 20X3

	£	£
Fixed assets		
Land and buildings (at valuation of £49,200 less accumulated depreciation of £5,000)		44,200
Plant (at cost of £70,000 less accumulated depreciation of £22,500)		47,500
Investments at cost		16,900
		108,600
Current Assets		
Stock	57,400	
Debtors	28,600	
Bank	1,200	
	87,200	
Creditors: amount falling due within one year		
Trade creditors	31,400	
Taxation	8,900	
	(40,300)	
Net current assets		46,900
Creditors: amount falling due after more than one year		
8% Loan notes		(43,200)
Net Assets		112,300

	£	£
Share capital and reserves:		
Ordinary shares of £1 each		25,000
Reserves:		
Share premium	5,000	
Revaluation reserve	12,000	
Profit and loss account	70,300	
		87,300
		112,300

Ledger account listings at 31 March 20X4

	Dr £	Cr £
Ordinary shares of £1 each		50,000
Share premium		8,000
Profit and loss reserve – 1 April 20X3		70,300
Profit before interest and tax – year to 31 March 20X4		17,900
Revaluation reserve		18,000
8% Loan notes		39,800
Trade creditors		26,700
Accrued loan interest		300
Taxation	1,100	
Land and buildings at valuation	62,300	
Plant at cost	84,600	
Buildings – accumulated depreciation 31 March 20X4		6,800
Plant – accumulated depreciation 31 March 20X4		37,600
Investments at cost	8,200	
Trade debtors	50,400	
Stock – 31 March 20X4	43,300	
Bank		1,900
Investment income		400
Loan interest	1,700	
Ordinary dividend	26,100	
	277,700	277,700

Notes

(i) There were no disposals of land and buildings during the year. The increase in the revaluation reserve was entirely due to the revaluation of the company's land.

(ii) Plant with a net book value of £12,000 (cost £23,500) was sold during the year for £7,800. The loss on sale has been included in the profit before interest and tax.

(iii) Investments with a cost of £8,700 were sold during the year for £11,000. The profit has been included in the profit before interest and tax. There were no further purchases of investments.

(iv) On 10 October 20X3 a bonus issue of 1 for 10 ordinary shares was made utilising the share premium account. The remainder of the increase in ordinary shares was due to an issue for cash on 30 October 20X3.

(v) The balance on the taxation account is after settlement of the provision made for the year to 31 March 20X3. A provision for the current year has not yet been made.

Required

From the above information, prepare a cash flow statement using the indirect method for Planter in accordance with FRS 1 'Cash Flow Statements' for the year to 31 March 20X4. **(25 marks)**

Note. The reconciliation of cash flows to the movement in net debt and analysis thereof is not required.

68 Bigwood (2.5 12/04 amended)

45 mins

Bigwood, a public company, is a high street retailer that sells clothing and food. The managing director is very disappointed with the current year's results. The company expanded its operations and commissioned a famous designer to restyle its clothing products. This has led to increased turnover in both retail lines, yet overall profits are down.

Details of the financial statements for the two years to 30 September 20X4 are shown below.

PROFIT AND LOSS ACCOUNT

	year to 30 September 20X4		year to 30 September 20X3	
	£'000	£'000	£'000	£'000
Turnover – clothing	16,000		15,600	
– food	7,000	23,000	4,000	19,600
Cost of sales – clothing	14,500		12,700	
– food	4,750		3,000	
		(19,250)		(15,700)
Gross profit		3,750		3,900
Other operating expenses		(2,750)		(1,900)
Operating profit		1,000		2,000
Interest expense		(300)		(80)
Profit before taxation		700		1,920
Taxation		(250)		(520)
Profit after taxation		450		1,400

BALANCE SHEETS AS AT:

	30 September 20X4		30 September 20X3	
	£'000	£'000	£'000	£'000
Fixed assets at cost		17,000		9,500
Accumulated depreciation		(5,000)		(3,000)
		12,000		6,500
Current assets				
Stock – clothing	2,700		1,360	
– food	200		140	
Debtors	100		50	
Bank	nil		450	
	3,000		2,000	
Creditors: amounts falling due within one year				
Bank overdraft	930		nil	
Trade creditors	3,100		2,150	
Taxation	220		450	
	(4,250)		(2,600)	
		(1,250)		(600)
Creditors: amounts falling due after more than one year				
Long-term loans		(3,000)		(1,000)
		7,750		4,900
Share capital and reserves				
Issued ordinary capital (£1 shares)		5,000		3,000
Share premium		1,000		nil
Profit and loss account		1,750		1,900
		7,750		4,900

The following information is relevant:

(i) The increase in fixed assets was due to the acquisition of five new stores and the refurbishment of some existing stores. The carrying value of fixtures scrapped at the refurbished stores was £1.2 million; they had originally cost £3 million. Bigwood did not receive any scrap proceeds for the fixtures, but did incur costs of

£50,000 to remove and dispose of them. The losses on the refurbishment have been charged to operating expenses. Depreciation is charged to cost of sales apportioned in relation to floor area (see below).

(ii)   The floor sales areas (in square metres) were:

	30 September 20X4	30 September 20X3
Clothing	48,000	35,000
Food	6,000	5,000
	54,000	40,000

(iii) The share price of Bigwood averaged £6·00 during the year to 30 September 20X3, but was only £3·00 at 30 September 20X4.

(iv) The following ratios have been calculated:

	20X4	20X3
Return on capital employed	9·3%	33·9%
Net assets turnover	2·1 times	3·3 times
Gross profit margin		
– clothing	9·4%	18·6%
– food	32·1%	25%
Net profit (after tax) margin	2·0%	7·1%
Current ratio	0·71:1	0·77 :1
Stock holding period		
– clothing	68 days	39 days
– food	15 days	17 days
Creditor payment period	59 days	50 days
Gearing	28%	17%
Interest cover	3·3 times	25 times

(v)   Dividends totaling £600,000 were paid in 20X3 and 20X4.

Required

(a)   Prepare, using the indirect method, a cash flow statement for Bigwood for the year to 30 September 20X4.

(12 marks)

Note. The analysis and movement of net debt are not required.

(b)   Write a report analysing the financial performance and financial position of Bigwood for the two years ended 30 September 20X4.   **(13 marks)**

Your report should utilise the above ratios and the information in your cash flow statement. It should refer to the relative performance of the clothing and food sales and be supported by any further ratios you consider appropriate.   **(Total = 25 marks)**

69 Casino (2.5 6/05)   45 mins

(a) Casino is a private company. Details of its balance sheets as at 31 March 20X5 and 20X4 are shown below together with other relevant information:

BALANCE SHEET AS AT

	31 March 20X5		31 March 20X4	
Fixed Assets (note (i))	£m	£m	£m	£m
Intangible assets		400		510
Tangible assets		880		760
		1,280		1,270
Current assets				
Stock	350		420	
Debtors	808		372	
Interest receivable	5		3	
Short term deposits	32		120	
Bank	15		75	
	1,210		990	
Creditors: amounts falling due within one year				
Creditors	530		515	
Bank overdraft	125		nil	
Taxation	15		110	
	(670)		(625)	
Net current assets		540		365
Creditors: amounts falling due after more than one year				
12% fixed interest loan note		nil		(150)
8% variable rate loan note	(160)		nil	
Provisions for liabilities				
Deferred tax		(90)		(75)
Net assets		1,570		1,410
Capital and reserves				
Ordinary Shares of £1 each		300		200
Reserves				
Share premium	60		nil	
Revaluation reserve	112		45	
Profit and loss account	1,098		1,165	
		1,270		1,210
		1,570		1,410

The following supporting information is available:

(i) Details relating to the fixed assets are:

Tangible fixed assets at:

	31 March 20X5			31 March 20X4		
	Cost/ Valuation	Depreciation	Carrying value	Cost/ Valuation	Depreciation	Carrying value
	£m	£m	£m	£m	£m	£m
Land and buildings	600	12	588	500	80	420
Plant	440	148	292	445	105	340
			880			760

Casino revalued the carrying value of its land and buildings by an increase of £70 million on 1 April 20X4. On 31 March 20X5 Casino transferred £3 million from the revaluation reserve to the profit and loss account reserve representing the realisation of the revaluation reserve due to the depreciation of buildings. During the year Casino acquired new plant at a cost of £60 million and sold some old plant for £15 million at a loss of £12 million.

There were no acquisitions or disposals of intangible assets.

(ii)   The following extract is from the draft profit and loss account for the year to 31 March 20X5:

	£m	£m
Operating loss		(32)
Interest receivable		12
Finance costs		(24)
Loss before tax		(44)
Corporation tax repayment claim	14	
Deferred tax charge	(15)	
		(1)
Loss for the period		(45)

The finance costs are made up of:

	£m
Interest expense	(16)
Penalty cost for early redemption of fixed rate loan	(6)
Issue costs of variable rate loan	(2)

(iii)   Dividends of £25 million were paid during the year.

Required

(a)   As far as the information permits, prepare a cash flow statement for Casino for the year to 31 March 20X5 in accordance with FRS 1 'Cash Flow Statements'.

Note: you are not required to prepare a reconciliation of net cash flow to movement in net debt or an analysis of changes in net debt.   **(20 marks)**

(b)   In recent years many analysts have commented on a growing disillusionment with the usefulness and reliability of the information contained in some companies' profit and loss accounts.

Required

Discuss the extent to which a company's cash flow statement may be more useful and reliable than its profit and loss account.   **(5 marks)**

(Total = 25 marks)

70 Tabba (2.5 12/05)

45 mins

The following draft financial statements relate to Tabba, a private company.

Balance sheets as at:

	30 September 20X5		30 September 20X4	
	£'000	£'000	£'000	£'000
Tangible fixed assets (note (ii))		10,600		15,800
Current assets				
Stocks	2,550		1,850	
Debtors	3,100		2,600	
Insurance claim (note (iii))	1,500		1,200	
Bank	850		nil	
	8,000		5,650	
Creditors: amounts falling due within one year				
Bank overdraft	nil		550	
Trade creditors	4,050		2,950	
Government grants (note (ii))	600		400	
Finance lease obligations (note (ii))	900		800	
Taxation	100		1,200	
	(5,650)		(5,900)	
Net current assets/(liabilities)		2,350		(250)
Creditors: amounts falling due after more than one year				
Government grants (note (ii))	1,400		900	
Finance lease obligations (note (ii))	2,000		1,700	
6% loan notes	800		nil	
10% loan notes	nil		4,000	
		(4,200)		(6,600)
Provisions for liabilities				
Deferred tax		(200)		(500)
		8,550		8,450
Capital and reserves				
Ordinary shares (£1 each)		6,000		6,000
Reserves				
Revaluation (note (ii))	nil		1,600	
Profit and loss reserve	2,550		850	
		2,550		2,450
		8,550		8,450

The following information is relevant:

(i)   Profit and loss account extract for the year ended 30 September 20X5:

	£'000
Operating profit before interest and tax	270
Interest expense	(260)
Interest receivable	40
Profit before tax	50
Net tax credit	50
Profit after tax	100

Note: the interest expense includes finance lease interest.

(ii)   The details of the tangible fixed assets are:

	Cost	Accumulated depreciation	Carrying value
	£'000	£'000	£'000
At 30 September 20X4	20,200	4,400	15,800
At 30 September 20X5	16,000	5,400	10,600

During the year Tabba sold its factory for its fair value £12 million and agreed to rent it back, under an operating lease, for a period of five years at £1 million per annum. At the date of sale it had a carrying value of £7·4 million based on a previous revaluation of £8·6 million less depreciation of £1·2 million since the revaluation. The profit on the sale of the factory has been included in operating profit. The surplus on the revaluation reserve related entirely to the factory. No other disposals of fixed assets were made during the year.

Plant acquired under finance leases during the year was £1·5 million. Other purchases of plant during the year qualified for government grants of £950,000.

Amortisation of government grants has been credited to cost of sales.

(iii) The insurance claim relates to flood damage to the company's stocks which occurred in September 20X4. The original estimate has been revised during the year after negotiations with the insurance company. The claim is expected to be settled in the near future.

Required

(a) Prepare a cash flow statement using the indirect method for Tabba in accordance with FRS 1 *Cash flow statements* for the year ended 30 September 20X5. **(17 marks)**

Note: The reconciliation of cash flows to the movement in net debt and analysis thereof is not required.

(b) Using the information in the question and your cash flow statement, comment on the change in the financial position of Tabba during the year ended 30 September 20X5. **(8 marks)**

Note: you are not required to calculate any ratios. **(Total = 25 marks)**

71 Minster (2.5 12/06)   45 mins

Minster is a publicly listed company. Details of its financial statements for the year ended 30 September 2006, together with a comparative balance sheet, are:

Balance sheet at	30 September 2006 £'000	30 September 2006 £'000	30 September 2005 £'000	30 September 2005 £'000
Fixed assets (note (i))				
Tangible		1,280		940
Software		135		Nil
Investments at fair value through profit and loss		150		125
		1,565		1,065
Current assets				
Stock	480		510	
Trade debtors	270		380	
Amounts due from long-term contracts	80		55	
Bank	nil		35	
	830		980	
Creditors: amounts falling due within one year				
Bank overdraft	25		40	
Trade creditors	350		555	
Taxation	60		50	
	(435)		(645)	
Net current assets		395		335
Creditors: amounts falling due after more than one year				
9% loan note		(120)		Nil
Provisions for liabilities				
Environmental provision	162		nil	
Deferred tax	18	(180)	25	(25)
Net assets		1,660		1,375

Balance sheet at	30 September 2006		30 September 2005	
	£'000	£'000	£'000	£'000
Share capital and reserves				
Equity shares of 25 pence each		500		300
Reserves				
Share premium (note (ii))	150		85	
Revaluation reserve	60		25	
Profit and loss account	950	1,160	965	1,075
		1,660		1,375

Profit and loss account for the year ended 30 September 2006

Turnover	1,397
Cost of sales	(1,110)
Gross profit	287
Operating expenses	(125)
	162
Investment income and gain on investments	20
Finance costs (note (i))	(40)
Profit before tax	142
Tax	(57)
Profit for the year	85

The following supporting information is available:

(i)   Included in tangible fixed assets is a coal mine and related plant that Minster purchased on 1 October 2005. Legislation requires that in ten years' time (the estimated life of the mine) Minster will have to landscape the area affected by the mining. The future cost of this has been estimated and discounted at a ratio of 8% to a present value of £150,000. This cost has been included in the carrying amount of the mine and together with the unwinding of the discount, has also been treated as a provision. The unwinding of the discount in included within finance costs in the profit and loss account.

Other land was revalued (upward) by £35,000 during the year.

Depreciation of tangible fixed assets fro the year was £255,000.

There were no disposals of tangible fixed assets during the year.

The software was purchased on 1 April 2006 for £180,000.

The market value of the investments had increased during the year by £15,000. there have been no sales of these investments during the year.

(ii)   On 1 April 2006 there was a bonus (scrip) issue of ordinary shares of one for every four held utilising the share premium reserve. A further cash share issue was made on 1 June 2006. No shares were redeemed during the year.

(iii)   A dividend of 5 pence per share was paid on 1 July 2006.

Required

(a)   Prepare a cash flow statement for Minster for the year to 30 September 2006 in accordance with FRS 1 *Cash flow statements*.

Note: you are not required to prepare a reconciliation of net cash flow to movement in net debt or an analysis of changes in net debt. **(15 marks)**

(b)   Comment on the financial performance and position of Minster as revealed by the above financial statements and your cash flow statements. **(10 marks)**

(Total = 25 marks)

72 Preparation question: Changing prices

The following information has been extracted from the accounts of Epsilon plc prepared under the historical cost convention for 20X6.

PROFIT AND LOSS ACCOUNT EXTRACTS 20X6

	£m
Turnover	200
Operating profit	15
Less interest payable	3
Net profit	12

SUMMARISED BALANCE SHEET AT 31 DECEMBER 20X6

	£m	£m
Fixed assets at cost less depreciation		60
Current assets		
Stocks	20	
Debtors	30	
Bank	2	
	52	
Current liabilities	30	
Net current assets		22
Total assets less current liabilities		82
Less 15% debentures		20
		62
Capital and reserves		62

The company's accountant has prepared the following current cost data.

	£m
Current cost adjustments for 20X6	
Depreciation adjustment	3
Cost of sales adjustment	5
Replacement cost at 31 December 20X6	
Fixed assets, net of depreciation	85
Stocks	21

Required

(a)   Calculate the current cost operating profit of Epsilon plc for 20X6 and the summarised current cost balance sheet of the company at 31 December 20X6, so far as the information permits.

(b)   Calculate the following ratios from both the historical cost accounts and current cost accounts:

(i)   Interest cover
(ii)   Rate of return on shareholders' equity
(iii) Debt/equity ratio.

(c)   Discuss the significance of the ratios calculated under (b) and of the reasons for differences between them.

Note. Ignore taxation.

Approaching the question

1   To save time in this question, the current cost adjustments are given to you. You should, of course, understand how they are calculated.

2   Part (b) is straightforward. Make sure you allow yourself time to give adequate weight to the discussion in part (c).

73 Update (2.5 6/03 part)   22 mins

Most companies prepare their financial statements under the historical cost convention. In times of rising prices it has been said that without modification such financial statements can be misleading.

Required

(a)   Explain the problems that can be encountered when users rely on financial statements prepared under the historical cost convention for their information needs.   **(6 marks)**

Note: your answer should consider problems with the profit and loss account and the balance sheet.

(b)   Update plc has been considering the effect of alternative methods of preparing their financial statements. As an example they picked an item of plant that they acquired from Suppliers plc on 1 April 20X0 at a cost of £250,000. The following details have been obtained:

- the company policy is to depreciate plant at 20% per annum on the reducing balance basis;

- the movement in the retail price index has been:

1 April 20X0	180
1 April 20X1	202
1 April 20X2	206
31 March 20X3	216

- Suppliers plc's price catalogue at 31 March 20X3 shows an item of similar plant at a cost of £320,000. On reading the specification it appears that the new model can produce 480 units per hour whereas the model owned by Update plc can only produce 420 units per hour.

Required

Calculate for Update plc the depreciation charge for the plant for the year to 31 March 20X3 (based on year end values) and its balance sheet carrying value on that date using:

- the historical cost basis;
- a current purchasing power basis; and
- a current cost basis.   **(6 marks)**

(Total = 12 marks)

QUESTIONS

108

Answers

1 Peterlee

(a)   The primary purpose of the *Statement* is to provide a frame of reference to help the ASB itself in developing new accounting standards and reviewing existing ones. Its main impact on accounting practice is therefore through its influence on the standard-setting process. It also has the following purposes:

- To assist auditors in forming an opinion as to whether financial statements conform with accounting standards.

- To help preparers of financial statements and auditors faced with new or emerging accounting issues to carry out an initial analysis of the issues involved.

- To provide a common set of principles for use by standard setters which is very similar to the IASB *Framework* and should therefore facilitate harmonisation of accounting practice.

The *Statement* is not an accounting standard and does not contain requirements on how financial statements should be prepared or presented. This is governed by company law and accounting standards and the overriding requirement of true and fair. It is also not the only influence on standard setting. Factors such as legal requirements, implementation issues and industry-specific issues also play a part.

(b)   *Assets* are defined as 'rights or access to future economic benefits controlled by an entity as a result of past transactions or events'. The use of 'controlled' agrees with FRS 5 in that where an entity may not legally 'own' an asset but has control of the rights to future economic benefits accruing from it, the asset should be recognised. The most obvious example of this is an asset held under a finance lease. This is not legally owned, but is shown on the balance sheet as a fixed asset. The emphasis on 'past transactions or events' prevents the recognition of contingent assets.

Liabilities are defined as 'obligations of an entity to transfer economic benefits as a result of past transactions or events'. This obligation may be legal or it may be constructive. For instance, a company may have no legal obligation to fulfil certain environmental requirements, but it may have created, by its previous actions, the expectation that it will do so. This will be regarded as a constructive obligation and the cost of carrying it out will be provided for. Again, 'past transactions or events' prevents the use of liabilities for 'profit smoothing'. An entity cannot set up a provision for an obligation which has not yet been incurred, such as a restructuring which it intends to carry out in the following year.

The emphasis placed upon correctly defining and recognising assets and liabilities underlines the importance of the balance sheet. The elements of financial statements identified in the *Statement*, other than assets and liabilities themselves, are measured in terms of changes in assets and liabilities. Ownership interest is the excess of assets over liabilities and gains and losses are defined as increases or decreases in ownership interest, aside from contributions from and distributions to owners. So correct identification and measurement of assets and liabilities is crucial to the preparation of financial statements which present a true and fair view.

2 Derringdo

(a)   *Statement of Principles*

The *Statement of Principles* states that the starting point for recognising income is whether or not there has been an increase or decrease in net assets (excluding share issues or dividends). An increase in net assets gives rise to income, and a decrease in net assets creates a loss. This in turn means that revenue recognition is driven by the recognition of assets and liabilities.

However, it also states that the traditional ideas of matching and identification of critical events also affect revenue recognition.

Normally the traditional and modern approach will give the same result; when goods are sold at a profit then there is also an increase in net assets.

However, there are occasions when conflicts arise; for example:

- The profit on the sale of property is recognised as income in the profit and loss account, whereas under SSAP 19 the revaluation of the same item would be taken directly to the revaluation reserve.

- Under SSAP 4, income from capital grants is deferred over the life of the related asset in accordance with the matching concept. However, deferred income does not meet the ASB's definition of a liability and so in theory the grant income should be recognised in full when it is received.

FRS 5 *Reporting the substance of transactions* seeks to apply a more theoretical approach to revenue recognition in a few areas where the traditional approach was giving a misleading impression. For example sale and repurchase agreements are now treated as loans rather than sales.

For the time being inconsistencies between theory, practice and standards will probably remain.

(b) *Sale of goods*

When selling the A grade goods, Derringdo acts as an agent for Gungho. The goods never belong to Derringdo, and so they do not appear in the balance sheet as stock or in the P&L as cost of sales. Instead Derringdo's turnover will only include the commissions earned on these sales.

The B grade goods are normal goods purchased for resale. The P&L will recognise the gross sales revenue and the related cost of sales.

		£'000
Turnover	(4,600 + 11,400)	16,000
Cost of sales		(8,550)
Gross profit		7,450

Workings

A grade goods		£'000	£'000
Revenues	(18,400 × 100 / 50)		36,800
Cost of sales	Opening stock	2,400	
	Purchases	18,000	
	Closing stock	(2,000)	
			(18,400)
Gross profit (50%)			18,400
Commission	36,800 @ 12.5%		4,600

B grade goods		£'000	£'000
Revenues	(8,550 × 100 / 75)		11,400
Cost of sales	Opening stock	1,000	
	Purchases	8,800	
	Closing stock	(1,250)	
			(8,550)
Gross profit (25%)			2,850

3 Regulatory framework

Text reference. Chapter 2.

Top tips. A basic knowledge of the structure and processes of the ASB would probably be enough to earn a pass mark, but parts of this question require a bit of thought. To earn a pass mark break each question down into its components and write a few lies on each. For example, in part (b) most people will sketch out the standard setting process, but make sure you also include a sentence or two on enforcing and on supplementing standards.

Easy marks. Part (a) is very straightforward and will earn you a maximum of ten easy marks. In part (b), five easy marks can be picked up by remembering the standard setting process.

Examiner's comments. Most answers were weak and very short. Enforcement issues were mostly ignored.

		Marks
(a)	1 mark per relevant point to a **maximum**	10
(b)	1 mark per relevant point to a **maximum**	10
(c)	1 mark per relevant point to a **maximum**	5
	Maximum for question	25

(a) The UK Regulatory Framework

There are two strands to the UK Regulatory Framework; legal regulation and professional regulation.

Legal Framework

The Companies Acts of 1985 and 1989 set out the basic format and content of published financial statements. These Acts implement European Union Directives, and so UK Company Law is basically the same as company law throughout the European Union.

The Companies Acts do not include detailed accounting rules. Instead they require companies to comply with generally accepted accounting practice. This gives legal backing to the accounting standards (SSAPs and FRSs) produced by the Accounting Standards Board (ASB).

From 2005 all publicly quoted companies based in the European Union must comply with International Financial Reporting Standards produced by the International Accounting Standards Board (IASB).

As a result, the professional regulations developed by the ASB and IASB now have legal force.

Professional Framework

In the UK professional regulation is supervised by the Financial Reporting Council. This oversees and provides funding for the ASB, the Financial Reporting Review Panel (FRRP) and the Urgent Issues Task Force (UITF).

The ASB develops and publishes Financial Reporting Standards (FRSs). For many years the ASB has aimed to produce accounting standards that comply with their international equivalents; for example FRS 12 published in 1998 is virtually the same as IAS 37. This harmonisation is set to increase now that listed companies in the UK must comply with IFRS.

The importance of the IASB has increased over the last decade. IFRSs already apply to EU listed companies, and as a result of a joint project with IOSCO they will soon be acceptable for all cross-border listings throughout the world.

Summary

Accounting regulation in the UK is dominated legally by the EU and professionally by the IASB. Companies quoted on the London Stock Exchange have to comply with an additional set of 'listing rules' as well as the legal and professional rules.

(b) The Standard Setting Process

Setting standards

The Financial Reporting Council sets the agenda for the ASB. This is done in discussion with all interested parties; preparers, users and auditors. When a topic has been selected the ASB produces a *Discussion Paper* that sets out the problems being addressed and outlines possible solutions. Public comments are invited, and these are taken into account when the first *Financial Reporting Exposure Draft* is produced. This is a draft FRS, and again the public are invited to comment. Finally, a *Financial Reporting Standard* is produced and published.

In future, the ASB's importance will decline, because IFRSs published by the IASB will be adopted in the UK with relatively minor amendments. The IASB has a similar process for producing its own standards.

Enforcing standards

The Companies Act assumes that financial statements must comply with applicable accounting standards in order to show a true and fair view. The auditors are the first line of enforcement in this process as they must identify and disclose any material departures from accounting standards.

Published financial statements are reviewed by the FRRP to ensure that they comply with all applicable accounting standards. It has the power to order companies to correct and republish their financial statements if there has been an unacceptable departure from these standards, and it can publicly censure auditors for not identifying and disclosing the breach in their audit report. The FRRP can take a company to court if it refuses to comply with its requests, but this has not yet occurred in practice.

Supplementing standards

The UITF provides rapid solutions to accounting problems not covered by existing standards, or clarification when existing standards are being misinterpreted. The 'consensus opinions' issued by the UITF have the same force as FRSs issued by the ASB.

(c)   Have the structure and processes been successful?

In order to move away from "fire-fighting" context within which some SSAPs were issued, the ASB developed a conceptual framework, the Statement of Principles. FRSs are based on the Statement of Principles, which ensures that they do not conflict with each other.

The ASB has established a reputation for high quality accounting standards. Its FRSs are drawn up after open discussion, they are based on sound theoretical principles, they have reduced allowable alternatives and they are consistent with each other. The FRRP has improved compliance with these standards compared with the previous system.

Some standards have been criticised for being too complicated. The move towards fair values, and income recognition based on balance sheet values, has also been attacked. Also, corporate failures still occur without warning. However, overall the accounting framework in existence today is better than that inherited by the ASB in 1990.

4 Winger

Text reference. Chapter 3.

Top tips. As with consolidated accounts questions, a question on the preparation of a single company's accounts needs a methodical approach. Lay out proformas and fill the numbers in gradually by systematically working through the question.

(a)　WINGER PLC
PROFIT AND LOSS ACCOUNT
FOR THE YEAR ENDED 31 MARCH 20X1

	£'000
Turnover (358,450 – 27,000)	331,450
Cost of sales (W1)	(208,550)
Gross profit	122,900
Distribution expenses	(28,700)
Administration expenses	(15,000)
Operating profit	79,200
Exceptional items	
Profit on disposal of land and buildings	
(95,000 – 80,000)	15,000
Loss on abandonment of research project	(30,000)
Profit on ordinary activities before interest	64,200
Interest expense (W3)	(11,200)
Profit before tax	53,000
Taxation (15,000 – 2,200)	(12,800)
Profit for the period	40,200

(b)　BALANCE SHEET AS AT 31 MARCH 20X1

	£'000	£'000
Fixed assets: tangible		
Land and buildings (200,000 – 6,000 (W2))		194,000
Plant and machinery (W4)		160,000
		354,000
Current assets		
Stock (28,240 + 22,500 (W1))	50,740	
Debtors (55,000 – 27,000 (W1))	28,000	
Cash	10,660	
	89,400	
Creditors due within one year		
Trade and other creditors (W5)	51,400	
Taxation	15,000	
	66,400	
Net current assets		23,000
Total assets less current liabilities		377,000
Creditors due after one year		
Lease creditor (W6)	(47,200)	
8% debentures	(50,000)	(97,200)
Net assets		279,800
Capital and reserves		
Ordinary shares 25p each		150,000
Profit and loss account (71,600 + 40,200 – 12,000 + 30,000		
transfer from revaluation reserve)		129,000
Shareholders' funds		279,800

Workings

1　*Cost of sales*

	£'000
Per question	185,050
Less sale/return goods (27,000 × 100/120)	(22,500)
Add depreciation (W2)	46,000
	208,550

2   *Depreciation*

	£'000
Building (100,000 ÷ 50)	2,000
Heating system (20,000 ÷ 10)	2,000
Lifts (30,000 ÷ 15)	2,000
	6,000
Leased plant (80,000 × 20%)	16,000
Owned plant (154,800 – 34,800) × 20%	24,000
	46,000

3   *Interest expense*

	£'000
Debenture interest (50,000 × 8%)	4,000
Finance lease (80,000 – 20,000) × 12%	7,200
	11,200

4   *Plant and machinery*

	£'000
Cost: owned plant	154,800
leased plant	80,000
	234,800
Depreciation: owned plant (34,800 + 24,000 (W2))	(58,800)
leased plant (80,000 × 20%)	(16,000)
	160,000

5   *Trade and other creditors*

	£'000
Trial balance	29,400
Lease creditor (W6)	20,000
Accrued debenture interest	2,000
	51,400

6   *Lease creditor*

	£'000
Total capital due	80,000
Less amount paid	(20,000)
	60,000
Add accrued interest (60,000 × 12%)	7,200
Total creditor	67,200
Due within one year	20,000
Due after one year	47,200

(c)   **Policy on depreciation of buildings**

Prior to the issue of FRS 15 *Tangible fixed assets*, companies often used to justify the non-depreciation of buildings on several grounds, including:

(i)   That the current value of the buildings was **higher than cost**.

(ii)   That the level of **maintenance** meant that no deterioration or consumption had taken place.

(iii)   That the depreciation charge would **not be material**.

FRS 15 dismisses the first two of them as being **insufficient grounds** for a policy of non-depreciation. Depreciation is **not** a **valuation model**; rather it is a means of **allocating the depreciable amount** of the asset to accounting periods.

However, it is **still permissible not to charge depreciation** on the grounds of **non-materiality**, but only when **both**:

(i)   The **depreciation charge** for the period **and**

(ii)   The **accumulated depreciation** that would have been charged against the value of the asset at that point in time,

are immaterial.

Thus assets with very long lives and/or high residual values may meet the criteria not to be depreciated. For depreciation to be classed as immaterial FRS 15 specifies certain conditions:

(i)   There must be a policy of **regular maintenance**.

(ii)   The asset is unlikely to **suffer obsolescence**.

(iii)   There is a policy **and** practice of disposing of similar assets long **before** the **end of their useful lives** at proceeds not materially less than their carrying amounts.

An annual **test for impairment** is also required (except for land).

On the facts given, Winger's policy may have complied with FRS 15.

5 Harrington

Text reference. Chapter 3.

Top tips. There is a lot to get through in this question. Work through the adjustments methodically, but keep an eye on the time. Make sure that you attempt all three statements.

Easy marks. Although there is a lot to do here, none of it is difficult. The self constructed asset may have caused some problems, but the rest is not complex.

Examiner's comments. This type of question has been asked many times and is useful for examining several areas of the syllabus. Most candidates did quite well. The most common errors were:

- failing to carry out easy calculations such as the interest charge and profit on the sale of plant
- incorrect calculation of the corporation tax charge
- errors dealing with entries to the revaluation reserve
- failing to note that the share issue had already been recorded

Marking scheme

			Marks
			Marks
(a)	Restated profit and loss		
	Turnover	1	
	Cost of sales	5	
	Other items	3	9
(b)	Rights issue	1	
	Surplus on land and buildings	2	
	Transfer to realised profits	1	
	Other items	2	6
(c)	Balance sheet		
	1 mark per item – max		10
			25

(a)　HARRINGTON LTD
　　　PROFIT AND LOSS ACCOUNT FOR THE YEAR ENDING 31 MARCH 20X5

		£'000
Turnover	13,700 – 300 proceeds	13,400
Cost of sales	W1	(8,910)
Gross profit		4,490
Operating expenses		(2,400)
Operating profit		2,090
Investment income	£1.2m × 10%	120
Interest payable	£500m × 10%	(50)
Profit before tax		2,160
Taxation	W5	(385)
Profit for the year		1,775

(b)　Movement on Capital and Reserves for the year-ending 31 March 20X5

	Share Capital £'000	Share Premium £'000	Revaluation Reserve £'000	P&L Account £'000	Total £'000
Opening (W6)	1,600	40	-	2,990	4,630
Share issue (W6)	400	560	-	-	960
Revaluation (W4)	-	-	1,800	-	1,800
Excess depreciation (W4)	-	-	(80)	80	-
Profit for the year	-	-	-	1,775	1,775
Dividends paid	-	-	-	(500)	(500)
Closing	2,000	600	1,720	4,345	8,665

(c)　BALANCE SHEET AS AT 31 MARCH 20X5

	£'000	£'000
Fixed assets		
Tangible fixed assets (W4)		8,060
Investments (£1.2m × 110%)		1,320
		9,380
Current assets		
Stocks	1,750	
Trade debtors	2,450	
Bank	350	
	4,550	
Creditors: amounts falling due within one year		
Trade creditors	4,130	
Accrued interest (£50m charged - £25m paid)	25	
Corporation Tax	260	
	4,415	
Net current assets		135
Total assets less current liabilities		9,515
Creditors: amounts falling due after more than one year		
Loan note		(500)
Provision for liabilities		
Deferred tax (£1.4m × 25%)		(350)
		8,665
Capital and reserves		
Share Capital		2,000
Share Premium		600
Revaluation reserve		1,720
P&L reserves		4,345
		8,665

Workings

1   *Cost of sales*

			£'000
From question			9,200
Less: profit on disposal	W2		(30)
Less: capitalisation	W3		(1,000)
Add: depreciation	W4		740
			8,910

2   *Disposal*

Proceeds	(transferred from sales)	300
Carrying value	(900 – 630)	(270)
Profit on disposal		30

3   *Capitalisation*

		£'000
Total costs incurred	(150 + 800 + 65 + 20)	1,035
Less: rectification costs	(10 + 25)	(35)
		1,000

4   *Tangible fixed assets*

		Land £'000		Buildings £'000		Plant £'000	Total £'000
Cost	Opening	1,000		4,000		5,200	
	Additions	-	W3	1,000		-	
	Disposals	-		-	W2	(900)	
	Revaluation	200		800		-	
	Closing	1,200		5,800		4,300	
Depreciation	Opening	-		800		3,130	
	Charge	-		290		450	
	Disposals	-		-	W2	(630)	
	Revaluation	-		(800)		-	
	Closing	-		290		2,950	
Net Book Value		1,200		5,510		1,350	8,060

Total revaluation	200 + 800 + 800 = £1,800,000
Total depreciation	290 + 450 = £740,000

Buildings

Revaluation of building excludes the addition during the year.
Depreciation: £5.8m/20 years = £290,000

		£'000
Excess depreciation on revaluation		
Revalued depreciation	£4.8m / 20 years	240
Historic cost depreciation	£3.2m / 20 years	160
Excess		80

		£'000
Depreciation on plant		
Cost		4,300
Cumulative depreciation	(3,130 – 630)	(2,500)
Balance		1,800
25% depreciation		450

W5   *Taxation*

		£'000	£'000
Estimate for current year	(current liability)		260
Under-provision for prior year			55
Deferred tax			
Provision required (£1.4m × 25%)	(non-current liability)	350	
Opening provision		(280)	
Increase			70
			385

W6 *Share issue*

The 1 for 4 rights issue means that there are five shares in issue at the year-end for every four in issue at the start. Therefore the opening capital must have been £2m × ⁴/₅ = £1.6m.

	Capital £'000	Premium £'000
Opening balance		
6.4m shares @ 25 pence each	1,600	40
1 for 4 rights issue at 60 pence		
Capital: 1.6m shares @ 25 pence	400	-
Premium: 1.6m shares @ 35 pence	-	560
	2,000	600

(The opening share premium is a balancing figure.)

6 Petra

Text references. Chapters 7 and 18.

Top tips. The main complications in Part (a) involve the treatment of agency sales and the treatment of tangible and intangible fixed assets.

Easy marks. There are five marks for two straightforward EPS calculations in part (c). Do these straight after Part (a) otherwise you might run out of time.

Examiner's comments. This was a familiar question requiring the preparation of a profit and loss account, balance sheet and two EPS calculations. The main errors were:

- Failure to understand the nature of the agency sale.

- Errors in calculating cost of sales – such as deducting depreciation and impairment and deducting closing inventory twice.

- Errors in calculating the tax charge, including dealing with the movement on deferred tax.

			Marks
(a)	Turnover	1	
	Cost of sales	6	
	Commission	1	
	Distribution and administration	1	
	Interest expense	1	
	Taxation	2	
		12	
	Maximum		10
(b)	Development costs	1	
	Fixed assets	2	
	Current assets	4	
	Current liabilities	2	
	Loan note	1	
	Deferred tax	1	
	Shares and share premium	1	
	Retained earnings	1	
		13	
	Maximum		10
(c)	Basic EPS	2	
	Diluted EPS	3	5
			25

(a)   PROFIT AND LOSS ACCOUNT FOR THE YEAR ENDING 30 SEPTEMBER 20X5

		£'000
Turnover	(W1)	185,800
Cost of sales	(W1)	(128,100)
Gross profit		57,700
Other operating income	(W1)	1,000
Distribution costs		(17,000)
Administration expenses		(18,000)
Operating profit		23,700
Interest expense	(£50m × 6%)	(3,000)
Profit before tax		20,700
Taxation	(W5)	(7,600)
Profit for the financial year		13,100

(b)   BALANCE SHEET AS AT 30 SEPTEMBER 20X5

		£'000	£'000
Fixed assets			
Intangible assets	(W4)		18,000
Tangible assets	(W2)		106,000
			124,000
Current assets			
Stocks		21,300	
Trade debtors		24,000	
Debtor for sale of plant	(W3)	6,900	
Bank		11,000	
		63,200	
Creditors: amounts falling due within one year			
Trade creditors		15,000	
Accrued Loan Note interest	$(£50m \times 6\% \times {}^6/_{12})$	1,500	
Taxation		4,000	
		20,500	
Net current assets			42,700
Total assets less current liabilities			166,700
Creditors: amounts falling due after more than one year			
6% Loan note			(50,000)
Provisions for liabilities			
Deferred tax			(17,600)
Net assets			99,100
Capital and reserves			
Share Capital			40,000
Share Premium			12,000
Profit and loss reserves	(34,000 + 13,100)		47,100
			99,100

Workings

W1   *Turnover and cost of sales*

		Turnover	Cost of Sales
		£'000	£'000
From TB		197,800	114,000
Commission sales		(12,000)	-
Cost of commission sales		-	(8,000)
Revenues due to Sharma		-	(3,000)
Depreciation on property	W2a	-	2,000
Depreciation on plant	W2b	-	6,000
Loss on disposal of asset	W3	-	3,100
Impairment of intangible	W4	-	14,000
		185,800	128,100

Petra earns £1m commission on the sales undertaken for Sharma. This is shown as other income (although it could also be included within turnover). Petra never owns or controls the goods that are being sold so the cost of these items should not be included in Petra's profit and loss account.

W2   *Tangible fixed assets*

	£'000
Property *W2a*	82,000
Plant *W2b*	24,000
	106,000

W2a   *Property*

			£'000	£'000
Cost				100,000
Depreciation	Opening		16,000	
	Charge	(100 − 40) / 30 years	2,000	
				(18,000)
				82,000

W2b   *Plant and equipment*

		Cost	Depreciation
		£'000	£'000
From TB		66,000	26,000
Disposal	See W3	(16,000)	(6,000)
		50,000	20,000
Depreciation charge	(£50m - £20m) ×20%	-	6,000
		50,000	26,000

Carrying value £24m

W3   *Loss on disposal*

	£'000	£'000
Proceeds: £7.5m × 92%		6,900
Cost	16,000	
Less depreciation	(6,000)	
NBV		(10,000)
Loss on disposal		(3,100)

W4   *Development expenditure*

	£'000
Cost	40,000
Less amortisation	(8,000)
Opening carrying value	32,000
Impairment and depreciation charge (balancing figure)	(14,000)
Impaired closing carrying value	18,000

W5   *Taxation*

	£'000
Tax on current year's profits	4,000
Under provision in prior year	1,000
Increase in deferred tax (£17.6m - £15m)	2,600
	7,600

(c)   Earnings per share

Basic

Earnings	£13,100,000	=	**8.2 pence**
Number of shares in issue (£40m ÷ £0.25)	160,000,000		

Fully diluted

Earnings	£13,100,000	=	**7.4 pence**
Number of shares in issue (see below)	176,000,000		

Existing shares			160,000,000
Dilutive shares			
Number of shares to be issued		24,000,000	
Proceeds of share option	£7,200,000		
Number of shares this would buy	£7.2m ÷ £0.90 =	(8,000,000)	
Dilutive shares issued for free			16,000,000
Total shares for diluted EPS calculation			176,000,000

7 Allgone

Text reference. Chapter 3.

Top tips. As well as examining you on the format and content of the financial statements, this question also tests your knowledge of six specific situations.

As always, be methodical and don't get bogged down in the detail.

Easy marks. Provided you are methodical, you should obtain at least 13 marks quite easily just by using the proformas and slotting in the figures that are straightforward.

Examiner's comments. Many candidates showed weakness in areas already examined in Paper 1.1 eg calculation and accrual of interest, depreciation on revalued assets and declared dividends. Also too many candidates did not produce a statement of total recognised gains and losses.

Marking scheme

			Marks
(a)	*Profit and loss account*		
	Sales revenue		1
	Cost of sales		3
	Operating costs		1
	Finance costs		2
	Taxation		2
		Available	**9**
		Maximum	**7**
(b)	*STRGL*		
	Revaluation		2
	Prior year adjustment		1
	Unrealised loss		2
		Maximum	**5**
(c)	*Balance sheet*		
	Software		3
	Tangible fixed assets		1
	Investments		1
	Stock		1
	Trade debtors and creditors		1
	In substance loan		1
	Share capital		1
	Revaluation reserve		2
	Profit and loss reserve		1
	Long-term liabilities		2
	Accrued finance costs		2
	Taxation provision		1
		Available	**17**
		Maximum	**13**
		Maximum for question	**25**

ALLGONE: PROFIT AND LOSS ACCOUNT FOR THE YEAR ENDED 31 MARCH 20X3

		£'000
Turnover	(236,200 – 8,000 (W1))	228,200
Cost of sales	W2	(150,000)
Gross profit		78,200
Operating expenses		(12,400)
Operating profit		65,800
Interest payable and similar charges	W3	(5,850)
Profit before tax		59,950
Tax	W4	(13,100)
Profit after tax		46,850

STATEMENT OF TOTAL RECOGNISED GAINS AND LOSSES FOR THE YEAR ENDED 31 MARCH 20X3

	£'000
Profit for the year	46,850
Revaluation (W5)	40,000
Unrealised loss on investments (W8)	(1,200)
Prior year adjustment (W10)	(32,000)
Total gains and losses recognised since last annual report	53,650

ALLGONE: BALANCE SHEET AS AT 31 MARCH 20X3

		£'000
Fixed assets		
Tangible fixed assets (W5)		177,000
Investments (W8)		10,800
		187,800
Current assets		
Stocks (W2)	14,300	
Trade debtors	23,000	
	37,300	
Creditors: amounts falling due within one year		
Trade creditors	15,200	
Bank overdraft	350	
Accruals (W9)	2,450	
Funders Bank	8,000	
Taxation payable	11,300	
	37,300	
Net current assets		–
Total assets less current liabilities		187,800
Creditors: amounts falling due after more than one year		
10% Redeemable preference shares	20,000	
12% Loan note	40,000	
		(60,000)
Provision for liabilities		
Deferred tax		(4,800)
Net assets		123,000

	£'000
Capital and Reserves	
Share capital	60,000
Revaluation reserve (W10)	42,800
Profit and loss account (W10)	20,200
	123,000

Workings

W1   *Sale to Funders Bank*

The substance of this transaction is a short-term loan. This is shown by the Bank's option to demand repurchase within one month of the year-end at cost plus £250,000, which means that Allgone still bears the risks and benefits of these items. Therefore, the revenue (£8m) and related cost of sales (£6m) will be removed from the P&L. The balance sheet will show a loan of £8m, and the stock will be shown at its original cost of £6m. The £250,000 is a finance cost which will be charged to the P&L. In the absence of detailed information about the timing of the initial transaction, this answer assumes that the full £250,000 should be charged this year.

W2   *Cost of sales and closing stocks*

	£'000	£'000
Purchases		127,850
Opening stocks		19,450
Closing stocks:		
From Note (i)	8,500	
Less NRV allowance (500 – 300)	(200)	
Add cost of stocks 'sold' to Funders Bank	6,000	
Value of closing stock		(14,300)
		133,000
Depreciation	W5	17,000
		150,000

W3   *Finance costs*

	£'000
Loans: £40m × $^9/_{12}$ × 12%: £2.4m paid + £1.2 m accrued	3,600
£20m 10% Preference shares: £1m paid + £1m accrued	2,000
Accrued finance charge to Funders Bank	250
	5,850

W4   *Taxation*

	£'000	£'000
Estimated Corporation Tax expense from the question		11,300
Deferred tax: brought forward per TB	3,000	
carried forward (£16m × 30%)	4,800	
increase		1,800
Tax charge for the year		13,100

W5   *Tangible fixed assets*

	Land	Buildings	Plant & Equipment	Software	Total
	£'000	£'000	£'000	£'000	£'000
Cost or valuation					
Opening	20,000	80,000	84,300	10,000	194,300
Revaluation	5,000	25,000	-	-	30,000
Closing	25,000	105,000	84,300	10,000	224,300
Depreciation					
Opening	-	10,000	24,300	6,000	40,300
Revaluation (W6)	-	(10,000)	-	-	(10,000)
Charge for the year (W6 & W7)	-	3,000	12,000	2,000	17,000
Closing	-	3,000	36,300	8,000	47,300
Net book value	25,000	102,000	48,000	2,000	177,000

Total revaluation surplus: £5m + £25m + £10m = £40m.

W6   *Depreciation and revaluation of the buildings*

At revaluation the property had been owned for 5 years out of an expected useful life of 40 years. The accumulated depreciation on the buildings was £80m × $^5/_{40}$ = £10m. This will be eliminated on revaluation.

The new valuation of £105m will be depreciated over the remaining 35 year useful life of the asset, giving an annual charge of £3m. This is charged to operating expenses.

The £1m difference between the revalued charge and the historic cost charge (£2m per annum) is adjusted for by a transfer of £1m per annum from the revaluation reserve to the profit and loss account.

W7   *Depreciation on plant and software*

	£'000
Plant & equipment: (20% reducing balance) (84,300 − 24,300) × 20%	12,000
Software (sum of the digits over 5 years) $^3/_{15}$ × £10m	2,000

W8   *Investments*

	Asset	Revaluation
	£'000	£'000
Opening valuation and related revaluation reserve @ £2.50	12,000	5,000
Change (balancing figure)	(1,200)	(1,200)
Closing valuation and related revaluation reserve @ £2.25	10,800	3,800

FRS 26 paragraph 55 (b) states that gains and losses on fair valuing available for sale financial assets shall be recognised directly in equity and reported in the statement of total recognised gains and losses.

W9   *Accruals*

	£'000
Interest on loan notes (W3)	1,200
Preference share dividend (W3)	1,000
Accrued finance charge to Funders Bank	250
	2,450

W10   *Reserves*

	Revaluation Reserve £'000	*Profit and Loss Reserve* £'000
Opening balance as previously stated	5,000	4,350
Correction of prior period error	–	(32,000)
Opening balance as restated	5,000	(27,650)
Revaluation surplus: Land & buildings (W5)	40,000	-
Investments (W8)	(1,200)	-
Transfer of depreciation on revaluation (W6)	(1,000)	1,000
Profit for the year	-	46,850
Closing balance	42,800	20,200

Prior period error

The fraud took place before the employee left in January 20X2, but was not discovered until the current accounting period. This means that the prior period financial statements were misstated. To correct prior period errors, FRS 3 requires all prior period financial statements to be restated correctly. The cumulative correction is reported as a restatement of the opening balance on reserves and also at the foot of the Statement of Total Recognised Gains and Losses.

8 Tadeon

Top tips. Start by working through (i) to (v). Read each requirement twice and then do neat workings which the marker can read. If you cannot do one of these, leave it.

Easy marks. The actual financial statements were easy once you had worked through the issues which needed to be brought in. You may have had trouble with the deferred tax but the depreciation and suspense account workings were easy. Don't spend time on any issues which you don't understand or can't do, just move on.

		Marks
(a)	*Profit and loss account*	
	Turnover	1
	Cost of sales	1
	Operating costs	1
	Investment income	1
	Finance costs	3
	Taxation	3
	Available	10
	Maximum	8
(b)	*Balance sheet*	
	Tangible fixed assets	3
	Investment	1
	Stock and trade debtors	1
	Trade creditors and overdraft	1
	Lease obligation (1 for current, 1 for long-term)	2
	Accrued finance lease costs	1
	Tax payable	1
	Loan note	2
	Deferred tax	1
	Share capital and premium	3
	Revaluation reserve	2
	Profit and loss account (including 1 mark for dividend paid)	2
	Available	20
	Maximum	17
	Maximum for question	25

(a) TADEON

PROFIT AND LOSS ACCOUNT FOR THE YEAR ENDED 30 SEPTEMBER 2006

	£'000
Turnover	277,800
Cost of sales (118,000 + 26,000 (W1))	(144,000)
Gross profit	133,800
Investment income	2,000
Operating expenses (40,000 + 1,200 (W3))	(41,200)
Finance cost (2,750 (W2) + 1,500 (W3))	(4,250)
Profit before tax	90,350
Taxation (W5)	(36,800)
Profit for the period	53,550

(b) TADEON
BALANCE SHEET AS AT 30 SEPTEMBER 2006

	£'000	£'000
Fixed assets		
Tangible fixed assets (W1)		299,000
Investments		42,000
		341,000
Current assets		
Stock	33,300	
Debtors	53,500	
	86,800	
Creditors – amounts falling due within one year		
Amount due under finance		
lease (W3)	(6,000)	
Trade creditors	(18,700)	
Taxation	(38,000)	
Overdraft	(1,900)	
	(64,600)	
Net current assets		22,200
Total assets less current liabilities		363,200
Creditors – amounts falling due after more than one year		
Amount due under finance		
lease (W3)	10,500	
Loan creditor (W2)	51,750	
		(62,250)
Provisions for liabilities		
Deferred tax (W5)		(14,800)
		286,150
Capital and reserves		
Called up share capital (150,000 + 50,000 (W6))		200,000
Share premium (W6)		28,000
Revaluation reserve (20,000 (W1) – 4,000 (W5))		16,000
Profit and loss account (18,600 + 53,550 – 30,000 (W6))		42,150
		286,150

Workings

1 *Tangible fixed assets*

	Property	Plant & equipment	Vehicle	Total
	£'000	£'000	£'000	£'000
Cost	225,000	181,000		406,000
Accumulated depreciation	(36,000)	(85,000)		(121,000)
Addition			20,000	20,000
Current year depreciation	(9,000)	(12,000)	(5,000)	(26,000)
Revaluation (W4)	20,000	-	-	20,000
	200,000	84,000	15,000	299,000

2 *Loan note*

	£'000
Proceeds	50,000
Interest @ 5.5%	2,750
Interest paid	(1,000)
Carrying value	51,750

3   *Finance lease*

	£'000
Fair value of asset	20,000
Deposit paid	(5,000)
	15,000
Interest to 30 September 2006	1,500
Balance at 1 October 2006	16,500
Amount due within one year	(6,000)
Amount due after one year	10,500

Therefore £1.2m is charged to operating lease rentals and £1.5m to finance costs on the finance lease.

4   *Revaluation*

	£'000
Carrying value of leasehold at 1 October 2005	189,000
Depreciation to 30 September 2006 (225,000/25)	(9,000)
	180,000
Revaluation	20,000
Carrying value at 30 September 2006	200,000
Revaluation reserve balance (20,000 – 4,000 (W5))	16,000

5   *Taxation*

	£'000
Current year tax charge	38,000
Transfer from deferred tax ((54,000 × 20%) – 12,000)	(1,200)
Profit and loss charge	36,800
Deferred tax balance (74,000 × 20%)	14,800

Note

Deferred tax on revaluation (20,000 × 20%) charged to revaluation reserve	4,000

6   *Suspense account*

	£'000
Dividend paid (750m shares @ 80p × 5%)	(30,000)
Rights issue – shares (250m × 20p)	50,000
Rights issue – premium (250m ×12p)	30,000
Issue costs – to share premium account	(2,000)
Balance on suspense account	48,000
Net amount to share premium (30,000 – 2,000)	28,000

9 Derringdo II

Grant

(a)   *Liability*

There are two issues here:

(1)   Should a capital grant be treated as deferred income in the financial statements, and

(2)   Should a liability be recognised for the potential repayment of the grant.

Derringdo has credited the £240,000 grant to a deferred income account which is shown as a liability in the balance sheet. It is then released to the P&L over the ten year life of the related asset. However, the *Statement of Principles* states that a liability should only be recognised if there is a probable outflow of economic benefits. This is not true for a grant; under normal circumstances the grant will not have to be repaid and so a liability does not exist.

This example is complicated by the possibility of having to repay the grant if the asset is sold. At the balance sheet date the asset has not been sold, and so there is no past event to give rise to a liability. Indeed, Derringdo intends to keep the asset for its ten year useful life. Nor can it be classified as a contingent liability. Under FRS 12 the 'uncertain future event' that creates a contingent liability must be 'not wholly within the control of the entity'. In this case Derringdo will make the decision to keep or sell the asset.

Following on from the above, the *Statement of Principles* would not permit the grant to be shown as a liability. Instead the grant would be claimed as income in the year that it was received (provided that there was no intention to sell the asset within the four year claw-back period). However, the treatment of the grant as deferred income is in accordance with SSAP 4 *Accounting for Government Grants*.

(b)   Extracts from the financial statements for the year-ending 31 March 20X3

Company policy

Profit and loss account			£
Operating expenses	Depreciation charge	(see below)	34,000
	Release of grant	(see below)	(12,000)
			22,000

Balance sheet

		£
Fixed assets	Plant and equipment	766,000
Creditors: amounts falling due within one year	Deferred income	24,000
Creditors: amounts falling after more than one year	Deferred income	204,000
		228,000

Workings

	£
Plant, equipment	
Cost gross, excluding grant	800,000
Depreciation 10 years straight line, 15% residual value for 6 months	
$800,000 \times 85\% \times 10\% \times {}^{6}/_{12}$	(34,000)
Net book value	766,000

Deferred income		£
Grant received	£800,000 × 30%	240,000
Release for this year	$£240,000 \times 10\% \times {}^{6}/_{12}$	(12,000)
Total balance at year-end		228,000

Presentation		
Current liability	£240,000 × 10%	24,000
Long-term liability	balance	204,000
		228,000

Theoretical approach under the Statement of Principles

Because the 'deferred' element of the grant cannot be recognised as a liability, the grant will be claimed in full in the year that it is received. The repayment clause will not affect this policy because, at the balance sheet date, Derringdo has not sold the asset and so no liability exists.

Profit and loss account		£
Operating expenses	Depreciation charge (as before)	34,000
	Grant received and claimed	(240,000)
		(206,000)

Balance sheet		£
Fixed assets:	Plant and equipment	766,000

10 Question with answer plan: Broadoak

Text reference. Chapter 4.

Top tips. This question required fairly comprehensive knowledge of FRS 15, Tangible fixed assets. Remember that revaluation is not compulsory but if one asset is revalued so must all other assets in that class.

Examiner's comments. Answers to this question were rather polarised: either very good or rather poor; however in general the answers were above average. The main areas of criticism were:

- for the cost of fixed assets, many students gave the roles relating to determining whether an asset was impaired and other incorrect answer discussed the fair value of assets. Candidates should ensure that they read the question carefully so that they know what it is asking.

- many candidates thought that revaluation was compulsory (it is not) and the treatment of gains and losses was not properly understood.

In part (c) the most common errors were:

- incorrect capitalisation of maintenance costs (in some cases all three years) and the installation error

- failure to capitalise the compulsory dismantling and restoration costs

- failure to depreciate the property in part (ii) or depreciating it over the wrong period

- debiting the whole revaluation loss to the revaluation reserve rather than also partly to the profit and loss account.

Answer plan

It always pays to answer the discussion parts first, as these will often highlight the particular difficulties to be found in the calculations.

Part (a)

(i) FRS 15: cost = purchase price + import duties + directly attributable costs.

Deal with each item separately. Mention costs that must be dealt with as expenses eg admin costs. Consider the capitalisation of borrowing costs.

Bonus points: mention the treatment of self-constructed assets and abnormal costs.

(ii) Subsequent expenditure – give treatment per FRS 15. For three marks, give three examples of subsequent expenditure.

Part (b)

Revaluation – measured reliably
- consistency
- whole class of asset
- regular revaluations
- up to date
- treatment of surplus
- treatment of deficit

Disposal – treatment of gains
- treatment of losses

Part (c)

(i) Use information given to calculate the initial capitalisation. Remember that you need to consider all the items in part (a)(i).

(ii) If you follow the points on revaluation in part (b), you will need the following extracts:

PROFIT AND LOSS ACCOUNT	20X1	20X2
	$	$
Amortisation	X	X
Revaluation loss		X
BALANCE SHEET		
Leasehold	X	X
Revaluation surplus	X	

(a) (i) When a tangible fixed asset is first capitalised it should be measured at its **cost.** Cost according to FRS 15 is the costs that are **directly attributable to bringing the asset into working condition for its intended use**. These directly attributable costs might include:

- Purchase price (after deducting any trade discount but not settlement discount)
- Other acquisition costs such as stamp duty, import duties and non-refundable purchase taxes
- Delivery costs
- Installation costs
- Site preparation and clearance costs
- Professional fees
- The labour costs of any of the company's own employees directly involved in the construction or acquisition of the specific tangible fixed asset
- Any costs of dismantling and removing the asset and restoring the site that would be recognised as a provision under FRS 12, Provisions, Contingent Liabilities and Contingent Assets.

Finance costs that are directly attributable to the construction of tangible fixed assets **may be capitalised** as part of this cost according to FRS 15. Companies are **not required to capitalise finance costs** but if they do adopt this policy then it **must be applied consistently**.

(ii) The key to determining whether any **subsequent expenditure** is to be capitalised is the standard of **performance** of the asset which was initially assessed to determine the asset's useful economic life and residual value. Subsequent expenditure that ensures that the asset maintains its **previously assessed standard of performance** should be recognised in the **profit and loss account** as revenue expenditure. However FRS 15 allows subsequent expenditure to be capitalised in three circumstances:

Where the subsequent expenditure provides **an enhancement of the economic benefits** of the fixed asset in excess of the previously assessed standard of performance, (for example expenditure which lengthens the economic life of the asset or increases its production capacity).

Where a component of the fixed asset which has been **treated separately for depreciation purposes is replaced or restored**. This relates to major elements of a fixed asset that are treated separately from the main asset such as the replacement of an engine on an aeroplane - the plane's body may be expected to last for 40 years but the engines must be replaced (say) every 8 years.

Where the subsequent expenditure **relates to a major inspection or overhaul** of a fixed asset that restores the economic benefits of the asset that have been consumed by the entity and have already been reflected in depreciation.

(b) Companies are **not required to revalue** their fixed assets according to FRS 15 but it does allow them to revalue if the directors wish to. However if a company chooses a policy of revaluation of fixed assets then **if**

one asset in a class of fixed assets is revalued then **all fixed assets in that class must be revalued**. This is to ensure that assets are not selectively revalued if the valuation is favourable but left at book value if the valuation is adverse.

The carrying value of revalued fixed assets should be their **current values at the balance sheet date**. This might imply a full valuation each year but FRS 15 allows that where properties are revalued a full valuation should take place at least every 5 years with an interim valuation in year 3 and at any other time when it is likely that there has been a material change in value.

Revaluation gains and losses are differences between the carrying value or net book value of the asset and the revalued amount. **Revaluation gains are normally recognised in the Statement of Total Recognised Gains and Losses (STRGL) and taken to a revaluation reserve**.

The treatment of revaluation losses however can be more complex and will depend upon their cause and the amount of the loss. If a revaluation loss is **clearly caused by a consumption of economic benefits**, such as damage to the asset, this loss should be **taken to the profit and loss account**. Other revaluation losses **should be taken to the revaluation reserve until the carrying amount is equivalent to depreciated historical cost** and then any further losses to the profit and loss account. However if the recoverable amount of the asset is greater than its revalued amount this amount of the loss can be taken to the revaluation reserve rather than the profit and loss account.

Any profit or loss on the disposal of a fixed asset is the **difference between the net disposal proceeds and the net book value or carrying value** of the asset at the date of disposal. This will be the case whether the asset is carried at cost or revaluation. This profit or loss should be **recognised in the profit and loss account** for the period in which the disposal takes place. There is then a reserve transfer of any remaining credit on the revaluation reserve relating to the asset disposed of to the profit and loss account reserve.

(c)   Initial cost of plant

	£
Purchase price (£240,000 × 87.5%)	210,000
Shipping and handling costs	2,750
Estimated pre-production testing	12,500
Electrical cable cost (14,000 − 6,000)	8,000
Concrete reinforcement	4,500
Own labour cost	7,500
Dismantling and restoration costs (15,000 + 3,000)	18,000
	263,250

Note

The items that are excluded from initial cost are:

- Maintenance contract as this is revenue expenditure
- Settlement discount (only trade discounts are deducted)
- The cost of the specification error – only normal costs should be capitalised.

(d)   **Broadoak plc - Profit and loss account extract**

	30 September 20X1 £	30 September 20X2 £
Amortisation (£240,000/12)	(20,000)	
(£231,000/11)		(21,000)
Impairment (W)		(25,000)

Broadoak plc - Statement of total recognised gains and losses extract

Surplus/ (deficit) on revaluation (W)	11,000	(10,000)

	30 September 20X1 £	30 September 20X2 £
Broadoak plc – Balance sheet extract		
Leasehold	231,000	175,000

Working

Revaluation and impairment

	£
Cost at 1 October 20X0	240,000
Amortisation to 30 September 20X1	(20,000)
Carrying value at 30 September 20X1	220,000
Revaluation gain	11,000
Valuation at 30 September 20X1	231,000
Amortisation to 30 September 20X2	(21,000)
Carrying value at 30 September 20X2	210,000
Revaluation loss to STRGL	
– down to depreciated historical cost	
$(210,000 - (240,000 \times 10/12))$	(10,000)
Impairment loss to profit and loss account	(25,000)
Valuation at 30 September 20X2	175,000

11 Elite Leisure

Elite Leisure's cruise ship

Although there is only one ship, the ship is a complex asset made up from a number of smaller assets with different costs and useful lives. Each of the component assets of the ship will be accounted for separately with its own cost, depreciation and profit or loss on disposal.

At 30 September 20X4 the ship is eight years old and its cost and carrying value is as follows:

	Cost £m	Depreciation period	Accumulated Depreciation £m	Carrying value £m
Ship's fabric	300	8 years / 25 years	96	204
Cabins and entertainment areas	150	8 years / 12 years	100	50
Propulsion system	100	30,000 hours / 40,000 hours	75	25
	550		271	279

Changes during Y/E 30 September 20X5

Replacing the propulsion system £140m

The old engines will be scrapped giving rise to a £25m loss on disposal.

The new engines will be capitalised and depreciated over their 50,000 hour working life. The charge for this year will be £140m × 5,000 hours / 50,000 hours = £14m.

Upgrading cabins and entertainment areas £60m

These costs can be capitalised because they are improvements and because they extend the useful life of the assets. The revised carrying value at 1 October 20X4 is £110m (£50m + £60m).

The depreciation charge for the year is £22m (£110 ÷ 5 years).

Repainting the ship's fabric £20m

This is a maintenance cost. It will be charged to the profit and loss account statement for the year. The depreciation for the ship itself will be £12m, based on its £300m cost and 25 year life.

Summary

Balance Sheet	Ship's Fabric £m	Cabins etc £m	Propulsion £m	Total £m
Opening carrying value	204	50	25	279
Disposals	-	-	(25)	(25)
Additions	-	60	140	200
Depreciation	(12)	(22)	(14)	(48)
Closing carrying value	192	88	126	406

Profit and Loss Account	£m
Depreciation	48
Loss on disposal	25
Repainting	20
Total charge	93

12 Myriad

(a) Investment properties are properties owned by a company which are **not used within its own operations** (or the operations of any other member of its group) but instead are held for two main purposes:

- To gain rental income from letting
- To gain on the capital appreciation of the properties.

In contrast owner-occupied properties are normal operational fixed assets of a company in that they are used within the operations of the company and their economic value is therefore consumed in the process of earning revenue.

The differences in nature of these two types of property are recognised in **SSAP 19, Accounting for investment properties**, by distinguishing investment properties from other property fixed assets. The different accounting treatment for investment properties is based upon the fact that investment properties are held to earn rental income and to gain in value.

The importance of the current value of the properties is recognised by their valuation in the balance sheet at current value or **open market value**. Any changes in this market value are **taken to the Statement of Total Recognised Gains and Losses** each year and **shown in an investment revaluation reserve**. The second important difference in accounting treatment is that as the investment properties are not being consumed within the business there is **no annual depreciation charge**. Depreciation recognises the economic consumption of assets but this is not appropriate for investment properties and therefore it should not be charged. There is an exception recognised in SSAP 19 in that **leasehold properties with less than 20 years remaining on their leases should be depreciated** each year although also shown at their open market value.

(b) **Myriad plc - Balance sheet extract**

		Cost/ valuation £'000	Accumulated depreciation £'000	Carrying value £'000
Land and buildings	– A (150/50 × 2)	150	6	144
Investment properties	– B	145	–	145
	– C	150	–	150

	£'000
Investment property revaluation reserve (W1)	73

Myriad plc – Profit and loss account extract

	£'000
Depreciation (3 (A) + 10 (C)) (W2)	13

Myriad plc – Statement of total recognised gains and losses - extract

	£'000
Unrealised loss on revaluation of investment properties (35 – 20) (W1)	(15)

Workings

1   *Investment property revaluation reserve*

		£'000
1 October 20X0	– B (180 – 120)	60
	– C (140 – 112)(W2)	28
		88
Year ended 30 September 20X1 – STRGL		
	– B (180 – 145)	(35)
	– C (150 – 130)(W2)	20
Balance at 30 September 20X1		73

2   As investment C has less than 20 years of its lease remaining it must be depreciated according to SSAP 19.

	£'000
Cost at 1 October 20W9	120
Depreciation to 30 September 20X0 (120/15)	(8)
Carrying value	112
Revaluation STRGL	28
Valuation at 30 September 20X0	140
Depreciation to 30 September 20X1 (140/14)	(10)
Carrying value	130
Revaluation STRGL	20
Valuation at 30 September 20X1	150

13 Merryview

PROFIT AND LOSS ACCOUNT (EXTRACTS) YEAR TO 31 MARCH 20X2

	£'000
Depreciation (W1)	312

BALANCE SHEET (EXTRACTS) AS AT 31 MARCH 20X2

	£'000
Fixed assets	
Land and buildings (W3)	2,940
Revaluation reserve (W4)	514

Workings

1   *Depreciation*

	£'000
Head office building:	
6 months to 1 October 20X1 (1,200/25 × 6/12)	24
6 months to 31 March 20X2 (1,350/22.5 × 6/12)	30
Training premises:	
6 months to 1 October 20X1 (900/25 × 6/12)	18
6 months to 31 March 20X2 (600/10 × 6/12)	30
	102
Impairment loss(W2)	210
	312

2	*Impairment loss*	£'000
	Original cost of training premises	900
	Depreciation at 1 October 20X1 (900/25 × 2.5)	(90)
	NBV	810
	Revalued amount	(600)
	Impairment loss	210

3	*Land and buildings*	£'000
	Land (700 + 350)	1,050
	Buildings:	
	Revalued amount (1,350 + 600)	1,950
	Depreciation since revaluation	(60)
		2,940

4 *Revaluation reserve*

			£'000
Land:			
Head office (700 – 500)	200		
Training premises (350 – 300)	50		
			250
Head office building:			
Revalued amount	1,350		
NBV at revaluation (1,200 × 22.5/25)	(1,080)		
			270
Less depreciation adjustment			
on head office building: (30 – 24) (W1)			(6)
			514

14 Myriad II

(a) According to **FRS 18, Accounting Policies**, companies should choose the **most appropriate accounting policies** for the entity. These accounting policies should be **reviewed regularly** to ensure that they are the most appropriate for the particular circumstances and **changed if they are no longer the most appropriate** for the entity. Any changes in **recognition, presentation or measurement basis** of an item in the financial statements is a **change in accounting policy**. A change in accounting policy should only occur **where the new policy is more appropriate** than the old policy or there has been a **change in accounting standards or requirements of the law**.

(b)

	30 September 20X1	30 September 20X0 (restated)
Myriad plc – Profit and loss account extract	£'000	£'000
Amortisation (1,060 × 25%)	265	
((1,060 – 400) × 25%)		165
Myriad plc – Balance sheet extract		
Development expenditure – cost	1,230	
cost (1,230 – 560)		670
amortisation (W1)	(505)	(240)
Net book value	725	430

Myriad plc – Statement of total recognised gains and losses extract

At the foot of the current years STRGL there would be a prior period adjustment of £430,000 (W2)

Workings

1   *Amortisation of development expenditure*

		£'000
Amortisation at 30 September 20X0		
20W9	300 × 25% × 2 years	150
20X0	360 × 25%	90
		240
Amortisation at 30 September 20X1		
20W9	300 × 25% × 3 years	225
20X0	360 × 25% × 2 years	180
20X1	400 × 25%	100
		505

2   *Prior period adjustment*

	£'000
Development costs at 30 September 20W9	420
Amortisation at 30 September 20W9 (300 × 25%)	(75)
Prior period adjustment at 30 September 20W9	345
Development costs for year ended 30 September 20X0	250
Amortisation for year ended 30 September 20X0	(165)
Prior period adjustment at 30 September 20X0	430

15 Dexterity

Text reference. Chapter 5.

Top tips. Part (a) is a test of memory. Follow the structure given to you in the question; discuss three situations (purchase, business combination, internal generation) for two assets (goodwill and other intangibles). This gives you a minimum of six marks out of ten.

Part (b) requires you to apply theory. Explain both the correct treatment and why alternative treatments have been rejected. For example in (b)(ii) explain why £12m can be capitalised and why £20m can't be.

Easy marks. If you know the standards, then part (a) should be 10 easy marks,

Examiner's comments. Part 9 (a) dealt with the treatment of goodwill and intangible assets. Part (b) included five scenarios to test the application of knowledge.

Candidates usually did very well in part (a) but performed really badly when it came to practical applications in part (b).

			Marks
(a)	Discussion of goodwill		3
	Other intangibles – separate transactions		2
	– part of an acquisition		3
	– internally developed		3
		Available	**11**
		Maximum	**10**

(b)	(i)	One mark for each item in balance sheet	4
	(ii)	Does it qualify as development expenditure	1
		The need for an active market	1
		Drugs are unique, not homogeneous	1
	(iii)	Neither an acquired asset nor internally generated	1
		Really recognition of goodwill	1
		Can recognise both the asset and the grant at fair value	1
		Or at cost – granted asset has zero cost	1
	(iv)	In reality a valuable asset, in accounting a pseudo-asset	1
		Cannot control workforce	1
		Does not meet recognition criteria	1
	(v)	Effective advertising really part of goodwill	1
		Cannot be recognised as a fixed asset	1
		Prepayment of £2.5 million	1
		Cannot spread over two years	1
		Available	**18**
		Maximum	**15**
		Maximum for question	**25**

(a) **Recognition and amortisation**

Goodwill

Only goodwill arising from a business combination is recognised. Under FRS 10 goodwill is the difference between the cost of the investment and the fair value of the acquired entity's identifiable assets and liabilities. Once recognised there is a rebuttable assumption that its useful life is 20 years or less, and so it is amortised over twenty years or less. However, an amortisation period longer than 20 years is allowed provided that it is reviewed for impairment at the end of each reporting period. If the goodwill has an indefinite life then it should not be amortised, provided that it is reviewed for impairment at the end of each reporting period.

One of the key aspects of goodwill is that it cannot be separated from the business that it belongs to. Therefore goodwill cannot be purchased separately from other assets. In addition, FRS 10 states that internally generated goodwill must not be capitalised.

Other intangible assets

Other intangibles can be recognised if they can be distinguished from goodwill; typically this means that they can be separated from the rest of the business, or that they arise from a legal or contractual right.

If an intangible is purchased separately then it will be recognised at cost. If the asset is not purchased for cash then its cost equals the fair value of the consideration.

Intangibles acquired as part of a business combination are recognised provided that they can be valued separately from goodwill. The acquirer will recognise an intangible even if the asset had not been recognised previously. If an intangible cannot be valued, then it will be subsumed into goodwill. Intangibles cannot be recognised if they create negative goodwill.

Internally generated intangibles can only be recognised if they are distinct from goodwill and if the expenditure is separate from the general cost of developing a business. For example, a brand name acquired in a business combination is capitalised whereas an internally generated brand isn't. There are also specific rules for capitalising development expenditure.

An internally generated intangible asset may only be capitalised if it has a readily ascertainable market value. This is unlikely, because most intangibles are unique. However, government licences and quotas are often bought and sold and therefore may be examples of these rare homogeneous intangibles.

The amortisation and impairment rules are the same for goodwill and other intangibles.

(b) **Dexterity**

(i) **Temerity**

The following assets will be recognised on acquisition:

	£m
Fair value of sundry net assets	15
Patent at fair value	10
Research carried out for customer	2
Goodwill (balancing figure)	8
Total consideration	35

The patent is recognised at its fair value at the date of acquisition, even if it hadn't previously been recognised by Temerity. It will be amortised over the remaining 8 years of its useful life with an assumed nil residual value.

The higher value of £15m can't be used because it depends on the successful outcome of the clinical trials. The extra £5m is a contingent asset. Under FRS 7 the value attributed to a contingent asset reflects the best estimate of the likely outcome. There is no information about the likely outcome of the trials, and so it is prudent not to recognise it.

Even if the trials are successful the patent cannot be revalued to £15m unless there is an active market in such patents, which is unlikely.

Although research is not capitalised, this research has been carried out for a customer and should be recognised as work-in-progress in current assets. It will be valued at the lower of cost and net realisable value unless it meets the definition of a long-term work-in-progress under SSAP 9.

The goodwill is capitalised at cost and amortised over its useful life.

(ii) **New drug**

Under SSAP 13 the £12m costs of developing this new drug are capitalised and then amortised over its commercial life. (The costs of researching a new drug are never capitalised.)

FRS 10 only allows intangibles to be held at valuation if there is a readily ascertainable market value. Patents are only given to unique products and so they cannot be revalued. Therefore the £20m valuation is irrelevant.

(iii) **Government licence**

The general rule for intangibles are that they are initially measured at cost (in this case £Nil) and then only revalued if an active market exists (which is not the case for this exclusive licence). Therefore the licence cannot be recognised.

(The rules under IFRS GAAP are different. IAS 38 Para 44 states that assets acquired as a result of a government grant may be capitalised at fair value, along with a corresponding credit for the value of the grant. Therefore Dexterity would recognise an asset and grant of £10m which are then amortised/released over the five year life of the license. The net effect on profits and on shareholders funds will be nil.)

(iv) **Training costs**

Although well trained staff add value to a business training costs cannot be capitalised. This is because a business does not have sufficient control over the expected future economic benefits arising from staff training; in other words trained staff are free to leave and work for someone else. Training is part of the general cost of developing a business as a whole.

(v) **Advertising costs**

Advertising and promotional costs should be recognised as an expense when incurred. This is because the expected future economic benefits are uncertain and they are beyond the control of the entity.

However, because the year-end is half way through the campaign there is a £2.5m prepayment to be recognised as a current asset.

16 Derwent

Advent

(a)   *Balance sheet extracts as at 30 September 20X4*

Fixed assets				£m
Tangible fixed assets	Note 1			316
Intangible assets	Note 2			100
				416

Note 1 Tangible fixed assets

		Land and buildings	Plant	Total
Cost		£m	£m	£m
Opening		280	150	430
Additions	W1	-	50	50
Revaluations		(15)	-	(15)
Closing		265	200	465
Depreciation				
Opening		40	105	145
Charge	W2/W1	9	35	44
Revaluation		(40)	-	(40)
Closing		9	140	149
Net Book Value				
30 September 20X4		256	60	316
30 September 20X3		240	45	285

Buildings are depreciated over 25 years and plant over 5 years.

On 1 October 20X3 the land and buildings were valued by XYZ, Chartered Surveyors, on an open market existing use basis.

W1   *Plant*

Installation and commissioning costs are included in the cost of the asset.

		£m
Depreciation		
Opening cost of £150m:	full year at 20%	30
Additions of £50m:	half year at 20%	5
		35

W2   *Property*

	Land	Buildings: Value	Total Value	Buildings: Dep'n	NBV
	£m	£m	£m	£m	£m
Opening	80	200	280	(40)	240
Revaluation	5	(20)	(15)	40	25
	85	180	265	-	265
Depreciation (20 years)	-	-	-	(9)	(9)
Closing	85	180	265	(9)	256

Note 2 Intangible assets: Telecommunications licence

	£m
Cost	
Opening and closing	300
Depreciation	
Opening	30
Charge	30
Impairment	140
Closing	200
Net book value	
30 September 20X4	100
30 September 20X3	270

The net book value must not exceed the impaired value of £100m; therefore the closing accumulated depreciation must be fixed at £200m. This in turn gives the impairment charge as a balancing figure of £140m.

The new carrying value of £100m will be depreciated over the remaining 8 year life of the license.

(b)   *Usefulness of the disclosures*

The disclosures give the reader more information about the nature and value of the fixed assets.

Firstly, there is the split between tangible assets (property, plant and equipment) and intangible assets. Lenders are less willing to use intangibles as security for loans than tangibles, and in the event of a winding up intangibles are often worthless without the business to support them.

Within tangible assets there is the split between land and buildings and the rest. Land and buildings are often seen as the best source of security by lenders.

Land and buildings can go up in value as well as down, and so the note indicates the effect of revaluations during the year. The revaluation reserve note elsewhere in the financial statements will show the total revaluation compared with original cost. Because valuations are subjective the identity and qualifications of the valuer are disclosed.

The rates of depreciation indicate how prudent (or otherwise) the depreciation policies are, and whether the reported profits are fairly stated. The ratio between carrying value and cost gives a rough idea of the age of the assets, and of how soon they will need replacing.

The disclosure of the impairment loss flags a bad investment; the shareholders will want more information about this at their annual general meeting.

17 Wilderness

Text reference. Chapters 5 and 6.

Top tips. Part (a) is a straight forward description of impairment and how it is accounted for.

Part (b) applies the theory. In (b) (ii) remember that the impairment of the brand name should have been accounted for when it happened in April 20X5. This is before the impairment review of the whole income generating unit in September.

Easy marks. Part (a) was 2 easy marks for very basic knowledge. In part (b) you must set out all your assumptions clearly.

Examiner's comments. This question tested the principles of impairment of assets. It was not a popular choice and candidates who attempted it scored on average less than half marks. Answers to part (a) were generally correct but lacked important detail. The numerical examples in (b) were less well answered, showing an inability to apply the principles. Part (b) (ii) answers were even worse. Many candidates did not realise the Phoenix brand name was an internally-generated asset and can could not be recognised. In some cases no attempt was made to apportion the impairment loss over the relevant assets.

Marking scheme

				Marks
(a)	(i)	Impairment – definition	1	
		Net realisable value	2	
		Value in use	2	
		IGU	1	
		Annual impairment review	$\underline{3}$	
			9	
		Maximum		6
	(ii)	Impairment loss and treatment	3	
		Application to IGU	$\underline{3}$	
			6	
		Maximum		5
(b)	(i)	Carrying value	2	
		Realisable value	2	
		Recoverable amount	1	
		Impairment loss	1	
		Depreciation	1	
		Closing carrying value	$\underline{1}$	
			8	
		Maximum		7
	(ii)	Brand	2	
		Stocks	2	
		Plant	1	
		Impairment loss	1	
		Land value	$\underline{1}$	
			8	
		Maximum		$\underline{7}$
				$\underline{25}$

(a) (i) *Define an impairment loss*

An impairment occurs when the carrying value of an asset exceeds its recoverable amount. Recoverable amount represents the amount of cash that an asset will generate either through use (value in use) or through disposal (net realisable value).

The value in use is the present value of all future cash flows derived from an asset, including any disposal proceeds at the end of the asset's life. The present value of future cash flows will be affected by the timing, volatility and uncertainty of the cash flows. This can be reflected in the forecasted cash flows or the discount rate used.

Very few business assets generate their own cash flows, and so assets are often grouped together into income generating units for impairment purposes. An income generating unit is the smallest group of assets generating independent cash flows

Net realisable value is the amount obtainable for an asset in an active market, less disposal costs. The market value of used assets with no active market will have to be estimated. Valuations based on a 'forced sale' value would not normally be used.

Impairment reviews

- At each reporting date an entity shall assess whether there are any indications that an impairment has occurred; if there are such indications then the recoverable amount of the asset must be estimated.

- Goodwill and intangible assets with indefinite lives (or with an estimated life of over 20 years) should be reviewed for impairment annually.

- Tangible assets with a remaining useful life greater than 50 years, or which are not depreciated on the grounds of materiality, should also be reviewed annually.

(ii) *Accounting for an impairment loss*

Impairment losses should be recognised immediately. They will normally be charged to the P&L alongside depreciation, but the impairment of a revalued asset should be taken directly to the revaluation reserve (unless the impairment is below depreciated historic cost). In the balance sheet the impairment will normally be included within accumulated depreciation, although it could be disclosed separately if material. Future depreciation charges will be based on the impaired value and the remaining useful life at the date of the impairment.

Impairments of income generating units must be apportioned to the individual assets within that unit. The impairment is firstly allocated to goodwill, then to other intangibles, and then it is apportioned to the remaining assets on a pro rata basis. However, individual assets are not impaired below their own realisable value; any unused impairment is re-apportioned to the other assets.

(b) (i) *Wilderness*

Summary

Profit and loss account		£
Depreciation	First six months	40,000
	Second six months	37,500
Impairment		50,000
		127,500

Balance Sheet 30 September 20X5	£
Cost	640,000
Accumulated depreciation and impairment (£400,000 + £40,000 + £50,000 + £37,500)	(527,500)
Carrying value	112,500

At 1 April 20X5 the asset should be restated at the lower of carrying value and recoverable amount. Recoverable amount is the higher of *value in use* and *fair value less costs to sell.*

Carrying value 1 April 20X5		£
Cost		640,000
Opening depreciation		(400,000)
Depreciation for 6 months	(£640,000 × 12$\frac{1}{2}$% × $^{6}/_{12}$)	(40,000)
Carrying value 1 April 20X5		200,000

Recoverable amount	£
Value in use (recoverable amount)	150,000
Fair value less costs to sell*	20,000

*Wilderness does not intend to replace the machine and so the trade-in value of £180,000 is irrelevant.

The asset is impaired and should be written down to the recoverable amount of £150,000, giving an impairment loss of £50,000. This new valuation will then be depreciated over the remaining useful life of the asset, which is two years from the date of the accident.

Carrying value 30 September 20X5:		£
Valuation 1 April 20X5		150,000
Depreciation for 6 months	(£150,000 × $^{6}/_{24}$)	(37,500)
Carrying value 1 April 20X5		112,500

(ii)   *Mossel*

The question raises four issues:

(a)   The value of the Quencher brand name,
(b)   The £1.5m upgrade costs,
(c)   The old bottles in stocks, and
(d)   The overall impairment of the whole operation.

(a)   *The value of the Quencher brand name*

The £7m Quencher brand name should have been written off when it was discontinued. The Phoenix brand name is internally generated and so it cannot be capitalised. This will reduce the carrying value of the net assets at 30 September to £25m.

(b)   *The £1.5m upgrade costs*

These costs reflect the directors' intentions for the coming year. There is no obligation to incur these costs and so they cannot be recognised in the current year. However they may be disclosed in the notes.

(c)   *The old bottles in stocks*

These should be stated at the lower of normal cost (£2m) and net realisable value (£2.75m), therefore they remain at their cost of £2m. The NRV is the normal sales price of £3m (normal cost of £2m plus 50%) less the £250,000 re-labelling costs.

(d)   *The overall impairment of the whole operation at September 20X5*

The value in use and recoverable amount of the whole operation has been reduced to £20m. This is less than the carrying value of £25m and so an impairment of £5m has to be accounted for and apportioned to the assets within the income generating unit. This is done as follows:

	Carrying value £'000	Impairment £'000	Recoverable amount £'000
Brand (already impaired)	–	–	–
Land	12,000	(3,000)	9,000
Plant	8,000	(2,000)	6,000
	20,000	(5,000)	15,000

18 Multiplex

(a) **Carrying value of assets**

The impairment losses are allocated as required by FRS 11 *Impairment of fixed assets and goodwill*.

	Asset at 1.1.20X1 £'000	1st provision (W1) £'000	Assets at 1.2.20X1 £'000	2nd provision (W2) £'000	Revised asset £'000
Goodwill	200	(200)	-	-	-
Operating licence	1,000	(300)	700	(100)	600
Property: stations/land	250	-	250	(50)	200
Rail track/coaches	250	-	250	(50)	200
Steam engines	1,000	(500)	500	-	500
Other net assets	300	-	300	-	300
	3,000	(1,000)	2,000	(200)	1,800

Workings

1   *First provision*

£500,000 relates directly to an engine and its recoverable amount can be assessed directly (ie zero). FRS 11 then requires goodwill to be written off. Any further impairment must be written off intangible assets.

2   *Second provision*

The first £100,000 of the impairment loss is applied to the operating licence to write it down to NRV. The remainder is applied pro rata to assets carried at other than their net selling prices.

(b) **Correct accounting treatment – closure of engineering division**

At the year end of 31 March 20X1, the company has committed itself to a **binding decision** to close the engineering operation. The expected losses on closure **must** therefore **be provided** for and, as they are **material**, they will be classed as **exceptional**. FRS 3 *Reporting financial performance* requires **separate disclosure** of losses on the closure of an operation on the face of the profit and loss account.

However, again under FRS 3, the closure of the division appears to meet **only three** of the four criteria for it to be treated as a discontinued operation, ie:

(i)   The activities have **ceased permanently**.
(ii)   The closure has a **material effect** on the nature and focus of Multiplex's operations.
(iii) The results are **separately distinguishable**.
(iv)   But the closure will *not* be completed **within three months** of the year end.

The provision must therefore be shown as part of **continuing operations**, although the circumstances may be explained in the notes to the financial statements.

The amount will be:

	£m
Loss on sale of net assets (46 – 30)	16.0
Other costs: redundancies	2.0
Professional costs	1.5
Penalty costs	3.0
	22.5

The treatment of the future operating losses of £4.5 million is less clear.

The company is 'demonstrably committed' to the sale, and therefore FRS 3 requires it to make a provision for losses up to the date of sale. However, FRS 12 *Provisions, contingent liabilities and contingent assets* does not allow any future operating losses to be recognised as a provision unless they relate to 'onerous contracts' (which is not indicated in this question). FRS 12 excludes provisions covered by another accounting standard and this presumably includes FRS 3. Commentators have pointed out this apparent conflict between the two standards.

There is a case for recognising a provision on the grounds that FRS 3 appears to require it. The pertinent question is: does the company have an obligation to incur the losses? In other words, has it any alternative to operating the business at a loss until the date of sale? If so, the spirit of FRS 12 suggests that a provision should not be recognised.

19 Preparation question: Research Ltd

Research Ltd balance sheet extracts

	20X1 £'000	20X0 £'000
Other net assets	2,270	1,600
Share capital	550	500
Revaluation reserve	120	–
Profit and loss reserve	1,600	1,100
	2,270	1,600

Statement of total recognised gains and losses

	20X1 £'000	20X0 £'000
Profit for the year	500	280
Unrealised surplus on revaluation of properties	120	–
Total recognised gains and losses relating to the year	620	280
Prior period adjustment	(360)	–
Total gains and losses recognised since last annual report	260	280

Reconciliation of movements in shareholders' funds

	20X1 £'000	20X0 £'000
Profit for the year (2,130 – 1,460 – 220 + 50)/(410 + 50 – 180)	500	280
Dividends	–	–
Other recognised gains and losses relating to the year (net)	120	–
New share capital subscribed	50	–
Net addition to shareholders' funds	670	280
Opening shareholders' funds (previously stated as £1,960,000 20X1 and £1,550,000* 20X0 before deducting prior year adjustment of £360,000 and £230,000** respectively)	1,600	1,320
Closing shareholders' funds	2,270	1,600

*(1,960 – 410)/ **(360 – 180 + 50)

Statement of movement in reserves

	£'000
b/f as previously stated	1,460
Prior year adjustment	(360)
As restated	1,100
Profit for the year (2,130 – 1,460 – 220 + 50)	500
Dividends	–
At 31 December 20X1	1,600

20 Derringdo III

Carpets

A change of accounting policy occurs when a new policy is used to report the same situations. In this case there is a new situation, Derringdo's terms of trade have changed, and so a new policy has been applied to report it. This is not a change of policy. The old trade will still be reported under the old method and the new trade will be reported under the new method.

	£'000
P&L	
Carpets fitted under the old terms of trade (these will not have been claimed in the previous year)	1,200
Carpets sold under the new terms of trade	23,000
Total revenue for this year	24,200

21 Telenorth

Text references. Chapters 7 and 18.

Top tips. This was a 'typical' published financial statements type question with an earnings per share calculation. Candidates had to prepare the financial statements from a trial balance and include several adjustments which were used to cover many areas of the syllabus.

Examiner's comment. This was the one question where some less methodical candidates appeared to run out of time. On the whole this was well answered and remarkably some candidates scored full marks on Part (a). Again the 'trickier' adjustments proved to be stumbling blocks. Two of the worst errors were:

(a)   Not providing for the second half of the debenture (loan) interest.

(b)   Incorrect calculation of basic depreciation charges and inclusion of them in the wrong category. (The question was specific as to where depreciation should be charged.)

Answers to Part (b), the calculation of the earnings per share figure, were surprisingly disappointing. A significant proportion of candidates did not even attempt this section, of those that did very few correctly handled the rights issue and several candidates thought that the question involved a dilution calculation.

(a) (i) **Telenorth plc - Profit and loss account for the year ending 30 September 20X1**

	£'000	£'000
Turnover		283,460
Cost of sales (W2)		(155,170)
Gross profit		128,290
Distribution expenses	(22,300)	
Administrative expenses (W4)	(42,200)	
		(64,500)
Operating profit		63,790
Interest payable and similar charges (W5)	(1,656)	
Investment income (W6)	1,500	
		(156)
Profit before tax		63,634
Tax (W7)		(24,600)
Profit after tax		39,034

(ii) **Telenorth plc - Balance sheet as at 30 September 20X1**

	£'000	£'000
Tangible fixed assets (W9)		83,440
Investments		34,500
		117,940
Current assets		
Stock (W1)	16,680	
Trade debtors		
(35,700 + 12,000) (W3)	47,700	
	64,380	
Creditors: amounts falling due within one year (W10)	(53,326)	
Net current assets		11,054
		128,994
Creditors: amounts falling due after more than one year		
6% Debentures	(10,000)	
8% Preference shares	(12,000)	
		(22,000)
Provision for liabilities		
Deferred tax (5,200 + 2,200)		(7,400)
		99,594
Share capital and reserves		
Ordinary shares of £1 each (20,000 + 40,000 + 6,000)		30,000
Share premium (W11)	16,000	
Revaluation reserve (3,400 – 1,000)	2,400	
Profit and loss account (W8)	51,194	69,594
		99,594

Workings

1 *Closing stock*

	£000
Value at 4 October	16,000
Add: sales (1,400 × 100/140)	1,000
sale or return (650 × 100/130)	500
Less: purchases	(820)
	16,680

2   *Cost of sales*

	£000
Opening stock	12,400
Purchases	147,200
Less: closing stock (W1)	(16,680)
	142,920
Leasehold depreciation (56,250/25)	2,250
Plant depreciation (55,000 – 5,000/5)	10,000
	155,170

3   *Debt factoring*

The risks and rewards of the debt that has been factored remain with Telenorth plc therefore the debt should not have been taken off the balance sheet. Instead the substance of the transaction is that Kwikfinance has provided a loan to Telenorth at an interest rate of 1% per month. This must be reflected in the balance sheet with subsequent adjustments in the profit and loss account.

The journal entry to reinstate the debtor and correctly record the transaction is:

		£000	£000
Debit	Debtors	12,000	
Credit	Loan		9,600
Credit	Administrative expenses		2,400
Debit	Interest payable (9,600 × 1%)	96	
Credit	Accruals		96

4   *Administrative expenses*

	£000
Per trial balance	34,440
Less: incorrect treatment of debt factoring (W3)	(2,400)
Add: computer depreciation	
((35,000 – 9,600) × 40%)	10,160
	42,200

5   *Interest payable and similar charges*

	£000
Debenture interest (10,000 × 6%)	600
Debt factor finance charge (W3)	96
Preference dividend (12,000 × 8%)	960
	1,656

6   *Investment income*

	£000
UK dividends	1,080
Interest received	420
	1,500

7   *Tax charge*

	£000
Provision required	23,400
Deferred tax	1,200
	24,600

8   *Profit and loss account*

	£000
Balance b/f	14,160
Profit for the period	39,034
Ordinary dividend paid	(2,000)
	51,194

9   *Tangible fixed assets*

	£000	£000
Leasehold		
Cost	56,250	
Depreciation (18,000 + 2,250)	20,250	
NBV		36,000
Plant and equipment		
Cost	55,000	
Depreciation (12,800 + 10,000)	22,800	
NBV		32,200
Computer system		
Cost	35,000	
Depreciation (9,600 + 10,160)	19,760	
NBV		15,240
		83,440

10   *Creditors: amounts falling due within one year*

	£000
Bank overdraft	1,680
Trade creditors	17,770
Taxation	23,400
Proposed preference dividend	480
Loan from factor	9,600
Accruals - debenture interest	300
debt factor finance charge (W3)	96
	53,326

11   *Share premium account*

	£000
Issue of options (4,000 × £1)	4,000
Rights issue (6,000 × £2)	12,000
	16,000

(b)

	£000
Earnings available for ordinary shareholders:	
Profit after tax	39,034

Rights issue - theoretical ex-rights price

	£
4 shares @ £4	16
1 share @ £3	3
5 shares @ £3.80 (bal fig)	19

Weighted average number of shares in issue:

	000s
24,000 × 9/12 × 4/3.80	18,947
30,000 × 3/12	7,500
	26,447

$$\text{Earnings per share} = \frac{£39,034}{26,447}$$

$$= 148 \text{ pence}$$

22 Tourmalet

Text references. Chapters 7 and 15.

Top tips. As well as examining you on the format and content of the profit and loss account and statement of total recognised gains and losses, this question also tests your knowledge of several specific situations.

One key point is to separate out the discontinued activities.

As always, be methodical and don't get bogged down in the detail.

Easy marks. Parts (a) and (c) are 9 easy marks. You should be able to answer these even if you get bogged down in the profit and loss account.

Examiner's comments. Part (a) covered the sale and leaseback of plant. Most candidates realised that this should be treated as a secured loan. However, some failed to recognise the correct treatment.

In part (b), candidates had to prepare a profit and loss account and this was generally well-answered. However some problems arose: discontinued operation, provision for slow moving stock, and the treatment of interest on the loan from part (a).

Part (c) was generally ignored. Those who did attempt the statement of total recognised gains and losses failed to realise that the preference shares should be treated as debt and so the preference dividend should be treated as a finance cost.

Marking scheme

			Marks
(a)	Should not be treated as sales/cost of sales		1
	Normally only the profit in income (may require disclosure)		1
	The substance of the transaction is a secured loan		1
	Plant should be left on balance sheet		1
	'Sale' proceeds of £50 million shown as loan		1
	Rentals are partly interest and partly capital repayments		1
		Available	6
		Maximum	5
(b)	*Profit and loss account*		
	Discontinuing operations figures		3
	Sales		2
	Cost of sales		5
	Distribution expenses		1
	Administration expenses		2
	Finance costs (including 1 for preference dividends)		2
	Loss on investment properties		1
	Investment income		1
	Taxation		2
		Available	19
		Maximum	17
(c)	*Statement of total recognised gains and losses*		
	Profit for period		1
	Deficit on investment property		1
	Total		1
		Maximum	3
		Maximum for question	25

(a)   *Sale of plant*

The substance of this transaction is a financing arrangement, not a sale.

- Tourmalet will continue to enjoy the risks and benefits of ownership for the remainder of the asset's life because of the leaseback deal.

- The lease appears to be a finance lease, so Tourmalet will continue to recognise the asset.

- Over the period of the lease Tourmalet will repay the sale proceeds in full, plus interest at 12%, indicating that this is a loan and not a sale.

Tourmalet should continue to recognise the asset at its original cost, and depreciate it as before. The sale proceeds will be treated as a loan, and the lease payments will be split between repayment of this loan and a finance charge. Even if the sale were a genuine sale, it should not have been included within normal trading turnover and cost of sales.

TOURMALET: PROFIT AND LOSS ACCOUNT FOR THE YEAR ENDED 30 SEPTEMBER 20X3

	Continuing £'000		Discontinued £'000		Total £'000
Turnover	247,800	(W1)	15,200		263,000
Cost of sales (W2)	(128,800)		(16,000)		(144,800)
Gross profit	119,000		(800)		118,200
Distribution costs	(26,400)		–		(26,400)
Administrative expenses (W3)	(20,000)	(W3)	(4,700)	(W6)	(24,700)
Operating profit	72,600		(5,500)		67,100
Other income					1,200
Finance costs (W4)					(3,800)
Profit before tax					64,500
Taxation (W5)					(7,100)
Profit after tax					57,400

STATEMENT OF TOTAL RECOGNISED GAINS AND LOSSES

	£'000
Profit for the financial year (profit after tax)	57,400
Unrealised deficit on investment property (10m – 9.8m)	(200)
Total gains and losses recognised since the last annual report	57,200

Workings

		£'000	£'000
1	*Turnover*		
	From TB		313,000
	Disposal of plant		(50,000)
	Discontinued activities		(15,200)
			247,800
2	*Cost of sales*		
	Opening stock		26,550
	Purchases		158,450
	Disposal of plant		(40,000)
	Closing stock: Cost	28,500	
	NRV allowance (4,500 – 2,000)	(2,500)	
			(26,000)
	Depreciation		
	Leased item £40m / 5 years		8,000
	Others (£98.6m - £24.6m) × 20%		14,800
	Buildings (£120m / 40 years)		3,000
	Total		144,800
	Discontinued activities		(16,000)
	Continuing activities		128,800

			£'000	£'000
3	*Administrative expenses*			
	From the TB			23,200
	Discontinued activities			(3,200)
				20,000
4	*Finance costs*			
	6% Redeemable preference shares			
	Interim dividend from the TB			900
	Accrued final dividend £30m × 6% × 6/12			900
	Finance cost of lease back £50m × 12% × 4/12			2,000
				3,800
5	*Taxation*			
	Over-provision from the trial balance			(2,100)
	Charge for the year			9,200
				7,100
6	*Discontinued operations*			
	Administration (3,200 + 1,500 termination penalty)			4,700

23 Partway

Text reference. Chapter 7.

Top tips. This question covers discontinued operations and changes of accounting policy. Not to be attempted unless you knew something about both of these. There are 5 separate parts to this question. Do something on each of them, do not get carried away with the profit and loss account.

Easy marks. (a) (i) and (ii) and (b) (i) were quite easy and you should have been to do well on them. (a) (iii) was not difficult but you may have ended up spending too long on it and (b) (ii) was a bit tricky. However you were asked to comment, so a sensible comment supported by the evidence would have secured you a mark or two.

Marking scheme

				Marks
(a)	(i)	definition itself		2
		usefulness of information		1
		why a rigorous definition is needed		1
			Maximum	**4**
	(ii)	discussion whether a discontinued operation		3
		conclusion		1
			Maximum	**4**
	(iii)	figures for turnover from continuing operations (2005 and 2006)		1
		figures for turnover from new business (2006)		1
		figures for turnover from discontinued operations (2005 and 2006)		1
		figures for profit before tax from continuing operations (2005 and 2006)		1
		figures for profit before tax from new business (2006)		1
		figures for profit before tax from discontinued operations (2005 and 2006)		1
			Maximum	**6**
(b)	(i)	1 mark per relevant point	**Maximum**	**5**
	(ii)	1 mark per relevant point	**Maximum**	**6**
			Maximum for question	**25**

(a)   (i)   A discontinued operation must meet all of the following conditions specified in FRS 3:

      (1)   The sale or termination must have been **completed** before the earlier of 3 months after the year end or the date the financial statements are approved.

      (2)   The former activity must have **ceased permanently**.

      (3)   The sale or termination has a **material effect** on the nature and focus of the entity's operations and represents a material reduction in its operating facilities resulting either from:

          •   Its withdrawal from a particular market; or from
          •   A material reduction in turnover in its continuing markets

      (4)   The assets, liabilities, results of operations and activities are **clearly distinguishable**, physically, operationally and for financial reporting purposes.

This very precise definition is needed to ensure that only operations which can properly be regarded as discontinued are classified as such. Users of accounts, particularly financial analysts, will be more interested in the results of continuing operations as a guide to the company's future profitability and it is not unacceptable for discontinued operations to show a loss. Companies could therefore be tempted to hide loss-making activities under the umbrella of discontinued operations, hence the rigorous requirement under (d) that the elements of the discontinued operation must be clearly distinguishable from those of continuing operations. It is also conceivable that a company could seek to include the results of a profitable operation which has been sold under continuing operations.

The separation of the results of continuing and discontinued operations and acquisitions on the face of the profit and loss account makes possible more meaningful year on year comparison. The inclusion of prior year information for discontinued operations means that it can be seen exactly how the continuing operations have performed, and to forecast more accurately how they can be expected to perform in the future with the addition of acquired operations.

(ii)   This can be correctly classified as a discontinued operation. The termination was completed before the accounts were approved and within 2 weeks of the year end date. The interested parties were notified at that time and an announcement was made in the press, making the decision irrevocable. The travel agency business has ceased permanently and represents a withdrawal from the over-the-counter market, which will entail a material reduction in its operating facilities. The results of the travel agency business are clearly distinguished.

(iii) PARTWAY
PROFIT AND LOSS ACCOUNT FOR THE YEAR ENDED

	31 October 2006		31 October 2005	
Turnover	£'000	£'000	£'000	£'000
Continuing operations	23,000		22,000	
Acquisitions	2,000		-	
	25,000		22,000	
Discontinued operations	14,000		18,000	
		39,000		40,000
Cost of sales		(36,000)		(32,000)
Gross profit		3,000		8,000
Net operating expenses		(2,600)		(2,000)
Operating profit				
Continuing operations	4,000		4,500	
Acquisitions	400		-	
	4,400		4,500	
Discontinued operations	(4,000)		1,500	
Profit before tax		400		6,000

(b)   (i)   Accounting policies can be described as the principles, conventions, rules and practices applied by an entity that prescribe how transactions and other events are to be reflected in its financial statements. This includes the recognition, presentation and measurement basis to be applied to assets, liabilities, gains, losses and changes to shareholders funds. Once these policies have been adopted, they are not expected to change frequently and comparability requires that ideally they do not change from year to year. However, FRS 18 does envisage situations where a change of accounting policy is required in the interests of presenting a true and fair view.

An entity may have to change an accounting policy in response to changes in a Standard or UITF Abstract or in applicable legislation. Or it may be an internal decision which can be justified on the basis of presenting a more true and fair view. An accounting policy adopted to deal with transactions or events which did not arise previously is not treated as a change of accounting policy.

Where a change of accounting policy has taken place it must be accounted for by retrospective restatement. This means that the comparative financial statements must be restated in the light of the new accounting policy. This makes it possible to compare results for these years as if the new accounting policy had always been in place. The financial statements must disclose the reason for the change of accounting policy and the effects of the change on the results for the previous year.

    (ii)   The directors' proposal here is that revenue recognition can be accelerated based on the imposition of compulsory holiday insurance. This is based on the presumption that the risk of not receiving the balance of the payment has now been covered. However, at the point when the deposit is received, Partway has not yet done anything to earn the revenue. Under UITF Abstract 40 *Revenue recognition and service contracts*, where the substance of a contract is that a right to consideration does not arise until the occurrence of a critical event, revenue does not arise until that event occurs. In this case, the critical event is the date the holiday is actually taken. The existing policy is therefore correct and should not be changed.

If this change were to be made it would not be a change in accounting policy as it is a change in timing, rather than recognition, presentation or measurement basis. The directors would of course prefer it not to be recognised as a change of accounting policy, as the restatement of comparatives would defeat the purpose of the change.

24 Preparation question: Simple consolidation

> **Top tips**. This is a very easy question giving you practice in all the basics of consolidation which are needed in all questions.

BOO GROUP
CONSOLIDATED PROFIT AND LOSS ACCOUNT
FOR THE YEAR ENDED 31 DECEMBER 20X8

	£'000
Sales (5,000 + 1,000 − 100)	5,900
Cost of sales (2,900 + 600 − 80)	3,420
Gross profit	2,480
Other expenses (1,700 + 320)	2,020
Profit before tax	460
Tax (130 + 25)	155
Profit after tax	305
Minority interest (20% × £55,000)	11
Group profit for the year	294

CONSOLIDATED BALANCE SHEET AS AT 31 DECEMBER 20X8

	£'000	£'000
Fixed assets (2,000 + 200 − 80)		2,120
Current assets		
Stock (500 + 120 + 80)	700	
Trade debtors (650 − 100 + 40)	590	
Bank and cash (390 + 35)	425	
	1,715	
Current liabilities		
Trade creditors (910 + 30)	940	
Tax (130 + 25)	155	
	1,095	
Net current assets		620
Total assets less current liabilities		2,740
Capital and reserves		
Share capital (Boo only)		2,000
Profit and loss account (W5)		672
Minority interest (W4)		68
		2,740

Workings

1 *Group structure*

Boo

| 80%

Goose (P/L reserve £nil on acquisition)

2 *Goodwill*

	£'000	£'000
Cost of investment		80
For:		
Share capital	100	
P/L reserve	-	
	× 80%	(80)
Goodwill		Nil

3 *Unrealised profit*

	£'000
Sales	100
Cost of sales	(80)
	20

4 *Minority interest*

	£'000
Net assets per question	340
Minority interest (20% × 340)	68

5   *Reserves*

	Boo	*Goose*
	£'000	£'000
Per question	500	240
Less: unrealised profit	(20)	
pre acquisition		(Nil)
Share of post acquisition		240
(240 × 80%)	192	
	672	

25 Hideaway

FRS 8 Related party disclosures

(a)   *Circumstances giving rise to related parties*

- Parties are related if:

- One party has direct or indirect control over the other (eg a parent and its subsidiary),

- The parties are under common control from the same source (eg two subsidiaries in the same group),

- One party has such influence over the operating and financial policies of the other that the other party might not be able to pursue its own interests (eg there is potential influence, even if it isn't being exercised),

- The parties to a transaction are both subject to influence from another party, to the extent that one of them has subordinated its own interests.

(b)   *Importance of related party disclosures*

Investors invest in a business on the assumption that it aims to maximise its own profits for the benefit of its own shareholders. This means that all transactions have been negotiated at arm's length between willing and informed parties. The existence of related parties may encourage directors to make decisions for the benefit of another entity at the expense of their own shareholders. This can be done actively by selling goods and services cheaply to related parties, or by buying in goods and services at an above market price. It can also happen when directors choose not to compete with a related party, or offer guarantees or collateral for other party's loans.

Disclosure is particularly important when a business is being sold. It may receive a lot of custom, supplies, services or general help and advice from family or group companies. When the company is sold these benefits may be withdrawn.

Related party transactions are not illegal, nor are they necessarily a bad thing. However shareholders and potential investors need to be informed of material related party transactions in order to make informed investment and stewardship decisions.

(c)   *Hideaway, Benedict and Depret*

The directors and shareholders of Hideaway, the parent, will maximise their wealth by diverting profitable trade into wholly owned subsidiaries. They have done this by instructing Depret (a 55% subsidiary) to sell goods to Benedict (a 100% subsidiary) at £5m below fair value. As a result the minority shareholders of Depret have been deprived of their 45% interest in those lost profits, amounting to £2.25m. The non-group directors of Depret will also lose out if their pay is linked to Depret's profits.

Because Depret's profits have been reduced, the minority shareholders might be persuaded to sell their shares to Hideaway for less than their true value. Certainly potential shareholders will not be willing to pay as much for Depret's shares as they would have if Depret's profits had been maximised.

The opposite possibility is that the Directors of Hideaway are boosting Benedict's reported performance with the intention of selling it off for an inflated price.

Depret's minority shareholders might be able to get legal redress because the majority shareholders appear to be using their power to oppress the minority. This, however, will depend on local law. The tax authorities might also suspect Depret of trying to avoid tax, especially if Benedict is in a different tax jurisdiction.

26 Highveldt

Text reference. Chapter 9.

Top tips. Don't forget **Part (b).** There are five marks here for explaining the purpose of consolidated financial statements. Do it first, before getting tied up with Part (a).

Part (a) Make sure that you read the question before doing anything. You are not asked to prepare a balance sheet; just the goodwill and reserves. This makes the question easier to manage as effectively you are just doing the workings without having to tie it all together in a set of financial statements.

Easy marks. Part (b) is the only easy marks here. For the rest, be very methodical. There are quite a few complications to consider. For each calculation go through each of the six additional pieces of information and make appropriate adjustments when relevant.

Examiner's comments. Many candidates got confused with the fair value and other adjustments, in particular the split between the pre- and post-acquisition element. The most common errors were:

- incorrect cost of investment
- omitting the brand from the goodwill calculation
- incorrect treatment of the development costs
- errors in the calculation of the minority interest
- not correctly accounting for unrealised profit in stock
- incorrect calculation of share premium and revaluation reserve

				Marks
(a)	(i)	**Goodwill**		
		Consideration	2	
		Share capital and premium	1	
		Pre-acquisition profit	2	
		Fair value adjustments	2	
		Goodwill amortisation	1	8
	(ii)	**Minority interest**		
		Share capital and premium	1	
		profit and loss reserve	2	
		fair value adjustment	1	4
	(iii)	**Consolidated reserves**		
		Share premium	1	
		Revaluation reserve	2	
		Profit and loss account		
		Post acquisition profit	2	
		Interest receivable	1	
		Finance cost	1	
		Amortisation of goodwill	1	8
(b)		1 mark per relevant point		5
				25

Group Structure as at 31 March 20X5

Highveldt
Parent

75%	Since 1-4-04

Samson
Subsidiary

(a) (i) *Goodwill in Samson*

	£m	£m
Cost of business combination		
80m shares × 75% × £3.50		210
Deferred consideration; £108m × $^1/_{1.08}$		100
		310
Share of the net assets acquired at fair value		
Carrying value of net assets at 1-4-20X4:		
Ordinary shares	80	
Share premium	40	
Retained earnings	134	
	254	
Fair valuation adjustments		
Revaluation of land at the date of acquisition	20	
Recognition of the fair value of brands acquired	40	
Derecognition of capitalised development expenditure	(18)	
Fair value of the net assets at acquisition	296	
75% Group share		(222)
Cost of Goodwill		88
Amortisation over four years; one year's charge		(22)
Net Book Value at 31 March 20X5		66

Notes (not required in the exam)

Goodwill is based on the present value of the deferred consideration. During the year the £8m discount will be charged to Highveldt's P&L as a finance cost. (In (a)(iii) the Group P&L Reserves will be adjusted for this accrued interest.)

Only the £20m fair valuation is relevant at the date of acquisition. The £4m arising post acquisition will be treated as a normal revaluation and credited to the revaluation reserve. (See (a)(iii) below.)

Samson was right not to capitalise an internally developed brand name because, without an active market, its value cannot be measured reliably. However the fair value of a brand name can be measured as part of an acquisition. Therefore the £40m fair value will be recognised at acquisition and an additional £4m amortisation will be charged in the consolidated P&L.

At acquisition Samson had capitalised £18m of development expenditure. Highveldt does not recognise this as an asset, so the net assets at acquisition are reduced by £18m. A further £32m is capitalised by Samson post acquisition; this will be written off in the consolidated P&L (net of the £10m amortisation already charged).

(ii) *Minority interest in Samson's net assets*

	£m
Samson's net assets from the question	330
Fair valuation of land at acquisition	20
Revaluation of land post acquisition	4
Carrying value of capitalised brand (£40m - £4m amortisation)	36
Less: carrying value of the capitalised development expenditure	
(£50m - £10m amortisation)	(40)
Less: allowance for unrealised profit ($^1/_3$ £6m)	(2)
Consolidated value of Samson's net assets	348
Minority 25% interest	87

(iii) *Consolidated Reserves*

Share premium   £80m

The share premium of a group, like the share capital, is the share premium of the parent only.

	£48m
Revaluation reserve	

	£m
Parent's own revaluation reserve	45
Group share of Samson's post acquisition revaluation; £4m × 75%	3
	48

Group profit and loss reserve

	Highveldt	Samson
	£m	£m
Per question	350	210
Accrued interest from Samson (£60m × 10%)	6	
Amortisation of brand (£40m / 10)		(4)
Write off development expenditure (£50m – £18m)		(32)
Write back amortisation of development expenditure		10
Allowance for unrealised profit in stock		(2)
Pre-acquisition		(134)
		48
Group share 75% x 48	36	
Amortisation of goodwill	(22)	
Unwinding of discount on deferred consideration	(8)	
Group profit and loss reserve	362	

(b) *Usefulness of consolidated financial statements*

The main reason for preparing consolidated accounts is that groups operate as a single economic unit, and it is not possible to understand the affairs of the parent company without taking into account the financial position and performance of all the companies that it controls. The directors of the parent company should be held fully accountable for all the money they have invested on their shareholders' behalf, whether that has been done directly by the parent or via a subsidiary.

There are also practical reasons why parent company accounts cannot show the full picture. The parent company's own financial statements only show the original cost of the investment and the dividends received from the subsidiary. As explained below, this hides the true value and nature of the investment in the subsidiary, and, without consolidation, could be used to manipulate the reported results of the parent.

- The cost of the investment will include a premium for goodwill, but this is only quantified and reported if consolidated accounts are prepared.

- A controlling interest in a subsidiary can be achieved with a 51% interest. The full value of the assets controlled by the group is only shown through consolidation when the minority's interest is taken into account.

- Without consolidation, the assets and liabilities of the subsidiary are disguised.

    – A subsidiary could be very highly geared, making its liquidity and profitability volatile.

    – A subsidiary's assets might consist of intangible assets, or other assets with highly subjective values.

- The parent company controls the dividend policy of the subsidiary, enabling it to smooth out profit fluctuations with a steady dividend. Consolidation reveals the underlying profits of the group.

- Over time the net assets of the subsidiary should increase, but the cost of the investment will stay fixed and will soon bear no relation to the true value of the subsidiary.

27 Hample

HAMPLE PLC
CONSOLIDATED BALANCE SHEET AS AT 31 MARCH 20X9

	£'000	£'000
Fixed assets		
Intangible: software (W2)	1,440	
Goodwill (W3)	480	
		1,920
Tangible: land and buildings (600 + 900 − 120 + 30) (W2)	1,410	
plant and equipment (1,520 + 1,090)	2,610	
		4,020
Investments (65 + 210)		275
		6,215
Current assets		
Stocks (719 + 560 − 5) (W4)	1,274	
Debtors (524 + 328)	852	
Cash (20 + 55 cash in transit)	75	
	2,201	
Creditors: amounts due within one year		
Trade creditors (475 + 472)	947	
Taxation (228 + 174)	402	
Overdraft	27	
	(1,376)	
Net current assets		825
Creditors: amounts due after one year		
Government grants (230 + 40)		(270)
Net assets		6,770
Share capital and reserves		
Ordinary shares of £1 each		2,000
Share premium		2,000
Profit and loss account (W5)		2,420
		6,420
Minority interest (W6)		350
		6,770

Workings

1   *Group structure*

Hample

         | 90% + loan note

Sopel   (P/L reserve £2,200,000 on acquisition)

2   Fair value adjustments

	At acquisition £'000	Movement £'000	At balance sheet date £'000
Leasehold property (4 yr life) – see note below	(120)	30	(90)
Software – see note below	(180)	(180)	(360)
	(300)	(150)	(450)

Note

Leasehold property

	Cash flow	Discount factor	Present value		NBV		Fair value adj
T_0	80	1	80				
T_{1-3}	80	2.5	200				
			280	-	400	=	(120)

Computer software

	1.4.X8 £'000	31.3.X9 £'000	
Fair value (2,400 × 4/5)	1,920	1,440	(2,400 × 3/5)
Net book value (2,400 × 7/8)	2,100	1,800	(2,400 × 6/8)
Fair value adj	(180)	(360)	

3   Goodwill

	£'000	£'000
Cost of investment - shares		4,110
For: (net assets including loan)		
Share capital	1,500	
Share premium	500	
P/L reserve	2,200	
Fair value adj (W2)	(300)	
	3,900	
Group share	× 90%	(3,510)
Goodwill		600
Amortised (1/5)		(120)
Unamortised		480

4   Unrealised profit

	£'000	%
Sales	25	125
Cost of sales	20	100
	5	25

5   Profit and loss account

	Hample £'000	Sopel £'000
Per question	2,900	1,955
FV adj (W2)		(150)
Unrealised profit		(5)
Pre acquisition		(2,200)
		(400)
Share of post acquisition loss in Sopel		
((400) × 90%)	(360)	
Less: goodwill amortised (W3)	(120)	
	2,420	

6   *Minority interest*

	£'000
Net assets per question	3,955
Less: unrealised profit	(5)
FV adj (W2)	(450)
	3,500
	×10%
	350

7   *Current accounts*

	£'000
In Hample's books	75
Cash in transit	(15)
In Sopel's books	60

Intra group loan	
In Hample's books	200
Cash in transit	(40)
In Sopel's books	160

> **Top tips.** Below is an alternative format which some people find easier to understand because it integrates the various aspects of the question.
>
> It is a format which groups use in practice, as you will realise, because once the spreadsheet is set up, they can go on adding subsequent years to it.
>
> Use the method which suits your way of thinking and are likely to find most efficient in an examination environment.

8   *Goodwill and minority interests*

	Total 100% £'000	At acquisition 90% £'000	Post acquisition 90% £'000	Minority interests 10% £'000
At acquisition				
Share capital	1,500	1,350	-	150
Share premium	500	450	-	50
Profits to beginning of year	2,200	1,980	-	220
Fair value adjustment - software				
(480) – 300)	(180)	(162)	-	(18)
- property	(120)	(108)	-	(12)
	3,900	3,510	-	390
Cost of investment		4,110	-	
Goodwill		600		

Post acquisition movements

Current year loss (1,955 – 2,200)	(245)	-	(220)	(25)
Additional depreciation	(180)	-	(162)	(18)
Over depreciation	30	-	27	3
Unrealised profit	(5)	-	(4)	(1)
Minority interest per P&L a/c*				(41)
Minority interest per B/S				349

Post acquisition profits of Sopel attributable to Hample	(359)
Add Profit and loss account of Hample	2,900
Goodwill amortisation (600 ÷ 5)	(120)
Consolidated profit and loss account (B/S)	2,421

* Not separately required for this particular question.

28 Preparation question: Acquisition during the year

(a)   PORT GROUP
CONSOLIDATED PROFIT AND LOSS ACCOUNT FOR THE YEAR ENDING 31 DECEMBER 20X4

	Port	Alfred 2/12	Adjustment	Group
	£'000	£'000		£'000
Turnover	100	166		266
Cost of sales	(36)	(43)		(79)
Gross profit				187
Interest on loan to Alfred	276	-	(46)	230
Other investment income	158	-		158
Operating expenses	(56)	(55)		(111)
Finance costs	-	(46)	46	–
Profit before tax				464
Taxation	(112)	(6)		(118)
Profit after tax				346
Minority interest (W4)				(4)
Group profit after tax				342

PORT GROUP CONSOLIDATED BALANCE SHEET AS AT 31 DECEMBER 20X4

	£'000	£'000
Fixed assets		
Goodwill (W2)		275
Tangible fixed assets (100 + 3,000)		3,100
Investments		600
		3,975
Current assets (800 + 139)	939	
Current liabilities (200 + 323)	(523)	
Net current assets		416
Net assets		4,391
Capital and reserves		
Share capital (W3)		235
Share premium (W3)		1,115
Retained earnings (W5)		2,912
		4,262
Minority interest (W4)		129
		4,391

Note that the loan to Alfred has been cancelled out.

Workings

1   *Group structure*

Port
75% Subsidiary Two months only
Alfred

2   *Calculation of the cost of investment and goodwill*

	£'000	£'000	£'000
Fair value of shares issued			650
Net assets at date of acquisition: (Note)			
Shares		100	
Share premium		85	
Retained earnings:			
Opening	235		
Add: accrued profit for the year: £96,000 × 10/12	80		
Pre-acquisition retained earnings		315	
Net assets		500	
Group share: 75%			(375)
Goodwill capitalised at cost			275

Note. The net assets at the date of acquisition are calculated by time-apportioning profits. The share capital and retained earnings brought forward obviously all arose before acquisition. The profit for the year is assumed to have arisen evenly over time.

3   *Issue of shares*

	Draft £'000	New issue £'000	Revised £'000
Share Capital	200	35	235
Share Premium	500	615	1,115
Fair value of proceeds		650	

4   *Minority interests*

Profit and loss account

The rule here is to time apportion the minority interest in the subsidiary acquired during the year. After all, you can only take out in respect of the minorities what was put in in the first place. So, if two months were consolidated then two months of minority interest will be deducted. (The same rule applies when a subsidiary is disposed of.)

£96,000 × 2/12 × 25% = £4,000.

Balance sheet

Alfred's equity is £516,000. The minority interest is 25% of that = £129,000.

5   *Group retained earnings*

	Port £'000	Alfred £'000
Per question	2,900	331
Less pre acquisition (W2)		(315)
		16
Share of Alfred: (16 × 75%)	12	
	2,912	

29 Hillusion

Text references. Chapters 9 and 10.

Top tips. Don't forget **Part (b)** There are five quick and easy marks here, but to score them all you must use numbers from your answer to Part (a). So, do Part (b) as soon as you have calculated the unrealised profit.

Part (a) This is a straight forward consolidation. Although there is a lot of time pressure on you to prepare the profit and loss account and the balance sheet, this is balanced by the absence of any serious complications in the question. A methodical approach will earn high marks.

(Although Hillusion intends to sell Skeptik within two to three years, Skeptik must still be consolidated. FRS 2 only allows non-consolidation if the subsidiary was acquired with the intention of selling it within twelve months.)

1   Sketch out the group structure, noting percentage holdings and the date of acquisition.

2   Prepare a pro-forma profit and loss account and balance sheet for your answer.

3   Note the adjustments for fair valuations, inter-company balances, inter-company trade and unrealised profit.

4   Calculate the carrying value of the goodwill in the subsidiary, and the amortisation charge in the profit and loss account.

5   Calculate the profit attributable to the parent and to the minority.

6   Calculate the minority interest in the subsidiary's net assets.

7   Calculate the Group retained earnings.

Easy marks. Part (b) is 5 easy marks.

Examiner's comments. This was a fairly straightforward consolidated profit and loss account and balance sheet. The adjustments involved were simpler than if just one statement had been required. The main concern was that a number of candidates used proportional consolidation to account for the subsidiary.

Part (b) was generally well understood and answered. However some candidates choose to answer how such profits arrive and how they are eliminated. The question asks **why** they are eliminated. Many candidates either did not answer this question or based their answer on the group statement instead of the entity's statements.

			Marks
(a)	Profit and loss account		
	Sales revenue		2
	Cost of sales		3
	Operating expenses including goodwill		2
	Loan interest		1
	Tax		1
	Minority interest		1
	Retained earnings b/f		1
	Balance Sheet:		
	Goodwill		3
	Tangible fixed assets		2
	Current assets		2
	Retained earnings		1
	Minority interest		2
	10% loan notes		1
	Current liabilities		2
		Available	**24**
		Maximum	**20**
(b)	1 mark per relevant point to	**Maximum**	**5**
		Maximum for question	**25**

(a) THE HILLUSION GROUP
CONSOLIDATED PROFIT AND LOSS ACCOUNT FOR THE YEAR ENDED 31 MARCH 20X3

		£'000
Turnover	$(60,000 + (^9/_{12} \times 24,000) - 12,000)$	66,000
Cost of sales	$(42,000 + (^9/_{12} \times 20,000) - 12,000 + 500 \text{ (W4)} + 600 \text{ (W3)}$	(46,100)
Gross profit		19,900
Amortisation of goodwill	(W2)	(300)
Operating expenses	$(6,000 + (^9/_{12} \times 200)$	(6,150)
Operating profit		13,450
Finance costs	$(75 \text{ cr} + (^9/_{12} \times 200) \text{ dr netted off})$	(75)
Profit before tax		13,375
Taxation	$(3,000 + (^9/_{12} \times 600))$	(3,450)
Profit for the year		9,925
Minority interest	(W5)	(330)
Retained profit for the year		9,595
Retained profit b/f	(Parent only in year of acquisition)	16,525
Retained profit c/d		26,120

CONSOLIDATED BALANCE SHEET AS AT 31 MARCH 20X3

	£'000
Fixed assets	
Intangible assets: Goodwill (W2)	900
Tangible assets (19,320 + 8,000 + 2,600 FV adjustment (W3))	29,920
Investments (11,280 – 10,280 W2 – 1,000 loan notes)	-
	30,820

	£'000	
Current assets (15,000 + 8,000 – 500 pup (W4) – 750 inter-company)	21,750	
Creditors: amounts falling due within one year (10,000 + 3,600 – 750)	(12,850)	
Net current assets		8,900
Total assets less current liabilities		39,720
Creditors: amounts falling due after more than one year		
10% Loan Notes (0 + 2,000 – 1,000 intercompany)		(1,000)
Net assets		38,720
Capital and reserves		
Called-up share capital (Parent only)		10,000
Profit and loss account (W6)		26,120
		36,120
Minority interest (10,400 + 2,600 (W3) × 20%)		2,600
		38,720

Workings

1   *Group Structure as at 31 March 20X3*

> **Hillusion**
>
> 80% purchased for £10.28m on 1 July 20X2.
> Skeptik is Hillusion's subsidiary for $^9/_{12}$ of the year.
>
> **Skeptik**

2   *Goodwill in Skeptik*

	£'000	£'000
Cost of business combination		10,280
Share of the net assets acquired at fair value		
Share Capital	2,000	
Opening retained earnings	5,400	
Time apportioned profits for the year; £3m × $^3/_{12}$	750	
Fair value increase for the plant	3,200	
Fair value of the net assets at acquisition	11,350	
80% Group share		(9,080)
Cost of Goodwill		1,200
Amortisation charge 1200/3 × 9/12	P&L	(300)
Net book value	B/S	900

3   *Fair valued plant*

		£'000
Fair value adjustment at acquisition		3,200
Movement: Depreciation over four years for four months; £3.2m × ¼ × $^9/_{12}$	P&L	(600)
Fair value adjustment at balance sheet date	B/S	2,600

The extra £600,000 depreciation is taken into account when apportioning the profit for the year between the parent and the minority interest. It also affects the group's retained earnings in the balance sheet and the minority interest.

4   *Inter-company trade and the provision for unrealised profit*

Group turnover and cost of sales are reduced by the £12m of inter-company sales at invoiced value. This adjustment does not affect profits.

An adjustment is made for the unrealised profit on goods sold by Hillusion to Skeptik but still unsold at the year-end. This increases the cost of sales in the P&L and reduces the balance sheet value of the stocks. The gross profit margin was 25% (£3m/£12m).

		£'000
Goods unsold at the year-end; £12m - £10m		2,000
Unrealised profit: £2m × 25%		500

5   *Minority interest*

		£'000
Time apportioned share of Skeptik's profits for the year	£3m × $^9/_{12}$ × 20%	450
Less: Depreciation on fair valuation (W3)	£600,000 × 20%	(120)
		330

6   *Group Profit and Loss Account*

	Hillusion	Skeptic
	£'000	£'000
Per question	25,600	8,400
Provision for unrealised profit (W4)	(500)	
Movement on FV adjustment (W3)		(600)
Pre-acquisition (5,400 + 750) (W2)		(6,150)
		1,650
Group share (1,650 × 80%)	1,320	
Amortisation of goodwill (W2)	(300)	
	26,120	

(b)   *Unrealised profits*

Unrealised profits arise when group companies trade with each other. In their own individual company accounts profits and losses will be claimed on these transactions, and goods bought from a fellow group company will be recorded at their invoiced cost by the purchaser.

However, consolidated accounts are drawn up on the principle that the group is a single economic entity. From a group point of view, no transaction occurs when goods are traded between group companies, and no profits or losses arise. Revenue and profits will only be claimed when the goods are sold onto a third party from outside of the group.

In this example, Hillusion sold £12m of goods to Skeptik making a profit of £3m. The sale by Hillusion and the purchase by Skeptik must be eliminated from the consolidated P&L. This adjustment will not affect profits because both the sales and the purchases have been reduced by the same amount.

By the year-end Skeptik had sold £10m of these items making a profit of £5m. From a group point of view, the profit on these items, including their share of the profit claimed by Hillusion, has now been realised. However, Skeptik still has £2m of goods bought from Hillusion. This valuation includes an element of profit (£500,000) that has not yet been realised and needs to be eliminated. This will reduce the net book value of the stock to the amount originally paid for them by Hillusion. If unrealised profits were not eliminated, then groups could boost their profits and asset values by selling goods to each other at inflated prices.

A future purchaser of Skeptik would obviously review Skeptik's own financial statements. These show a £3.6m profit before tax, which gives a very healthy 15% net profit on revenues. However, over 60% of Skeptik's revenue comes from selling goods supplied by Hillusion. The gross profit earned on these items is £5m, which is more than the £4m gross profit for the company as a whole. A new owner might not get such favourable terms from Hillusion, leaving them with the loss making products. Nobody would be interested in buying such a business, but this information cannot be gleaned from the entity's own financial statements.

Hillusion also makes no management charge to Skeptik, which further inflates Skeptik's profits. Hillusion has a record of selling subsidiaries after a few years at a profit, and its accounting practices are probably adopted with this aim in mind.

30 Hydan

Text references. Chapters 9 and 10.

Top tips. Note that Systan made a **loss** in the post-acquisition period – therefore the retained earnings at acquisition were **higher** than the retained earnings at the year end. This means that, in the profit and loss account, the minority will be allocated their share of a loss. This is unusual – do not be put off by it.

Easy marks. In general this was an easier consolidation question than many we have seen. You were told what the additional depreciation was on the fair value adjustment, and the unrealised profit calculation was simple. The rest was straightforward consolidation procedure, with easy marks for issues such as cancelling out the intercompany loan. The information in the question and your answer to (a) will have told you all you needed to know to answer (b), and there were five easy marks available there.

Examiner's comments. The most common errors in this question were:

- Incorrect cost of investment. Some candidates included the loan and some were unable to calculate the value of the shares.

- Post-acquisition results of subsidiary treated as profits.

- Fair value adjustments omitted.

- Problems with minority interest.

- Errors dealing with intra-group transactions, tax relief and unrealised profit.

Marking scheme

			Marks
(a)	**Profit and loss account**		
	Turnover	2	
	Cost of sales	3	
	Operating expenses including 1 mark for goodwill	2	
	Interest receivable/payable	1	
	Tax	1	
	Minority interest	2	
	Balance sheet		
	Goodwill	3	
	Tangible fixed assets	2	
	Investments	1	
	Current assets/creditors due within one year	2	
	7% bank loan	1	
	Elimination of 10% intra-group loan	1	
	Minority interest	2	
	Share capital and share premium	1	
	Profit and loss account reserve	1	
	Available	25	
	Maximum		20
(b)	1 mark per relevant point to **Maximum**		5
	Maximum for question		25

(a) HYDAN CONSOLIDATED PROFIT AND LOSS ACCOUNT YEAR ENDED 31 MARCH 20X6

	£'000
Turnover (98,000 + 35,200 − 30,000 intra-group)	103,200
Cost of sales (W2)	(77,500)
Gross profit	25,700
Operating expenses (11,800 + 8,000 + 375 (W1))	(20,175)
Interest receivable (W3)	150
Interest payable	(420)
Profit before tax	5,255
Taxation (4,200 − 1,000)	(3,200)
Profit after tax	2,055
Minority interest (W4)	1,400
Profit for the financial year	3,455

HYDAN CONSOLIDATED BALANCE SHEET AT 31 MARCH 20X6

	£'000	£'000
Fixed assets		
Intangible: Goodwill (W1)		2,625
Tangible (18,400 + 9,500 + 1,200 − 300 (W2))		28,800
Investments (16,000 − 10,800 (W1) − 4,000)		1,200
Current assets (W5)	24,000	
Creditors: amounts falling due within one year: (W6)	(14,300)	
Net current assets		9,700
		42,325
Creditors: amounts falling due after more than one year:		
7% bank loan		(6,000)
Net assets		36,325
Capital and reserves		
Share capital		10,000
Share premium		5,000
Profit and loss account (W7)		17,525
		32,525
Minority interest (W8)		3,800
		36,325

Workings

1 *Goodwill in Systan*

	£'000	£'000
Cost of acquisition (1,200 × £9)		10,800
Share of net assets acquired:		
Share capital	2,000	
Share premium	500	
Pre-acquisition reserves (6,300 + 3,000)	9,300	
Fair value adjustment	1,200	
	13,000	
Group share 60%		(7,800)
Goodwill		3,000
Amortisation: (3,000 / 4 × 6 months)		375

2   *Cost of sales*

	£'000
Hydan	76,000
Systan	31,000
Intra-group purchases	(30,000)
Unrealised profit in stock (4,000 × 5%)	200
FVA – additional depreciation	300
	77,500

3   *Interest receivable*

	£'000
Per Hydan profit and loss account	350
Intra-company (4,000 × 10% × 6/12)	(200)
	150

4   *Minority interest: profit and loss account*

	£'000
Post-acquisition loss	3,000
Unrealised profit in stock (W2)	200
Additional depreciation (W2)	300
Adjusted loss	3,500
Minority share 40%	1,400

5   *Current assets*

	£'000
Hydan	18,000
Systan	7,200
Unrealised profit in stock	(200)
Intra-group debt	(1,000)
	24,000

6   *Creditors: amounts falling due within one year*

	£'000
Hydan	11,400
Systan	3,900
Intra-group debt	(1,000)
	14,300

7   *Group profit and loss account*

	Hydan	Systan
	£'000	£'000
Per question	20,000	6,300
Pre-acquisition		(9,300)
Unrealised profit in stock		(200)
Additional depreciation		(300)
Goodwill amortisation	(375)	
	19,625	(3,500)
Group share of Systan ((3,500) × 60%)	(2,100)	
	17,525	

8   *Minority interest: balance sheet*

	£'000
Share capital	2,000
Share premium	500
Profit and loss account	6,300
Unrealised profit in stock	(200)
Additional depreciation	(300)
Fair value adjustment	1,200
	9,500
Minority share 40%	3,800

(b)   If we look at Systan's pre-acquisition operating performance, we can see a gross profit margin of 25% and a net profit margin of 15%. During the post-acquisition 6-month period turnover is up by 46% but the gross profit margin is only 12% and the company has made a net loss of 8.5%. Clearly this requires some explanation.

Hydan obtained a controlling interest in Systan in order to secure its supplies of components. In the post-acquisition period £30m of Systan's £35m sales were to Hydan and realised 5% gross profit. In order to compensate for this, Systan has substantially increased the price charged to its other customers to give a 50% gross profit margin on those sales. The eventual result of this may be that it will no longer have any other customers.

Systan's results for the second half-year have also suffered from a large rise in operating expenses – from £1.2m in the pre-acquisition half year to £8m in the post-acquisition half year. It looks as though Systan has been charged a large share of group operating expenses. Hydan itself has operating expenses for the year of £11.8m on a turnover of £98m, while Systan has expenses of £8m on 6 months turnover of £35m. As there are no current account balances outstanding, Systan has obviously had to pay the intra-group portion of this £8m, facilitated by a loan from Hydan at 10%. At the same time, Hydan owes Systan £1m on which no interest is being paid.

The overall conclusion must be that Systan's position has been adversely affected by the acquisition and by the resulting related party transactions. Hydan has used transfer pricing and inter-company charges to transfer profits from the subsidiary to the parent company, thus benefiting its own shareholders at the expense of the minority.

31 Hydrate

Text references. Chapters 9 and 10.

Top tips. This question is in itself quite straightforward. If you take a methodical approach then you should earn high marks. The question originally also tested merger accounting, which is no longer examinable. As amended, it is no longer exam length

1   Note percentage holdings and the date of acquisition.

2   Prepare a pro-forma profit and loss account and balance sheet for your answer, including the assets and liabilities of the parent and its subsidiary.

3   Adjust for the fair valuation.

4   Calculate the carrying value of the goodwill in the subsidiary.

5   Calculate the balance on the consolidated retained earnings.

Easy marks. An easy question and you should gain 10 marks just by being methodical.

Examiner's comments. This was a fairly straightforward question and was generally well answered. In the balance sheet, the calculations of goodwill, share capital and reserves caused problems. Some poorly prepared candidates calculated minority interest when the question stated that the parent had acquired 100% of the subsidiary.

Consolidated profit and loss account – year to 30 September 20X2

	£'000
Turnover (24,000 + 10,000)	34,000
Cost of sales (16,600 + 5,900)	(22,500)
Gross profit	11,500
Operating expenses (1,600 + 500 + 3,000 (W1))	5,100
Operating profit	6,400
Taxation (2,000 + 1,500)	(3,500)
Profit after tax	2,900

Consolidated balance sheet as at 30 September 20X2

	£'000	£'000
Fixed assets		
Goodwill (W1)		27,000
Land and buildings (20,000 + 15,000)		35,000
Plant (44,000 + 20,000)		64,000
Investment (12,800 + 5,000)		17,800
		143,800
Current assets		
Stock (22,800 + 23,600)	46,400	
Debtors (16,400 + 24,200)	40,600	
Bank (500 + 200)	700	
	87,700	
Creditors: amounts falling due within one year		
Trade creditors (15,300 + 17,700)	33,000	
Taxation (2,200 + 3,000)	5,200	
	(38,200)	
Net current assets		49,500
Creditors: amounts falling due after more than one year		
8% loan note (5,000 + 18,000)		(23,000)
Net assets		170,300

	£'000	£'000
Capital and reserves		
Ordinary shares of £1 (W3)		35,000
Share premium (W3)		79,000
Profit and loss account (W2)		56,300
		170,300

Workings

1		£'000	£'000
	Cost of acquisition (15,000 shares × £6)		90,000
	Share capital	12,000	
	Profit and loss account (45,100 – 2,100)	43,000	
	Fair value adjustment	5,000	
		(60,000)	
	Goodwill		30,000
	Allocated to year ended 30.9.20X2		
	((30,000/5) × 6/12)		(3,000)
	Carrying value at 30.9.20X2		27,000

2	*Reserves: profit and loss account*	
		£'000
	Hydrate	57,200
	Sulphate (4,200 × 6/12)	2,100
	Goodwill (W1)	(3,000)
		56,300

3	*Share capital*	
		£'000
	Prior to acquisition	20,000
	New shares issued (nominal value)	15,000
		35,000
	Share premium:	
	Prior to acquisition	4,000
	15,000 shares @ £5	75,000
		79,000

32 Preparation question: Laurel Ltd

LAUREL LTD

Consolidated balance sheet as at 31 December 20X9

	£'000	£'000
Fixed assets		
Intangible (W4)		5.0
Tangible (220 + 160 + (W3) 3)		383.0
Investment in associate (W5)		75.5
		463.5
Current assets		
Stocks (384 + 234 – (W2) 10)	608.0	
Debtors (275 + 166)	441.0	
Cash (42 + 10)	52.0	
	1,101.0	
Creditors: amounts falling due within one year		
Trade creditors (457 + 343)	800.0	
Net current assets		301.0
		764.5

ANSWERS

	£'000	£'000
Capital and reserves		
£1 ordinary shares		400.0
Share premium account		16.0
Profit and loss reserve (W7)		302.5
		718.5
Minority interest (W6)		46.0
		764.5

Workings

1   *Group structure*

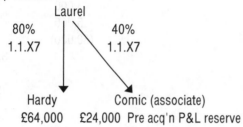

2   *Unrealised profit*

Laurel's sales to Hardy: £32,000 – £22,000 = £10,000

| Dr P&L reserve (Laurel) | £10,000 |
| Cr group stocks | £10,000 |

Laurel's sales to Comic (associate) (£22,000 – £10,000) × ½ × 40% share = £2,400.

| Dr P&L reserve (Laurel) | £2,400 |
| Cr Investment in associate | £2,400 |

3   *Fair value adjustments*

	At acquisition date £'000	Movement £'000	At B/S date £'000
Fixed assets (57 – 45)	+12	(9)*	+3
*Extra depreciation £12,000 × ¾			
	Goodwill	P&L reserve	FA/MI

4   *Goodwill*

	Hardy Ltd		Comic Ltd	
	£'000	£'000	£'000	£'000
Cost of acquired entity		160		70
Share of net assets acquired:				
Share capital	96		80	
Share premium	3		–	
P&L reserve	64		24	
Fair value adjustment (W3)	12		–	
	175 × 80%	(140)	104 × 40%	(41.6)
Goodwill		20		28.4
Amortisation (³/₄)		(15)		(21.3)
		5		7.1

5	Investment in associate	
		£'000
	Share of net assets (177 × 40%)	70.8
	Unamortised goodwill (W4)	7.1
	Unrealised profit (W2)	(2.4)
		75.5

6	Minority interest		
		£'000	£'000
	Net assets per question	227	
	Fair value adjustment (W3)	3	
		230 × 20%	46

7 Consolidated profit and loss reserve

	Laurel £'000	Hardy £'000	Comic £'000
P&L reserve per question	278.0	128.0	97.0
Less: PUP re Hardy (W2)	(10.0)		
PUP re Comic (W2)	(2.4)		
Fair value adjustment movement (W3)		(9.0)	
	265.6	119.0	97.0
Less: pre-acquisition P&L reserve		(64.0)	(24.0)
		55.0	73
Hardy (55 × 80%)	44.0		
Comic (73 × 40%)	29.2		
Less: amortisation of goodwill (W4) (15 + 21.3)	(36.3)		
	302.5		

33 Preparation question: Tyson plc

Tyson Ltd
Consolidated profit and loss account for the year ended 31 December 20X9

	£'000	£'000
Turnover (500 + 150 − 66)		584.0
Cost of sales (270 + 80 − 66 + (W2) 18)		(302.0)
Gross profit		282.0
Operating expenses (150 + 20 + (W3) 15.2)		(185.2)
Group operating profit		96.8
Share of operating profit in associate [(25 × 40%) − (W3) 2.4]		7.6
		104.4
Interest receivable (group)		25.0
Interest payable		
Group	(20.0)	
Associate (10 × 40%)	(4.0)	
		(24.0)
Profit before tax		105.4
Taxation		
Group (25 + 15)	(40.0)	
Associate (5 × 40%)	(2.0)	
		(42.0)
Profit after tax		63.4
Minority interest [(45 − (W2) 18) × 20%]		(5.4)
Profit after tax and minority interest		58.0

Workings

1   *Group structure*

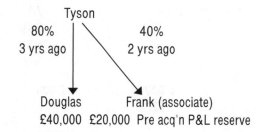

2   *Unrealised profit*

	£'000
Selling price	66
Cost	(48)
PUP	18

3   *Goodwill*

		In Douglas Ltd £'000		In Frank Ltd £'000
Cost of acquired entity		188		60
Net assets acquired:				
Share capital	100		100	
Profit and loss reserve	40		20	
	140		120	
Group share	× 80%	(112)	× 40%	(48)
		76		12
Annual amortisation	76/5 =	15.2	12/5 =	2.4

34 Question with analysis: Hepburn

(a)   HEPBURN PLC
       CONSOLIDATED PROFIT AND LOSS ACCOUNT
       FOR THE YEAR ENDED 31 MARCH 20X1

	£'000
Turnover (W1)	1,600
Cost of sales (W2)	(890)
Gross profit	710
Operating expenses (W3)	(184)
Debenture interest (12 × 6/12)	(6)
Profit before tax	520
Taxation (100 + (40 × 6/12))	(120)
Profit after tax	400
Minority interest (200 × 20% × 6/12)	(20)
Profit after tax and minority interest	380

HEPBURN PLC
CONSOLIDATED BALANCE SHEET
AS AT 31 MARCH 20X1

	£'000	£'000
Fixed assets		
Intangible: goodwill (W4)		180
Tangible fixed assets		
Land and buildings (400 + 150 + 125)		675
Plant and machinery (220 + 510)		730
Investments (20 + 10)		30
		1,615
Current assets		
Stock (240 + 280 − 10 (W2))	510	
Debtors (170 + 210 − 56)	324	
Bank (20 + 40 + 20)	80	
	914	
Creditors: amounts due < 1 year		
Trade creditors (170 + 155 - 36)	289	
Taxation (50 + 45)	95	
	384	
Net current assets		530
		2,145
Creditors: amounts due > 1 year		
8% Debentures		(150)
Net Assets		1,995
Capital and reserves		
Ordinary shares £1 each (400 + 300 (W4))		700
Share premium account (900 − 300 (W4))		600
Profit and loss account (W5)		500
		1,800
Minority interests (W6)		195
Shareholders' funds		1,995

Workings

1	*Turnover*	£'000
	Hepburn	1,200
	Salter (1,000 × 6/12)	500
	Intercompany sale	(100)
		1,600

2	*Cost of sales*	£'000
	Hepburn	650
	Salter (660 × 6/12)	330
	Intercompany sales	(100)
	Unrealised profit in stock (100 × 50% × 25/125)	10
		890

3	*Operating expenses*	£'000
	Hepburn	120
	Salter (88 × 6/12)	44
	Goodwill amortisation (W4)	20
		184

		£'000	£'000
4	*Goodwill*		
	Cost of investment in Salter 150 × 80% × 5/2 (= 300) × £3		900
	Fair value of net assets acquired		
	Share capital	150	
	Profit and loss account		
	At 1 April 20X0 (700 - 200)	500	
	Profit to 1 Oct 20X0 (200 × 6/12)	100	
	Fair value adjustment	125	
		875	
	Group share (80%)		700
	Goodwill		200
	Amortisation (200 ÷ 5 × 6/12)		20
	Unamortised		180

		Hepburn plc	Salter Ltd
5	*Profit and loss account*	£'000	£'000
	As per accounts 31.3.20X1	450	700
	Unrealised profit in stock (W2)	(10)	
	Pre-acquisition profit At 1 April 20X0 (W4)		(500)
	Profit to 1 Oct 20X0		(100)
			100
	Group share of Salter Ltd (100 × 80%)	80	
	Goodwill amortisation (W4)	(20)	
		500	

		£'000
6	*Minority interest*	
	Share capital: 20% × 150	30
	Profit and loss account: 20% × 700	140
	Fair value adjustment of land: 20% × 125	25
		195

(b)   In **voting rights**, Hepburn's interest in Woodbridge Ltd is **60%**; however it is correct that it is only entitled to 6,000/24,000 = 25% of any dividends paid.

The approach taken by Hepburn to its investment in Woodbridge seems to be based on the view that, with a **25% equity holding**, the investment would normally be treated as an associate and equity accounting applied. However, Hepburn does not exert any significant influence over Woodbridge and hence under FRS 9 *Associates and joint ventures* it can rebut the presumption of associate status.

> Key point

This overlooks the fact that FRS 2 *Accounting for subsidiary undertakings* bases the treatment of an investment in another entity on the notion of control rather than **ownership**. Hepburn can control Woodbridge by virtue of its holding the **majority of the voting rights** in the company.

Woodbridge is thus a **subsidiary** and should be **consolidated in full** in Hepburn's group accounts, **from the date of acquisition**.

Hepburn's directors may wish to avoid consolidation because of Woodbridge's **losses**. But these **losses** may indicate that the **value of the investment** in Woodbridge in Hepburn's own individual accounts may be **overstated**. A test for **impairment**, as required by FRS 11 *Impairment of fixed assets and goodwill* may reveal that the **recoverable amount** of the investment has fallen below £20,000, thus requiring a write down in Hepburn's own accounts and a write down of Woodbridge's assets in the consolidated accounts.

35 Holdrite

Text references. Chapters 10 and 11.

Top tips. **Part (a)** The acquisitions take place in the middle of the year and so the post tax profits have to be time apportioned in order to calculate the net assets at acquisition. Both the consideration and the net assets acquired need to be fair valued.

Part (b) This is a straight forward consolidated profit and loss account.

1   Sketch out the group structure, noting percentage holdings and dates of acquisition.

2   Prepare a pro-forma profit and loss account for your answer. Remember the line for "Share of profit of associate".

3   Time apportion the income and expenses of the subsidiary, the share of the associate's profit, and the minority interest.

4   Note the adjustments for inter-company balances and unrealised profit.

5   The goodwill amortisation charge is given in the question.

Part (c) The parent had no subsidiaries at the start of the year.

Easy marks. You should be able to obtain half marks (13 marks) just by being methodical.

Examiner's comments. The main part of this question required a consolidated profit and loss account. In general this question was very well answered. However there were problems with goodwill and minority interest.

			Marks
(a)	*Goodwill of Staybrite:*		
	Value of shares exchanged		1
	8% loan notes issued		1
	Equity shares and share premium		1
	Pre-acquisition reserves		1
	Fair value adjustments		1
	Goodwill of Allbrite:		
	Value of shares exchanged		1
	Cash paid		1
	Equity shares and share premium		1
	Pre-acquisition reserves		1
		Available	9
		Maximum	8
(b)	*Profit and loss account*		
	Revenue		2
	Cost of sales		4
	Operating expenses		2
	Interest expense		1
	Income from associate		2
	Taxation		2
	Minority interest		2
			3
		Available	16
		Maximum	15
(c)	Dividends		1
	Retained profits b/f and c/f		1
		Maximum	2
		Maximum for question	25

(a) Goodwill

Goodwill in Staybrite

	£'000	£'000
Cost of acquisition		
Share exchange: (2/3 × 75% × 10m shares) × £6		30,000
Loan Note: (100/250 × 75% × 10m shares) × £1		3,000
		33,000
Share of the net assets acquired at fair value		
Share Capital	10,000	
Share premium	4,000	
Opening retained earnings	7,500	
Time apportioned profits for the year; £9m × $^6/_{12}$	4,500	
Fair value increase for the land (23 – 20)	3,000	
Fair value increase for the plant (30 – 25)	5,000	
Fair value of the net assets at acquisition	34,000	
75% Group share		(25,500)
Cost of Goodwill		7,500
Amortisation: £7.5m × $^1/_5$ × $^6/_{12}$		750

The fair value of the share exchange is the market price of the shares issued by the acquirer.

The fair value of the loan note is its nominal value.

Goodwill in Allbrite

	£'000	£'000
Cost of acquisition		
Share exchange: (3/4 × 40% × 5m shares) × £6		9,000
Cash: (£1 × 40% × 5m shares)		2,000
		11,000
Share of the net assets acquired at fair value		
Share Capital	5,000	
Share premium	2,000	
Opening retained earnings	6,000	
Time apportioned profits for the year; £4m × $^6/_{12}$	2,000	
Fair value of the net assets at acquisition	15,000	
40% Group share		(6,000)
Cost of Goodwill		5,000
Amortisation: £5m × $^1/_5$ × $^6/_{12}$		500

(b) THE HOLDRITE GROUP

CONSOLIDATED PROFIT AND LOSS ACCOUNT FOR THE YEAR ENDED 30 SEPTEMBER 20X4

		£'000	£'000
Turnover	W2		85,350
Cost of sales	W2		(48,750)
Gross profit			36,600
Operating expenses	W2		(15,730)
Operating profit			20,870
Share of profit of associate	W3		700
			21,570
Finance costs			(170)
Profit before tax			21,400
Taxation: Group	4,800 + ($^6/_{12}$ × 3,000)	6,300	
Associate	2,000 × $^6/_{12}$ × 40%	400	
			(6,700)
Profit for the year			14,700
Minority interest	W4		(1,000)
Group			13,700

Workings

1   *Group Structure as at 30 September 20X4*

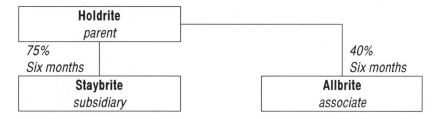

2 Turnover and expenses

	Turnover	Cost of sales	Operating Expenses
	£'000	£'000	£'000
Parent	75,000	47,400	10,480
Six months time apportioned from subsidiary's own P&L	20,350	9,850	4,500
Inter-company trade	(10,000)	(10,000)	-
Extra depreciation on fair valuation	-	500	-
Unrealised profit (£4m × ¼ in parent's books)	-	1,000	-
Amortisation of goodwill (Part(a))	-	-	750
	85,350	48,750	15,730

3 Share of profit of associate

	£'000
$^{6}/_{12}$ × 40% × operating profit of £6m	1,200
Less: amortisation of goodwill (Part (a))	(500)
	700

4 Minority interest

	£'000
Subsidiary's own profit after tax, time apportioned: $^{6}/_{12}$ × £9m	4,500
Less: extra depreciation on fair valuation	(500)
	4,000
25% Minority share	1,000

(c) Movement on consolidated profit and loss reserve

	£'000
Opening (Parent only, as there were no subsidiaries or associates.)	18,000
Profit for the year attributable to parent company shareholders	13,700
Equity dividends paid	(5,000)
	26,700

36 Hapsburg

Text references. Chapters 9 and 11.

Top tips. Don't forget **Part (b).** There are five marks here for rehearsing some of the criticisms of the equity method. Do it first, before getting bogged down in Part (a).

Part (a) This consolidated balance sheet includes an associate accounted for using the equity method. The interest in the associate was acquired during the year and so profits will have to be time apportioned in order to find the net assets acquired.

As always, be methodical.

- Sketch out the group structure, noting percentage holdings and the date of acquisition.

- Prepare a pro-forma balance sheet for your answer.

- Note the adjustments for fair valuations, inter-company balances and unrealised profit.

- Calculate the carrying value of the goodwill in the subsidiary. Don't forget amortisation.

- Calculate the carrying value of the associate. This is the group's share of the associate's net assets plus the goodwill less amortisation.

- Calculate the minority interest in the subsidiary's net assets.

- Calculate the group profit and loss reserve.

Easy marks. Part (b) is five easy marks.

Examiner's comments. The question asked for a consolidated balance sheet for a group including a subsidiary and an associate.

Part (a) required the consolidated balance sheet and was very well-answered, although there are still some candidates who persist in using proportional consolidation.

Part (b) required a discussion of equity accounting and was either ignored or very badly answered. Even candidates who had used equity accounting correctly to account for the associate in part (a) had very little idea why this was the treatment.

		Marks
(a)	Balance sheet	5
	Goodwill (four for total figure, one for depreciation)	1
	Land and buildings	2
	Plant	2
	Investment in associate	3
	Other investments	1
	Stock	2
	Trade debtors and cash	1
	Current liabilities	1
	10% loan notes	1
	Deferred consideration	2
	Minority interest	2
	Share capital and share premium	1
	Retained earnings	3
	Available	25
	Maximum	20
(b)	Reasoning behind equity accounting	3
	Discussion of off balance sheet financing	2
	Maximum	5
	Maximum for question	25

(a)   THE HAPSBURG GROUP
        CONSOLIDATED BALANCE SHEET AS AT 31 MARCH 20X4

	£'000	£'000
Fixed assets		
Tangible fixed assets (16,600 + 24,400 + 9,700 + 25,100 + 3,750)		79,550
Intangible fixed assets: Goodwill (W4)		12,800
Investments at fair value		4,500
Investment in associate (W7)		15,150
		112,000
Current assets		
Stocks (9,900 + 4,800 – 300 (W3))	14,400	
Trade and other debtors (13,600 + 8,600)	22,200	
Cash and cash equivalents (1,200 + 3,800)	5,000	
	41,600	
Creditors: amounts falling due within one year		
Trade and other creditors (16,500 + 6,900)	23,400	
Taxation (9,600 + 3,400)	13,000	
	36,400	
Net current assets		5,200
Total assets less current liabilities		117,200
Creditors: amounts falling due within one year		
Loans (16,000 + 4,200)	20,200	
Deferred consideration (W5)	19,800	
		(40,000)
Net assets		77,200

	£'000	£'000
Capital and reserves		
Share capital (Parent only) (20,000 + (24m shares × $^2/_3$ × £1))		36,000
Share premium (Parent only) (8,000 + (24m shares × $^2/_3$ × £1))		24,000
Profit and loss reserve (W8)		8,050
		68,050
Minority interest (W9)		9,150
		77,200

Workings

1   *Group Structure as at 31 March 20X4*

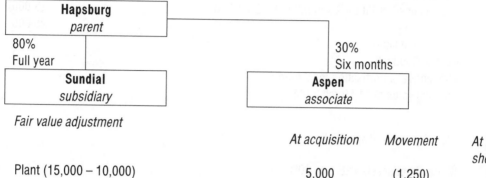

2   *Fair value adjustment*

	At acquisition	Movement	At balance sheet date
Plant (15,000 – 10,000)	5,000	(1,250)	3,750
Investments (4,500 – 3,000)	1,500	-	1,500
	6,500	(1,250)	5,250
	↓	↓	↓
	Goodwill	Profit and loss reserve	Fixed assets and minority interest

The subsidiary's profit and loss reserve will be reduced by £1,250,000. This will affect both the group's share of those earnings and the minority interest.

3   *Unrealised profit on associate's sales*

£1.6m profit was made on sales of £4m. Only £2.5m is left on hand, including profit of £1m.

Because the sale was made by the associate, only the group's 30% share will be accounted for, which is £300,000. These items are part of the parent's stock, and so group stocks will be reduced by £300,000.

4   *Goodwill in Sundial*

	£'000	£'000
Cost of investment		
24m shares × 2/3 × £2 (share exchange)		32,000
24m shares × £0.75 × (deferred consideration of £1 in three years time)		18,000
		50,000
Share of the net assets acquired at fair value		
Share capital	30,000	
Share premium	2,000	
Profit and loss reserve (8,500 – 4,500)	4,000	
Fair value increase for the plant (15,000 – 10,000)	5,000	
Fair value increase for the investments (4,500 – 3,000)	1,500	
Fair value of the net assets at acquisition	42,500	
80% Group share		(34,000)
Goodwill at acquisition		16,000
Amortisation over five years; one year's charge to date		(3,200)
Carrying value at 31 March 20X4		12,800

5   *Deferred consideration*

	£'000
Present value of consideration at acquisition (W4)	18,000
Finance cost @ 10% (reduces group profit and loss reserve)	1,800
Carrying value 31 March 20X4	19,800

6   *Goodwill in associate*

	£'000	£'000
Cost of investment		15,000
Share of net assets acquired		
Net assets at 31 March 20X4	28,000	
Less retained profit for six months (6/12 × £6m)	(3,000)	
	25,000	
30% Group share		(7,500)
Cost of Goodwill		7,500
20% annual amortisation for 6 months		(750)
Carrying value at 31 March 20X4		6,750

7   *Carrying value of associate*

	£'000
Share of net assets £28m × 30%	8,400
Carrying value of goodwill (W6)	6,750
	15,150

8   *Minority interest*

	£'000	£'000
Sundial's net assets from the question		40,500
Carrying value of fair value increase for plant W3		3,750
Fair value increase for investments		1,500
		45,750
Minority 20% interest		9,150

9   *Group Profit and Loss Reserve*

	Hapsburg	Sundial	Aspen
Per question	10,600	8,500	8,000
Fair value adjustment movement (W2)		(1,250)	
Unrealised profit (W3)			(1,000)
Unwinding of discount on deferred consideration (W5)	(1,800)		
Pre-acquisition			
Sundial (8,500 − 4,500)		(4,000)	
Aspen (8,000 − ($^{6}/_{12}$ × 6,000))			(5,000)
	8,800	3,250	2,000
Group share:			
Sundial 80%	2,600		
Aspen 30%	600		
Amortisation to date:			
Sundial (W4)	(3,200)		
Aspen (W6)	(750)		
	8,050		

(b)   *The Equity method*

Associates normally arise when an investing company acquires between 20% and 50% of the equity of another, giving it significant influence (but not control) over its investment; in particular it is able to participate in the financial and operating policy decisions of the investee, including its dividend policy. Before the equity method was introduced, such investments were held at cost in the balance sheet even if the underlying net assets had increased, and the profit and loss account only recognised dividends received. As a result shareholders were unable to tell how well (or badly) these investments were performing. Also, directors could manipulate reported profits by encouraging the associate to pay large dividends (provided the other shareholders were willing).

Under FRS 9 the carrying value of an associate is the investor's share of its net assets, plus un-amortised goodwill. The P&L recognises the group's share of the associate's operating result, interest and tax.

As a result it is harder for the investor to manipulate profits, and the underlying performance of the associate is reported by the investor. However, this method has the disadvantage that the financial risks affecting the associate are hidden. For example if the net assets are £3m this could represent £4m of assets and £1m of liabilities (which is safe) or it could be £100m of assets and £97m of liabilities (which is high risk). Likewise in the P&L such key performance indicators as gross profit are hidden (although interest cover can be calculated).

To counter this, FRS 9 requires additional disclosure about a group's aggregate share of its associates' fixed assets, current assets, current liabilities, long-term liabilities and turnover if its total investment in associates exceeds a materiality threshold. This threshold is reached if the group's aggregate share of its associates gross assets, or gross liabilities, or turnover, or operating results exceeds 15% of the group values for these items. More disclosures are required if a 25% threshold is reached.

Proportional consolidation would solve some of these problems by recognising the investee's share of each item in the profit and loss account and balance sheet. This method is not allowed by FRS 9 because it implies that the investor has control over a part of the associate's trade and net assets, rather than influence over all of it.

37 Hedra

Text references. Chapters 9 and 11.

Top tips. This is a big question, but as always a methodical approach will ensure a good score.

Look out for the fair value adjustments to Salvador, and remember that increases in fair value *after* acquisition are treated as normal revaluations. The deferred consideration is now payable, which will increase the goodwill and be recognised as a creditor.

Aragon's net assets at acquisition and fair value of consideration must be calculated.

Easy marks. There are no particular easy marks here. Read the question carefully and make your workings very clear.

Examiner's comments. A majority of candidates show a good knowledge of the basic principles of consolidation. The main errors were:

- Use of proportional consolidation for the subsidiary. This demonstrates that a candidate has not studied the most important topic in the syllabus and has not attempted past questions.

- Use of full consolidation or proportional consolidation (rather than equity accounting) for the associate.

- Incorrectly calculating cost of the investment in the subsidiary.

- Now including fair adjustments in minority interest.

		Marks
(a)	Goodwill and amortisation	6
	Fixed assets and investments	7
	Current assets	2
	Current liabilities	3
	Deferred tax	1
	Elimination of loan note	1
	Minority interest	4
	Share capital	1
	Revaluation reserve	2
	Retained earnings	3
	Available	30
	Maximum	25

Group Structure as at 30 September 20X5

Hedra	40%	Aragon
Parent	01-04-X5	*associate*

60% | 01-10-X4

Salvador
Subsidiary

CONSOLIDATED BALANCE SHEET AS AT 30 SEPTEMBER 20X5

			£m	£m
Fixed Assets				
Goodwill	(W1)			80
Land and buildings	(W2)			350
Plant	(W2)			300
Investment in associate	(W3)			214
Investment in Salvador:	Equity	(195 taken to cost of control)		-
	Loan Notes	(50 inter-company)		-
Investments				45
				989
Current assets				
Stocks	(130 + 80)		210	
Trade debtors	(142 + 97)		239	
Cash at bank			4	
			453	
Creditors: amounts falling due within one year				
Trade creditors	(118 + 141)		259	
Bank overdraft			12	
Current tax payable			50	
Deferred consideration now due	(W1)		49	
			370	
Net current assets				83
Total assets less current liabilities				1,072
Creditors: amounts falling due after more than one year				
8% Loan Notes	(50 inter-company)			-
Provision for liabilities				
Deferred tax	(45 – 10 (tax losses))			(35)
Net assets				1,037

		£m	£m
Capital and reserves			
Share capital	(Parent only; 400 + 80) (W3)		480
Share premium	(Parent only; 40 + 120) (W3)		160
Revaluation reserve	(15 + (5 × 60%) + 12)		30
Profit and loss reserve	(W4)		255
			925
Minority interest	(W5)		112
			1,037

Workings

1   *Goodwill in Salvador*

		£m	£m
Cost of acquisition			
Cash			195
Deferred consideration now payable			49
			244
Share of the net assets acquired at fair value			
Carrying value of net assets at 1-4-20X4:			
Ordinary shares		120	
Share premium		50	
Profit and loss reserve		20	
Fair valuation adjustments:			
Land		20	
Plant		20	
Tax loss (£40m × 25%)		10	
Fair value of the net assets at acquisition		240	
60% Group share			(144)
Goodwill			100
Amortisation @ 20% for 12 months			(20)
Carrying value at 30 September 20X5			80

Salvador's profits have exceeded the agreed amount and the £49m deferred consideration is now payable. It will increase the consideration and be accrued for as a current liability.

The £5m increase in the fair value of Salvador's land post acquisition is treated as a revaluation. This will be shared between the parent (60% = £3m) and the minority (40% = £2m).

2   *Tangible fixed assets*

	L&B	Plant
	£m	£m
Hedra	208	150
Revaluation	12	-
Salvador	105	135
Fair valuation increase of land	20	-
Revaluation of land	5	-
Fair valuation increase of plant	-	20
25% Depreciation on fair valuation	-	(5)
	350	300

3   *40% Investment in associate*

		£m
Share of net assets	(40% × £400m)	160
Goodwill	see below	54
		214

Goodwill		£m	£m
Consideration	see below		200
Net assets acquired	Net assets at 30 September 20X5	400	
	Less six month's profit ((300 – 200) × ½)	(50)	
	Net assets at acquisition	350	
	40% share		(140)
Goodwill			60
Amortisation	(Over five years for six months £60m × 20% × ½)		(6)
			54

Consideration: nominal value and premium of shares issued	£m
Nominal value of shares issued (£1)	80
Share premium (balancing figure)	120
Fair value (£2.50)	200

2 shares in Hedra issued for each of 40m shares acquired in Aragon
Fair value = 80m shares × £2.50 = £200m

4   *Group profit and loss reserves*

	Hedra	Salvador
	£m	£m
Per question	240	60
Additional depreciation		(5)
Pre-acquisition		(20)
		35
Group share 60%	21	
Amortisation of goodwill:		
Salvador	(20)	
Aragon	(6)	
Group share of Aragon's post acquisition retained earnings:		
((300 – 200) × 40% × $^6/_{12}$)	20	
Group reserves at 30 September 20X5	255	

5   *Minority interest in Salvador's net assets*

	£m
Salvador's net assets from the question	230
Fair valuation of unrelieved tax losses (£40m × 25%)	10
Fair value increase of land at acquisition	20
Revaluation of land post acquisition	5
Fair value increase of plant at acquisition	20
Less: depreciation on fair value adjustment	(5)
Consolidated value of Salvador's net assets	280
Minority 40% interest	112

38 Hosterling

Text references. Chapters 10 and 11.

Top tips. This is a consolidated profit and loss account including an associate, less common than a consolidated balance sheet but with no serious problems. Start by noting down the shareholdings and the number of months during which the investment in the associate has been held, then do (a) and (b) and get the proforma down for (c).

Easy marks. The only complex part of this question was dealing with the associate. Accounting for the subsidiary was very straightforward and you should have had no trouble with the unrealised profit or the fair value adjustment. So make sure you get these simple parts of the question correct.

		Marks
(a)	Goodwill of Sunlee:	
	consideration	1
	equity shares	1
	pre acquisition reserves	1
	fair value adjustments	2
	Maximum	**5**
(b)	Carrying amount of Amber:	
	cost of investment at acquisition	1
	net assets other than goodwill at acquisition	1
	carrying amount of goodwill at 30 September 2006	2
	Maximum	**4**
(c)	Profit and loss account:	
	turnover	2
	cost of sales	4
	distribution costs and administrative expenses	1
	amortisation of goodwill in Sunlee	1
	share of associate's losses	1
	amortisation of goodwill in Amber	1
	finance costs	1
	taxation – group	1
	– associate	1
	minority interests	2
	eliminate dividend from Sunlee	1
	Maximum	**16**
	Maximum for question	**25**

(a) **Goodwill in Sunlee**

	£'000	£'000
Consideration (16,000 × 5 × 3/5)		48,000
Shares	20,000	
Profit and loss account	18,000	
Fair value adjustment (W)	12,000	
	50,000	
Group share 80%		(40,000)
Goodwill		8,000

Working

Total fair value adjustment = 4,000 + 3,000 + 5,000 =	£12m

(b) **Investment in Amber**

	£'000
Cost of investment (6m × £4)	24,000
Share of post-acquisition loss (20m × 3/12 × 40%)	(2,000)
Goodwill amortisation (W)	(500)
	21,500

Working

Goodwill

	£'000	£'000
Consideration (as above)		24,000
Shares	15,000	
Profit and loss account:		
Prior year	35,000	
Current year ((20m) × 9/12)	(15,000)	
	35,000	
Group share 40%		(14,000)
Goodwill		10,000
Amortisation (10m /5 × 3/12)		500

Alternative calculation:

Investment in Amber

	£'000
Share of net assets ((15,000 + 35,000 − 20,000) × 40%)	12,000
Unamortised goodwill (10,000 − 500)	9,500
	21,500

(c) HOSTERLING GROUP
CONSOLIDATED PROFIT AND LOSS ACCOUNT FOR THE YEAR ENDED 30 SEPTEMBER 2006

	£,000	£,000
Turnover (105,000 + 62,000 − 18,000)		149,000
Cost of sales (W1)		(89,000)
Gross profit		60,000
Distribution costs (4,000 + 2,000)		(6,000)
Administrative expenses (W2)		(16,100)
Group operating profit		37,900
Share of loss of associate (W3)		(2,900)
Finance costs (1,200 + 900)		(2,100)
Profit before tax		32,900
Tax – group (8,700 + 2,600)	(11,300)	
– associate (4,000 × 3/12 ×40%)	400	
		(10,900)
Profit after tax		22,000
Minority interest (13,000 − 1,000 (W1)) × 20%		(2,400)
Profit for the financial year		19,600

Workings

1 *Cost of sales*

	£'000
Hosterling	68,000
Sunlee	36,500
Intra-group	(18,000)
Unrealised profit in stock (7,500 ×25/125)	1,500
Depreciation on fair value adjustment (5,000/5)	1,000
	89,000

2 *Administrative expenses*

Hosterling	7,500
Sunlee	7,000
Goodwill amortisation (8,000/5)	1,600
	16,100

3   *Share of loss of associate*

Share of loss before tax (24,000 × 3/12 × 40%)	2,400
Goodwill amortisation ((b) above)	500
	2,900

39 Preparation question: Contract

	Contract 1 £ (W1)	Contract 2 £ (W2)	Contract 3 £ (W3)	Contract 4 £ (W4)
PROFIT AND LOSS ACCOUNT				
Turnover	54,000	6,000	84,000	125,000
Cost of sales	(43,200)	(6,000)	(108,000)	(105,000)
Gross profit/(loss)	10,800	–	(24,000)	20,000
BALANCE SHEET				
Stocks				
Long-term contracts				
Net cost	4,800			5,600
Payments on account in excess of turnover	–			–
	4,800			5,600
Debtors				
Amounts recoverable on contracts	3,600	6,000	7,200	4,800
Provisions for liabilities			(4,800)	

Workings

1   *Contract 1*

Turnover	45% ×120,000 =	54,000
COS	45% × (48,000 + 48,000) =	43,200
WIP	48,000 – 43,200 =	4,800
Debtors	54,000 – 50,400 =	3,600

2   *Contract 2*

Turnover = COS

COS	10% × (6,000 + 54,000) =	6,000
WIP	6,000 – 6,000 =	0
Debtors	6,000 – 0 =	6,000

3   *Contract 3*

Turnover	35% × 240,000 =	84,000
COS calc	35% × (103,200 + 160,800) =	(92,400)
Loss		(8,400)
∴ Forseeable loss		(15,600)
Total loss	240,000 – (103,200 + 160,800) =	(24,000)
∴ Total COS	84,000 + 24,000 =	108,000

Made up of:

Provision	(15,600)		
WIP	103,200 – 92,400 = 10,800 – 15,600 =	(4,800)	

∴ Disclose as Nil.

Debtors	84,000 – 76,800 =	7,200
Provision		(4,800)

4   *Contract 4*

Turnover	(70% × 500,000) – 225,000 =	125,000
COS	(70% × 420,000) – 189,000 =	105,000
WIP	299,600 – 105,000 – 189,000 =	5,600
Debtors	225,000 + 125,000 – 345,200 =	4,800

40 Merryview

(a)   MERRYVIEW PLC
PROFIT AND LOSS ACCOUNT (EXTRACTS) TO 31 MARCH 20X1

	£'000
Revenue (W4)	14,000
Cost of sales (W1)	(9,100)
Profit (W3)	4,900

BALANCE SHEET (EXTRACTS) AS AT 31 MARCH 20X1

	£'000
Fixed assets	
Plant and machinery (3,000 – 300)	2,700
Current assets	
Amounts recoverable on contracts (W6)	1,200
Stocks and WIP	300

Workings

1.   *Cost of sales*

	£'000
Costs to date per question	7,100
Overheads (3,500 × 40%)	1,400
Depreciation (9 months) (W5)	900
Closing stock	(300)
	9,100

2.   *Total expected cost*

	£'000
Cost of sales as above	9,100
Costs to complete	14,800
Balance of depreciation	2,100
	26,000

3.   *Profit to date*

Expected total profit (40,000 – 26,000)	14,000
Profit to date:	
$14,000 \times \dfrac{9,100}{26,000}$	4,900

4. *Revenue*

$$40,000 \times \frac{9,100}{26,000}$$

14,000

5. *Depreciation*

Depreciable amount (3,600 – 600)	3,000
Depreciation period	30 months
Depreciation rate is therefore	100 per month
9 months to 31.3.X1	900
12 months to 31.3.X2	1,200

6. *Amount recoverable on contract*

	£'000
Sales revenue	14,000
Progress payment	(12,800)
Recoverable	1,200

(b) PROFIT AND LOSS ACCOUNT (EXTRACTS) TO 31 MARCH 20X2

	£'000
Revenue (W4)	16,000
Cost of sales (W1)	(13,400)
Profit (W3)	2,600

BALANCE SHEET (EXTRACTS) AS AT 31 MARCH 20X2

	£'000
Fixed assets	
Plant and machinery (3,000 – 900 – 1,200)	900
Current assets	
Amounts recoverable on contracts (W5)	1,000
Stocks and WIP	-

Workings

1 *Cost of sales*

	£'000
Costs to date	20,400
Depreciation	2,100
	22,500
Less costs attributable to prior year	(9,100)
	13,400

2 *Total expected cost*

	£'000
Costs to date	22,500
Costs to complete	6,600
Balance of depreciation	900
	30,000

3 *Profit to date*

	£'000
Expected total profit (40,000 – 30,000)	10,000
Profit to date:	

$$10,000 \times \frac{22,500}{30,000}$$

7,500

Less profit attributed to prior year	(4,900)
	2,600

4   Revenue

		£'000
$40,000 \times \dfrac{22,500}{30,000}$		30,000
Less attributed to prior year		(14,000)
		16,000

5   Amounts recoverable on contract

		£'000
Sales revenue to date		30,000
Progress payments received:	12, 800	
	16, 200	
		(29,000)
		1,000

41 Linnet

(a)   *Two methods of accounting for contracts*

Long-term contracts which span more than one accounting period bring in the problem of whether or not any profit can be recognised before the contract is complete. If the principle is followed that profit cannot be recognised until it is realised, then no profit would be recognised until the end of the contract. This does distort reported performance from one year to the next, but it is applicable in certain circumstances.

When the outcome of a contract can be estimated reliably, then turnover is recognised by reference to the stage of completion of contract activity. As a result turnover reflects the value of work done and profit is claimed in proportion to the work done. This is an application of the accruals principle and is referred to as the stage of completion method.

If the outcome of a contract cannot be estimated reliably (for example if the contract has only just begun) then the amount of turnover claimed will not exceed the costs incurred. This means that turnover reflects the cost of work done rather than its value and no profit is claimed. This is known as the completed contracts basis. This conforms with the prudence concept. As soon as the outcome of the contract is known turnover should be based on the stage of completion. This means that profits might be artificially low in the early stages of a contract and then unrealistically high in the period when the change to the stage of completion method occurs.

Losses are always provided for in full as soon as they are foreseen, regardless of how turnover is being calculated.

(b)   *Football stadium*

P&L (extracts)	£m
Turnover	70
Cost of sales	(81)
Gross loss	(11)

Balance sheet (extracts)	£m
Current assets	
Stocks	
Long-term contract work in progress	19
Debtors	
Amounts recoverable on contracts	40

Workings

This year's turnover, cost of sales and profit is the difference between the cumulative amounts at the beginning and end of the year. The rectification costs will be charged in full as they are incurred. As they cannot be recovered from the customer they will be excluded from the calculation of attributable turnover and profit.

P&L

		Turnover		*Cost of sales*		*Total*
Cumulative to 31 March 20X4	a	220	b	176	c	44
Cumulative to 31 March 20X3 (from question)		(150)		(112)		(38)
Recognised this year		70		64		6
Rectification costs				17		(17)
				81		(11)

(i) *Turnover*

£180m of progress payments received for work done to 29 February 20X4
= 90% of value of work done.

→ 100% value of work done to 29 February 20X4	200
Value of further work done to 31 March 20X4	20
Total work done to 31 March 20X4	220

(ii) *Cost of sales*

Balancing figure; 220 (turnover) − 44 (profit) = 176 (cost of sales).

(iii) *Profit*

Contract price	300
Costs to date	(195)
Costs to complete	(45)
Expected contract profit	60

Recognised to date:

Value of work done to date: $\dfrac{220}{300} \times 60 =$ 44
Total contract price

Balance Sheet

Debtors

Amounts recoverable on contracts	£m
Turnover recognised to date	220
Less: progress payments received	(180)
	40

The amounts recoverable on long-term contracts includes an element of profit. It is the difference between the turnover claimed in the P&L and the cash received from customers.

Stocks

Long-term contract work in progress		£m
Costs to date	195 + 17	212
Less: costs charged to the P&L	112 + 81	(193)
		19

Long term contract work in progress is stated at cost. It is the difference between the costs incurred and the costs charged to the P&L.

42 Torrent

Alfa

Profit and loss account	£m
Turnover $((12.6 - 5.4) \times 100/90)$	8
Cost of sales (balancing figure)	(7)
Profit (W1)	1

Balance sheet	
Long-term contract balance (W2)	1.0
Amount recoverable on contract (W3)	1.4

Workings

1   *Profit*

	£m	£m
At 31 March 20X5		
Total expected profit	5.0	
Invoiced to date $(5.4 \times 100/90)$	6.0	
Profit recognised $(5 \times 6/20)$		1.5
At 31 March 20X6		
Total expected profit	5.0	
Invoiced to date $(12.6 \times 100/90)$	14.0	
Profit recognised $(5 \times 14/20)$		3.5
Less recognised in 20X5		(1.5)
Less rectification costs		(1.0)
Profit 20X6		1.0

2   *Long-term contract balance*

	£m	£m
Costs to date		12.5
Transferred to cost of sales:		
Turnover $(6 + 8)$	14.0	
Profit $(1.5 + 1)$	(2.5)	(11.5)
Long term contract balance		1.0

3   *Amount recoverable on contract*

	£m
Amount invoiced $(12.6 \times 100/90)$	14.0
Progress payments received	(12.6)
Amount recoverable on contract	1.4

Beta

	£m
Profit and loss account	
Turnover $(1.8 \times 100/90)$	2.0
Cost of sales (balancing figure)	(3.5)
Loss for the year (total loss on contract now recognised)	(1.5)
Balance sheet	
Long term contract balance	Nil
Amount recoverable on contract $(2 - 1.8)$	0.2

Ceta

Profit and loss account

	£m
Turnover (balancing figure)	4.8
Cost of sales	(4.0)
Profit (2 × 4/10)	0.8

Balance sheet

Long term contract balance	Nil
Amount recoverable on contract	4.8

Total

Profit and loss account

	£m
Turnover (8 + 2 + 4.8)	14.8
Cost of sales (7 + 3.5 + 4)	(14.5)
Profit/(Loss) (1 + (1.5) + 0.8)	0.3

Balance sheet

Long term contract balances (1 + 0 + 0)	1.0
Amounts recoverable on contracts (1.4 + 0.2 + 4.8)	6.4

43 Multiplex II

Financial statement extracts

	£m
Profit and loss account	
Turnover (W2)	18.0
Cost of sales (balancing figure)	(14.1)
Profit (W3)	3.9
Balance sheet	
Current assets	
Long-term contract balances (W5)	6.0
Debtors: amounts recoverable on long-term contracts (W6)	5.0

Workings

1   *Percentage completion*

$$\text{Percentage completion} = \frac{\text{Work certified}}{\text{Contract price}}$$

20X0	*20X1 (including variation)*
$\dfrac{£12m}{£40m} = 30\%$	$\dfrac{£30m}{£45m} = 66.7\%$ (ie $^2/_3$)

2   *Turnover*

Accumulated turnover to 31 March 20X1 = £45m × $^2/_3$ = £30m

In 20X1 turnover = £30m − £12m (20X0) = £18m

3   *Profit*

Revised estimated total profit = £45m − £30m = £15m

Accumulated to 31 March 20X1 = £15m × $^2/_3$ = £10m

Total profit for year ended 31 March 20X1:

	£m
Accumulated to date	10.0
Less 20X0 profit taken (W4)	(3.6)
Less rectification costs	(2.5)
	3.9

4 *Profit for 20X0*

	£m
Turnover	12.0
Cost of sales (bal fig)	(8.4)
Profit = (£40m − £28m) × 30%	3.6

5 *Long-term contract balance*

		£m
Costs incurred to 31 March 20X1		28.5
Cost of sales charged:	20X0 (W4)	(8.4)
	20X1	(14.1)
		6.0

6 *Debtors: amounts recoverable*

	£m
Value of work certified 31 March 20X1	30.0
Payments on account	(25.0)
Amounts due	5.0

44 Bodyline

Text reference. Chapter 13.

Top tips. Parts (a) and (b) require you to rehearse the standard discussion about the nature of provisions and the need for FRS 12. The well-prepared candidate should score highly.

The calculations in Part (c) can be tricky, but if you lay out your workings in a methodical manner then you should score good marks even if you don't get the answer perfectly right.

Part (d) requires you to criticise the directors' proposed treatment and then to outline and explain the correct accounting treatment.

Easy marks. The discussion parts (a) and (b) represent 12 easy marks.

Examiner's comments. This question dealt with the nature and treatment of provisions. Parts (a) and (b) were discursive; while (c) and (d) were practical examples of the application.

Generally candidates answered parts (a) and (b) well, but failed to deal with the practical applications in part (c) and (d).

Marking scheme

		Marks
(a)	One mark per valid point to max	6
(b)	The need for the Standard and examples to a max of 2 each	6
(c)	28 day refund policy – constructive obligation	1
	Calculation of provision for unrealised profits where goods resold at full price	1
	Calculation of provision for loss on goods sold at half normal price	1
	The product warranties are treated collectively	1
	Warranty cost can be estimated reliably therefore a liability, not a contingency	1
	Faulty goods other than from Header – not a loss, but	1
	Must remove profit made on them – quantified	1
	Return of faulty goods manufactured by Header creates a loss	1
	Quantification of loss	1
	Available	**9**
	Maximum	**8**
(b)	Director's treatment is incorrect	1
	This is an example of an asset with component parts	1
	Depreciation is £1.65m per annum plus £1,500 per machine hour	2
	Replacement does not meet the definition of a liability **Maximum**	**5**
	Maximum for question	**25**

(a)   *Provisions and FRS 12*

Provisions are liabilities of uncertain timing or amount. Because they are liabilities they must meet the recognition criteria for liabilities - that is there must be:

- a present obligation arising from past transactions or events,
- the transfer of economic benefits to settle the obligation must be probable,
- a reliable estimate can be made of the amount of the obligation.

The obligation giving rise to a provision can be legal or constructive. A constructive obligation can arise when the actions or statements made by an entity create an expectation that they will meet certain obligations, even if there is no legal requirement for them to do so; for example they may have a well- known policy of replacing goods beyond the normal warranty period.

Provisions are recognised in full as soon as an entity is aware of them, but long term provisions are recognised at present value. As time goes by the discount unwinds, increasing the provision. The increase in the provision is charged to the profit and loss account as a finance cost.

If an obligation depends upon a future event, then it is a contingent liability, not a provision. Also, if the amount of an obligation cannot be measured reliably, then it is a contingent liability. Contingent liabilities are not recognised in the financial statements, although they need to be disclosed unless the possibility of an outflow of economic benefits is remote.

(b)   *The need for a standard*

Although provisions have been a key area of financial reporting for many years, FRS 12 was the first standard to address this issue. Before FRS 12 there were no rules governing the

- definition,
- recognition,
- measurement,

207

- use, and
- presentation

of provisions.

The FRS 12 definition of a provision as a liability of uncertain timing or amount means that provisions must meet the recognition criteria for liabilities. This means that provisions cannot be created to suit management needs. In the past provisions were often created and released in order to smooth profits, rather than to provide for a specific liability. These were sometimes called 'big bath' provisions because they could be used for any and every purpose.

A specific example of this was the creation of provisions for reorganisation or restructuring. The charge to set these provisions up could be explained away by management to their investors as one-off exceptional items, but the release of the provision in the future would boost profits. Under FRS 12 provisions for restructuring can only be recognised if the restructuring has begun or if the restructuring has been announced publicly.

The measurement rules have standardised practice in an area where there were genuine differences of opinion. For example there are at least three ways in which the cost of cleaning up an industrial site after it is closed down (restoration costs) can be accounted for:

- ignore the costs until the site is abandoned,
- accrue the costs evenly over the productive life of the site, or
- provide for the costs in full immediately.

FRS 12 states that these costs should be provided for in full immediately, but at their present value.

Under FRS 12 provisions can only be used for the purpose that they were created for; if a provision is no longer needed it must be released. In the past provisions were sometimes created for one purpose and then used to cover the costs of another.

FRS 12 includes detailed disclosure requirements, including the movement on provisions during the year and an explanation of what each provision has been created for. This ensures that the rules set out above have been complied with.

(c)   *Bodyline*

This provision can be reliably measured on the basis of past experience. Although Bodyline does not know which items will be returned or develop faults, it can make an estimate of the total value of returns and faults that there will probably be.

The question does not make it clear whether the 28 day refund is part of the sales contract (in which case it is a legal obligation) or whether it is just a well-known and established part of Bodyline's trading practices (in which case it is a constructive obligation). Either way, an obligation exists that needs to be provided for.

The provision itself can be reliably measured on the basis of past experience. Although Bodyline does not know which items will be returned or develop faults, it can make an estimate of the total value of returns and faults that there will probably be.

The returns provision is £52,850, calculated as follows:

- Of the 10% of sales that are returned under this policy, 70% are resold at the full price. Therefore only the profit element is provided against on these items.

- A further 30% are sold at half the normal sales price, so the provision required will be half of the sale proceeds.

		£
70% resold at full price		
Goods from Header	£1.75m × 20% × 10% × 70% × 40/140	7,000
Other goods	£1.75m × 80% × 10% × 70% × 25/125	19,600
		26,600
30% resold at half price	£1.75m × 10% × 30% × ½	26,250
		52,850

The faulty goods provision is £57,600, calculated as follows::

- 20% of the goods returned will have been supplied by Header; Bodyline will suffer the loss in full on these items.

- Bodyline reclaims the cost of the other 80% returned. Only the profit element is provided for.

		£
Goods from Header	£160,000 × 20%	32,000
Other goods	£160,000 × 80% × 25/125	25,600
		57,600

(d) *Rockbuster*

No obligation exists to replace the engine and so it is wrong to create a provision for its replacement. Rockbuster may decide to trade in the earthmover rather than replace the engine. Also, the £2.4m depreciation charge includes an element in respect of the engine, so to make a provision as well is double-counting.

Instead FRS 15 Accounting for Fixed Assets states that the earth-mover should be treated as an asset with two separate components (the engine and the rest) with different useful lives. The engine (cost £7.5m) will be depreciated on a machine hours basis over 5,000 hours, while the rest of the machine (cost £16.5m) will be depreciated over ten years.

	Cost £'000	Depreciation charge
Engine	7,500	Depreciated on a machine hours basis over 5,000 hours. The charge is £1,500 per hour
The rest	16,500	Depreciated on a straight line basis over its ten year useful life. The charge is £1,650,000 per annum.
Total	24,000	

When the engine is replaced the cost and accumulated depreciation on the existing engine will be retired and the cost of the new engine will be capitalised and depreciated over its working life.

45 Myriad III

The scenario given introduces a number of issues relating to events after the balance sheet date, provisions and contingent liabilities.

The stock of paper had originally cost £48 per pack. It was eventually sold on 20 October at £45, being the normal price of £50 less the 10% price reduction that was introduced on 12 October due to competitive pressures. The paper was cut and repackaged due to the water damage at a cost of £4 per pack. The figures for cost and net realisable value therefore are as follows:

	Per pack £
Cost	48
Net realisable value (45 – 4)	41
Loss per pack	7

It therefore has to be decided whether the closing stock valuation at 30 September should be reduced to reflect this loss. The problem however is that the loss has two separate causes.

Part of the reason for the net realisable value of the paper being £7 per pack lower than its cost was that the paper had been damaged by water before the year end. This is an **adjusting event after the balance sheet date** and should lead to a **write down of the value of the closing stock**. However £5 of the loss per pack is due to the reduction of prices after the balance sheet date which is a **non-adjusting event after the balance sheet date**.

Therefore it would seem sensible that the closing stock should be written down by £2 (the adjusting post balance sheet event element) per pack at the balance sheet date with the loss being recognised in the year ending 30 September 20X1. The remaining £5 per pack loss however relates to the following year, to 30 September 20X2, and should be recognised in that period. If the £5 per pack reduction in price is material then it should be **disclosed** in the 20X1 financial statements as a non-adjusting post balance sheet event.

There is then a further problem to consider, the complaint from Securiprint plc. If the marks on the paper are due to either the manufacturing process or the damage that occurred to the paper then Myriad plc will probably be liable to Securiprint for compensation. If the liability is probable then a **provision should be made in the 20X1 financial statements** for the amount likely to be payable to Securiprint. If the marks on the paper were not caused by Myriad plc then no provision would be required but at this stage it is probably difficult to determine this categorically. It is therefore likely that a **contingent liability** for compensation should be disclosed in the 20X1 financial statements to reflect the possibility of liability. It must also be considered that if the marks on the paper are due to Myriad then it is possible that the entire stock of this paper is affected. If stocks have been sold to other customers then the possibility of a provision for compensation to them should also be considered. If however the paper has not yet been sold then the year end stock value **may need to be further reduced** to reflect the reduction in value of this damaged stock.

46 Peterlee II

(i)   The goodwill in Trantor is purchased goodwill and can be capitalised and shown as an asset in the consolidated balance sheet at the value calculated. However, the goodwill in Peterlee itself is internally generated goodwill, and per FRS 10 it cannot be capitalised because it cannot be reliably measured. So the directors will be allowed to include the goodwill in Trantor of £2.5 million in the financial statements, but the goodwill estimated to exist in Peterlee cannot be recognised.

(ii)   Per FRS 12 this treatment is not correct. The £2 million present value of the landscaping cost should be recognised as a provision at 31 March 20X6. The debit will be to the asset account, giving an asset value for the mine of £8 million. This total value will be depreciated over 10 years. In this way the landscaping cost will be charged to the profit and loss account over the life of the mine. At the same time, the discount to present value will 'unwind' over the 10 year period. This will be credited to the provision and charged as a finance cost. At the end of 10 years, the amount in the provision account should equal the amount due to be paid.

(iii)   As this is a convertible loan, it must be apportioned between debt and equity. Per FRS 25 this is calculated as follows:

	£'000
Present value of the principal: £5 million × 0.75	3,750
Present value of interest: £0.4 million × 2.49 (0.91 + 0.83 + 0.75)	996
Debt element	4,746
Equity element (balancing figure)	254
Proceeds of issue	5,000

The debt element of the loan is therefore £4.746 million. £0.254 million will be shown as conversion rights under *Capital and reserves*.

The profit and loss account and balance sheet amounts will be as follows:

	£'000	£'000
Debt element of loan		4,746
Interest at 10% (profit and loss account)	475	
Interest paid	(400)	
Balance due		75
Balance of loan at 31 March 20X6 (balance sheet)		4,821

47 Jedders

> **Tutor's hint**. This is a type of question which is likely to arise in this paper, covering various standards. In this case, you need to know about FRS 15 and FRS 25.

(a) (i) FRS 15 *Tangible fixed assets* does not allow **selective revaluations** of tangible fixed assets: if one asset is revalued, all in that class must be revalued, thus avoiding 'cherry picking' of asset gains where others in the class may have fallen in value. In addition, non-recording of a fall in value of an asset cannot be justified on the basis that a recovery in market prices is expected in the future.

(ii) PROFIT AND LOSS ACCOUNT (EXTRACTS)

	£'000
Depreciation charge	
North ((£1.2m × 80%)/20 years)	48
Central ((£4.8m × 140%)/40 years)	168
South (£2.25m/30 years)	75
	291
Loss on revaluation	
(20% × £1.2m)	240

BALANCE SHEET (EXTRACTS)

	Cost/revaluation	Depreciation	NBV
	£'000	£'000	£'000
North	960	48	912
Central	6,720	168	6,552
South	2,250	75	2,175
	9,930	291	9,639

At 1 January 20X0 the accumulated depreciation of the Central property is £1.2m, which represents 10 years' worth of depreciation, leaving 40 years remaining life. For the South and North properties, the respective lives on these calculations are 30 and 20 years. If there is no previous revaluation surplus on the North property, then the loss in the current year is classed as an impairment and must be taken to the profit and loss account.

(b) A statement of how the debt should be treated:

Group A. These are normal non-factor debts and the debtors' allowance should be calculated as usual.

Group B. Although these debts have been factored, the risks of late collection and bad debts remain with Jedders. Thus, the outstanding balance less the debtors' allowance should still appear in Jedders' balance sheet, with a liability recorded for the amount received from Fab Factors. In addition, an interest charge would be made for the 1% charge for the monies advanced.

Group C. In a non-recourse situation such as this, Jedders has effectively sold its debtors for 95% of their value. The debtors would therefore be taken off Jedders' balance sheet, leaving cash and a residual finance charge.

Applying these treatments to the figures given:

PROFIT AND LOSS ACCOUNT (EXTRACT)

		£
Debtors' allowance		
Group A	(20% × (1,250 × 20%))	50,000
Group B	(20% × (1,500 × 10%))	30,000
Group C		nil
		80,000
Finance charge		
Group A		nil
Group B	(1% × 1,500) + (1% × 900) + (1% × 450)	28,500
Group C	(5% × 2,000)	160,000
		128,500

BALANCE SHEET (EXTRACTS)

Trade receivables		Less allowance %	Net balance £
Group A	(1,250 × 20%)	20	200,000
Group B	(1,500 × 10%)	20	120,000
Group C		Nil	Nil
			320,000

(c) FRS 25 *Financial instruments: Presentation* requires the issuer of a **hybrid or compound instrument** of this nature – containing elements that are characteristic of both debt and equity – to separate out the components of the instrument and classify them separately. Fab Factors are thus wrong in their advice that such instruments should be recorded and shown as debt.

The proceeds of issue should be split between the amounts attributable to the conversion rights, which are classed as **equity**, and the remainder which must be classed as a **liability**. Although there are several methods that might be used, the question only gives sufficient information to allow the amounts of debt liability to be calculated, leaving the equity element as the residual.

Year	Cash flows £'000	Factor at 10%	Present value £'000
1 Interest (£15m × 7%)	1,050	0.91	955.5
2	1,050	0.83	871.5
3	1,050	0.75	787.5
4	1,050	0.68	714.0
5 Interest + capital	16,050	0.62	9,951.0
Total debt component			13,279.5
Proceeds of issue			15,000.0
Equity component (residual)			1,720.5

PROFIT AND LOSS ACCOUNT (EXTRACTS)

	£'000
Interest paid (7% × £15m)	1,050
Provision for additional finance costs ((10% × £13.2795m) – £1.05m) (rounded)	278
	1,328

BALANCE SHEET (EXTRACTS)

	£'000
Long-term liabilities	
7% convertible debentures	13,279.5
Provision for additional finance costs	278.0
	13,557.5
Equity	
Option to convert to equity	1,720.5

48 Triangle

Text reference. Chapters 13 and 15.

Top tips. Four questions on four very different topics; clean-up provisions, events after the balance sheet date, contingent assets and the substance of transactions. Start with the one you feel happiest with but do not overrun. Strict time control is needed to maximise marks.

Easy marks.(ii) and (iii) are probably the easiest scenarios, but you almost make an intelligent effort at all four to receive a pass.

Examiner's comments. This question was relatively unpopular and poorly answered. However it was fairly straightforward and covered areas that had been examined previously. In (i) many candidates ignored the treatment of the decontamination costs, which was the main point of the question. (ii) was answered better, although almost no-one suggested reclassifying the cost of the fraud from cost of sales to expenses. In (iii) many candidates failed to realise that they were dealing with a contingent asset. In (iv) most candidates correctly recognised the substance of the transaction, as a financing arrangement.

Marking scheme

			Marks
(i)	Treatment of provision	2	
	Cost of plant	1	
	Revised depreciation	1	
	Profit and loss charges	2	
	Other items	2	8
(ii)	Adjusting event/effect on presentation	2	
	Correct treatment and disclosure	3	5
(iii)	Contingent asset	1	
	Correct treatment	3	4
(iv)	Identify substance	2	
	Evaluate repurchase option	3	
	Correct treatment	3	8
			25

(i)   *Contamination*

There are two errors in the current accounting treatment.

Firstly, the obligation to clean up the contamination existed in full from the day that the plant was brought into use. Therefore the provision should be recognised in full immediately at present value; it should not be accrued incrementally over the life of the plant. Over the next ten years the present value will increase as the discount unwinds. This will be reported by increasing the provision and charging the increase to the P&L as a finance cost.

Secondly, on initial recognition, the cost of the plant should include the present value of the decontamination.

The plant and the provision should be reported as follows:

		£'000
Plant (a fixed asset)		
1 April 20X4: cost	(£15m + £5m)	20,000
Depreciation	(£20m/10 years)	(2,000)
31 March 20X5: NBV		18,000

	£'000
Provision	
1 April 20X4	5,000
Finance cost @ 8%	400
31 March 20X5	5,400

(ii) *Fraud*

The fraud means that the draft financial statements for the year-ended 31 March 2005 are incorrect. This probably won't affect the net profit for the year, but it will affect the amounts shown for cost of sales and gross profit.

The discovery of this fraud provides new evidence about conditions existing at the balance sheet date, and so it is classified as an adjusting event. The £210,000 fraud that occurred during the year will be charged to the income statement as an operating expense and disclosed.

The £30,000 fraud occurring after the year-end does not affect conditions existing at the balance sheet date and so it will not be adjusted for. However, it will be disclosed if it is considered to be material in its own right.

(iii) *Insurance claim*

The insurance claim gives rise to a contingent asset for £240,000. However, under FRS 12 contingent assets are not recognised unless the realisation of income is virtually certain, and this is not the case here because the insurers are disputing the claim.

A contingent asset is disclosed when an inflow of economic benefits is probable, but without legal opinion it is not possible to regard the success of the claim as probable.

Following on from the above, the insurance claim should be ignored altogether in the financial statements for the year-ending 31 March 20X5.

(iv) *Factorall*

The £5m proceeds from Factorall cannot be claimed as income because the substance of the transaction appears to be a £5m loan secured on the maturing stock.

This is because Triangle still retains the cost and benefits of ownership through its option to repurchase the stock before 31 March 2008. Although legally Triangle could refuse to repurchase the stock, there is evidence of a constructive obligation to do so as noted below:

- The initial sale was below market price, and so there is an opportunity cost arising from not repurchasing.

- The repurchase price is based on the sales price plus interest rather than on its true market value at the date of repurchase. The market price will probably be higher, suggesting an additional opportunity cost from not repurchasing.

- Factorall, as a finance house, will not have the expertise to bring the product to market, and so it will be expecting Triangle to repurchase. If Triangle refuses to repurchase then it is unlikely that Factorall (or any similar company) will be willing to enter into such an agreement with Triangle again.

Because there is a constructive obligation to repurchase the stock Triangle should recognise this as a liability (at present value) and continue to recognise the stock at cost (including the storage costs).

For Factorall the benefit of this arrangement is the 10% compound interest debtor, not the purchase of the product.

The correct accounting treatment for this transaction in Triangle's books is as follows:

P&L

Finance costs	(£5m @ 10%)	£500,000
Balance sheet		
Current assets		
Stock	(£3m + £300,000 holding costs)	£3,300,000
Creditors due after one year		
Secured loan	(£5m + 10%)	£5,500,000

The journal to correct the old treatment is as follows:

				Debit £'000	Credit £'000
Debit	P&L	Sales	Proceeds	5,000	
Credit	B/S	Secured loan	Proceeds		5,000
Debit	B/S	Stock	Cost of stock	3,000	
Credit	P&L	Cost of sales	Cost of stock		3,000
Debit	B/S	Stock	Holding costs	300	
Credit	B/S	Debtors	Holding costs		300
Debit	P&L	Finance costs	10% interest	500	
Credit	B/S	Secured loan	10% interest		500

49 Forest

Text reference. Chapter 15.

Top tips. Examples other than the ones we discuss might have gained marks. This is not an easy question; although you should have the arguments in (a) to hand, (b) requires more thought. Also, be careful to follow the time allocations.

(a)   The general aim of accounting is to reflect the **economic reality** of transactions undertaken by entities. this can be undermined by structuring transactions so that, if treated according to the letter of the law, the accounts would show a very different effect. The main aim in most cases where legal form does not accord with economic reality is to **take liabilities off balance sheet**. Entities have used various methods for this, the most prevalent of which was the use of '**quasi-subsidiary**' vehicles, into which debt could be loaded, but which was not consolidated into the group accounts.

Showing legal form rather than economic substance therefore **undermines** the relevance of financial reports and produces information that is of little use to users of accounts. Other types of manipulation include **profit-smoothing** over time, often using provisions and accruals, and undertaking **window dressing** transactions around the year end, often to improve specific performance measures.

(b)   In any transaction, there will be a **variety of features** that will indicate its underlying substance. Similarly, there are certain features that frequently indicate where legal form and substance are likely to be different. Each of these features would need to be investigated thoroughly to determine the substance of a transaction.

    (i)   Transactions may be set up where it appears that an asset has been sold, and legal title has passed to another party, whereas in fact the '**vendor**' **still enjoys** substantially all the **benefits** of ownership (and similarly is exposed to substantially all the risks of ownership). If legal form was followed, an asset could be removed from the vendor's balance sheet, along with the ability to pay for it. The principle of ascribing ownership to the beneficial user underpins SSAP 21 *Accounting for leases and live purchase contracts*, which requires finance leases to be accounted for by the lessee as if the lessee owned the asset. Although legal title is held by the lessor, it is the lessee that has the risks and rewards of ownership.

        Applying the **substance over form rule** to some transactions where ownership is separated form beneficial use can have **significant results**. For example, in sale and leaseback situations where full use of an asset is retained by the 'vendor', the transaction would be treated as a **borrowing against the security of the asset** not a sale.

(ii) Where a transaction appears not to make sense economically, eg it has been transacted at a substantial over or under value, it may be that it is linked to other transactions. **Only when looked at as a whole will the series of transactions make economic sense**. A good example is where an asset, say stocks of maturing whisky, are 'sold' to another party. However, at the same time the 'vendor' is given an option to repurchase the stock at a future date, often at a pre-determined amount. When both transactions are viewed together, it becomes clear (where it is the case) that the deal has been set up to give the 'purchaser' of the stock a lender's return, ie the transactions when viewed together are in substance a borrowing against the security of the stocks.

In these situations is it important to assess the **true economic effect** of the option. Options are used frequently by entities, quite legitimately, to reduce risks. However, in a linked transactions situation it will often by the case that it is almost certain that the option will (or in come cases, will not) be exercised. In other words, it is not a true option.

(iii) As noted in (ii) above, transactions undertaken at an **over- or under-value** are likely to be **linked to another transaction**, such that both together create in substance a very different transaction from when each is considered separately For example, an entity may sell an asset to another party for an amount less than its fair value. The asset is then leased back over future years at a rental below normal commercial rates. As the profit foregone on the sale is compensated for by the reduced rental levels, the profit on sale is effectively 'smoothed' over future years.

(c) (i) **Legal form basis**

Year ended 31 March	20X2 £'000	20X3 £'000	20X4 £'000	Total £'000
Income statement				
Sales	15,000	nil	25,000	40,000
Cost of sales	(12,000)	nil	(19,965)	(31,965)
Gross profit	3,000	nil	5,035	8,035
Balance sheet				
Stock	Nil	nil	nil	
Loan	Nil	nil	nil	

(ii) **Substance of the transaction**

Year ended 31 March	20X2 £'000	20X3 £'000	20X4 £'000	Total £'000
Income statement				
Sales	nil	nil	25,000	25,000
Cost of sales	nil	nil	(12,000)	(12,000)
Gross profit	nil	nil	13,000	13,000
Interest @ 10%	(1,500)	(1,650)	(1,815)	(4,965)
Net profit/loss	(1,500)	(1,650)	11,185	8,035
Balance sheet				
Stock	12,000	12,000	Nil	
Loan: principle	15,000	15,000	15,000	
interest	1,500	3,150	4,965	
			19,965	
Repaid 31 March 20X4			(19,965)	
			-	

Using **legal form** only, **profits have been spread over two years** (20X2 and 20X4), whereas the **substance of the transaction** is that a **loss is made in the first two years** as interest accrues to the lender. Also, using the legal form only allows sales to be inflated, by showing two sales and purchases, rather then the one 'true' sales, as shown in (ii). The substance of the transaction approach shows the interest charge, which is otherwise completely lost under the legal form approach.

Both methods report the same profit in the end, but the substance of the transaction as shown in the accounts will indicate that this is in fact a **borrowing against stock assets**; it is not a sale and repurchase with normal commercial features.

50 Atkins

(a) *Retail car showrooms*

This problem arises whenever goods are delivered on a consignment stock basis, with deferred payment and the option to return unsold goods. The question is, who should recognise the goods as an asset between the date of delivery and the date of payment?

The party that bears the risks and benefits of the cars recognises them as assets in their balance sheet. Even though the cars are held at one of Atkins plc's showrooms does not mean to say that Atkins plc recognises them as assets. If the benefits are shared between the two parties, then the party that bears most of the risks will recognise the asset.

If the manufacturer still bears the risks and benefits then the manufacturer recognises the cars in its own balance sheet as stock at production cost. No revenue or profit is claimed by the manufacturer, and no purchase or stock item is recognised by Atkins plc.

If Atkins plc bears the risks and rewards of ownership of the cars, then Atkins plc will recognise them as assets at their purchase price, along with the related liability to pay for them. The manufacturer will no longer recognise the cars; instead it will claim a sale and recognise a trade debtor.

In this situation the risks and benefits are borne as follows:

- The price paid by Atkins plc is fixed at the date of delivery. This means that Atkins plc bears any risk (or benefit) of price changes arising after that date. (If the retail price falls, then Atkins plc will lose out because its own purchase price is based on 80% of the retail price on delivery. Likewise if the retail price rises Atkins plc gets extra profit because its own purchase price is fixed.)

- The 1.5% per month 'display charge' represents interest on the money owed by Atkins plc to the manufacturer from the date of delivery. This means that Atkins plc bears the risk of slow moving cars, because Atkins plc will be charged interest for as long as a car remains unsold (or until six months has passed and Atkins plc pays for the car in full).

- Atkins plc's right to return unsold cars could, in theory, offset the risk of price cuts and slow moving items. However, in practice Atkins plc has never taken advantage of this right and so it suggests that for commercial reasons it cannot be exercised (for example the manufacturer may stop supplying cars to Atkins if the right is exercised frequently).

- The one area where the manufacturer still appears to have some rights of ownership is in its right to recall or transfer cars held at Atkins' showrooms.

It is clear from this that Atkins bears all the risks attached to these assets from the date of delivery. Therefore Atkins will recognise them as assets from the date of delivery, along with the related trade creditor. The 'display charge' will be accrued as it is incurred over time.

The manufacturer will recognise a sale as soon as the cars are delivered, and claim the display charge over time. The manufacturer's experience of trading with Atkins will decide the level of provision needed in respect of returns.

(b)   *Landbank*

The legal form of this transaction is that Atkins has sold three plots of land costing £1.2m for £2.4m making a profit of £1.2m. However, there are a number of points that suggest that this is a financing arrangement rather than a true sale:

The sale is for below the market price. Why would Atkins make a genuine sale for £800,000 less than its open market value?

On 30 September 2004 Atkins has the option to repurchase at £3.2m. On that day the open market value may be higher, in which case Atkins can repurchase and resell again. Atkins will then benefit from any price rises occurring after the original sale in 20X1.

If on 30 September 20X4 the price has fallen below £3.2m, and Atkins does not want to exercise its right to repurchase, then Atkins can be forced to repurchase the following day. Atkins will therefore bear any fall in value arising after 20X1.

The difference between the £2.4m sales price in 20X1 and the £3.2m repurchase price in 20X4 represents interest at the market rate of 10% per annum.

The probability that Atkins will benefit from any future price rises and suffer from any price falls, along with the finance charge implicit in the sale and repurchase prices, suggests that this is a secured loan rather than a true sale.

Extracts from the financial statements for the year to 30 September 20X2

Legal form (the land is considered to be sold by Atkins)

	£'000
Profit and loss account	
Revenue	2,400
Cost of sales	(1,200)
Gross profit	1,200

	£'000
Balance sheet	
Fixed assets	
Land at cost (£2m - £1.2m)	800

Commercial substance (the transaction is a £2.4m loan secured on the land)

	£'000
Profit and loss account	
Gross profit	-
Finance cost(£2.4m @ 10%)	(240)

	£'000
Balance sheet	
Fixed assets	
Land at cost	2,000
Creditors: amount due after more than one year	
Secured loan due 2004(2,400 + 240)	2,640

51 Angelino

> **Text reference.** Chapter 15.
>
> **Top tips.** This was not a question to attempt unless you knew something about the various issues involved in off balance sheet finance. (a) may look like something you can waffle your way through, but that is not the case. In scenarios like (b) it is always worth taking the time to read the information twice, then you will understand the situation before you try to evaluate it.
>
> **Easy marks.** (a) may have looked like easy marks, but only if you knew something about the issues. If you did know enough to answer (a), then (b) was easy marks. These were all classic off balance sheet situations and you should have had no trouble dealing with them.

Marking scheme

				Marks
(a)		1 mark per relevant point to a	**Maximum**	9
(b)	(i)	1 mark per relevant point to a	**Maximum**	5
	(ii)	sale price not at fair value raises substance issues		1
		leaseback is not a finance lease		1
		treat building as sold (derecognise) at a profit of £2.5m		1
		rental treated as: £800,000 rental cost		1
		£200,000 finance cost		1
		£300,000 loan repayment		1
			Maximum	6
	(iii)	general discussion of risk and rewards re consignment goods		2
		Issues and accounting treatment relating to supplies from Monza		2
		Issues and accounting treatment relating to supplies from Capri		2
			available	6
			Maximum	5
			Maximum for question	25

(a) Off balance sheet finance is a form of creative accounting which seeks to obscure financial transactions. It has been described as 'the funding or refinancing of a company's operations in such a way that, under legal requirements and existing accounting conventions, some or all of the finance may not be shown on its balance sheet.'

In practice, most off balance sheet finance transactions are intended to keep debt off the balance sheet. In order to achieve this, the related asset is also kept off the balance sheet. An example of this is where an asset is actually acquired under a finance lease. Rather than show the asset and the related loan creditor, the acquirer may decide that the asset is not to be capitalised and the lease is accounted for as an operating lease. Or stock may be purchased on consignment, under a legal agreement which allows the purchaser to not record the current asset or the related creditor. Potential suppliers doing a credit reference check on the company will not discover the true value of its existing trade creditors or be able to accurately assess its payment record. Another example can be where an asset is 'sold' and 'repurchased' under an arrangement which is in substance a loan secured on the asset. The asset disappears from the balance sheet and the loan is represented as sale proceeds.

Obviously, this conflicts with the requirement to produce 'true and fair' financial statements and the ASB has sought to deal with the off balance sheet problem by means of the definitions and recognition criteria for assets and liabilities in the *Statement of Principles* and more specifically in FRS 5 *Reporting the substance of transactions*. FRS 5 lays out criteria for recognition or derecognition of an asset, based on which party bears the risks and rewards of ownership.

Why do companies want to keep debt off the balance sheet? Mainly to improve the appearance of the balance sheet and avoid any impact on gearing. They want to satisfy the expectations of analysts. An increase in borrowing brings an increase in interest payments, which reduces the amount left to distribute to shareholders. An increase in borrowing above a certain limit can therefore be negatively perceived by investors, leading to a possible fall in the share price. A fall in the share price can leave the company vulnerable to takeover.

A company which is short of funds and needs to raise further loans also needs to convince lenders that it is a good risk. If it already has large loans outstanding, lenders will be less willing to make further loans, or will require a higher rate of interest to compensate for the increased risk of default. The company may therefore seek to move some of its borrowing off balance sheet (perhaps by paying off one loan with another disguised as a sale and repurchase) and thereby reduce its gearing to a more acceptable level.

Off balance sheet finance is to some degree a dynamic issue; new forms of it will continue to arise and it will continue to be a problem for standard setters, auditors, lenders and investors. A number of the high-profile collapses of recent years have revealed substantial amounts of borrowing off balance sheet.

(b) (i) In this situation the debts have been factored 'with recourse'. Angelino still bears the risks of slow payment (they receive a residual amount depending upon how quickly customers pay) and non-payment (they refund to Omar any balances uncollected after six months). The substance of the transaction is therefore that Omar is providing a loan to Angelino on the security of the debtors.

The debtors have therefore not been sold and should not be derecognised. The payment from Omar should be accounted for as a loan. When a debtor pays, the amount lent in respect of his balance should be debited to the loan and credited to his account and the balance needed to clear his balance should be charged to loan interest/ debt collection expenses.

(ii) This is a sale and leaseback transaction in which the sale price has been inflated to include a loan and the lease payments have been inflated to include interest and loan repayments.

Taking the transaction at its face value, Angelino could record the sale at £12m, showing a profit on disposal of £4.5m. The lease payments of £1.3m per annum would be charged to profit and loss as rent.

However, representing the substance of the transaction, the sale should be recorded at market value of £10m, giving a profit on disposal of £2.5m and the additional £2m should be recorded as a long-term loan. The £0.5m per annum above market value in the lease payments should be treated as loan repayments.

The loan will be accounted for as follows:

	£'000	£'000
Initial balance 1.10.05	2,000	
Finance cost 10%	200	
Instalment paid	(500)	
Balance 30.9.06	1,700	
Creditors – amounts due within one year (500 – 170)		330
Creditors – amounts due after one year (1,700 – 330)		1,370
		1,700

(iii) Angelino's contract with Monza is a typical consignment agreement. The cars remain the property of Monza and Angelino bears none of the risks of ownership. When Angelino sells a car or decides to keep it at the end of three months, it purchases it at that point from Monza, at the list price in force at that date. This is therefore the point at which the risks and rewards pass to Angelino. Up to that point there is no sale and the cars should not appear in stock.

The agreement with Capri is of the nature of purchase under a credit agreement. Angelino pays a 10% deposit and obtains ownership of the vehicles at that point. If it fails to pay the balance, it forfeits its deposit and has to return the cars at its own expense, so it has taken on the risks of ownership, principally the risk of not being able to sell the vehicle. In this case Angelino should show the cars in stock and set up a creditor for the list price, less the deposit paid. The 1% display charge should be accounted for as interest.

52 Preparation question: Branch Ltd

PROFIT AND LOSS ACCOUNT (EXTRACT)

	£
Depreciation (W1)	5,000
Interest payable and similar charges	2,074

BALANCE SHEET (EXTRACT)

Tangible fixed assets include assets held under finance lease with a net book value of £15,000

Creditors: amounts falling due within one year	
Obligations under finance leases (W2) (16,924 – 14,786)	2,138

Creditors: amounts falling due after more than one year	
Obligations under finance leases (W2)	14,786

Workings

1 *Depreciation*

$$\frac{20,000}{4} = £5,000 \text{ pa}$$

2 *Obligations under finance leases*

		£
Year ended 31 December 20X1		
1.1.X1	Liability b/d	20,000
1.1.X1	Deposit	(1,150)
		18,850
1.1.X1 – 31.12.X1	Interest at 11%	2,074
31.12.X1	Instalment	(4,000)
31.12.X1	Liability c/d	16,924
Year ended 31 December 20X2		
1.1.X2 – 31.12.X2	Interest at 11%	1,862
31.12.X2	Instalment	(4,000)
31.12.X2	Liability c/d	14,786

53 Evans

PROFIT AND LOSS ACCOUNT EXTRACT

	20X3
	£
Operating profit (note 1)	X
Interest payable and similar charges (note 2)	1,171
Profit on ordinary activities before taxation	X

BALANCE SHEET EXTRACT

	20X3
	£
Tangible assets (note 3)	X
	X
Creditors: amounts falling due within one year (note 4)	X
Creditors: amounts falling due after more than one year (note 5)	X

Notes

1   *Operating profit*

Operating profit is arrived at after charging:

	20X3
	£
Depreciation of owned assets	X
Depreciation of assets held under finance leases	6,157
Hire of plant and machinery - operating leases	10,000

2   *Interest payable and similar charges*

	£
Finance charges payable - finance leases (W2)	1,171

3   *Tangible assets*

	£
Cost at 1 January 20X3	X
Additions	X
Cost at 31 December 20X3	X
Accumulated depreciation at 1 January 20X3	X
Charge for the year	X
Accumulated depreciation at 31 December 20X3	X
Net book value at 31 December 20X3	X
Net book value at 1 January 20X3	X

The net book value of fixed assets of £X includes an amount of £55,413 in respect of assets held under finance leases.

4   *Creditors: amounts falling due within one year*

	£
Trade creditors	X
Obligations under finance leases (note 6)	8,708
	X

5   *Creditors: amounts falling due after more than one year*

	£
Debenture loans	X
Obligations under finance leases (note 6)	51,033
	X

6   *Obligations under finance leases*

The minimum lease payments to which the company was committed at 31 December 20X3 are as follows.

	£	£
Under one year		12,000
Over one year		
In the second to fifth years inclusive	48,000	
Over five years	15,000	
		63,000
		75,000
Less: Interest allocated to future periods (W4)		15,259
(W2)		59,741
Due within one year (W3)		8,708
Due after more than one year (W3)		51,033
(W2)		59,741

7   *Commitments under operating leases*

At 31 December 20X3 the company had an annual commitment of £10,000 under a non-cancellable operating lease, in respect of plant and machinery, which expires after more than five years from the balance sheet date.

Workings

1   *Depreciation charge for the year*

	£
Cost of asset	61,570
Useful life	10 years
Depreciation charge	£6,157

2   *Obligation to date*

	£
Cash price	61,570
Instalment 1 October 20X3	(3,000)
	58,570
Interest October – December 20X3 (2%)	1,171
Balance 31 December 20X3 (c/d)	59,741

3   *Obligation under one year*

	Balance	Interest	Payments
Balance 31 December 20X3 (b/d)	59,741		
Instalment 1 January 20X4	(3,000)		3,000
	56,741		
Interest January - March 20X4 (2%)	1,135	1,135	
Balance 31 March 20X4	57,876		
Instalment 1 April 20X4	(3,000)		3,000
	54,876		
Interest April - June 20X4 (2%)	1,098	1,098	
Balance 30 June 20X4	55,974		
Instalment 1 July 20X4	(3,000)		3,000
	52,974		
Interest July - September 20X4 (2%)	1,059	1,059	
Balance 30 September 20X4	54,033		
Instalment 1 October 20X4	(3,000)		3,000
	51,033		
Instalments due under one year			12,000
Interest for next year		3,292	(3,292)
Obligation due within one year			8,708

4   *Interest analysis*

	£
Total payments (£3,000 × 26)	78,000
Cash price	(61,570)
Total interest	16,430
Interest to date (W1)	(1,171)
Interest in respect of future periods	15,259

54 Bowtock

SSAP 21 and Leased assets

The first task is to decide what sort of lease the asset is held under. This is a finance lease because it transfers substantially all the risks and rewards of ownership to the lessee, as shown by the length of the lease and its cost:

- The asset's useful life is five years (as shown by the 20% straight line depreciation policy) and the lease is also for five years. Therefore the asset is being held for the whole of its useful life.

- The minimum lease payments are £60,000 spread over four years. The present value of these payments at an 8% discount rate is £51,745, which is 99.5% of their fair value. Leases are assumed to be finance leases if the present value of the minimum lease payments is more the 90% of the asset's fair value.

The asset is capitalised at the lower of the fair value and the present value of the minimum lease payments and depreciated over its five year useful life; the obligation to make lease payments is recognised as a liability.

As the fair value is a close approximation to the present value of the minimum lease payments, the fair value has been used in the following calculations.

Extracts from Bowtock's financial statements for the year ending 30 September 20X3

Profit and loss account	£
Depreciation charge (£52,000 × 20%)	10,400
Finance costs [800 (W3a) + 1,872(W3b)]	2,672

Balance sheet	
Fixed assets	
Assets held under finance leases (W1)	33,800

Creditors: amounts falling due within one year	
Obligations under finance leases (W2)	11,376

Creditors: amounts falling due after more than one year	
Obligations under finance leases (W2)	21,696

W1   *Net book value of asset*

	£	£
1 January 20X2: Fair value of lease and asset		52,000
Depreciation to 30 September 20X2 £52,000 × 20% × 9/12	7,800	
Depreciation to 30 September 20X3 £52,000 × 20%	10,400	
		(18,200)
Net book value 30 September 20X3		33,800

W2   *Presentation of the lease liability*

		£
Total balance 30 September 20X3	(W3c)	33,072
Capital amount due within 12 months		
Payment 1 January 20X4		12,000
Less un-accrued interest on £31,200 at 8% for 3 months		(624)
Creditors: amounts falling due within one year		11,376
Creditors: amounts falling due after more than one year		
£33,072 - £11,376		21,696

W3   *Movement on the lease liability*

		£
1 January 20X2: Fair value of lease and asset		52,000
First payment 1.1.X2		(12,000)
Balance 1.1.X2		40,000
Interest on £40,000 at 8% for 9 months		2,400
Balance 30 September 20X2		42,400
Interest on £40,000 at 8% for 3 months	(W3a)	800
Second payment 1.1.X3		(12,000)
Balance 1.1.X3		31,200
Interest on £31,200 at 8% for 9 months	(W3b)	1,872
Balance 30 September 20X3	(W3c)	33,072
Interest due to 1.1.X4 (£31,200 × 8% for 3 months)		624
		33,696

55 Preparation question: Julian Co

Deferred tax implications

(i)   Accelerated capital allowances: full provision should be made for the excess capital allowances. The provision should be discounted based on a calculation of the timing of its reversal.

(ii)   Revaluation: assuming there is no binding contract to sell the property, no provision is required.

Provision:

	£m
Accelerated capital allowances (W1)	36.0
Discount	(2.9)
Discounted provision for deferred tax	33.1

Working

1   *Capital allowances*

Timing differences £120m

∴ undiscounted provision £120m × 30% = £36m

Years to come	Reversal of timing difference £m	Deferred tax liability (× 30%) £m	Discount factor	Discounted liability £m
X2	30	9	.962	8.7
X3	40	12	.925	11.1
X4	50	15	.889	13.3
	120	36		33.1

56 Deferred taxation

Nature and purpose of deferred taxation

Accounting profits and taxable profits are not the same. There are several reasons for this but they may conveniently be considered under two headings: permanent differences and timing differences.

(i)   **Permanent differences** arise because certain expenditure, such as entertainment of UK customers, is not allowed as a deduction for tax purposes although it is quite properly deducted in arriving at accounting profit. Similarly, certain income (such as franked investment income) is not subject to corporation tax, although it forms part of accounting profit.

(ii)   **Timing differences** arise because certain items are included in the accounts in a period different from that in which they are dealt with for taxation purposes.

Deferred tax is a means of ironing out the tax inequalities arising from timing differences. In years when corporation tax is saved by timing differences such as **accelerated capital allowances**, a charge for **deferred taxation** is made in the profit and loss account and a provision set up in the balance sheet; in years when timing **differences reverse**, because the depreciation charge exceeds the capital allowances available, a **deferred tax credit** is made in the profit and loss account and the balance sheet provision is reduced.

The tax actually payable to the Inland Revenue is the **corporation tax liability**. The credit balance on the deferred taxation account represents an estimate of tax saved because of timing differences but expected ultimately to become payable when those differences reverse.

The main categories in which timing differences can occur are as follows.

(i)   **Short-term timing differences**. These arise because taxable profits are calculated on a receipts and payments basis, whereas accounting profits are calculated on an accruals basis.

        For example, general allowances for bad debts in the financial accounts are not allowable for tax purposes until they crystallise into specific bad debts.

(ii)   **Accelerated capital allowances**. When new assets are purchased, capital allowances may be available against taxable profits which exceed the amount of depreciation chargeable on the assets in the financial accounts for the year of purchase. These can be very large now, with 100% first year allowances available for 'small' companies on computers and software.

(iii)   **Revaluation surpluses on fixed assets** for which a taxation charge does not arise until the fixed assets are eventually realised.

(iv)   **Surpluses on disposals of fixed assets** which are subject to rollover relief.

Deferred taxation is therefore an accounting convention which is introduced in order to apply the **accruals concept to income reporting** where **timing differences** occur.

57 Bowtock II

(a)   *Principles of deferred tax*

        In the UK different rules are used for calculating accounting profit (as used by investors) and taxable profit. There are two kinds of difference between the two profits; permanent differences and temporary differences.

        •   Permanent differences arise when either certain items of expenditure are not allowed for tax purposes (such as entertainment) or when some income is not subject to tax (grants, for example). There is no deferred tax on these items.

- Temporary differences arise when income or expenditure is recognised in the financial statements in one year, but is charged or allowed for tax in another. Deferred tax needs to be provided for on these items.

The most important temporary difference is that between depreciation charged in the financial statements and capital allowances in the tax computation. In practice capital allowances tend to be at a higher rate than depreciation charges, resulting in accounting profits being higher than taxable profits. This means that the Corporation Tax charge is too low in comparison with accounting profits. However, these differences even out over the life of an asset, and so at some point in the future the accounting profits will be lower than the taxable profits, resulting in a relatively high Corporation Tax charge.

These differences are misleading for investors who value companies on the basis of their post tax profits (by using EPS for example). Deferred tax adjusts the reported tax expense for these differences. As a result the reported tax charge (the Corporation Tax for the period plus the deferred tax) will be comparable to the reported profits, and in the balance sheet a provision is built up for the expected increase in the tax charge in the future.

There are many ways that deferred tax could be calculated. FRS 19 applies the liability method. Deferred Tax is provided if, at the balance sheet date, there is an obligation to pay more tax in the future as a result of transactions that have occurred in the past. The main exception to this is that deferred tax is not provided on revaluation gains unless there is a commitment to sell the item.

(b)   *Bowtock*

The provision for deferred tax in Bowtock's balance sheet at 30 September 20X3 will be the potential tax on the difference between the accumulated depreciation of £600,000 and the cumulative tax allowance of £768,000. The difference is £632,000 and the tax on the difference is £158,000.

The charge (or credit) for deferred tax in profit and loss account is the increase (or decrease) in the provision during the year. The closing provision of £158,000 is less than the opening provision of £160,000, so there is a credit for £2,000 in respect of this year.

Movement in the provision for deferred tax for the year-ending 30 September 20X3

	£
Opening provision	160,000
Credit released to the profit and loss account	(2,000)
Closing provision	158,000

Workings

		Depreciation £		Tax allowance £	Difference £	Tax @ 25% £
Y/E 09/X1						
Charge	W1	200,000	W2	800,000		
Balance		200,000		800,000	600,000	150,000
Y/E 09/X2						
Charge		200,000	W3	240,000		
Balance		400,000		1,040,000	640,000	160,000
Y/E 09/X3						
Charge		200,000	W4	192,000		
Balance		600,000		1,232,000	632,000	158,000

(W1)   £2,000,000 cost - £400,000 residual value over 8 years.
(W2)   £2,000,000 × 40%
(W3)   £1,200,000 × 20%
(W3)   £960,000 × 20%

58 Preparation question: Fenton plc

(a) Fenton plc

Date	Narrative	Shares	Time	Bonus fraction	Weighted average
1.1.X1	b/d	5,000,000	$\times \frac{1}{12}$	$\times \frac{2.00}{1.95} \times \frac{11}{10}$	470,085
31.1.X1	Rights issue	+ 1,250,000			
		6,250,000	$\times \frac{5}{12}$	$\times \frac{11}{10}$	2,864,583
30.6.X1	FMP	+ 125,000			
		6,375,000	$\times \frac{5}{12}$	$\times \frac{11}{10}$	2,921,875
30.11.X1	Bonus issue	+ 637,500			
		7,012,500	$\times \frac{1}{12}$		584,375
					6,840,918

TERP	4 @ 2	=	8.00
	1 @ 1.75	=	1.75
	5		9.75
	$\therefore$ 1.95		

EPS for y/e 31.12.X1 = $\dfrac{2,900,000}{6,840,918}$ = 42.4p

Restated EPS for y/e 31.12.X0 = 46.4p $\times \dfrac{1.95}{2.00} \times \frac{10}{11}$ = 41.1p

(b) Sinbad plc

Basic EPS = $\dfrac{£644,000}{10,000,000}$ = 6.44p

Diluted EPS

	£
Earnings	
P.A.T.	644,000
Interest saving 1,200,000 @ 5% × 70%	42,000
	686,000
Number of shares	
Basic	10,000,000
On conversion	4,800,000
	14,800,000

Diluted EPS = $\dfrac{£686,000}{14,800,000}$ = 4.64p

(c) Talbot plc

Basic EPS = $\dfrac{£540,000}{5,000,000}$ = 10.8p

Diluted EPS:

Consideration on exercise 400,000 × £1.10 = £440,000

Shares acquired at FV £440,000/£1.60 = 275,000

$\therefore$ shares issued for no consideration (400,000 – 275,000) = 125,000

EPS = $\dfrac{£540,000}{5,000,000 + 125,000}$ = 10.5p

59 Savoir

Shares in issue

	Shares 25p
1 April 20X3	40,000,000
1 July 20X3 FMP	8,000,000
	48,000,000
1 January 20X4 Bonus issue (48/4)	12,000,000
31 March 20X4	60,000,000

(a) *Year ended 31 March 20X4*

	m
Shares:	
Existing	40
New issue (8m × 9/12 months)	6
Bonus issue (48/4)	12
	58

Earnings £13.8m, therefore EPS = 13.8/58 = 24p

Comparative

The EPS for 20X3 would be restated to allow for the dilutive effect of the bonus issue as follows:

25p × 48/60* = 20p

* Existing shares + new issue = 48

  Existing shares + new issue + bonus issue = 60

  Note that the 8m shares issued at full price are non-dilutive and are therefore added to both sides of the fraction.

Year ended 31 March 20X5

'2 for 5' rights issue takes place halfway through the year and results in 24m additional shares.

Weighted average number of shares calculated as follows:

60 × 6/12 × 2.4 / 2 (market price / theoretical ex-rights price (W))	36
84 × 6/12	42
	78

Earnings £19.5m, therefore EPS = 19.5 / 78 = 25p

Comparative

The EPS for 20X4 is now restated following the rights issue in October 20X4 as follows:

24p × theoretical ex-rights price (W) /market price = 24p × 2 / 2.40 = 20p

Working

	£
Theoretical ex-rights price	
5 shares at market price (5 × 2.4)	12
2 shares at £1	2
	14/7 = 2

(b)   Basic EPS = £25.2m / 84m = 30p

Diluted EPS:

	Shares m	Earnings £m
Existing	84.0	25.2
Loan stock	10.0	1.2 (W1)
Share options	4.8 (W2)	–
	98.8	26.4

EPS = 26.4 / 98.8 = 26.7p

Workings

1   *Loan stock*

	£m
When conversion takes place there will be a saving of:	
Interest (20m × 8%)	1.6
Less tax (1.6 × 25%)	(0.4)
	1.2

2   *Share options*

Shares issued will be 12m @ £1.50 = £18m.

At market price of £2.50 the value would be £30m.

The shortfall is £12m, which is equivalent to 4.8m shares at market price.

60 Niagara

(a)   *Dividend cover*

Dividend cover is a basic measure of risk which describes how many times the equity dividend is covered by the profits attributable to the equity holders. A high ratio (say above three) means that the company could maintain its present level of dividend even if profits were to fall in future years; this makes the company attractive to some investors because there is a lower risk of a reduction in investment income. If this ratio is low (say less than 2) then any reduction in profits could easily lead to a forced reduction in the level of equity dividend. This increases the risks of investing in the company, and makes the company less attractive to investors. A ratio below 1 means that the company is using previous year's profits to pay this year's dividend. This is unsustainable in the long run.

Niagara's dividend cover is 2.02. This is not in the danger zone, but it is unspectacular. Although Niagara may not have to reduce its dividend unless profits halve, there is no room for increasing the dividend unless profits rise.

Workings

Niagara's draft accounts show a £2,585,000 profit attributable to the equity holders, but this is before accounting for the preference dividends. The revised profit attributable to the equity shareholders is as follows:

	£
Draft equity shareholders profit	2,585,000
£1m 8% preference shares (full year)	(80,000)
£1m 6% preference shares (half year)	(30,000)
Revised profits attributable to the equity shareholders	2,475,000

Niagara has declared two equity dividends for the year. The interim dividend was paid to its original shareholders, but the final dividend will also be paid to the new shares arising from the one-for-five rights issue:

	Share capital	Nominal Value	Number of shares	Dividend per share	Total dividend £
Interim	£3m	25 pence	12,000,000	3 pence	360,000
Final	£3.6m	25 pence	14,400,000	6 pence	864,000
					1,224,000

Dividend cover = £2,475,000 / £1,224,000 = **2.02**

(b) *Basic earnings per share*

This is the profits attributable to the ordinary equity holders of the parent divided by the weighted average number of ordinary shares outstanding during the period. This year's calculation takes into account the rights issue half way through the year. Last year's reported EPS of 24p will have to be adjusted for the bonus element of the rights issue.

Basic EPS

20X3	17.7 pence
20X2 (restated)	22.5 pence

20X3 Basic EPS

$$\frac{\text{Profit attributable to the ordinary equity holders of the parent}}{\text{Weighted average number of ordinary shares outstanding during the period}}$$

$$\frac{£2,475,000 \text{ (see above)}}{14,000,000 \text{ shares (see below)}} = \textbf{17.7 pence}$$

Weighted average number of ordinary shares

Share holding	Number of shares	Weighting	
Original holding plus 'Bonus' element	12,800,000	12/12	12,800,000
Full market value' element of rights issue	1,600,000	9/12	1,200,000
Closing holding	14,400,000		14,000,000

'Bonus' and 'full market' elements of rights issue:

Theoretical ex-rights price

	Number of shares	Price	Market capitalisation £
Original holding	12,000,000	£2.40	28,800,000
Rights issue	2,400,000	£1.50	3,600,000
	14,400,000		32,400,000

Theoretical ex-rights price = £32.4m / 14.4m shares = £2.25 per share

Original shareholding grossed-up for 'bonus' issue

Original holding of 12m shares $\times \dfrac{£2.40}{£2.25}$ = 12,800,000 shares

'Full market value' issue

2,400,000 shares less 800,000 bonus issue = 1,600,000 at full market value.

(1,600,000× £2.25 = £3,600,000 / 2,400,000 × £1.50 = £3,600,000)

20X2 Restated EPS

Original EPS scaled down for 'bonus' issue

24 pence as originally reported × $\frac{£2.25}{£2.40}$ = **22.5 pence**

(c) **Fully diluted earnings per share**

Investors need to be aware of circumstances that might reduce earnings per share in the future. Diluted EPS measures the effect that existing commitments might have on future EPS. The two examples in this question are typical:

When the convertible loan stock is converted into ordinary shares there will be an increase in the number of shares that the earnings must be shared between. However, there will also be an increase in available earnings because the loan interest will no longer be paid.

When the directors receive their free shares in 20X5 there will also be an increase in the number of equity shares, but this time with no compensating increase in profits.'

The net effect of increases in profits and shares can increase or reduce EPS. If the diluted EPS is less than the basic EPS then it must be reported in the financial statements.

Niagara's fully diluted EPS is 16.5 pence, about 7% less than the basic EPS of 17.7 pence. This is not a prediction of what Niagara's EPS will be in 20X5, merely an illustration of how this year's profits would have been shared had these events already taken place. It serves to warn investors of the effects of existing obligations to issue shares.

Workings

Revised earnings for the year (W1 below) $\frac{£2,573,000}{15,550,000}$ = **16.5 pence**
Revised number of shares in issue (W2 below)

1 *Revised earnings*

	£'000
Basic earnings	2,475
Add: Interest saved (£2m × 7%)	140
Less: Tax charge (£140,000 @ 25%)	(42)
Diluted earnings	2,573

2 *Revised number of shares*

Weighted average number of shares in issue this year	14,000,000
Maximum conversion of loan stock: £2m × 40 shares / £100	800,000
Directors' warrants	750,000
Diluted number of shares in issue	15,550,000

61 Preparation question: Analytical review

Top tips. Try not to calculate too many ratios. The question gives a big hint as to those you should provide. Remember however that it is your analysis which is as important as the ratios.

(a)

		20X7	20X6	20X5	20X4	20X3
1	Net profit before tax: sales	18.3%	11.1%	14.0%	9.4%	6.9%
2	Net profit before tax: total assets less current liabilities	31.6%	20.8%	28.0%	19.5%	14.7%
3	Working capital ratio	×1.77	×1.68	×1.40	×1.77	×1.65
4	Liquidity ratio	0.60	0.50	0.54	0.68	0.70
5	Sales: fixed assets	×2.65	×3.00	×2.77	×3.54	×3.48
6	Stock turnover (cost of sales:stock ratio)	×1.78	×1.50	×2.03	×2.29	×2.53
7	Debtors collection period (average debtors ÷ sales × 365) (Average debtors taken as average value of opening and closing debtors)	51 days	53 days	62 days	62 days	-
8	Age of stock (average stock ÷ cost of sales × 365)	199 days	198 days	162 days	143 days	-
9	Sales growth (% pa)	21%	35%	18%	16%	-
10	Cost of sales growth (% pa)	25%	16%	11%	15%	-
11	Net profit growth (% pa)	100%	7%	75%	60%	-
12	Plant/machinery growth (% pa)	60%	67%	50%	33%	-
13	Working capital per £1 sales	20p	20p	14p	20p	18p
14	Gearing ratio (debt including overdraft:equity ratio)	90%	130%	60%	89%	126%
15	Gross profit/sales	46%	47%	39%	35%	34%
16	Creditors*/cost of sales × 365	98 days	139 days	174 days	93 days	84 days

*excluding overdraft

(b) (i) **Analysis of the financing proposals**

The company needs some long-term funds, to redeem the debenture stock in 20X9 and to finance further sales growth.

The amount of **extra long-term capital** required is uncertain; £1.5m is needed to redeem the stock. The sales growth has been fairly strong for the last four years, and if similar growth rates continue, the company will need funding for extra working capital and for new fixed assets.

It is perhaps significant that the **percentage growth** in **fixed assets** has been well **in excess of sales growth**, indicating perhaps that the company is having to purchase more expensive equipment to remain competitive. Both gross profit/sales and net profit/sales have improved over the years, indicating that in spite of the growth in fixed assets, profitability is improving (due perhaps to greater productivity).

However, **sales as a proportion of fixed assets** was relatively **low** in 20X7, suggesting perhaps that asset utilisation is below capacity and could be improved, thus reducing the requirement for fixed asset purchases.

The source of **additional long-term capital will be debt capital or equity**. The company's net profits are probably insufficient to provide finance from retained profits, and so extra finance will be needed from debt capital or a new issue of equity.

The company's **financial gearing**, although fluctuating, has been **high**. This raises doubts about whether sufficient debt capital can be raised to meet all the company's finance requirements. Presumably, the existing debentures are secured; a new issue of debentures maturing in 20X9 will also need security. The bank overdraft will probably also be secured by a charge, perhaps a floating charge on the company's stocks and debtors. Plant and machinery does not usually provide good security, and so there would be doubts about whether the company could raise sufficient extra loan capital, because of inadequate security (and excessive gearing).

(ii) **Reasonableness of figures**

The **five-year results** show a continuing growth in sales and profits, with a return and profit ratio currently higher than the industry average.

A comparison with the average statistics for the industry indicates that the **control of working capital** by AB plc is not as good as it might be. Although the company has maintained a fairly steady ratio of working capital per £1 of sales at around 20p, its current ratio and liquidity ratio are lower than the industry average.

In spite of this, **turnover of stock is slower** than the industry average, the average **debt collection period** a little **longer** and the **age of stock greater**. This suggests that the company is taking longer-than-average credit from suppliers, in spite of the improvement in 20X7. The figures therefore suggest that some attention should be given to working capital and cash flow, with a view to improving stock turnover, better credit management and improving liquidity. The stock valuation may not be accurate, which would affect the profit figure.

62 Rytetrend

Text references. Chapters 19 and 21.

Top tips. Part (a) Cash flow questions are a good choice in an exam. The format and content are straightforward and easy to learn. All the information needed for your answer must be given to you in the question. A methodical approach will generate good marks.

Part (b) This question refers to operating performance and financial position, and so the profit and loss account and balance sheet need to be discussed along with the cash flow statement. Note that more marks are available for this analysis than for the cash flow statement itself, so make sure that you leave yourself enough time for Part (b). Also, with only about 20 to 25 minutes available, you must be economical with the number of ratios you calculate and concentrate on making comments.

Easy marks. Part (a) is 12 easy marks.

Examiner's comments. This question consisted of a cash flow statement and an interpretation of it.

Part (a), the cash flow statement, was relatively straightforward but candidates are still not adjusting for non-cash elements. Also many candidates described inflows as outflows and vice versa.

Part (b), the report analysing performance, was poorly answered. As has happened in the past, candidates calculated ratios but then failed to explain why the ratio had moved. Other candidates calculated too many ratios. The marking scheme gave five marks to calculation and 9 marks to 'appropriate comments'.

			Marks
(a)	Operating profit		1
	Depreciation adjustment		1
	Loss on sale of plant		1
	Warranty provision		1
	Working capital changes		2
	Interest paid		1
	Tax paid		1
	Purchase of fixed assets		2
	Share issue; issue/redemption of loan		2
	Ordinary dividends		1
	Decrease in cash		1
		Available	**14**
		Maximum	**12**
(b)	Relevant ratios	**Available**	**5**
	Appropriate comments	**Available**	**9**
			14
		Maximum	**13**
		Maximum for question	**25**

(a)　RYTETREND
RECONCILIATION OF OPERATING PROFIT TO NET CASH INFLOW FROM OPERATING ACTIVITIES

		£'000
Operating profit	(W1)	4,100
Adjustments for:		
Depreciation	(W2)	7,410
Loss on disposal of fixed assets	(W2)	700
Warranty charge		580
Warranty costs paid	(150 + 580 – 500)	(230)
(Increase) decrease in stocks	(2,650 – 3,270)	620
(Increase) decrease in trade debtors	(1,100 – 1,950)	850
Increase (decrease) in trade creditors	(2,850 – 1,980)	870
Net cash inflow from operating activities		14,900

CASH FLOW STATEMENT FOR THE YEAR ENDED 31 MARCH 20X3

	£'000	£'000
Net cash inflow from operating activities		14,900
Servicing of finance: Interest paid		(460)
Taxation paid *(630 + 1,000 – 720)*		(910)
Capital expenditure: Purchase of fixed assets (W2) (15,750 – 500 + 300)		(15,550)
		(2,020)
Equity dividends paid		(430)
		(2,450)
Financing		
Proceeds from issue of share capital *(13,000 – 10,000)*	3,000	
Proceeds of 6% Loan Notes	2,000	
Repayment of 10% Loan Notes	(4,000)	
		1,000
Net decrease in cash *(400 in hand to 1,050 o/d)*		(1,450)

Workings

1   *Construction costs and profit before tax*

The cash flow statement must take into account the changes to assets and profits caused by capitalising £300,000 of construction costs.

	£'000
Operating profit in the draft P&L	3,860
Add back capitalised installation costs	300
Less 20% depreciation on these costs	(60)
	4,100

2   *Fixed Assets*

Movement for the year

		Cost £'000	Depreciation £'000
Opening balance		27,500	10,200
Disposal: Cost		(6,000)	-
Depreciation £6m × 20% × 4 years		-	(4,800)
Additions	balancing figure	15,750	-
Depreciation	balancing figure	-	7,350
Closing balance	in draft accounts	37,250	12,750
Capitalised installation costs		300	60
Revised closing balance		37,550	12,810

Depreciation charge

		£'000
Draft	from above	7,350
Installation costs	from above	60
Total charge		7,410

Loss on disposal

		£'000
Proceeds	trade in allowance	500
Net book value of disposals	6,000 – 4,800	(1,200)
Loss		700

Payments for additions

		£'000
Draft	from above	15,750
Installation costs	from above	300
Less trade in allowance		(500)
Total cost		15,550

(b)   **Commentary**

Operating performance

Rytetrend has posted a 35% increase in turnover, which is exceptionally good (assuming that inflation is negligible). One way to boost revenues is to cut the selling price in the hope of attracting more customers on the basis of price. This would lead to a steep fall in the gross profit margin. In this case Rytetrend's gross profit margin has fallen from 31.9% to 29.2%, which is only a modest fall. Maybe Rytetrend has attracted new customers owing to the quality of its products as well as because of its prices.

Although operating expenses have increased, they now only account for 17% of turnover rather than 20%. This suggests that Rytetrend has benefited from economies of scale as their business has increased.

Rytetrend's return on capital employed has improved from 14.4% to 18%. This is good, especially considering the £16m of capital expenditure during the year. Next year should be even better as a full year's profits will be earned from these new assets.

Financial position

Although the cash flow statement shows a net decrease in cash of £1.45m, Rytetrend is in a much better financial position now than at the start of the year.

- Rytetrend has generated £14.9m from its operations, which covers its finance costs (£460,000) and dividends (£430,000) sixteen times over.

- The only reason why net cash has decreased is because £15.55m has been invested in new equipment, which should boost profits and cash flows even more next year.

- The burden of Rytetrend's loan finance has been reduced in two ways. Firstly the total amount of debt has been reduced from £4m to £2m. Secondly, the cost of debt has been reduced from 10% to 6%. In the future Rytetrend's finance costs should only be £120,000 instead of £400,000. This reduction was made possible by an extra £3m of share capital raised during the year.

Controls over working capital have also been tightened.

- Stock days have been reduced from 75 to 43 days. This is good for cash flow and it also reduces the likelihood of obsolescence.

- The cash collection period from trade debtors has been reduced from 30 to 13 days. As well as boosting cash flows this also reduces the chances of debts going bad. This reduction could have been caused by better credit control, or by fewer sales being made on credit.

- The supplier payment period has remained at about 45 days. This is acceptable to most suppliers and also helps Rytetrend's cash flow.

The net effect of these changes is that the working capital cycle has been reduced from 60 days to 10 days, which is good. It also means that the current ratio has reduced from 2.0 to 0.7. In the past this would have been considered worrying, but today's thinking is that this reflects an efficient use of resources, especially by a retail business with strong cash generation.

Overall this business is generating a lot of cash. It will only take 25 working days to pay off the overdraft, and the modest level of dividends compared to profits or investment suggests that the management take a prudent view of their stewardship of the company.

Summary of ratios (based on adjusted financial statements)

	20X3	20X2
Increase in turnover	+35%	
Gross profit margin	29.2%	31.9%
Operating expense %		
$\dfrac{\text{Operating expenses}}{\text{Turnover}}$	17%	20%
Interest cover		
$\dfrac{\text{Profit before finance costs}}{\text{Finance costs}}$	8.9	5.8
Net profit margin		
$\dfrac{\text{Profit before tax}}{\text{Turnover}}$	11.4%	10.2%
Return on capital employed		
$\dfrac{\text{Profit before finance costs}}{\text{Assets}-\text{current liabilities}}$	18%	14.4%
Stock days		
$\dfrac{\text{Stock}}{\text{Cost of sales}}\times 365$	43 days	75 days

	20X3	20X2
Debtors days		
$\dfrac{\text{Trade debtors}}{\text{Turnover}} \times 365$	13 days	30 days
Creditor days		
$\dfrac{\text{Trade creditors}}{\text{Cost of sales}} \times 365$	46 days	45 days
Working capital cycle	10 days	60 days
Current ratio		
$\dfrac{\text{Current assets}}{\text{Current liabilities}}$	0.7	2.0

63 Harper

Text references. Chapters 18, 19 and 20.

Top tips. **Part (a)** There are seven marks here for some quite basic comments and calculations. Remember though that the information on acquisitions is not required by FRS 3.

Part (b) There are more marks for explanations than for calculations here. If you can remember the reasons for calculating basic and diluted EPS then you should be able to score most of the marks.

Part (c) Basically this question is asking you to explain the calculations and adjustments you make when calculating taxable profits, the tax charge, and tax paid, all of which should be familiar to you.

Easy marks. Part (a) is 7 easy marks.

Examiner's comments. This question was poorly answered with many candidates failing to read the question correctly. A frequent mistake was including discontinued operations when calculating the following year's profit in part (a).

Part (b) was better answered, although some candidates failed to realise that EPS is based on profit.

Part (c) was well answered but some candidates gave only brief outlines and little depth apart from timing differences.

Marking scheme

				Marks
(a)	(i)	1 mark per relevant point to a	**Maximum**	3
	(ii)	£110 for both companies if no information available		1
		Applying the information available – £77 million for Gamma		1
		– £209 million for Toga		2
			Maximum	4
(b)	(i)	1 mark per relevant point to a	**Maximum**	3
	(ii)	Number of shares re loan stock		1
		Interest saved		1
		Dilutive number of share re options		2
		Calculation of diluted EPS		1
			Maximum	5
	(iii)	1 mark per relevant point to a	**Maximum**	4
(c)		1 mark per relevant point to a	**Maximum**	6
			Maximum for question	25

(a)   (i)   *Usefulness*

Investors use the historic information in financial statements in order to forecast the future performance of a company. If a material part of a business has been discontinued during the year then the results of that business need to be excluded from the forecast, because those profits and losses are not going to recur.

Normally entities will want to sell off poorly performing businesses, so the disposal will hopefully boost future performance. If a profitable business is being sold off then shareholders will want to know why. Is the entity being forced to sell off good businesses in order to pay off debts, or is it a shrewd move, selling a business at its peak when its value is highest?

(ii)   *Gamma and Toga*

On the basis of the operating profit alone, both companies are making £100m this year and will be expected to make £110m next year, so there is nothing to choose between them. However, the expected results are very different if the information about discontinued activities and acquisitions is taken into account. With this information, Gamma is expected to make £77m next year and Toga £209m (see below), therefore Mrs Harper should invest in Toga.

		£m
Gamma's forecast operating profits		
Continuing activities	£70m × 110%	77
Acquisitions (none disclosed)		
Discontinued activities		-
Total expected operating profits		77
Toga's forecast operating profits		£m
Continuing activities	£90m × 110%	99
Acquisitions (adjusted for a full year)	£50m × 12/6 × 110%	110
Discontinued activities		-
Total expected operating profits		209

There are two aspects to the change in the forecast; the exclusion of the discontinued activities and adjusting profits from acquisitions to cover a full twelve months.

(b)   (i)   *Trends in EPS and profits*

The trend in reported profits shows the overall increase in an entity's profits over time. This increase could have been caused by

(1)   expansion and/or improvement in the entity's own business financed by retained profits or borrowings, or,

(2)   an increase in the size of the business financed by an issue of new shares,

In the first situation all of the increase in profits will belong to the existing shareholders, and so the trend in reported profits and EPS will be the same. In the second situation the increased profits will have to be shared with the new shareholders as well. This means that the increase in EPS will be less than the increase in reported profits. The cake may have got bigger, but it is being shared between more people.

The small investor will be more concerned with the change in profits attributable to their own shareholding, because this will determine the size of their potential dividends in the long run. Therefore Earnings Per Share is a more useful measure of performance for Mrs Harper.

(ii)   *Diluted EPS for 20X2*

$$\frac{\text{Adjusted earnings}}{\text{Diluted number of shares}} \quad \frac{£62m}{£360m} \quad \text{Earnings per share} = 17.2 \text{ pence}$$

		£m	£m
Adjusted earnings			
Original earnings			50
Interest saved on conversion	£200m × 8%	16	
Less tax at 25%		(4)	
			12
			62

Diluted number of shares

	Number (m)
Original	200
Conversion of loan stock (£200m × 70 shares/£100)	140
Directors options	
Proceeds (50 million shares @ £1.50) = £75m	
£75m buys 30m shares at the market price of £2.50	30
The directors will receive 50m shares	50
The dilution is 20m shares	20
Total diluted number of shares	360

(iii)   *Relevance of diluted EPS*

Investors use historic EPS to forecast future EPS. Obviously future EPS will depend on future profitability, but it will also be affected by the entity's existing commitments to issue shares in the future. These may reduce existing shareholders' share of profits even if the reported profits stay the same. Therefore investors need to know what the maximum potential reduction in their share of earnings could be based on the entity's existing obligations.

Two common causes of dilution are the conversion of loan stock (or preference shares), and share options that entitle the option holder to purchase shares at below the market rate.

The conversion of loan stock tends to increase earnings because the entity no longer has to pay interest on the loan. However, if this benefit is outweighed by a large increase in the number of shares in issue then existing shareholders will see their share of profits reduced.

An option to purchase shares at below market price always dilutes profits, because the benefit of the finance raised will be less than the number of shares issued.

In this question the diluted EPS is 17.2 cents. This is not a prediction of future EPS; that will depend on how many shares are issued, and what the future profits of Taylor will be.

(c)   *Tax*

The income tax rate of 25% applies to the taxable profits for the year. Not all income is taxable, and some items of expenditure are not allowable for tax. Therefore the taxable profits for the year may be more or less than the accounting profits, giving rise to an effective rate of tax on accounting profits above or below the expected rate.

The tax charge in the accounts also contains other items. In particular there is an adjustment for any over or under provision in previous years. If a material error was made when estimating the income tax in the previous year then the charge for this year will be materially affected by the correction.

The other common item in the tax charge is the increase or decrease in the deferred tax provision. This adjustment tends to bring the charge in the income statement closer to the prevailing rate of tax, as it smoothes out timing differences between when profits are recognised for tax purposes and for accounting purposes.

The difference between the charge for tax in the income statement and the tax paid in the cash flow statement is caused by two things;

(1)   Tax tends to be paid in the year following the period in which the tax was charged. So, tax charged in this year's income statement will be paid and reported in next year's cash flow statement.

(2)   Deferred tax (mentioned above) provides for tax that may not be payable for many years to come. So, although it is charged in the income statement as it arises, it may be many years before it becomes payable.

64 Comparator

Text reference. Chapters 19 and 20.

Top tips. **Part (a)** You should be familiar with the standard points discussing the limitations of ratio analysis. Make sure that you refer to inter-firm comparison services.

Part (b) Only six marks for calculating the ratios. Don't exceed your time allowance here.

Part (c) Do not merely describe the ratio in words, or say that it has gone up or down. Your comments should be on the possible reasons for differences in the accounting ratios, and the possible consequences of those differences. Accounting ratios tend to raise questions rather than provide answers.

Easy marks. Part (b) is 6 easy marks but do not go overboard with your calculations – you have 11 minutes only. See also the examiner's comments.

Examiner's comments. Answers to this question were generally just above average. Once again candidates wanted to calculate too many ratios. Also the answers to part (c) on interpretation of the ratios were very weak and lacked depth. Candidates need to relate the ratios to the business and make suggestions on why the ratios have changed.

Marking scheme

			Marks
(a)	Up to 1 mark for each limitation	**Maximum**	7
	Note: a good answer must refer to interfirm comparison issues		
(b)	½ mark for each relevant ratio	**Maximum**	6
(c)	Format		1
	Discussion of: Profitability		3
	Liquidity (and working capital ratios)		4
	Gearing		2
	Investment ratios		3
	Other issues		2
	Summary		1
		Available	16
		Maximum	12
		Maximum for question	25

(a) **Comparisons**

Accounting ratios can be used to assess the strength and performance of a company. They are mainly used to compare a company's performance over time or to compare one company with another (or to the average for similar companies).

Accounting ratios are calculated from published financial statements, and so they are subject to the same estimates and judgements as the statements. Accounting ratios tend to raise questions rather than answer them; for example a declining gross profit margin might indicate increased input costs or a declining sales price. Because of this, ratio analysis is often used in practice to identify areas that need further investigation.

More problems arise when companies are being compared, as it is difficult to find two companies that really are comparable:

- Big, publicly quoted companies often have diverse business interests located around the globe, unlike their smaller rivals which are more localised and less diversified.

- Different accounting policies can affect key ratios. For example a company that capitalises borrowing costs will have higher profits and net assets than one that doesn't.

- Different business practices may affect reported profits and assets. For example a business operating from rented premises and using rented equipment will have a very low capital employed compared with a similar business that owns its own premises and equipment.

- Balance sheet values may not be typical for the year as a whole. This might be because of seasonal fluctuations (for example a farming business) or because of a deliberate attempt to tidy up the balance sheet for the year-end by collecting in debtors and delaying the payment of suppliers.

- The dividend policy of a publicly quoted company will be very different from that of a small family company.

- Big companies tend to have different economies of scale than smaller companies.

The use of a comparison service will exaggerate these problems:

- Users will not know which firms have been used in the comparison. Because companies themselves are diverse, averages calculated may not be comparable to the user's company. For example, a small brewery may be focused on its core activity of brewing beer, but its competitor companies used by the comparison service may have diversified into hotels, retailing and other leisure activities.

- The year-ends of companies used will affect the ratios calculated.

- Averaged information will not tell you what the typical (model) ratio is, nor will it tell you what the normal range of ratios is.

Overall, although it is a useful and informative exercise to compare ratios, care must be taken to ensure that like is being compared with like.

(b) **Calculations**

	Comparator	Sector average
Return on capital employed	33.1%	22.1%
$\dfrac{\text{Profit before finance costs}}{\text{Assets} - \text{current liabilities}}$	$\dfrac{186 + 34}{1,135 - 470}$	
Net asset turnover	3.6	1.8
$\dfrac{\text{Turnover}}{\text{Assets} - \text{current liabilities}}$	$\dfrac{2,425}{1,135 - 470}$	
Gross profit margin	22.9%	30%
$\dfrac{\text{Gross profit}}{\text{Turnover}}$	$\dfrac{555}{2,425}$	
Net profit margin	7.7%	12.5%
$\dfrac{\text{Profit before tax}}{\text{Turnover}}$	$\dfrac{186}{2,425}$	
Net profit margin excluding write-off	12.6%	12.5%
$\dfrac{\text{Profit before tax} + \text{write off}}{\text{Turnover}}$	$\dfrac{186 + 120}{2,425}$	
ROCE excluding write off	51.1%	22.1%
$\dfrac{\text{Profit before finance costs} + \text{write off}}{\text{Assets} - \text{current liabilities}}$	$\dfrac{186 + 34 + 120}{665}$	
Current ratio	1.3 : 1	1.6 : 1
$\dfrac{\text{Current assets}}{\text{Current liabilities}}$	$\dfrac{595}{470}$	

	Comparator	Sector average
Quick ratio	0.7 : 1	0.9 : 1
$\dfrac{\text{Current assets} - \text{stocks}}{\text{Current liabilities}}$	$\dfrac{595 - 275}{470}$	
Stock holding period	54 days	46 days
$\dfrac{\text{Stock}}{\text{Cost of sales}} \times 365$	$\dfrac{275}{1,870} \times 365$	
Debtors' collection period	48 days	45 days
$\dfrac{\text{Trade debtors}}{\text{Turnover}} \times 365$	$\dfrac{320}{2,425} \times 365$	
Creditors' payment period	68 days	55 days
$\dfrac{\text{Trade creditors}}{\text{Cost of sales}} \times 365$	$\dfrac{350}{1,870} \times 365$	
Working capital cycle	34 days	36 days
	54 + 48 - 68	46 + 45 - 55
Debt to Equity	82%	40%
$\dfrac{\text{Interest bearing borrowings}}{\text{Equity}}$	$\dfrac{300}{365}$	
Dividend yield	1.7%	6%
$\dfrac{\text{Dividends paid per share}^*}{\text{Market price per share}}$	$\dfrac{10 \text{ pence}}{£6}$	
Dividend cover	1.6 times	3 times
$\dfrac{\text{Profit for the year}}{\text{Dividends paid}}$	$\dfrac{96}{60}$	

*Dividend per share

$$\frac{\text{Total dividend}}{\text{Number of shares in issue}} = \frac{£60,000}{150,000 \times 4} = 10 \text{ pence}$$

(c) **REPORT**

To: xxx
From: A N Accountant
Date: xxx
Subject: Financial performance of Comparator

Analysis of the financial performance of Comparator compared with the sector averages

Operating performance

The high ROCE of 33.1% (compared with 22.1% for all companies) shows that Comparator's assets are being used relatively efficiently. This is despite Comparator having a disappointing gross profit margin (22.9% compared with 30%) and net profit margin (7.7% compared with 12.5%). Comparator has made up for this low level of profitability by having a very high level of asset utilisation, as shown by an asset turnover ratio of 3.6 times, which is twice the average of 1.8 times.

There are two things that complicate the analysis above:

(i)   The age of Comparator's fixed assets, and
(ii)   The write off of stock.

These are discussed below:

(i)   The net book value of Comparator's fixed assets is only 15% of their cost, suggesting that these assets are quite old. This will have boosted the ROCE compared with a company with newer assets with a higher net book value. However, there is not enough information to investigate this further. Also, these assets will probably need replacing soon, and because Comparator has no cash it will need to borrow more money. This will be extremely difficult (and probably expensive) as Comparator's gearing ratio is already very high (82%) compared with the sector average (40%).

(ii)   Comparator's net profit margin is distorted by the £120,000 charge for writing off stock. Without this the net profit margin would have been 12.6%, which is greater than the average of 12.5%. If this write-off really is a one-off not-to-be-repeated event then this suggests that the underlying return on capital employed is 51.1%. However, the sector averages do not include similar information on one-off costs.

Financial position

Long term

As mentioned above, Comparator's gearing ratio is already high and the need to replace old plant and equipment could push it higher. As the existing equipment cost £3.6m some years ago Comparator could expect to spend as much again today, all of it on borrowed money. This would require a gearing ratio of 1,100%, which the banks would almost certainly not tolerate. The alternative would be to raise more share capital. At the current market price of £6 a share a further 600,000 shares would need to be issued, which would double the number of shares. This also seems an unlikely prospect. However, without new loans or share capital there can be no new equipment.

Short term

Comparator's quick and current ratios are below the industry average, which suggests that there may be short term cash flow problems and poor financial management.

Although the working capital cycle is relatively good (34 days compared with 36), the individual components are worse implying that there is poor stock control, poor credit control, and a shortage of cash to pay suppliers. Poor stock control may have caused the build up of obsolete stock (leading to the £120,000 write-off), and poor credit control can lead to an increase in bad debts. Delaying paying suppliers (who now have to wait 68 days to be paid) is a short term fix, but it can back-fire if suppliers lose patience with Comparator and demand cash on delivery, or refuse to deliver at all.

Interest cover, dividends, tax and overdraft

Although the interest cover of ten is good in terms of profits, there is no cash to pay the interest. Likewise there is £85,000 tax to pay. We are not told what the overdraft limit is, but it appears that Comparator can only meet its obligations if the overdraft is increased.

Investment ratios

Comparator's dividend yield of 1.7% is very low compared with the average of 6%, which will dissuade many investors from subscribing to a new share issue. On the other hand it suggests that the share price is relatively high. This might be because investors are aware of additional information that promises a brighter future for Comparator, or maybe the share price will drop when these results are published.

The dividend cover of 1.6 is also worrying; Comparator is paying out almost its entire earnings at a time when it needs to generate cash to pay off its liabilities and invest in new equipment.

Summary and conclusion

At first sight Comparator's operating performance appears to be good compared with its rivals, but further analysis suggests that this might be boosted by old plant and equipment. Comparator's financial position is worrying both in the short term and the long term, and it is difficult to see how Comparator will be able to meet its obligations and invest in the future. Unless things improve Comparator's going concern status must be in doubt.

65 Breadline

Text reference. Chapter 20.

Top tips. Part (a) The question gives the game away by asking you to consider related party issues. If you mentally go through the normal consolidation adjustments you should be able to think of five ways in which they could affect the perceived performance of a subsidiary.

Part (b) Financial analysis is a key part of the syllabus and a key skill throughout your professional career. The first thing you must do is to identify who you are performing the analysis for and why. In this case you are reporting to your own Chief Executive. The purpose of the report is not so clear. The body of the question refers to the possibility of acquiring Breadline and the recoverability of the money owed to Judicious, but the requirement itself asks you to analyse the overall financial performance of Breadline. The question also reminds you to refer to areas that cause concern or require further investigation. The second thing you should do is to review the financial statements to pick out obvious changes from one year to the next. When you have identified these, then you can switch on your calculator and calculate the ratios. Finally, remember that the marks are for your comments, not for the calculations.

Easy marks. Part (a) should be 5 easy marks.

Examiner's comments. Part (a) was a discussion of issues that may arise in part (b), although several candidates failed to realise this. Part (b) was generally well answered, although far too many answers gave the movements without discussing reasons for those movements. The notes given to the financial statements contained vital information that was ignored by too many candidates.

Marking scheme

		Marks
(a)	1 mark per relevant point to a maximum of	5
(b)	Format and presentation of report	1
	Calculation of relevant ratios – up to	6
	Appropriate comments on above ratios	10
	References to areas of concern	5
	Available	22
	Maximum	20
	Maximum for question	25

(a) **Assessing a subsidiary's performance**

The trade of a subsidiary is carried out for the benefit of the group as a whole, not for the benefit of the subsidiary itself. Therefore there will be transactions, assets and liabilities that only exist because of the subsidiary's position within the group. The value of these transactions (and the transaction itself) will not have been agreed on an 'arm's length' basis. Some typical examples are noted below:

Sales and cost of sales

Group companies often trade between themselves at an agreed price. This price may be above or below the market price. Either way it means that one group company will be reporting a higher gross profit at the expense of another.

Also, these transactions might not take place at all if the companies were independent. For example, a baker might buy its flour from a subsidiary, but would choose a completely different supplier if the companies were independent.

Group companies normally don't compete against each other. This means that a subsidiary might refrain from making sales that it would otherwise have made. Also, it might be protected against competition from other group companies.

Shared costs and benefits

Group companies often pool resources in order to get economies of scale. For example office buildings and administration costs can be shared, reducing the cost to each company. Marketing, distribution, research and development will also be better and cheaper if they are shared across a group.

Finance is often raised at competitive rates for the group as a whole, with the funds then being passed on to the subsidiaries. Sometimes the finance for a subsidiary will be deliberately subsidised via an inter-company loan account.

All of the above practices are legitimate and make sound business sense. However, they all distort the reported performance of an individual subsidiary company. If the subsidiary were independent its trade and its profitability would be very different.

(b)   **Report to the Chief Executive of Judicious plc on the financial position of Breadline Ltd**

From: Assistant Financial Controller

Introduction

This report investigates the overall financial position of Breadline Ltd, with particular reference to the possibility of acquiring Breadline Ltd and the recoverability of the amounts owed to Judicious plc.

This report is based on the published financial statements of Breadline Ltd for the year ending 31 December 20X1. Breadline Ltd is a wholly owned subsidiary of Wheatmaster plc.

There are a number of areas that cause concern, or where further investigation is necessary. These are highlighted in the report.

Sales and profitability

Breadline Ltd has increased sales by 31% and increased its reported gross profit margin from 26% to 30%. On the face of it this looks like good sustainable growth.

However, the notes to the accounts report that the profit on disposal of the freehold premises was credited to cost of sales. This will have reduced the cost of sales and inflated gross profit. It is a one off profit that cannot be repeated in the future. The financial effect of this sale is not known but it can be estimated. The company's business address and trading premises have not changed; this suggests that the company is still occupying the same buildings. In 20X0 Breadline Ltd had freehold buildings valued at £1,250,000 and no leasehold buildings. In 20X1 Breadline Ltd had no freeholds but owned a leasehold costing £2,500,000. This suggests a sale and lease back arrangement. Because the proceeds of the freehold must have been greater than the cost of the leasehold this puts a minimum value on the sale proceeds of £2.5m and a minimum profit of £1.25m. If 20X1's cost of sales are adjusted for this then the gross profit in 20X1 would be £1.3m and the gross profit margin only 15%. This suggests that Breadline Ltd has boosted sales by cutting its selling price. This has reduced operating profits in the current year and is unsustainable in the long run.

Interest cover

Although the reported interest cover has dropped from 206 to 100 it is still at an extremely safe level (interest cover of 6 would be adequate). However, excluding the profit on disposal of the freehold reduces profit before interest in 20X1 to £740,000. Also, Breadline Ltd has taken out a £500,000 loan note at a 2% interest rate. This is below the market rate of 8%. In one way or another Breadline Ltd will have to pay the market rate of interest, either by offering a premium on redemption or conversion rights, and so the true interest charge on the loan notes will be £40,000, not £10,000. This makes the total interest charge for the year £50,000 and reduces the interest cover to 15.

Interest cover of fifteen is still good, but with the overdraft increasing and profitability declining the chances are that this is going to deteriorate further over the coming years.

Working capital management

Stock levels have remained steady at about 18 days. Debtors have increased from 34 days to 41 days. This may have been because the credit control department has been unable to cope with the 31% increase in sales. However, 41 days is acceptable. Likewise creditors have edged up from 45 days to 52 days. Overall, the working capital cycle has remained steady at 7.8 days this year compared with 7.1 days last year.

What is worrying for Judicious plc is that Breadline Ltd has not been paying us as quickly as other suppliers. Last year the balance owed to Judicious plc was 45.6 days old which was close to the average of 44.8 days. This year the balance is 103.4 days, which is twice the average. This difference could have been caused by increased sales by Judicious plc in the last two months of the year, or more likely by Breadline Ltd favouring other creditors over Judicious plc. Maybe Breadline Ltd is paying amounts owing to group companies before it is paying its third party creditors.

Financing

Breadline Ltd has received £600,000 from issuing new shares (£400,000 par value + £200,000 premium) and £500,000 from issuing a loan note. The shares were issued to Wheatmaster plc, its parent, and the loan note was also probably issued to a related party. (That would account for the below market rate of interest.) In total £1,100,000 has been raised, but then £900,000 has been paid out by way of dividend. It would have been much more efficient to have foregone the shares and loans and not paid a dividend either. The only explanation for this money-go-round is that it has transferred £900,000 of distributable profits up to the parent.

The dividend is particularly worrying because Breadline Ltd could only pay it by distributing the profit made on disposal of the freehold property. This is reducing Breadline Ltd's capital base.

Breadline Ltd has also received a substantial (but unknown) amount from the disposal of property. The only obvious investment during the year is the purchase of another £870,000 of plant.

Despite all this cash coming in, during the year the bank balance has fallen from £250,000 in hand to an overdraft of £220,000, a cash outflow of £470,000.

Conclusion

Breadline Ltd's apparent progress and prosperity does not survive detailed examination. Its profits and cash flows appear to have been manipulated for the benefit of its parent, and to inflate the reported profits before selling the business. The dividends and sale and leaseback transactions also suggest that Wheatmaster plc is trying to extract as much value from the business as possible before selling it. Therefore I would not recommend that Judicious plc should acquire Breadline Ltd.

Also, Judicious plc should seek to recover the amount owed to it for supplies, and to enforce stricter credit control in the future.

Summary of ratios

		20X1	20X0
Increase in sales:	(£8,500 – £6,500)/£6,500	31%	
Gross profit margins:	£2,550/£8,500 (£1,690/£6,500)	30%	26%
Revised gross profit in 20X1:	£2,550,000 – £1,250,000	£1.3m	
Revised gross profit margin in 20X1:	£1.3m/£8.5m	15%	
Reported interest cover:	20X1 (£2,550 – £560)/£20	100	
	20X0 (£1,690 – £660)/£5		206
Revised profit before interest 20X1:	(£2,550 – £1,250 – £560)	£740K	
Revised interest 20X1:	(£500,000 × 8%) + £10,000	£50K	
Revised interest cover 20X1:	£740,000/£50,000	15	

Working capital management
Stock days
Based on a revised cost of sales in 20X1 of £7,200 (£5,950 + £1,250)

20X1: (370/7,200) × 365 days 20X0:	(240/4,810) × 365 days	18.8	18.2

Debtor days

20X1: (960/8,500) × 365 days 20X0:	(600/6,500) × 365 days	41.2	33.7

Creditor days

	20X1	20X0
Based on a revised cost of sales in 20X1 of £7,200		
20X1: (1,030/7,200) × 365 days 20X0: (590/4,810) × 365 days	52.2	44.8
Working capital cycle (days):	7.8	7.1
Ageing of the amounts owed to Judicious plc		
20X1: (340/1,200) × 365 days 20X0: (100/800) × 365 days	103.4	45.6

66 Preparation question: Dickson Ltd

Dickson Ltd
Cash flow statement for year ended 31 March 20X8

	£'000	£'000
Net cash inflow from operating activities (Note 1)		
Cash receipts from customers (W4)	1,526	
Cash payments to suppliers (W5)	(1,195)	
Cash payments to and on behalf of employees	(20)	
		311
Returns on investments and servicing of finance		
Interest paid		(15)
Taxation		
Corporation tax paid (W3)		(256)
Capital expenditure		
Payments to acquire development expenditure	(190)	
Payments to acquire tangible fixed assets (W2)	(248)	
Receipts from sale of tangible fixed assets	110	
		(328)
Equity dividends paid		(136)
Management of liquid resources		
Purchase of government bonds		(97)
Financing		
Issue of ordinary share capital (800 – 500)	300	
Issue of debenture loan	50	
		350
Decrease in cash		(171)

Note

Reconciliation of operating profit to net cash inflow from operating activities

	£'000
Profit before interest and tax (342 + 15)	357
Depreciation	57
Amortisation (W1)	60
Profit on disposal of fixed assets	(7)
Increase in stocks (360 – 227)	(133)
Decrease in debtors (274 – 324)	50
Decrease in creditors (291 – 364)	(73)
Net cash inflow from operating activities	311

Workings

1   *Development expenditure amortisation*

Intangible fixed assets

	£'000		£'000
Bal b/f	260		
		∴ Amortisation	60
Expenditure	190		
		Bal c/f	<u>390</u>
	<u>450</u>		<u>450</u>

2   *Payments to acquire tangible fixed assets*

Tangible fixed assets

	£'000		£'000
Bal b/f	637	Depreciation	57
Revaluations	100	Disposals	103
∴ Additions	<u>248</u>	Bal c/f	<u>825</u>
	<u>985</u>		<u>985</u>

3   *Taxation paid*

Taxation payable

	£'000		£'000
		Bal b/f	198
∴ Paid	256	P&L account	162
Bal c/f	<u>104</u>		
	<u>360</u>		<u>360</u>

4   *Cash receipts from customers*

Debtors

	£'000		£'000
Bal b/f	324		
		∴ Receipts	1,526
Turnover	1,476		
		Bal c/f	<u>274</u>
	<u>1,800</u>		<u>1,800</u>

5   *Cash paid to suppliers*

Creditors

	£'000		£'000
∴ Payments	1,195	Bal b/f	364
Bal c/f	291	Purchases (W6)	1,122
	<u>1,486</u>		<u>1,486</u>
			<u>1,486</u>

6   *Purchases*

	£'000	£'000
COS & expenses (962 + 172)		1,134
Stock adjustments:		
Opening stocks	(227)	
Closing stocks	360	
Non cash expenses:		133
Amortisation	(60)	
Depreciation	(57)	
Profit on disposal	7	
Disclosed separately:		(110)
Staff costs	(20)	
Interest	(15)	
		(35)
		1,122

67 Planter

Text reference. Chapter 21.

Top tips. An unusually straightforward cash flow question; they are normally combined with a written explanation or analysis. Any candidate who had practised this topic would score well.

Easy marks. 25 very easy marks if you work methodically through the question.

Examiner's comments. This question was popular and well answered. Common errors included:

- Wrong treatment of the interest accrual
- Failure to calculate tax correctly
- Failure to exclude non-cash items
- Inability to deal with the bonus issue

Marking scheme

	Marks
Reconciliation of operating profit to operating cash flows, one per item	8
Interest paid	2
Investment income	1
Taxation	2
Purchase of plant	2
Purchase of land and buildings	2
Sale of plant	1
Sale of investments	1
Ordinary dividend	2
Issue of ordinary shares	2
Redemption of loan notes	2
Decrease in cash	1
Available	**26**
Maximum for question	**25**

PLANTER

Reconciliation of operating profit to net cash inflow from operating activities

		£
Operating profit		17,900
Depreciation	W1	28,400
Loss on disposal of fixed assets	£7,800 - £12,000	4,200
Profit on disposal of investments	£11,000 - £8,700	(2,300)
(Increase) decrease in stocks	43,300 – 57,400	14,100
(Increase) decrease in debtors	50,400 – 28,600	(21,800)
Increase (decrease) in trade creditors	26,700 – 31,400	(4,700)
Net cash inflow from operating activities		35,800

CASH FLOW STATEMENT FOR THE YEAR ENDED 31 MARCH 20X4

		£	£
Net cash inflow from operating activities			35,800
Returns on investment and servicing of finance			
Investment income		400	
Interest paid	1,700 - 300	(1,400)	
			(1,000)
Taxation	8,900 + 1,100		(10,000)
Capital expenditure			
Receipts from sales of investments		11,000	
Receipts from sales of tangible fixed assets		7,800	
Payments to acquire tangible fixed assets	W1	(45,200)	
			(26,400)
			(1,600)
Equity dividends paid			(26,100)
			(27,700)
Financing activities			
Proceeds from issue of share capital	W2	28,000	
Repayment of loan	39,800 – 43,200	(3,400)	
			24,600
Net decrease in cash	-1,900 – 1,200		(3,100)

Workings

1   *Tangible fixed assets*

Summary

	Purchases	Depreciation
	£	£
Buildings	7,100	1,800
Plant	38,100	26,600
	45,200	28,400

Land and buildings

		Cost	Depreciation
		£	£
Opening		49,200	5,000
Revaluation	18,000 – 12,000	6,000	-
Depreciation	balancing figure	-	1,800
Purchases	Balancing figure	7,100	-
Closing		62,300	6,800

Plant

		Cost £	Depreciation £
Opening		70,000	22,500
Disposal		(23,500)	(11,500)
		46,500	11,000
Depreciation	Balancing figure	-	26,600
Purchases	Balancing figure	38,100	-
Closing		84,600	37,600

2 *Share issues*

	Capital £	Premium £	Total £
Opening	25,000	5,000	30,000
1 for 10 bonus issue	2,500	(2,500)	-
Cash issue (balancing figure)	22,500	5,500	28,000
Closing	50,000	8,000	58,000

68 Bigwood

Text reference. Chapters 19 and 21.

Top tips. This is a typical cash flow statement question, with half the marks for preparing the statement and half for interpretation. Make sure that you ring-fence half of your time for the interpretation in Part (b). Even if you haven't finished the cash flow statement, you will have identified the key points about Bigwood's financial position and performance. Also note that the question gives you the relevant ratios; you must explain the possible causes and consequences of these ratios.

Easy marks. The cash flow statement is 12 easy marks.

Examiner's comments. This required a cash flow statement, followed by analysis.

Part (a) was generally well answered although some candidates had trouble with disposal of fixed assets and the increase in the loan.

Part (b) on interpretation was very mixed. Disappointingly, few candidates calculated extra ratios and very few commented on the cash flow statement in part (a).

Marking scheme

		Marks
(a)	Net profit before tax	1
	Depreciation	1
	Loss on disposal	1
	Working capital items	3
	Interest paid	1
	Income tax paid	1
	Capital expenditure	1
	Disposal proceeds	1
	Equity dividends	1
	Financing – equity shares	1
	– loans	1
	Decrease in cash	1
	Available	**14**
	Maximum	**12**
(b)	Up to 3 marks for additional ratios	3
	1 mark per relevant point including 1 mark for format	10
	Maximum	**13**
	Maximum for question	**25**

(a) BIGWOOD

Reconciliation of operating profit to net cash inflow from operating activities

		£'000	£'000
Operating profit	P&L		1,000
Depreciation	W1		3,800
Loss on disposal of fixed assets			1,250
(Increase) decrease in trade debtors	(100 – 50)		(50)
(Increase) decrease in stocks	(2,900 – 1,500)		(1,400)
Increase (decrease) in trade creditors	(3,100 – 2,150)		950
Net cash inflow from operating activities			5,550

CASH FLOW STATEMENT FOR THE YEAR ENDED 30 SEPTEMBER 20X4

		£'000	£'000
Net cash inflow from operating activities			5,550
Returns on investments and servicing of finance			
Interest paid			(300)
Taxation	(450 + 250 – 220)		(480)
Capital expenditure			
Costs of disposal		(50)	
Payments to acquire tangible fixed assets	W1	(10,500)	
			(10,550)
			(5,780)
Equity dividends paid			(600)
			(6,380)
Financing			
Proceeds from issue of share capital	(5,000 + 1,000 – 3,000)	3,000	
Receipt of loan	(3,000 – 1,000)	2,000	
			5,000
Decrease in cash	(-930 – 450)		(1,380)

Working for tangible fixed assets

		Cost	Depreciation	NBV
		£'000	£'000	£'000
Opening		9,500	3,000	6,500
Scrapped		(3,000)	(1,800)	(1,200)
Depreciation	Balancing figure	-	3,800	(3,800)
Purchases	Balancing figure	10,500	-	10,500
Closing		17,000	5,000	12,000

Loss on disposal; NBV (£1,200,000) + disposal costs (£50,000) = £1,250,000.

(b)

Bigwood
Financial Position and Performance
Two years ending 30 September 20X4

Performance

During the year sales area increased by 35% (from 40,000m^2 to 54,000m^2), helping to increase sales by 17% (from £19.6m to £23m). The low increase in sales compared with floor space may be explained by the timing of the increase and the disruptions caused during refurbishment. The full benefit of the expansion may only be felt next year.

The relative performance of the two lines of trade suggests that the expansion has been misdirected towards clothing at the expense of food. Food floor space has increased by only 20%, but this has yielded a 75% increase in turnover accompanied by an increase in the gross profit margin from 25% to 32.1%. Clothing floor space increased by 37% but sales only rose by 2.5% and the gross profit margin halved from 18.6% to 9.4%.

The food lines are obviously popular, as sales and margins have grown. This demand for food has probably helped to decrease the stock holding period from 17 days to 15 days, which is always a good thing for perishable products like food.

The situation with clothing is the reverse; the fall in margins and barely static sales suggests that prices have had to be slashed to shift stock. This is not sustainable in the long run. Even with discounted prices, the level of unsold clothes has mounted from 39 days to 68 days. This is worrying in a seasonal and fashionable business like clothing, and may suggest that further price cuts will be needed to shift clothing before it becomes out of date.

One puzzling statistic is that the margin on food is higher than that on clothing. Normally food sells at a very low margin compensated for by high turnover. This suggests that Bigwood has specialised in high value-added foods rather than basic groceries.

The information given encourages depreciation to be apportioned between the products on the basis of floor space. This apportionment results in a loss of £1,878,000 after depreciation for clothing, wiping out the £1,828,000 profit made by food. These figures must be treated with caution because the refrigeration equipment needed to sell food will have a higher depreciation charge than the coat hangers needed to sell clothes.

Operating expenses have grown faster than sales, rising from 9.7% of turnovers to 12%. Normally expenses are expected to decrease as a percentage of sales as economies of scale kick in. This increase suggests either poor cost control (which is worrying) or some one-off costs associated with the expansion and refurbishment.

The high level of investment and poor profitability is reflected by the decline in the ROCE from 33.9% to 9.3%. Hopefully next year will see a full year of profits from the enlarged and refurbished business and a reduction in costs.

Liquidity

The current ratio has deteriorated slightly from 0.77 to 0.71; however this low ratio is not unusual for retailers and is often seen as a sign of efficient working capital management. The increase in the accounts creditor payment period from 50 to 59 days is not a problem as long as it does not rise further next year; a longer payment period might create bad will amongst Bigwood's suppliers.

At first glance it appears that the long-term liquidity of Bigwood gives cause for concern, with a net outflow of cash of £1.38m, an increase in gearing from 17% to 28% and a fall in interest cover from 25 times to 3.3 times. However, the situation is healthier than it looks as is explained below.

Bigwood has lost £1.38m of cash despite £3m of new share capital and £2m of new loans. But this new finance only covered half of the £10.5m of capital expenditure. This means that £4m of the expenditure came from cash generated during the year. If Bigwood takes a rest from expansion next year then it should generate another £4m of free cash which is enough to payoff the £930,000 overdraft and the £3m of loans.

Although the P&L reports a fall in interest cover from 25 to 3.3, the cash flow statement shows that cash generated from operations is 18.5 times the interest paid, which is quite comfortable.

Investor ratios

The fall in the share price from £6 to £3 shows that investors are pessimistic about Bigwood's future, although some of the fall will have been caused by the dilution from the share issue. The dividend per share will have decreased from 20 cents to 12 cents because of this issue, which will depress the share price.

The total dividend has been maintained at the cost of reducing the dividend cover from 2.33 to 0.75. Paying out dividends bigger than profits is unsustainable, but it may be intended to advertise the management's confidence in Bigwood's future. Net cash inflows from operating activities of £4.77m are about 8 times the dividend paid, and so the relatively high dividend will not be an immediate problem.

Summary

The results for 20X4 are disappointing considering the amount of investment put into the business. However, the future should be better for the following reasons:

The business generates £4m of free cash each year. This will reduce Bigwood's debts and finance costs, and provide funds for further expansion.

Next year should see a full year of increased profits from this year's capital expenditure, without the disruption caused by the redevelopment.

Management could help Bigwood's recovery by allocating more resources to the profitable food lines and by purchasing more popular clothing.

Additional ratios

Floor space	20X4	20X3	
Clothes	48,000	35,000	+ 37%
Food	6,000	5,000	+ 20%
Total	54,000	40,000	+ 35%

Sales			
Clothes	16,000	15,600	+ 2.5%
Food	7,000	4,000	+ 75%
Total	23,000	19,600	+ 17.3%

Profitability			
20X4	Clothes	Food	Total
Sales	16,000	7,000	23,000
Cost of sales	(14,500)	(4,750)	(19,250)
Gross profit	1,500	2,250	3,750
Depreciation	(3,378)	(422)	(3,800)
	(1,878)	1,828	(50)

Operating expense %			
20X4	Expense	2,750	= 12%
	Turnover	23,000	
20X3		1,900	
		19,600	= 9.7%

Interest cover in cash

Cash from operations	£5,550,000	= 18.5 times
Interest paid	£300,000	

Dividend cover

20X4	450/600	= 0.75
20X3	1,400/600	= 2.33

69 Casino

Text reference. Chapter 21.

Top tips. The cash flow itself is reasonably straight forward, although there are small complications involving property and finance costs. Start with the pro-forma and set your workings out clearly.

Easy marks. Do not neglect the 5 easy marks in part (b).

Examiner's comments. This question was well-answered and many candidates scored high marks. Some candidates had trouble with fixed assets and depreciation.

Other problem areas were:

- inflows treated as outflows and vice versa
- cash flow for interest paid and received and dividends
- ignoring effect of deferred tax
- poor format knowledge

Marking scheme

		Marks
(a)	Operating loss	1
	Depreciation and loss on sale	4
	Working capital items	3
	Taxation	2
	Capital expenditure	4
	Equity dividends	1
	Management of liquid resources	2
	Financing	3
	Max	20
(b)	1 mark per relevant point	5
		25

(a)   CASINO
        RECONCILIATION OF OPERATING LOSS TO NET CASH OUTFLOW FROM OPERATING ACTIVITIES

		£m
Operating loss		(32)
Depreciation	W1	93
Amortisation	(510 – 400)	110
Loss on disposal of fixed assets	from question	12
(Increase) decrease in trade & other debtors	(350 – 420)	70
(Increase) decrease in stocks	(808 – 372)	(436)
Increase (decrease) in trade creditors	(530 – 515)	15
Net cash outflow from operating activities		(168)

CASH FLOW STATEMENT FOR THE YEAR ENDED 31 MARCH 20X5

		£m	£m
Net cash outflow from operating activities			(168)
Return on investments and servicing of finance			
Investment income	(3 + 12 – 5)	10	
Interest paid		(16)	
			(6)
Taxation	W2		(81)
Capital expenditure			
Receipts from sales of tangible fixed assets	from question	15	
Payments to acquire tangible fixed assets	W1	(170)	
			(155)
			(410)
Equity dividends paid	from question		(25)
			(435)
Management of liquid resources	(120-32)		88
Financing			
Proceeds from issue of share capital	[(300 + 60) – 200]	160	
Proceeds of loan	(160 – 2 issue costs)	158	
Repayment of loan	(150 + 6 penalty)	(156)	
			162
Decrease in cash	W3		(185)

Workings

1   *Property, plant and equipment*

        Summary

	Purchases	Depreciation
	£m	£m
Buildings	110	12
Plant	60	81
	170	93

        Land and buildings at carrying value

		£m
Opening		420
Revaluation	from question	70
Depreciation	See * below	(12)
		478
Purchases	Balancing figure	110
Closing		588

*The revaluation will have cleared out the opening depreciation, so the charge must be the same as the closing balance.

Plant at carrying value

		£m
Opening		340
Additions	from question	60
Disposals	see below	(27)
		373
Depreciation	Balancing figure	(81)
Closing		292

Carrying value of disposals; proceeds £15m, loss £12m, carrying value £27m.

2   *Tax*

C/d	Current	15	B/f	Current	110
	Deferred	90		Deferred	75
			Charge		1
Cash paid	balance	81			-
		186			186

3   *Cash and overdrafts*

	20X5 £m	20X4 £m
Bank and cash in hand	15	75
Overdrafts	(125)	-
Net cash	(110)	75
Decrease	(185)	

(b)   *Usefulness and reliability*

It is often said that cash flow statements are more useful and reliable than profit and loss accounts. This claim is made because cash is the life blood of a business. Without cash the business cannot grow, repay its borrowings, service its finance, or pay a dividend. Without cash a business will wither and eventually fail. Therefore cash generation is more important than profitability.

Cash flow statements are also seen as being more reliable than income statements. Profit is based on the accruals concept which requires asset lives, provisions, fair values, contract profitability, impairment and so on to be estimated. Because this is subjective it is possible to have two different, but equally valid, profit figures. Cash is not subjective; cash inflows and outflows are all a question of fact.

However, cash flow statements are not as objective as they first seem. Cash inflow can be boosted by cutting back on investment and delaying the payment of creditors. This will give the illusion of success in the short run, but is bottling up investment expense and supplier bad will for the future. Even honest managers would be reluctant to make long-term investments if they thought that they would be judged solely on short-term cash generation. By matching income and expenditure, the P&L gives the reader a better understanding of the long term profitability of the company.

The cash flow statement and profit and loss account are meant to complement each other. The quality of the profits claimed in the P&L can be assessed by comparing them with the cash generated from operations in the cash flow statement. The sustainability of dividends can also be assessed with reference to the cash flow statement.

70 Tabba

Marking scheme

			Marks
(a)	Reconciliation of operating profit to cash flows	8	
	Interest paid and received	2	
	Taxation	2	
	Sale of factory	1	
	Purchase of fixed assets	1	
	Government grant	1	
	Loan redemption and issue	2	
	Repayment of finance lease	2	
	Increase in cash	1	
		20	
	Maximum		17
(b)	1 mark per relevant point		8
			25

(a) TABBA
RECONCILIATION OF OPERATING PROFIT TO NET CASH OUTFLOW FROM OPERATING ACTIVITIES

		£m	£m
Profit before interest and taxation			270
Adjustments for:			
Depreciation	W1		2,200
Profit on disposal of fixed assets	W1		(4,600)
Release of grant	W2		(250)
Increase in insurance claim debtor	1,500 – 1,200		(300)
Working capital adjustments			
(Increase) decrease in stocks	(2,550 – 1,850)		(700)
(Increase) decrease in trade & other debtors	(3,100 – 2,600)		(500)
Increase (decrease) in trade creditors	(4,050 – 2,950)		1,100
Net cash outflow from operating activities			(2,780)

CASH FLOW STATEMENT FOR THE YEAR ENDED 30 SEPTEMBER 20X5

		£m	£m
Net cash outflow from operating activities			(2,780)
Returns on investments and servicing of finance			
Interest received		40	
Interest paid		(260)	
			(220)
Taxation	W3		(1,350)
Capital expenditure			
Proceeds of grants	From question	950	
Proceeds from sale of factory	From question	12,000	
Purchase of fixed assets	W1	(2,900)	
			10,050
			5,700
Financing			
Proceeds of loan	6% loan received	800	
Repayment of loan	10% loan repaid	(4,000)	
Payments on finance leases	W4	(1,100)	
			(4,300)
Increase in cash	550 o/d to 850 in hand		1,400

Workings

W1 *Fixed assets*

	Cost	Depreciation	Carrying value	Revaluation
	£'000	£'000	£'000	£'000
Opening	20,200	4,400	15,800	1,600
Finance lease additions	1,500	-	1,500	
Disposals	(8,600)	(1,200)	(7,400)	(1,600)
Subtotal	13,100	3,200	9,900	-
Additions*	2,900	-	2,900	
Depreciation charge*	-	2,200	(2,200)	-
Closing	16,000	5,400	10,600	-

*Balancing figures

W2 *Release of grant*

		£'000
Opening	400 + 900	1,300
Received	from question	950
Released	Balancing figure	(250)
Closing	1,400 + 600	2,000

W3

			Tax			
C/d	Current	100	B/f	Current	1,200
	Deferred	200		Deferred	500
P&L credit		50			
Cash paid	balance	1,350			-
		1,700			1,700

W4

			Movement on finance lease			
C/d	Current	2,000	B/f	Current	1,700
	Non-current	900		Non-current	800
			New		1,500
Cash paid	balance	1,350			-
		4,000			4,000

(b)   Changes in Tabba's financial position

The last section of the cash flow statement reveals a healthy increase in cash of £1.4m. However, Tabba is losing cash hand over foot and its going concern status must be in doubt.

To survive and thrive businesses must generate cash from their operations; but Tabba has absorbed £2.78m. Whereas most companies report higher operating cash inflows than profits, Tabba has reported the reverse. The only reason Tabba was able to report a profit was because of the one-off £4.6m surplus on disposal. There were two other items that inflated profits without generating cash; a £300,000 increase in the insurance claim debtor and a £250,000 release of a government grant. Without these three items Tabba would have reported a £5.1m loss before tax.

Were it not for the disposal proceeds Tabba would be reporting a £10.6m net decrease in cash. Tabba has no other major assets to sell and so the coming year will see a large outflow of cash unless Tabba's trading position improves. When the current operating lease expires in four years time there will probably be a rent hike, further damaging Tabba's profitability and cash flows.

The high tax bill for the previous year suggests that Tabba's fall from profitability has been swift and steep. Despite this downturn in trade Tabba's stocks and debtors have increased, suggesting poor financial management. This in turn damages cash flow, which is indicated by the increase in the level of creditors.

There are some good signs though. Investment in fixed assets has continued, although £1.5m of this was on finance leases which are often a sign of cash shortages. Some of the disposal proceeds have been used to redeem the expensive £4m 10% loan and replace it with a smaller and cheaper £800,000 6% loan. This will save £352,000 per annum.

Tabba's recovery may depend on whether the circumstances causing the slump in profits and cash flow will either disappear of their own accord or whether Tabba can learn to live with them. The cash flow statement has however highlighted some serious issues for the shareholders to discuss with the directors at the annual general meeting.

71 Minster

Text references. Chapters 19 and 21.

Top tips. In this question 40% of the marks were for commenting on the financial position and performance of the company. This was not that simple, and it was important not to spend too long on the cash flow statement and leave insufficient time for (b).

Easy marks. The easy marks here were the cash flow statement. There were a few complexities such as the unwinding of the discount, on which you should not have wasted much time, but it was otherwise straightforward and you should have scored good marks on it. Part (b) was not that easy because there were no obvious issues to report on. The company was not failing or overtrading or doing tremendously well either. So it was important to look at the information in the question and the cash flow statement and see what you could learn from them, rather than computing a raft of ratios.

Marks

(a) cash from operating activity

operating profit	1
depreciation/amortisation	2
working capital items	2
finance costs	2
investment income	1
income taxes paid	2
capital expenditure	3
financing – issue of ordinary shares	1
– issue of 9% loan	1
dividend paid	1
decrease in cash	1
available	17
Maximum	**15**

(b) 1 mark per relevant point

	10
Maximum for question	25

(a) MINSTER

CASH FLOW STATEMENT FOR THE YEAR ENDED 30 SEPTEMBER 2006

	£'000	£'000
Net cash inflow from operating activities (Note 1)		372
Returns on investments and servicing of finance		
Investment income received (20 – 15 (investment gain))	5	
Finance costs (40 – 12 (unwinding of discount))	(28)	
Net cash outflow from returns on investments and servicing of finance		(23)
Taxation (W1)		(54)
Capital expenditure		
Tangible fixed assets (W2)	(410)	
Software	(180)	
Investments (150 – 125 – 15)	(10)	
Net cash outflow from capital expenditure		(600)
Equity dividends paid (500 × 4 × 5p)		(100)
Cash outflow before financing		(405)
Financing		
9% loan note	120	
Share issue (125 share cap + 140 premium)	265	
Net cash inflow from financing		385
Decrease in cash		(20)

Note 1

Reconciliation of operating profit to net cash inflow from operating activities

	£'000	£'000
Operating profit		162
Depreciation		255
Software amortisation (180 – 135)		45
		462
Working capital adjustments:		
Decrease in stock	30	
Decrease in debtors	110	
Decrease in creditors	(205)	
Increase in amounts due from long-term contracts	(25)	
		(90)
Net cash inflow from operating activities		372

Workings

1   *Taxation*

	£'000
Balance b/f	50
Charge for year	57
Reduction in deferred tax provision	7
Tax paid (balancing figure)	(54)
Balance c/f	60

2   *Tangible fixed assets*

Balance b/f	940
Environmental provision	150
Revaluation (60 – 25)	35
Depreciation	(255)
Acquisitions (balancing figure)	410
Balance c/f	1,280

(b)   **Re: financial performance and position of Minster**

Minster's net assets have increased by £285,000 over the year. The company shows a gross profit percentage of 20% and a net profit percentage of 10% - both quite healthy - and its net cash from operating activities is £372,000. However, the profit and loss account balance has decreased by £15,000 due to the payment of a dividend in excess of the net profit after tax. There has also been a bonus issue during the year, so Minster's shareholders have been well rewarded.

There are some significant changes in working capital levels over the year. Stock and creditors have both decreased. This could be due to more efficient purchasing and stock control, perhaps the introduction of a JIT system. The level of debtors has also declined, perhaps due to more efficient credit collection. Conversely, these changes could be due to a reduction in the level of activity, rather than any increase in efficiency but, looking at the large investment in fixed assets, it appears unlikely that the business is 'winding down' to any degree. This is borne out by the increase in long-term contract WIP.

The most noticeable feature in the cash flow statement is the heavy investment in fixed assets. As there are no disposals and no fixed assets were scrapped, this suggests expansion into new business activities or processes, rather than replacement of worn out or obsolete machinery. In addition to £410,000 on tangible fixed assets, £180,000 has been spent on software licences, which suggests that the new fixed assets comprise equipment which will computerise some of Minster's processes. This reflects positive expectations about the future trading environment.

This investment has been funded by a 9% loan note and a share issue, presumably a rights issue. The rights issue yielded £265,000, reflecting the confidence of shareholders. The loan note issue, offset by the share issue, takes Minster's gearing to just over 7%. This is still low and the interest, while fairly high, is at least tax-deductible. There would have to be a very significant downturn in the business for it to be unable to afford the interest payments and, if the extra investment pays off and profits rise, the returns to shareholders will be greater than if more funds had been raised from another equity issue, which would have diluted shareholdings.

72 Preparation question: Changing prices

Top tips. In this question the current cost adjustments are given to you but you must understand how they are calculated.

(a)   CURRENT COST OPERATING PROFIT FOR 20X6

	£m	£m
Historical cost operating profit		15
Current cost adjustments:		
Depreciation adjustment	3	
Cost of sales adjustment	5	
		(8)
Current cost operating profit		7

SUMMARISED CURRENT COST BALANCE SHEET
AS AT 31 DECEMBER 20X6

	£m	£m
Fixed assets		85
Current assets		
Stocks	21	
Debtors	30	
Bank	2	
	53	
Current liabilities	30	
		23
		108
Long-term liability		(20)
		88
Capital and reserves		88

(b)   (i)   **Interest cover**

       HC accounts: 15 ÷ 3 = 5 times
       CC accounts: 7 ÷ 3 = 2.3 times

    (ii)   **Return on shareholders' equity**

       HC accounts: 12 ÷ 62 = 19.4%
       CC accounts: 4 ÷ 88 = 4.5%

    (iii) **Debt/equity ratio**

       HC accounts: 20 ÷ 62 = 32.3%
       CC accounts: 20 ÷ 88 = 22.7%

(c)   (i)   **Interest cover**

       Companies must maintain their capital base if they wish to stay in business. The significance of the interest cover calculation is that it indicates the extent to which profits after tax are being eaten into by payments to finance external capital. The figures calculated above indicate that only one-fifth of historical cost profit is being absorbed in this way, while four-fifths are being retained to finance future growth. On the face of it, this might seem satisfactory; however, the current cost interest cover is only 2.3 times indicating that, after allowing for the impact of rising prices, interest payments absorb nearly half of profits after tax.

(ii)   **Return on shareholders' equity**

This is the ratio of profits earned for shareholders (ie profits after interest) to shareholders' equity. Once again, the position disclosed by the historical cost accounts is more favourable than appears from the current cost ratio. The historical cost profit is higher than the current cost profit because no allowance is made for the adverse impact of rising prices; and at the same time the denominator in the historical cost fraction is lower because shareholders' capital is stated at historical values rather than their higher current values.

The significance of the ratio is that it enables shareholders to assess the rate of return on their investment and to compare it with alternative investments that might be available to them.

(iii)   **Debt/equity ratio**

The significance of this ratio is as a measure of the extent to which the company's net assets are financed by external borrowing and shareholders' funds respectively.

In times of rising prices it can be beneficial to finance assets from loan capital. While the assets appreciate in value over time (and the gain accrues to shareholders), the liability is fixed in monetary amount. The effect of this is that current cost accounts tend to give a more favourable picture of the debt/equity ratio than historical cost accounts. In the ratios calculated above, the amount of debt is £20m in both balance sheets. This represents nearly one-third of the historical cost value of shareholders' funds, but only one-fifth of the equity calculated on a current cost basis.

73 Update

(a)   *Problems with historic cost*

Although retail price inflation has eased throughout the developed world, it is still a big issue for many businesses.

The net book values of property and other assets with long useful lives soon become unrealistic if based on historic cost, leading to the following problems:

- Even with modest inflation, the depreciation charge on these assets will be too low in comparison with the revenues that the assets are generating, inflating operating profits.

- The return on capital employed is doubly distorted; not only are operating profits overstated, but the related net assets will be understated, resulting in a flattering and unrealistic return. This makes it difficult to compare two companies with similar assets if those assets were bought at different times.

- Low asset values reduce the net assets of a business. This exaggerates the gearing ratio, which might dissuade banks from advancing loans to the business. It might also cause the stock market to undervalue a business.

The traditional solution to these problems is to revalue certain items. However, this creates a hybrid set of financial statements, with some assets at historic cost and others at valuation.

(b)   *Alternative methods*

	Historic cost £		CPP £		Current cost £
Cost / Valuation	250,000	(a)	300,000	(b)	280,000
Net book value based on 2 years depreciation (c)	160,000		192,000		179,200
Net book value based on 3 years depreciation (d)	128,000		153,600		143,360
Depreciation charge for this year (c – d = e)	32,000		38,400		35,840

(i)   The original cost of £250,000 will be indexed up for the change in the retail price index between the date of purchase and the balance sheet date.

£250,000 × 216 / 180 = £300,000

(ii)   The current cost will be reduced to reflect the lower productivity of the old asset.

£320,000 × 420 / 480 = £280,000

(iii)   The net book value after two years depreciation at 20% reducing balance will be 64% of the gross amount (0.8 × 0.8).

(iv)   The net book value after three years depreciation at 20% reducing balance will be 51.2% of the gross amount (0.8 × 0.8 × 0.8).

(v)   This years charge will be the difference between (c) and (d).

Mock Exams

ACCA Fundamentals Level

Paper F7

Financial Reporting

(UK)

Mock Examination 1

Question Paper	
Time allowed	
Reading and Planning Writing	**15 minutes** **3 hours**
Answer all FIVE questions	

DO NOT OPEN THIS PAPER UNTIL YOU ARE READY TO START UNDER EXAMINATION CONDITIONS

Question 1 Horsefield

Horsefield plc acquired 90% of Sandfly plc's ordinary shares on 1 April 20X0 paying £3 per share. The balance on Sandfly plc's profit and loss account reserve at this date was £800,000. On 1 October 20X1, Horsefield plc acquired 30% of Anthill plc's £1 ordinary shares for £3.50 per share. The balance sheets of the three companies at 31 March 20X2 are shown below:

	Horsefield plc		Sandfly plc		Anthill plc	
	£'000	£'000	£'000	£'000	£'000	£'000
Fixed assets						
Leasehold	3,200		2,000		1,000	
Plant	4,850		1,600		650	
		8,050		3,600		1,650
Investments		4,000		910		nil
		12,050		4,510		1,650
Current assets						
Stock	830		340		250	
Debtors	520		290		350	
Bank	240		nil		100	
	1,590		630		700	
Creditors: amounts falling due within one year						
Creditors	420		960		200	
Taxation	220		250		150	
Overdraft	nil		190		nil	
	(640)		(1,400)		(350)	
Net current assets (liabilities)		950		(770)		350
Creditors: amounts falling due after more than one year						
10% loan notes		(500)		(240)		(nil)
Net assets		12,500		3,500		2,000
Share capital and reserves:						
Ordinary shares of £1 each		5,000		1,200		600
Reserves:						
Profit and loss account b/f	6,000		1,400		800	
Profit year to 31 March 20X2	1,500		900		600	
		7,500		2,300		1,400
		12,500		3,500		2,000

The following information is relevant.

(i)   Fair value adjustments.

On 1 April 20X0 Sandfly plc owned an investment property that had a fair value of £120,000 in excess of its book value. The value of this property has not changed since acquisition.

Just prior to its acquisition, Sandfly plc was successful in applying for a six-year licence to dispose of hazardous waste. The licence was granted by the government at no cost, however Horsefield plc estimated that the licence was worth £180,000 at the date of acquisition.

(ii)   In January 20X2 Horsefield plc sold goods to Anthill plc for £65,000. These were transferred at a mark up of 30% on cost. Two thirds of these goods were still in the stock of Anthill plc at 31 March 20X2.

(iii)   To facilitate the consolidation procedures the group insists that all inter company creditor balances are settled prior to the year end. However, a cheque for £40,000 from Sandfly plc to Horsefield plc was not received until early April 20X2. Inter company balances are included in debtors and creditors as appropriate.

(iv)   The group accounting policy for goodwill is to write it off on a straight-line basis over a period of five years, with a proportionate charge where it arises part way through an accounting period.

(v)   Anthill plc is to be treated as an associated company of Horsefield plc.

Required

(a)   Prepare the consolidated balance sheet of Horsefield plc at 31 March 20X2   **(20 marks)**

(b)   Discuss the matters to consider in determining whether an investment in another company constitutes associated company status   **(5 marks)**

(Total = 25 marks)

Question 2 Tintagel

Reproduced below is the draft balance sheet of Tintagel, a public listed company, as at 31 March 20X4.

	£'000	£'000
Tangible fixed assets (note (i))		
Freehold property		126,000
Plant		110,000
Investment property (note (ii))		15,000
		251,000
Current assets		
Stock (note (iii))	60,400	
Trade debtors and prepayments	31,200	
Bank	13,800	
	105,400	
Creditors: amounts falling due within one year		
Trade creditors (note (iii))	47,400	
Provision for plant overhaul (note (iv))	12,000	
Taxation	4,200	
	(63,600)	
Net current assets		41,800
Provisions for liabilities		
Deferred tax – at 1 April 20X3 (note (v))		(18,700)
Suspense account (note (vi))		(14,100)
Net assets		260,000
Share capital and reserves		
Ordinary shares of 25p each		150,000
Reserves:		
Share premium	10,000	
Investment property revaluation reserve (note (ii))	3,400	
Profit and loss account – 1 April 20X3	48,100	
– Year to 31 March 20X4	48,500	
		110,000
		260,000

The following information is relevant.

(i)   The profit and loss account has been charged with £3·2 million being the first of four equal annual rental payments for an item of plant. This first payment was made on 1 April 20X3. Tintagel has been advised that this is a finance lease. The plant had a cash price of £11·2 million at the inception of the lease, which has an implicit interest rate of 10% per annum. Rentals are paid in advance.

None of the fixed assets have been depreciated for the current year. The freehold property should be depreciated at 2% on its cost of £130 million. Plant in the balance sheet comprises:

	£'000
Heavy excavating plant	50,000
Other plant	60,000
	110,000

Plant other than heavy excavating plant and leased plant is depreciated at 20% on a reducing balance basis. Leased plant is depreciated on a straight line basis over four years. Information about heavy excavating plant is in note (iv).

(ii) The investment property is a freehold property carried at its valuation on 31 March 20X3. Its value at 31 March 20X4 has been assessed by a qualified surveyor at £12·4 million.

(iii) During a stock count on 31 March 20X4 items that had cost £6 million were identified as being either damaged or slow moving. It is estimated that they will only realise £4 million in total, on which sales commission of 10% will be payable. An invoice for materials delivered on 12 March 20X4 for £500,000 has been discovered. It has not been recorded in Tintagel's bookkeeping system, although the materials were included in the stock count.

(iv) Tintagel operates some heavy excavating plant which requires a major overhaul every three years. The overhaul is estimated to cost £18 million and is due to be carried out in April 20X5. The provision of £12 million represents two annual amounts of £6 million made in the years to 31 March 20X3 and 20X4. The plant was purchased for £60m on 1 April 20X2 and it has a 6 year life. It is depreciated on a straight line basis.

(v) The deferred tax provision required at 31 March 20X4 has been calculated at £22·5 million.

(vi) The suspense account contains the credit entry relating to the issue on 1 October 20X3 of a £15 million 8% loan note. It was issued at a discount of 5% and incurred direct issue costs of £150,000. It is redeemable after four years at a premium of 10%. Interest is payable every six months in arrears. The first payment of interest has not been accrued and is due on 1 April 20X4. The effective rate of interest is 12.1%.

Required

(a) Commencing with the profit and loss account reserve figures in the above balance sheet (£48·1 million and £48·5 million), prepare a schedule of adjustments required to these figures taking into account any adjustments required by notes (i) to (vi) above. **(10 marks)**

(b) Redraft the balance sheet of Tintagel as at 31 March 20X4 taking into account the adjustments required in notes (i) to (vi) above. **(15 marks)**

Notes to the financial statements are NOT required. **(Total = 25 marks)**

Question 3 Nedberg

The financial statements of Nedberg plc for the year to 30 September 20X2, together with the comparative balance sheet as at 30 September 20X1 are shown below.

PROFIT AND LOSS ACCOUNT
YEAR TO 30 SEPTEMBER 20X2

	£m
Turnover	3,820
Cost of sales (note (1))	(2,620)
Gross profit for period	1,200
Operating expenses (note (1))	(300)
	900
Interest – loan note	(30)
Profit before tax	870
Taxation	(270)
Profit after tax	600

BALANCE SHEETS AS AT 30 SEPTEMBER

	20X2		20X1	
	£m	£m	£m	£m
Fixed assets				
Intangible assets (note (2))		650		300
Tangible assets		1,890		1,830
		2,540		2,130
Current assets				
Stock	1,420		940	
Debtors	990		680	
Cash	70		nil	
	2,480		1,620	
Creditors: amounts falling due within one year (note (3))	(1,020)		(1,010)	
Net current assets		1,460		610
Creditors: amounts falling due after more than one year				
10% Loan note		(300)		(100)
Provisions for liabilities (note (4))		(570)		(440)
Net assets		3,130		2,200
Share capital and reserves				
Ordinary shares of £1 each		750		500
Reserves:				
Share premium	350		100	
Revaluation	140		nil	
Profit and loss reserve	1,890	2,380	1,600	1,700
		3,130		2,200

Notes to the financial statements

(1) Cost of sales includes depreciation of tangible fixed assets of £320 million and a loss on the sale of plant of £50 million. It also includes a credit for the amortisation of government grants. Operating expenses include a charge of £20 million for the amortisation of goodwill.

(2)　Intangible fixed assets

	20X2	20X1
	£m	£m
Deferred development expenditure	470	100
Goodwill	180	200
	650	300

(3)　Creditors: amounts falling due within one year

	20X2	20X1
	£m	£m
Creditors	875	730
Bank overdraft	nil	115
Accrued loan interest	15	5
Taxation	130	160
	1,020	1,010

(4)　Provisions for liabilities.

	20X2	20X1
	£m	£m
Government grants	260	300
Deferred tax	310	140
	570	440

The following additional information is relevant.

(i)　**Intangible fixed assets**

The company successfully completed the development of a new product during the current year, capitalising a further £500 million before amortisation charges for the period.

(ii)　**Tangible fixed assets/revaluation reserve**

- The company revalued its buildings by £200 million on 1 October 20X1. The surplus was credited to a revaluation reserve.

- New plant was acquired during the year at a cost of £250 million and a government grant of £50 million was received for this plant.

- On 1 October 20X1 a bonus issue of 1 new share for every 10 held was made from the revaluation reserve.

- £10 million has been transferred from the revaluation reserve to realised profits as a year-end adjustment in respect of the additional depreciation created by the revaluation.

- The remaining movement on tangible fixed assets was due to the disposal of obsolete plant.

(iii)　**Share issues**

In addition to the bonus issue referred to above Nedberg plc made a further issue of ordinary shares for cash.

(iv)　**Dividends**

Dividends paid during the year totalled £320,000.

Required

(a)　A cash flow statement for Nedberg plc for the year to 30 September 20X2 prepared in accordance with FRS 1 'Cash flow statements'. **(20 marks)**

Note. A reconciliation and analysis of net debt is not required.

(b)　Comment briefly on the financial position of Nedberg plc as portrayed by the information in your cash flow statement. **(5 marks)**

(Total = 25 marks)

Question 4 Shiplake

Shiplake plc is preparing its financial statements to 31 March 20X2. The following situations have been identified by an impairment review team.

(a)   On 1 April 20X1 Shiplake plc acquired two wholly owned subsidiary companies, Halyard plc and Mainstay plc, in separate acquisitions. Consolidated goodwill was calculated as:

	Halyard plc £'000	Mainstay plc £'000
Purchase consideration	12,000	4,500
Estimated fair value of net assets	(8,000)	(3,000)
Consolidated goodwill	4,000	1,500

A review of the fair value of each subsidiary's net assets was undertaken in March 20X2. Unfortunately both companies' net assets had declined in value. The estimated value of Halyard plc's net assets as at 1 April 20X1 was now only £7 million. This was due to more detailed information becoming available about the market value of its specialised properties. Mainstay plc's net assets were estimated to have a fair value of £500,000 less than their carrying value. This fall was due to some physical damage occurring to its plant and machinery. Shiplake plc amortises all goodwill over a five year life.

(3 marks)

(b)   Shiplake plc has an item of earth-moving plant, which is hired out to companies on short-term contracts. Its carrying value, based on depreciated historical cost, is £400,000. The estimated selling price of this asset is only £250,000, with associated selling expenses of £5,000. A recent review of its value in use based on its forecast future cash flows was estimated at £500,000. Since this review was undertaken there has been a dramatic increase in interest rates that has significantly increased the cost of capital used by Shiplake plc to discount the future cash flows of the plant.   **(4 marks)**

(c)   Shiplake plc is engaged in a research and development project to produce a new product. In the year to 31 March 20X1 the company spent £120,000 on research that concluded that there were sufficient grounds to carry the project on to its development stage and a further £75,000 has been spent on development. At that date management had decided that they were not sufficiently confident in the ultimate profitability of the project and wrote off all the expenditure to date to the profit and loss account. In the current year further direct development costs have been incurred of £80,000 and the development work is now almost complete with only an estimated £10,000 of costs to be incurred in the future. Production is expected to commence within the next few months. Unfortunately the total trading profit from sales of the new product is not expected to be as good as market research data originally forecast and is estimated at only £150,000. As the future benefits are greater than the remaining future costs, the project will be completed, but due to overall deficit expected, the directors have again decided to write off all the development expenditure.   **(4 marks)**

(d)   Shiplake plc owns a company called Klassic Kars. Extracts from Shiplake plc's consolidated balance sheet relating to Klassic Kars are:

	£'000
Goodwill	80,000
Franchise costs	50,000
Restored vehicles (at cost)	90,000
Plant	100,000
Other net assets	50,000
	370,000

The restored vehicles have an estimated realisable value of £115 million. The franchise agreement contains a 'sell back' clause, which allows Klassic Kars to relinquish the franchise and gain a repayment of £30 million from the franchiser. An impairment review at 31 March 20X2 has estimated that the value of Klassic Kars as a going concern is only £240 million   **(4 marks)**

Required

Explain, with numerical illustrations where possible, how the information in (i) to (iv) above would affect the preparation of Shiplake plc's consolidated financial statements to 31 March 20X2. **(15 marks as indicated)**

Question 5 Creative accounting

(a) Explain, with relevant example, what is generally meant by the term 'creative accounting'. **(5 marks)**

(b) Explain why it is important to record the substance rather than the legal form of transactions and describe the features that may indicate that the substance of a transaction is different from its legal form. **(5 marks)**

(Total = 10 marks)

Answers

DO NOT TURN THIS PAGE UNTIL YOU HAVE
COMPLETED THE MOCK EXAM

A PLAN OF ATTACK

If this were the real Financial Reporting exam and you had been told to turn over and begin, what would be going through your mind?

Perhaps you're having a panic. You've spent most your study time on groups and interpretation of accounts (because that's what your tutor/BPP study Text told you to do), plus a selection of other topics, and you're really not sure that you know enough. The good news is that you can always get a solid start by tackling the first question, which is **always on group accounts.** So calm down. Spend the first few moments or so **looking at the paper,** and develop a **plan of attack.**

Looking through the paper

As it will be in the real exam, Question 1 is on group accounts. Here you have a consolidated balance sheet with one subsidiary and one associate, together with a discussion of associate status.

- Question 2 requires adjustments to draft accounts and preparing a restated balance sheet.

- Question 3 is a cash flow statement and comment on financial position.

- Question 4 is a scenario question on impairment of assets.

- Question 5 is a discussion on creative accounting.

All of these questions are compulsory

Question 1 is straightforward as long as you are able to deal with an associate.

Question 2 looks nasty but in fact the numbers are not difficult and you should get marks for detailed workings

Question 3 is a cash flow statement. Always a good one to go for. Remember to set up your pro-forma and work logically through the points.

Question 4 requires good knowledge of FRS 11.

Question 5 requires some thought. All the points you make must be relevant.

Allocating your time

BPP's advice is always allocate your time **according to the marks for the question** in total and for the parts of the question. But **use common sense.** If you're doing Question 4 but haven't a clue how to do Part (b), you might be advised to re-allocate you time and pick up more marks on, say, Question 5, where you can always add something to your discussion.

After the exam…Forget about it!

And don't worry if you found the paper difficult. More than likely other candidates will too. If this were the real thing you would need to **forget** the exam the minute you left the exam hall and **think about the next one.** Or, if it's the last one, **celebrate**!

Learn from this Mock

This mock is difficult. No one said it was going to be easy. **Do not brood** on your lack of knowledge in certain areas. Make a note of holes in your knowledge and do your best to plug them. This may mean redoing the bits where you are weak.

Remember technique is important.

- Know **what you are going to do** when you open the exam on the day.

- Know that you will select questions **after a thorough review.**

- Know that you can throw down **pro formas** when you attempt the accounts preparation questions.

- Know that **written answers** are so much better when each point is presented in a **separate paragraph** (lots of white space makes the marker's job easier and you can always go back, if you have time, and add a point you have just remembered without the page looking like an ink covered spider has been break dancing all over it).

- Know that you are the **only one** who knows the best way to approach the exam

Most important of all, focus on the **positive** things you have done in attempting this exam. You may have spent the allocated time on each question. You may have realised that you only answer three questions in Section B. You may know enough to pass every question in this Mock. Only change to improve. **Good luck.**

Question 1 Horsefield

Text references. Chapters 9 and 11.

Top tips. Start with **Part (b)**. There are five easy marks here that can be scored quickly, leaving you with ample time for the computational question. State the definition of an associate and then discuss the factors that may give rise to "significant influence but not control".

Part (a) Although there are quite a few parts to this question, each part is in itself quite straightforward. If you take a methodical approach then you should earn high marks.

(i) Sketch out the group structure, noting percentage holdings and the date of acquisition.

(ii) Prepare a pro-forma balance sheet for your answer, including the assets and liabilities of the parent and its subsidiary.

(iii) Note the adjustments for fair valuations, cash in transit and inter-company stocks. (In this question the unrealised profit allowance affects the investment in the associate. See below.)

(iv) Calculate the carrying value of the goodwill in the subsidiary.

(v) Calculate the carrying value of the associate.

(vi) Calculate the minority interest in the subsidiary.

(vii) Calculate the balance on the consolidated retained earnings.

Easy marks. Part (b) is 5 easy marks. Do it first to give yourself confidence.

Examiner's comments. This question was generally well answered. However, the examiner was worried by the fact that some candidates did not know that associates are accounted for by the equity method. Other errors included:

- Incorrect calculation of goodwill
- No account taken of unrealised profit on stock
- Fair value adjustments ignored or calculated incorrectly
- Addition errors
- No adjustment for cash in transit

Marking scheme

		Marks
(a)	Calculation of goodwill and its amortisation	3
	Licence	2
	Leasehold	1
	Property, plant and equipment	1
	Associate	3
	Other investments	2
	Stock	1
	Debtors	1
	Bank and overdraft (shown separate)	1
	Tax	1
	Share capital	1
	Minority interest	3
	Retained earnings	4
	Available	24
	Maximum	20
(b)	1 mark per relevant point to **Maximum**	5
	Maximum for question	25

(a)   HORSEFIELD PLC
      CONSOLIDATED BALANCE SHEET AS AT 31 MARCH 20X2

	£'000	£'000
Intangible fixed assets		
Goodwill (1,170 – 468) (W1)	702	
Waste disposal licence (180 – 60) (W3)	120	
		822
Tangible fixed assets		
Leasehold (3,200 + 2,000)	5,200	
Plant (4,850 + 1,600)	6,450	
		11,650
Investments		
Associated undertaking (W4)	705	
Other fixed asset investments		
(4,000 + 910 – 3,240 (Sandfly) – 630 (Anthill) +120)	1,160	
		1,865
		14,337
Current assets		
Stocks (830 + 340)	1,170	
Debtors (520 + 290 – 40)	770	
Cash (240 + 40)	280	
	2,220	
Creditors – amounts falling due within one year		
Creditors (420 + 960)	1,380	
Taxation due (220 + 250)	470	
Overdraft	190	
	2,040	
Net current assets		180
Creditors – amounts falling due after more than one year		
10% loan notes		(740)
Net assets		13,777
Share capital and reserves		
Ordinary share capital		5,000
Retained earnings (W3)		8,403
Minority interest (W2)		374
		13,777

Workings

1   *Goodwill*

	£'000	£'000
Cost of investment in Sandfly (1,200 × 90% × 3)		3,240
Shares	1,200	
Profit and loss account	800	
Fair value adjustment	120	
Licence	180	
	2,300	
Group share 90%		(2,070)
Goodwill		1,170
Amortisation – 2/5 years		(468)
Carrying value		702

	£'000	£'000
Cost of investment in Anthill (600 × 30% × 3.5)		630
Shares	600	
Pre-acquisition profits (800 + 600/2)	1,100	
	1,700	
Group share 30%		(510)
Goodwill		120
6 months amortisation (120/10)		(12)
Carrying value		108

2 *Minority interest*

	£'000	£'000
Share capital	1,200	
Reserves	2,300	
Fair value adjustment	120	
Licence	180	
Licence depreciation (2 years)	(60)	
		3,740
Minority share 10%		374

3 *Retained earnings*

	£'000	£'000
Horsefield		
Per question	7,500	
Provision for unrealised profit (10 × 30%)	(3)	
		7,497
Sandfly		
Post-acquisition	1,500	
Licence depreciation	(60)	
	1,440	
Group share 90%		1,296
Anthill		
Post-acquisition (1,400 − 800 − (600 × 50%))	300	
Group share 30%		90
		8,883
Goodwill amortisation		
Sandfly	468	
Anthill	12	
		(480)
		8,403

4 *Investment in associate*

	£'000
Investment at cost	630
Post acquisition profit (30% × (600 × 50%))	90
Amortisation of goodwill (W1)	(12)
Provision for unrealised profit (W3)	(3)
	705

(b) **Associated company status**

FRS 9 states that an associate is an entity in which the investor has a **participating interest** and over whose operating and financial policies the investor exercises a **significant influence**. In order to be a participating interest, the investor's interest must be held on a long-term basis for the purpose of securing benefits by the exercise of control or influence arising from or relating to that interest. There is a rebuttable presumption in the Companies Act that a shareholding of 20% or more of the voting rights constitutes a participating interest.

A shareholding of 20% can be shown not to constitute a participating interest where there is no exercise of significant influence. Similarly, a case could be made for associated company status where the share of voting rights is less than 20% but significant influence is exercised.

FRS 9 describes significant influence as active involvement and the ability to influence decisions on strategic issues such as business expansion or contraction, new markets, changes in products or activities and dividend policy.

Question 2 Tintagel

Text references. Chapters 3, 13 and 16.

Top tips. The balance sheet in Part (b) should be straightforward after calculating the adjustments required in Part (a), but don't underestimate the time that it will take to draft it.

The adjustments are quite straightforward; work through them methodically and keep an eye on the time. Extend your workings to show the corrected balance at the year-end.

Easy marks. There are no easy marks for this question! However, if you are very happy with double entry, you may find part (a) straightforward. If so, this is 10 easy marks.

Examiner's comments. Some candidates find it very hard to redraft financial statements instead of preparing them from scratch. However most candidates did well. Common errors included: treatment of the lease as if it were payments in arrears; treatment of the deficit on the investment property; and treatment of the loan note.

Marking scheme

			Marks
(a)	Profit and loss reserve		2
	Reversal of overhaul provision		3
	Depreciation charge		1
	Add back lease rental		1
	Lease interest		1
	Loan interest		1
	Loss on investment property		1
	Stock write down		1
	Unrecorded creditor		1
	Deferred tax		1
		Available	13
		Maximum	10
(b)	*Balance sheet*		
	Freehold property		1
	Plant		2
	Investment property		1
	Stock		2
	Debtors and creditors and bank		1
	Trade debtors		1
	Accrued lease interest		1
	Accrued loan interest		1
	Lease obligation (current liability)		1
	Taxation		1
	Lease obligation (long-term liability)		1
	8% loan note		2
	Deferred tax		1
	Ordinary shares and share premium		1
		Available	17
		Maximum	15
	Maximum for question		25

(a) *Schedule of Adjustments*

	Opening profit and loss reserve £'000	Profit for year £'000	Closing profit and loss reserve £'000
From question	48,100	48,500	96,600
(i) Lease restated as a finance lease *(W1)*			
Remove existing rental		3,200	3,200
Interest *((£11.2m – £3.2m) × 10%)*		(800)	(800)
Depreciation *(£11.2m/4 years)*		(2,800)	(2,800)
Depreciation			
Freehold property *(£130m × 2%)*		(2,600)	(2,600)
Sundry plant *(£60m × 20%)*		(12,000)	(12,000)
Heavy excavating plant *(See (iv) below)*			

(ii) The fall in value of the investment property is charged to the revaluation reserve, so there is no impact on the profit and loss account.

		Opening profit and loss reserve £'000	Profit for year £'000	Closing profit and loss reserve £'000
(iii)	Stock			
	NRV (£6m – (£4m × 90%))		(2,400)	(2,400)
	GRNI accrual		(500)	(500)
(iv)	Heavy excavating plant overhaul (W2)			
	Reverse overhaul provision	6,000	6,000	12,000
	Reverse old depreciation	10,000	-	10,000
	Charge new depreciation	(13,000)	(13,000)	(26,000)
(v)	Deferred tax			
	Increase (£22.5m – £18.7m)		(3,800)	(3,800)
(vi)	Loan Note (W3)			
	Interest expense		(853)	(853)
	Revised balances	51,100	18,947	70,047

Workings

1   *Lease restated as a finance lease*

		Capital	Interest	
1.4.X3	Asset	11,200		
	Instalment 1	(3,200)		
		8,000		
31.3.X4	Interest		800	(To profit and loss account)
	(8,000 × 10%)			
	Liability at 31.3.X4	8,000	800	
1.4.X4	– Creditors: amounts due within one year	(2,400)	(800)	
	Creditors: amounts due after more than one year	5,600		

2   *Overhaul costs*

The £12m provision for plant overhaul does not meet the criteria for a liability because there is no obligation to overhaul the asset (it could be sold or abandoned instead). The provision of £12m should be reversed. This increases the opening reserves by £6m and the profit for the current year by a further £6m.

The need for a periodic overhaul will be reflected in the depreciation charge. The total cost of £60m will be apportioned between £18m which will be consumed over three years (the overhaul costs) and the balance which will last for six years.

In the opening reserves the original depreciation of £10m is reversed and replaced with the new charge of £13m. The charge for this year is £13m.

		Total cost £'000	Overhaul 3 years £'000	Balance 6 years £'000
1-4-X2	Cost	60,000	18,000	42,000
	Depreciation	(13,000)	(6,000)	(7,000)
31-3-X3	Carrying value	47,000	12,000	35,000
	Depreciation	(13,000)	(6,000)	(7,000)
31-3-X4	Carrying value	34,000	6,000	28,000

3   *Loan Note*

The interest expense will reflect the full cost of this loan note (discount, interest, premium etc) rather than just the interest paid. This is charged using the loan note's internal rate of return which is given in the question as 12.1% pa.

	£'000
Received:	
Nominal value	15,000
Discount (5%)	(750)
Issue costs	(150)
Net cash received	14,100

Balance outstanding on loan notes at 31 March 20X4

	£'000
Net amount received	14,100
Interest at 12.1% (14,100 × 12.1% × 6/12)	853
Interest payable 1 April 20X4 (accrual)	(600)
Balance at 31 March 20X4	14,353

Note

The amount repayable at the end of the four years is £16,500,000 (£15m + 10% premium).

The effective interest rate allocates the cost as follows:

	£'000
Net amount received (as above)	14,100
Interest at 12.1%	1,706
Interest paid (15m × 8%)	(1,200)
Balance due 30.9.X4	14,606
Interest charge (14,606 × 12.1%)	1,767
Interest paid	(1,200)
Balance due 30.9.X5	15,173
Interest charge	1,836
Interest paid	(1,200)
Balance due 30.9.X6	15,809
Interest charge (balancing figure)	1,891
Interest paid	(1,200)
Balance to be repaid 30.9.X7	16,500

You do not need to do this whole calculation in order to answer the question and will probably not need to do it in an exam, but this is how it works. As we are dealing in £'000, the numbers are rounded, so the final interest charge is a balancing figure.

4   *Investment property*

	£'000
Opening investment revaluation reserve	3,400
Fall in value (£15m - £12.4m)	(2,600)
Closing balance	800

(b)   TINTAGEL BALANCE SHEET AS AT 31 MARCH 20X4

	£'000	£'000
Fixed assets		
Freehold property *(126,000 – 2,600)*		123,400
Heavy excavating plant *(W2)*		34,000
Sundry plant *(60,000 – 12,000)*		48,000
Leased plant *(11,200 – 2,800)*		8,400
Investment property		12,400
		226,200
Current assets		
Stocks *(60,400 – 2,400)*	58,000	
Trade debtors and prepayments	31,200	
Bank	13,800	
	103,000	
Creditors: amounts falling due within one year		
Trade creditors *(47,400 + 500)*	47,900	
Finance lease obligations *(W1)*	2,400	
Accrued finance lease interest *(W1)*	800	
Accrued Loan Note interest *(W3)*	600	
Corporation Tax	4,200	
	55,900	
Net current assets		47,100
Total assets less current liabilities		273,300
Creditors: amounts falling due after one year		
Finance lease obligations *(W1)*	5,600	
Loan note *(W3)*	14,353	
Deferred tax	22,500	
		(42,453)
Net assets		230,847
Capital and reserves		
Share Capital		150,000
Share Premium		10,000
Investment revaluation reserve *(W4)*		800
Profit and loss account *(Part (a))*		70,047
		230,847

Question 3 Nedburg

Text reference. Chapter 21.

Top tips. **Part (a)**. Cash flow questions are a good choice in an exam. The format and content are straightforward and easy to learn. All the information needed for your answer must be given to you in the question. A lot of marks can be scored if you take a methodical approach.

Part (b). Comments on a cash flow statement will always revolve around liquidity and cash generation. Comment on each section of the cash flow statement in turn. All sensible comments will be awarded marks.

Easy marks. The cash flow statement is straightforward and represents 20 easy marks.

Examiner's comments. This question was generally well answered and part (a) in particular was extremely well answered. However candidates still made mistakes in including non-cash items. Part (b) was poorly answered, some candidates making no effort to answer it at all. Most answers were superficial, giving general trends without commenting on them.

Marking scheme

		Marks
(a)	Net cash flows from operating activities	
	1 mark per item	8
	Returns on investment	2
	Taxation	2
	Capital expenditure – proceeds from the sale of the plant	2
	– other items, 1 mark per component	3
	Financing –equity shares	2
	– loan note	1
	Equity dividends	2
	Movement in cash for the year	1
	Available	**23**
	Maximum	**20**
(b)	1 mark per relevant point to (a)	**Maximum**	**5**
	Maximum for question	**25**

(a) Reconciliation of operating profit to net cash inflow from operating activities

	£m	£m
Profit before interest and tax		900
Depreciation		320
Amortisation – development expenditure (W1)	130	
– government grant (300 + 50 – 260)	(90)	
– goodwill	20	
		60
Loss on sale of plant		50
Increase in stocks (1,420 – 940)	(480)	
Increase in debtors (990 – 680)	(310)	
Increase in creditors (875 – 730)	145	
		(645)
Net cash inflow from operating activities		685

Cash flow statement

	£m
Net cash inflow from operating activities	685
Returns on investment and servicing of finance (Note 1)	(20)
Taxation (W2)	(130)
Capital expenditure (Note 2)	(680)
Equity dividends paid	(320)
Financing (Note 3)	650
Increase in cash	185

Notes

1   *Returns on investment and servicing of finance*

	£m	£m
Interest paid (300 × 10% - (15 – 5))		(20)

2 *Capital expenditure*

Purchase of plant (W3)	(250)
Deferred development costs	(500)
Government grant	50
Proceeds of sale of plant (W3)	20
	(680)

3 *Financing*

Proceeds of share issue (W4)	450
Proceeds of loan note issue (300 – 100)	200
	650

Workings

1 *Development expenditure*

Capitalised during the year	500
Increase in carrying amount	(370)
Balance – amount amortised	130

2 *Taxation*

Opening provisions (160 + 140)	300
Charge for the year	270
Closing provisions (130 + 310)	(440)
Tax paid (balance)	130

3 *Tangible fixed assets*

Opening balance	1,830
Revaluation	200
Purchase of new plant	250
Depreciation	(320)
Closing balance	(1,890)
Balance – NBV of plant disposed of	70
Loss on sale of plant	(50)
Disposal proceeds	20

4 *Share issue*

Closing share capital/share premium (750 + 350)	1,100
Opening share capital/share premium (500 + 100)	(600)
Increase	500
Bonus issue from revaluation reserve	(50)
Balance – proceeds of share issue	450

(b) **Commentary**

Nedberg has positive cash flow, generating £685m from operations which is sufficient to cover interest (£20m), tax (£130m) and dividends (£320m).

Unusually, the cash flow from operations is less than the operating profit of £900m. The cause of this appears to be the increase in current assets; stocks have increased by 51% and debtors by 46%. Without the comparative profit and loss account it is impossible to say whether these increases are in line with increased activity or whether this is the result of poor working capital management.

Nedberg has paid out £250m on new plant and capitalised £500m of development costs. In theory this is a good thing, as these investments will generate profits and cash flows in the future. However, Nedberg has had to raise £650m externally in order to pay for these investments, and this cannot be repeated year after year. Nedberg would be advised to reduce its capital investment for a year or two to enable it to get its finances back in order.

The financing section reveals that Nedberg has paid out in dividends half of the money it has received by issuing loans and shares. This seems pointless; the shareholders are getting back money that they have just invested (and they might have to pay tax on the dividends that they have received). The dividend for the year is also high compared with the profits after tax; Nedberg should reduce its dividends to a more modest and sustainable amount.

Overall, Nedberg has a healthy cash flow from operating activities. However, management need to:

- monitor working capital,
- scale back capital expenditure, and
- practise dividend restraint.

Question 4 Shiplake

(a) As the revision in value of Halyard plc's net assets is a re-estimate of the value of its net assets at the date of acquisition, it results in an adjustment to the original valuation, not a recognised impairment loss. Reducing the fair value of the net assets to £7 million will result in goodwill of £5 million. The charge for amortisation of goodwill will therefore increase from £800,000 to £1 million per annum.

(b) If the value in use falls due to the interest rate rise, but does not fall below £400,000, no impairment loss will be recognised. If the value in use falls to below £400,000 but is above £245,000, the impairment loss will be the difference between £400,00 and the recalculated value in use. If the value in use falls to below £245,000, the recoverable amount will be the net realisable value of £245,000. So the maximum impairment loss will be £155,000 (400,000 – 245,000).

(c) Per SSAP 13, the directors can write off all of the development expenditure if they wish to do so. Having written off the development costs to date, the company now has no deferred development expenditure brought forward. This means that it meets one of the SSAP 13 requirements for deferral, in that the aggregate of deferred development costs (0) and any further development costs (£80,000 + £10,000) is expected to be exceeded by future profits (£150,000). If the first £75,000 of development costs had not been written off, this would not be the case. The project does satisfy the other SSAP 13 deferral requirements, so the directors can choose whether or not to defer the £80,000 development costs.`

(d) Shiplake's investment in Klassic Kars has suffered an impairment loss of £130 million. The order in which this loss should be allocated per FRS 11 is:

- first to any goodwill in the unit;
- thereafter to any capitalised intangible asset in the unit;
- finally to the tangible assets, on a pro rata basis

We know that none of this loss can be allocated to the vehicles, which are carried at £90m and have an NRV of £115m. Only £20m of the loss can be allocated to the franchise, which has an NRV of £30m. The loss will be allocated to the goodwill, then £20m to the franchise and then pro rata to the other assets, as follows:

	Original value £'000	Impairment loss £'000	Restated value £'000
Goodwill	80,000	(80,000)	–
Franchise costs	50,000	(20,000)	30,000
Restored vehicles	90,000	–	90,000
Plant	100,000	(20,000)	80,000
Other net assets	50,000	(10,000)	40,000
	370,000	(130,000)	240,000

Question 5 Creative accounting

(a)   *Explanation*

Creative accounting is the selection of accounting policies that will portray an entity's financial position and performance in the best possible light. The policies chosen will comply with all existing professional and legal standards. In itself creative accounting is not illegal, although when taken to extremes the financial statements may no longer reflect fairly the underlying financial position and performance of the business.

Creative accounting policies are normally chosen in order to boost liquidity ratios in the balance sheet, or to increase or smooth out profits in the income statement.

Modern accounting standards have reduced the number of allowed alternatives, and so the opportunities for creative accounting are being reduced. FRS 5 deals with the following issues:

- Non-consolidation of 'quasi-subsidiaries'
- Sale and repurchase agreements, where secured loans are treated as 'sales'
- The treatment of consignment stock – determining who owns the asset

Other opportunities for creative accounting include:

- Capitalising interest or development costs in order to boost profits in the short term.

- Revaluing or not revaluing a class of assets. (Revaluing tends to improve gearing, but it reduces the return on capital employed.)

- Accounting for a joint venture using the equity method, thereby hiding the impact that the joint venture has on the entity's gross profit, finance costs, capital employed and borrowings.

There are also occasions where management deliberately overestimate the useful lives of assets, or underestimate provisions, or fail to apply appropriate policies. These practices are probably closer to fraud than to creative accounting.

(b)   *Substance of transactions*

FRS 5 requires financial statements to reflect the substance of transactions rather than just their legal form. This improves the reliability of the financial statements.

Most of the time there is no difference between the substance of a transaction and its legal form. For example the contract date for most sales is when the exchange of goods takes place, at which point all the rights of ownership pass from the seller to the buyer. The buyer recognises the asset, and also recognises the liability to pay for it. The seller ceases to recognise the old asset, but recognises a trade receivable instead. However there are occasions when the seller retains some of the rights of ownership. This raises the question of what assets and liabilities should be recognised, and when profits can be claimed. The legal form of these transactions often tends to overstate profits and hide liabilities.

Typical features of transactions where the substance may be different from the legal form are as follows:

- The seller continues to enjoy the risks and benefits of ownership by using the asset.
- The seller has a constructive obligation to repurchase the asset sold.
- The agreed selling price is markedly different from the market price.

The substance of these transactions are often secured loans, even though the legal form is a sale. If the legal form was reported then the 'seller' would claim a profit and ignore the obligation to repurchase the asset. This is obviously misleading to the user of the accounts.

ACCA Fundamentals Level

Paper F7

Financial Reporting

(UK)

Mock Examination 2

Question Paper	
Time allowed	
Reading and Planning Writing	**15 minutes** **3 hours**
Answer all FIVE questions	

**DO NOT OPEN THIS PAPER UNTIL YOU ARE READY TO START UNDER
EXAMINATION CONDITIONS**

Question 1 Hanford

Hanford plc acquired six million of Stopple plc's ordinary shares on 1 April 20X1 for an agreed consideration of £25 million. The consideration was settled by a share exchange of five new shares in Hanford plc for every three shares acquired in Stopple plc, and a cash payment of £5 million. The cash transaction has been recorded, but the share exchange has not.

The draft balance sheets of the two companies at 30 September 20X1 are:

	Hanford plc		Stopple plc	
	£'000	£'000	£'000	£'000
Fixed assets				
Land and buildings		32,060		9,400
Plant and equipment		46,480		17,780
Investment in Stopple plc		5,000		nil
		83,540		27,180
Current assets				
Stock	7,450		4,310	
Debtors	12,960		4,330	
Cash and bank	nil		520	
	20,410		9,160	
Creditors: amounts falling due within one year				
Creditors and accruals	5,920		4,160	
Bank overdraft	1,700		nil	
Taxation	1,870		1,380	
	(9,490)		(5,540)	
Net current assets		10,920		3,620
Creditors: amounts falling due after more than one year				
8% Debentures 20X4		nil		(6,000)
Net assets		94,460		24,800
Share capital and reserves				
Ordinary shares of £1 each		20,000		8,000
Reserves				
Share premium	10,000		2,000	
Profit and loss account b/f 1 October 20X0	51,260		6,000	
Profit for the year to 30 September 20X1	13,200	74,460	8,800	16,800
		94,460		24,800

The following information is relevant:

(i) The fair value of Stopple plc's land at the date of acquisition was £4 million in excess of its carrying value. Stopple plc's financial statements contain a note of a contingent asset for an insurance claim of £800,000 relating to some stock that was damaged by a flood on 5 March 20X1. The insurance company is disputing the claim. Hanford plc has taken legal advice on the claim and believes that it is highly likely that the insurance company will settle it in full in the near future.

The fair values of Stopple plc's other net assets approximated to their carrying value.

(ii) At the date of acquisition Hanford plc sold an item of plant to Stopple plc for £2.4 million. This plant had cost Hanford plc £2 million. Stopple plc has charged depreciation of £240,000 on this plant since it was acquired.

(iii) Hanford plc's current account debit balance of £820,000 with Stopple plc does not agree with the corresponding balance in Stopple plc's books. Investigations revealed that on 26 September 20X1 Hanford plc billed Stopple plc £200,000 for its share of central administration costs. Stopple plc has not yet recorded this invoice. Inter company current accounts are included in debtors or creditors as appropriate.

(iv)   Stopple plc paid a dividend of £400,000 on 30 September 20X1. The profit and dividend of Stopple plc are deemed to accrue evenly throughout the year. Stopple's retained profit of £8.8 million for the year to 30 September 20X1 as shown in its balance sheet is after the deduction of the dividend. Hanford plc's policy is to credit to income only those dividends received from post acquisition profits. Hanford plc has not yet accounted for the dividend from Stopple plc. The cheque has been received but not banked.

(v)   Consolidated goodwill is written off on a straight-line basis over a five year life, with time apportionment in the year of acquisition.

Required

(a)   Prepare the consolidated balance sheet of Hanford plc at 30 September 20X1.   **(20 marks)**

(b)   Suggest reasons why a parent company may not wish to consolidate a subsidiary company, and describe the circumstances in which non-consolidation of subsidiaries is permitted.   **(5 marks)**

(Total = 25 marks)

Question 2 Chamberlain

The following trial balance relates to Chamberlain, a publicly listed company, at 30 September 20X4:

	£'000	£'000
Ordinary share capital		200,000
Profit and loss reserve 1 October 20X3		162,000
6% Loan note (issued in 20X2)		50,000
Deferred tax (note (iv))		17,500
Land and buildings at cost (land element £163 million (note (i)))	403,000	
Plant and equipment at cost (note (i))	124,000	
Accumulated depreciation 1 October 20X3 – buildings		60,000
– plant and equipment		44,000
Trade debtors	48,000	
Stock – 1 October 20X3	35,500	
Bank	52,500	
Trade creditors		45,000
Turnover		246,500
Purchases	78,500	
Long term contract balance (note (ii))	5,000	
Operating expenses	29,000	
Loan interest paid	1,500	
Interim dividend	8,000	
Research and development expenditure (note (iii))	40,000	
	825,000	825,000

The following notes are relevant:

(i)   The building had an estimated life of 40 years when it was acquired and is being depreciated on a straight-line basis. Plant and equipment, other than the leased plant, is depreciated at 12.5% per annum using the reducing balance basis. Depreciation of buildings and plant and equipment is charged to cost of sales.

(ii)   The long term contract balance represents costs incurred to date of £35 million less progress payments received of £30 million on a two year construction contract that commenced on 1 October 20X3. The total contract price has been agreed at £125 million and Chamberlain expects the total contract cost to be £75 million. The company policy is to accrue for profit on uncompleted contracts by applying the percentage of completion to the total estimated profit. The percentage of completion is determined by the proportion of the contract costs to date compared to the total estimated contract costs. At 30 September 20X4, £5 million of the £35 million costs incurred to date related to unused stocks of materials on site.

Other stock at 30 September 20X4 amounted to £38.5 million at cost.

(iii)   The research and development expenditure is made up of £25 million of research, the remainder being development expenditure. The directors are confident of the success of this project which is likely to be completed in March 20X5 and wish to capitalise the maximum amount permitted under current accounting standards.

(iv)   The directors have estimated the provision for corporation tax for the year to 30 September 20X4 at £22 million. The deferred tax provision at 30 September 20X4 is to be adjusted to a credit balance of £14 million.

Required

Prepare for Chamberlain:

(a)   A profit and loss account for the year to 30 September 20X4; and   **(12 marks)**

(b)   A balance sheet as at 30 September 20X4 in accordance with the Companies Acts and current UK Accounting Standards as far as the information permits.   **(13 marks)**

Note. A Statement of Total Recognised Gains and Losses is NOT required.

Disclosure notes are ONLY required for the leased plant in item (ii) above.   **(Total = 25 marks)**

Question 3 Boston

Shown below are the summarized financial statements for Boston, a publicly listed company, for the years ended 31 March 20X5 and 20X6, together with some segment information analysed by class of business for the year ended 31 March 20X6 only:

	Carpeting £m	Hotels £m	House building £m	Total 31 March 20X6 £m	Total 31 March 20X5 £m
Turnover	90	130	280	500	450
Cost of sales (note (i))	(30)	(95)	(168)	(293)	(260)
Gross profit	60	35	112	207	190
Operating expenses	(25)	(15)	(32)	(72)	(60)
Segment profit	35	20	80	135	130
Common costs				(60)	(50)
Operating profit				75	80
Finance costs				(10)	(5)
Profit before tax				65	75
Taxation				(25)	(30)
Profit for the period				40	45

	Carpeting £m	Hotels £m	House building £m	Total 31 March 20X6 £m	Total 31 March 20X5 £m
Tangible fixed assets	40	140	200	380	332
Current assets	40	40	75	155	130
Current liabilities – tax	(4)	(9)	(12)	(25)	(30)
– other	(4)	(51)	(53)	(108)	(115)
Segment net assets (note (ii))	72	120	210	402	317
Bank balance				15	(5)
Unallocated loans				(65)	(40)
Net assets				352	272
Ordinary share capital				100	80
Share premium				20	nil
Profit and loss reserve				232	192
				352	272

The following notes are relevant.

(i)   Depreciation for the year to 31 March 20X6 was £35 million. During the year a hotel with a carrying amount of £40 million was sold at a loss of £12 million. Depreciation and the loss on the sale of fixed assets are charged to cost of sales. There were no other fixed asset disposals. As part of the company's overall acquisition of new fixed assets, the hotel segment acquired £104 million of new hotels during the year.

(ii)   The above figures are based on historical cost values. The fair values of the segment net assets are:

	Carpeting £m	Hotels £m	House building £m
at 31 March 20X5	80	150	250
at 31 March 20X6	97	240	265

(iii)   The following ratios (which can be taken to be correct) have been calculated based on the overall group results:

Year ended:	31 March 20X6	31 March 20X5
Return on capital employed	18·0%	27.5%
Gross profit margin	41·4%	42·2%
Operating profit margin	15%	17.8%
Net assets turnover	1.2 times	1.4 times
Current ratio	1.3: 1	0.9:1
Gearing	15.6%	12.8%

(iv)   The following segment ratios (which can be taken to be correct) have been calculated for the year ended 31 March 20X6 only:

	Carpeting	Hotels	House building
Segment return on net assets	48.6%	16.7%	38.1%
Segment asset turnover (times)	1.3	1.1	1.3
Gross profit margin	66.7%	26.9%	40%
Net profit margin	38.9%	15.4%	28.6%
Current ratio (excluding bank)	5:1	0.7:1	1.2:1

Required

(a)   Prepare a cash flow statement for Boston for the year ended 31 March 20X6.   **(10 marks)**

        Note. You are not required to show separate segmental cash flows or the analysis and movement of net debt.

(b)   Using the ratios provided, write a report to the Board of Boston analysing the company's financial performance and position for the year ended 31 March 20X6.   **(15 marks)**

        Your answer should make reference to your cash flow statement and the segmental information and consider the implication of the fair value information.

                                                                                            (Total = 25 marks)

Note. Segmental reporting is not in your syllabus. The segment information is provided simply to give you information about the different areas of the business for use in your answer to (b).

Question 4 Atomic Power

You are preparing a technical note to all your clients regarding the effects of FRS 12 *Provisions, contingent liabilities and contingent assets*, which became effective for accounting periods ending on or after 23 March 1999. Amongst other things, FRS 12 replaces SSAP 18 *Accounting for contingencies*.

One of your clients, Atomic Power plc, has asked for further help in applying FRS 12 because the company is concerned it may not be applying the standard correctly.

Atomic Power operates nuclear power stations that supply power to international, national and regional electricity companies. Environmental clear up costs can be a substantial item of expenditure for nuclear power plant operators; in some countries Atomic Power's licences have, by law, environmental clean-up commitments written in as part of the agreement, whereas in other countries there is no legal requirement to provide for them.

Atomic Power has brought into commission, on 1 July 20X1, a new nuclear power station, built at a cost of £600m. The plant has a licence to supply electricity for 12 years, which is the estimated life of the power station. At the end of 12 years, the station must be demolished and all the waste product (ie spent fuel) buried over 100m underground in an area sealed for contamination purposes. During the station's life the company will have to pay for the clean up of any contamination leaks from the plant's water cooling system.

The company has estimated the cost of demolition and waste disposal in 12 years' time at £540m, the discounted value of which, at an appropriate rate, is £360m. Past experience suggests that there is a 30% chance of a contamination leak occurring in any 12 month period, and the cost of cleaning it up will be between £60m and £120m a time, depending on its extent.

The company has sent you extracts from its draft financial statements in relation to the power plant, showing the following:

PROFIT AND LOSS ACCOUNT (EXTRACTS)

	£m
Fixed asset depreciation: power station (1/12 × £600m)	50
Provision for demolition and waste disposal (1/12 × £540m)	45
Provision for contamination leak clean-up (30% × £90m (average))	27
	122

BALANCE SHEET (EXTRACTS)

Tangible fixed assets	£m
Power station at cost	600
Depreciation	(50)
	550
Provisions for liabilities and charges	
Environmental costs (45 + 27)	72

No contamination leaks occurred in the year ended 30 June 20X2.

Required

(a) Draft a technical note for your clients that explains why there is a need for an accounting standard in respect of provisions. **(2 marks)**

(b) Advise Atomic Power plc on the acceptability of its current accounting policy and redraft the extracts of the financial statements for the company in line with FRS 12. **(8 marks)**

(c) Explain the effect it would have on your answer to (b) if Atomic Power was operating this nuclear power station in a country that does not legislate in respect of the above types of environmental costs. **(5 marks)**

(Total = 15 marks)

Question 5 Impairment

It is generally recognised in practice that fixed assets should not be carried in a balance sheet at values that are greater than they are 'worth'. In the past there has been little guidance in this area with the result that impairment losses were not recognised on a consistent or timely basis or were not recognised at all. FRS 11 *'Impairment of Fixed Assets and Goodwill'* was issued in July 1998 on this topic.

Required

(a)   Define an impairment loss and explain when companies should carry out a review for impairment of fixed assets and goodwill.   **(3 marks)**

(b)   Describe the circumstances that may indicate that a company's assets have become impaired.   **(7 marks)**

(Total = 10 marks)

Answers

DO NOT TURN THIS PAGE UNTIL YOU HAVE
COMPLETED THE MOCK EXAM

A plan of attack

Managing your nerves

As you turn the pages to start this mock exam a number of thoughts are likely to cross your mind. At best, examinations cause anxiety so it is important to stay focused on your task for the next three hours! Developing an awareness of what is going on emotionally within you may help you manage your nerves. Remember, you are unlikely to banish the flow of adrenaline, but the key is to harness it to help you work steadily and quickly through your answers.

Working through this mock exam will help you develop the exam stamina you will need to keep going for three hours.

Managing your time

Planning and time management are two of the key skills which complement the technical knowledge you need to succeed. To keep yourself on time, do not be afraid to jot down your target completion times for each question, perhaps next to the title of the question on the paper. As all the questions are compulsory, you do not have to spend time wondering which question to answer!

Focusing on scoring marks

When completing written answers, remember to communicate the critical points, which represent marks, and avoid padding and waffle. Sometimes it is possible to analyse a long sentence into more than one point. Always try to maximise the mark potential of what you write.

As you read through the questions, jot down on the question paper, any points you think you might forget. There is nothing more upsetting than coming out of an exam having forgotten to write a point you knew!

Structure and signpost your answers

As you read through the paper, highlight the key words and phrases in the examiner's requirements. This will help you focus precisely on what the examiner wants.

Also, where possible try to use headings and subheadings, to give a logical and easy-to-follow structure to your response. A well structured and sign-posted answer is more likely to convince the examiner that you know your subject.

Doing the exam

Actually doing the exam is a personal experience. There is not a single *right way*. As long as you submit complete answers to 5 questions after the three hours are up, then your approach obviously works.

Looking through the paper

Question 1, as always, is on **group accounts**. This time it requires a balance sheet for a parent company and subsidiary. Do not neglect part (b).

- Question 2 is on **preparing financial statements for an individual company**.
- Question 3 is a cash flow statement and interpretation of accounts
- Question 4 requires good understanding of provisions
- Question 5 is a discussion question on impairment

Allocating your time

BPP's advice is to always allocate your time **according to the marks for the question.** However, **use common sense.** If you're doing a question but haven't a clue how to do part (c), you might be better off re-allocating your time and getting more marks on another question, where you can add something you didn't have time for earlier on.

Question 1 Hanford

Text references. Chapter 9.

Top tips. This consolidated balance sheet has a number of complications. Watch out for the pre-acquisition dividend, the recognition of the contingent asset and adjustments for unrealised profits and inter-group transactions.

Examiner's comments. This was generally the best answered question on the paper. Most candidates had a good knowledge of the basic consolidation principles, but there were some problems with the adjusting items, notably:

- incorrect treatment of the pre-acquisition dividend
- incorrect fair value adjustment for the plant
- failure to adjust the share capital or calculate the premium for the share exchange
- treating invoiced administration costs as cash in transit

Some candidates were confused between profit and loss account and balance sheet issues, arising from the fact that the acquisition was half way through the year.

In part (b) some candidates did not consider other possible reasons why a parent company might not want to consolidate a subsidiary, even if permitted to do so.

(a) HANFORD PLC
     CONSOLIDATED BALANCE SHEET AS AT 30 SEPTEMBER 20X1

	£'000	£'000
Intangible fixed assets:		
Goodwill (W1)		5,355
Tangible fixed assets:		
Land and buildings		
(32,060 + 9,400 + 4,000)		45,460
Plant and equipment (W3)		63,900
		114,715
Current assets:		
Stock (7,450 + 4,310)	11,760	
Debtors (12,960 + 4,330 - 820)	16,470	
Insurance claim	800	
Cash and bank (520 + 300 (dividend))	820	
	29,850	
Creditors: amounts falling due within one year		
Creditors and accruals		
(5,920 + 4,160 - 620)	9,460	
Bank overdraft	1,700	
Taxation (1,870 + 1,380)	3,250	
	14,410	
Net current assets		15,440
		130,155
Creditors: amounts falling due after more than one year		
8% Debentures		(6,000)
		124,155
Share capital and reserves:		
Ordinary share capital (20,000 + 10,000)(W4)		30,000
Share premium (10,000 + 10,000) (W4)		20,000
Profit and loss account (W5)		66,805
		116,805
Minority interest (W6)		7,350
		124,155

Workings

1   *Goodwill*

	£'000	£'000
Consideration		25,000
Less: pre-acquisition dividend (W2)		(150)
		24,850
Share of net assets acquired		
Balance sheet value (24,800 – 4,400)	20,400	
Revaluation of land	4,000	
Contingent asset	800	
	25,200	
Group share 75%		18,900
Goodwill		5,950
Amortisation (5,950/5 × 6/12)		(595)
Balance sheet balance		5,355

2   *Pre-acquisition dividend*

	£'000
Dividend paid	400
Group share (400 × 75%)	300
Post-acquisition (300 × 6/12)	150
Pre-acquisition dividend	150

3   *Plant and equipment*

	£'000
Hanford	46,480
Stopple	17,780
Unrealised profit on sale	(400)
Additional depreciation charged	40
	63,900

4   *Ordinary share capital*

	£'000
Number of shares acquired in Stopple (8,000 × 75%)	6,000
Number of shares in Hanford issued (6,000 × 5/3)	10,000
Value of shares	
Nominal value (10,000 × £1)	10,000
Share premium (bal fig)	10,000
Total value of shares issued (25,000 - 5,000)	20,000

5   *Consolidated profit and loss reserve*

	£'000	£'000
Hanford		64,460
Less: unrealised profit on sale of plant (400 – 40)*		(360)
Post acquisition dividend (W2)		150
		64,250
Stopple post acquisition (8,800 × 6/12)	4,400	
Less: administration charge	(200)	
	4,200	
Group share 75%		3,150
		67,400
Less: goodwill amortised		(595)
		66,805

* The excess depreciation is deducted from the unrealised profit.

6   *Minority interest*

	£'000
Net assets per balance sheet	24,800
Fair value adjustment – land	4,000
– insurance	800
Management charge	(200)
	29,400
Minority interest (29,400 × 25%)	7,350

(b)   A parent company may wish not to consolidate a subsidiary because the **Companies Act** or **FRS 2, Accounting for subsidiary undertakings**, either allow or require the subsidiary not to be consolidated. In other instances a parent company may wish not to consolidate a subsidiary due to the **poor performance** of the subsidiary which they do not wish to include in the consolidated financial statements as the parent would like the consolidated financial statements to show the position of the group in the best possible light.

If the results of a poorly performing subsidiary are consolidated then this will impact on the consolidated balance sheet and profit and loss account. Consolidation of the subsidiary may **lower the consolidated return on capital employed, worsen the perceived consolidated liquidity position or increase the consolidated gearing level**. If a subsidiary therefore has operating losses, poor liquidity or high gearing levels then the parent company may wish not to consolidate that subsidiary.

In order to ensure that consolidated financial statements are **not manipulated** to improve perceived performance by non-consolidation of subsidiaries **both the Companies Act and FRS 2 have criteria regarding the non-consolidation of subsidiary companies**.

FRS 2 requires a subsidiary to be excluded from the consolidation when the subsidiary operates under **severe long-term restrictions** as in such cases the parent no longer has control of the subsidiary. The Companies Act permits exclusion on this basis.

FRS 2 also requires a subsidiary to be excluded from consolidation where the interest in the subsidiary is **held exclusively with a view to subsequent resale** and the subsidiary has not previously been consolidated in the group accounts of the parent. The Companies Act permits exclusion for this reason.

Question 2 Chamberlain

Top tips. As well as examining you on the format and content of the profit and loss account and balance sheet, this question also tests your knowledge of four specific situations. Work through these first, noting their effect on the profit and loss account and balance sheet.

As always, be methodical and don't get bogged down in the detail.

Easy marks. There are no easy marks with this question. However, a methodical approach should see you through.

Examiner's comments. This was the most popular and best answered of the optional questions. Problems occurred with: construction contracts, R & D and deferred tax.

		Marks
(a)	*Profit and loss account*	
	Turnover	2
	Cost of sales	6
	Operating costs	1
	Interest expense	2
	Taxation	2
	Available	**13**
	Maximum	**12**
(b)	*Balance sheet*	
	Development costs	1
	Property, plant and equipment	2
	Amounts due from construction contract customers	2
	Stock and debtors	1
	Accrued finance income	1
	Bank and trade creditors	1
	Accrued finance costs	1
	Corporation tax provision	1
	Long-term liabilities	2
	Share capital and reserves (including 1 mark for dividend paid)	2
	Available	**14**
	Maximum	**13**
	Maximum for question	**25**

(a) CHAMBERLAIN: PROFIT AND LOSS ACCOUNT FOR THE YEAR ENDED 30 SEPTEMBER 20X4

		£'000
Turnover	(246,500 + 50,000 (W3))	296,500
Cost of sales	(W1)	(146,500)
Gross profit		150,000
Operating expenses		(29,000)
Operating profit		121,000
Interest payable	£50m × 6%	(3,000)
Profit before tax		118,000
Taxation	(22,000 – 3,500)	(18,500)
Profit for the year		99,500

(b)   CHAMBERLAIN: BALANCE SHEET AS AT 30 SEPTEMBER 20X4

	£'000	£'000
Fixed assets		
Intangible fixed assets: Development expenditure (W4)		15,000
Tangible fixed assets (W2)		407,000
		422,000
Current assets		
Stocks (£38.5m + £5m unused raw materials (W3))	43,500	
Amounts recoverable on long term contracts (W3)	20,000	
Trade debtors	48,000	
Bank and cash	52,500	
	164,000	
Creditors: amounts falling due within one year		
Trade creditors	45,000	
Accrued interest (£3,000 charge – £1,500 paid)	1,500	
Corporation Tax	22,000	
	68,500	
Net current assets		95,500
Total assets less current liabilities		517,500
Creditors: amounts falling due after more than one year		
6% Loan Note		(50,000)
Provision for liabilities		
Deferred tax		(14,000)
Net assets		453,500
Capital and Reserves		
Share capital		200,000
Profit and loss account (162,000 + 99,500 profit – 8,000 dividend)		253,500
		453,500

Workings

1   Cost of sales

		£'000
Opening stock	from TB	35,500
Purchases	from TB	78,500
Depreciation	W2	16,000
Construction contract costs	W3	30,000
Closing stock	from question	(38,500)
Research expenditure	from question	25,000
		146,500

2   Property, plant, equipment

Total depreciation   £6m + £10m = £16m
Total carrying value   £337m + £70m = £407m

		£'000	£'000
Land & buildings:			
Cost			403,000
Depreciation	b/f	60,000	
	Charge (403m – 163m) × $^1/_{40}$	6,000	
	c/d		(66,000)
Carrying value			337,000

			£'000	£'000
Plant and equipment:				
Cost				124,000
Depreciation	b/f		44,000	
	Charge	(124m – 44m) × 12.5%	10,000	
	c/d			(54,000)
Carrying value				70,000

3 *Construction contract*

Profit and loss account

Contract turnover is matched with contract costs incurred in reaching the current stage of completion. (The costs incurred for this calculation exclude the raw materials purchased for the contract but not yet used.)

$$\frac{\text{Costs incurred to date}}{\text{Total costs}} \times \text{Contract price} = \text{contract turnover recognised}$$

$$\frac{\text{£35m} - \text{£5m raw materials}}{\text{£75m}} \times \text{£125m} = \text{£50m}$$

The attributable profit to date is 30/75 × total profit £50m = £20m

The cost of sales is the balancing figure of £50m – £20m = £30m

Balance sheet

	£'000
Turnover recognised	50,000
Less: progress payments received	(30,000)
Amount recoverable from customers	20,000
Raw materials allocated to contract	5,000

4 *Research and development*

		£'000
Research	Charge to P&L as incurred	25,000
Development	Capitalise in B/S	15,000
Total		40,000

Question 3 Boston

Text references. Chapters 19 and 21.

Top tips. These financial statements may have looked a bit confusing to start with, which is why you must take time to go through the question carefully and make sure you understand it. Once you had found your way round the numbers, the cash flow statement was fairly simple and more marks were available for the report in (b). In this case, the ratios were already provided, so you just had to analyse the information. As this is worth 15 marks, you should have taken time to analyse the information properly and come to some useful conclusions.

Easy marks. The cash flow statement was easy but was only worth 10 marks. 15 marks were available for the report and there was no reason not to do well on this part. Make notes before you start and cover the issues methodically.

Examiner's comments. Overall, most candidates did well on the cash flow with many receiving full marks for this section, but interpretation of the company's performance was mixed. Some simply commented on whether a particular ratio had gone up or down. This is not interpretation and attracts few marks. It is necessary to suggest what the underlying causes of the changes might be.

Marking scheme

		Marks
(a)	Operating profit	1
	Depreciation	1
	Loss on sale of hotel	1
	Increase in current assets	1
	Decrease in current liabilities	1
	Interest paid	1
	Tax paid	1
	Purchase of fixed assets	1
	Sale of fixed assets	1
	Share issue	1
	Issue of loan	1
	Increase in cash	1
	Available	12
	Maximum	10
(b)	One mark per valid point to maximum	15
	Maximum for question	25

(a) BOSTON
CASH FLOW STATEMENT FOR THE YEAR ENDED 31 MARCH 2006

	£m	£m
Net cash flow from operating activities		90
Returns on investment and servicing of finance		
Interest paid		(10)
Taxation paid		(30)
Capital expenditure		
Purchase of fixed assets (W)	(123)	
Proceeds of sale of fixed assets (40 – 12)	28	(95)
Financing		
Loan taken out (65 – 40)	25	
Proceeds of share issue (120 – 80)	40	65
Increase in cash		20

Note
Reconciliation of operating profit to net cash flow from operating activities

Operating profit	75
Depreciation	35
Loss on sale of fixed asset	12
Increase in current assets	(25)
Reduction in current liabilities	(7)
Net cash flow from operating activities	90

Working

Fixed assets – balance b/f	332
Depreciation	(35)
Carrying value of disposal	(40)
Purchase of fixed assets (balancing figure)	123
Balance c/f	380

(b)   **To: The Board, Boston**
      From: A N Accountant
      Report on financial performance and position for the year ended 31 March 20X6

All of Boston's profitability ratios have declined between 31 March 20X5 and 31 March 20X6. The overall ROCE has fallen from 27.5% to 18%. In spite of an increased turnover and a small increase in gross profit, the operating profit has fallen. This is due to a rise in operating expenses of 8% above the rise in turnover, which should be investigated. The fall in the gross profit margin can be attributed to the £12m loss on sale of fixed assets, which was charged to cost of sales. Without this, the gross profit margin would have been 43.8%.

If ROCE were to be recalculated using fair values it would be 16.7% for 20X5 and 12.5% for 20X6. Although this is much lower overall, the gap between the ROCE for 20X5 and 20X6 is much reduced. The ROCE for 2006 has been to some extent penalised by the addition of £64m assets to the hotels segment. These assets may not yet be producing much return.

If we look at the segments individually, carpeting is the most profitable segment and the hotel segment is the least profitable. However, if the loss on sale of fixed assets were not included in cost of sales, the hotel segment would show a gross profit of 36% - not far below house building. If we adjust the segment return on net assets for fair values, we get 36% carpeting, 8% hotels and 30% house building. This narrows the gap between carpeting and house building, but makes the hotel sector look unviable. However it is worth bearing in mind that the hotel sector currently holds £120m of unrealised profit on fixed assets, which could be realised if needed.

Boston's current ratio has improved in the year to 31.3.X6, but this ignores the increase of £25m in loans. The cash flow statement shows a decrease in cash before financing of £45m. This can be accounted for by £123m net spending on hotel properties. The company's gearing has increased due to the new loans, partly offset by the share issue, and it will now be facing higher interest payments. However, its gearing level is still not high, and the company is not currently running an overdraft, on which it would pay a higher rate of interest.

Question 4 Atomic Power

Text reference. Chapter 13.

Top tips. FRS 12 is an important 'anti-abuse' standard in the ASB repertoire. The definitions and recognition criteria you are required to discuss in (a) are fundamental to the standard. You must learn them thoroughly to be able to apply FRS 12 effectively in the exam.

Again, use headings and sub-headings to help both yourself and the marker.

(a)   TECHNICAL NOTE
      FRS 12 PROVISIONS, CONTINGENT LIABILITIES AND CONTINGENT ASSETS

The need for issuing FRS 12

The overall objective of FRS 12 is to obviate the practice of 'smoothing' results.

The use of provisions has created substantial opportunities for the **manipulation** of **reported profits**. One reason for this is that provisions are **pervasive**; they may arise in relation to almost all areas of a company's operations.

The **recognition** and **measurement** of provisions both rely greatly on the **judgement** of management. There is thus substantial scope for adjustment of provisions.

A particular issue is the way management use provisions to **'smooth' profits**; provisions are created for future expenditure in years when profits are healthy and then released to the profit and loss account as the expenditure arises, thus **reducing the volatility of reported profits** over time. FRS 12 is designed to prevent this.

Another difficult area is the use of provisions for future losses when one business acquires another. By **creating provisions for restructuring on acquisition** as part of the **fair value exercise**, the acquiring business can **increase** the **future profitability** of the **acquired entity**, again by releasing the provisions in future periods against the expenditure.

This practice has the perverse effect of increasing goodwill the greater the restructuring charges! This has been largely prevented, not only by FRS 12, but also by FRS 10 *Goodwill and intangibles* and FRS 7 *Fair values in acquisition accounting.*

(b) **Advice on present accounting policy on provisions**

Atomic Power's current accounting policies regarding accounting for provisions is no longer acceptable under FRS 12. Where an entity has a present obligation that will (probably) lead to a transfer of economic benefits as a result of a past transaction or event, then a provision should be made of the full amount of the expected liability.

Where that amount is expressed in **future prices** then these must be **discounted back** at a **nominal rate**. Atomic Power should thus recognise £360m as a liability, not £540m, for environmental costs on 1 July 20X1.

The credit side of the accounting entry is thus to the balance sheet heading 'Provisions for liabilities and charges'. The treatment of the corresponding debit entry required by FRS 12 is controversial; it must be added to the cost of the asset, to be released as the asset is depreciated over its useful life. This effectively 'grosses up' the assets and liabilities of the balance sheet and has called into question the nature of the assets recognised in this way in relation to how assets are defined in the ASB's *Statement of Principles.*

In Atomic Power's case, the effect of all this (barring the error in using £540m instead of £360m), on profits will not be much different under FRS 12 than the previous policy. The value of the power station plus the provision for environmental costs will be written off over its 12 year life.

The treatment of the possible costs of contamination leaks is more problematic. The main issue is whether a 'past event' has taken place. Is the past event the leak itself, or is it the generation of the electricity that could lead to a leak? There is also the question of the probability of a leak. Generally, if there is a greater than 50% chance of a liability occurring, it should be provided for, but if below 50%, then presumably the liability would be classed as contingent only, and disclosed in the notes rather than provided.

The probability of a leak is only 30% in any year and indeed one did not occur this year. Over 12 years of generation of electricity, it seems that a leak will occur about four times (ie one year in three). The cost of each leak is £60m-£120m; so taking the mid-cost, the cost of three leaks will be £90m × 4 = £360m. Over 12 years, therefore, the company would provide £30m per year. Applying the above, the revised accounts extracts are as follows.

PROFIT AND LOSS ACCOUNT (EXTRACTS)

	£m
Fixed asset depreciation: power station: 1/12 × (600 +360)	80
Provision for clean-up costs: 1/12 × (90 × 4)	30
	110

BALANCE SHEET (EXTRACTS)

Fixed assets	£m
Power station at cost	960
Depreciation (as above)	(80)
	880
Provision for liabilities	
Provision for environmental and clean-up costs (360 + 30)	390

(c)   **Impact of alternative national scenarios**

Where there is no statutory requirement to clean up environmental damage, one might expect FRS 12 not to require a provision because there is no obligation to transfer economic benefits. However, FRS 12 also includes the notion of a 'constructive obligation'. A constructive obligation arises from the company's own actions and behaviour, either as a pattern of past practice, or statements of intention or policy.

In Atomic Power's case, the company has a track record for cleaning up environmental damage or pollution, or if it has stated its intention to do so in terms of specific or general commitment, then the provisions should be made as in (b) above. However, if the company has not raised any expectations that it will clean up environmental damage, then no provisions would be required and the power station would simply be recorded at a cost of £600m and depreciated by £50m a year over 12 years.

Question 5 Impairment

(a)   FRS 11 defines an impairment loss as a reduction in the recoverable amount of a fixed asset or goodwill below its carrying amount. The recoverable amount is defined as the higher of the assets net realisable value (the amount at which it could be disposed of, less any direct selling costs) and its value in use (the present value of the future cash flows obtainable as a result of the assets continued use, including those resulting from its ultimate disposal). Where the cash flows attributable to an individual asset cannot be measured, value in use should be calculated at the level of the income-generating unit to which the asset belongs.

FRS 11 requires an impairment review to be carried out whenever events or changes in circumstances indicate that the carrying amount of an asset may not be recoverable. FRS 10 additionally requires that goodwill and intangible assets should be reviewed at the end of the first full financial year following acquisition, and at the end of each reporting period thereafter, if amortised over a period exceeding 20 years.

(b)   FRS 11 gives the following indicators of impairment:

- a current period operating loss, combined with past or expected future operating losses

- a current period net cash outflow from operating activities, combined with a past or expected future net cash outflow

- a significant decline in the asset's market value during the period

- obsolescence of, or physical damage to, the asset

- adverse changes in the business, or the market, in which the asset is involved, for instance the entrance of a major competitor

- adverse changes in the statutory or other regulatory environment

- a planned reorganisation or restructuring

- a major loss of key employees

- a significant increase in interest rates which are likely to affect the asset's discounted future cash flows, and therefore its value in use

ACCA Fundamentals Level

Paper F7

Financial Reporting

(UK)

Mock Examination 3

Question Paper	
Time allowed	
Reading and Planning Writing	**15 minutes** **3 hours**
Answer all FIVE questions	

DO NOT OPEN THIS PAPER UNTIL YOU ARE READY TO START UNDER EXAMINATION CONDITIONS

ALL FIVE questions are compulsory and MUST be attempted

1   On 1 October 2005 Pumice acquired the following fixed asset investments:
    –   80% of the equity share capital of Silverton at a cost of £13.6 million
    –   50% of Silverton's 10% loan notes at par
    –   1.6 million equity shares in Amok at a cost of £6.25 each.

    The summarised draft balance sheets of the three companies at 31 March 2006 are:

	Pumice		Silverton		Amok	
	£'000	£'000	£'000	£'000	£'000	£'000
Tangible fixed assets		20,000		8,500		16,500
Investments		26,000		nil		1,500
		46,000		8,500		18,000
Current assets	15,000		8,000		11,000	
Creditors: amounts falling due within one year	(10,000)		(3,500)		(5,000)	
Net current assets		5,000		4,500		6,000
Total assets less current liabilities		51,000		13,000		24,000
Creditors: amounts falling after more than one year						
8% Loan note		(4,000)		nil		nil
10% Loan note		nil		(2,000)		nil
		47,000		11,000		24,000
Capital and reserves						
Equity shares of £1 each		10,000		3,000		4,000
Profit and loss account		37,000		8,000		20,000
		47,000		11,000		24,000

The following information is relevant:

(i)   The fair values of Silverton's assets were equal to their carrying amounts with the exception of land and plant. Silverton's land had a fair value of £400,000 in excess of its carrying amount and plant had a fair value of £1.6 million in excess of its carrying amount. The plant had a remaining life of four years (straight-line depreciation) at the date of acquisition.

(ii)   In the post acquisition period Pumice sold goods to Silverton at a price of £6 million. These goods had cost Pumice £4 million. Half of these goods were still in the stock of Silverton at 31 March 2006. Silverton had a balance of £1.5 million owing to Pumice at 31 March 2006 which agreed with Pumice's records.

(iii) The net profit after tax for the year ended 31 March 2006 was £2 million for Silverton and £8 million for Amok. Assume profits accrued evenly throughout the year.

(iv)   Consolidated goodwill is to be written off over a five-year life using time apportionment in the year of acquisition.

(v)   No dividends were paid during the year by any of the companies.

Required:

(a) **Discuss how the investments purchased by Pumice on 1 October 2005 should be treated in its consolidated financial statements.**   (5 marks)

(b) **Prepare the consolidated balance sheet for Pumice as at 31 March 2006.**   (20 marks)

                                                                                                   (25 marks)

2   The following trial balance relates to Kala, a publicly listed company, at 31 March 2006:

	£'000	£'000
Land and buildings at cost (note (i))	270,000	
Plant – at cost (note (i))	156,000	
Investment properties – valuation at 1 April 2005 (note (i))	90,000	
Purchases	78,200	
Operating expenses	15,500	
Loan interest paid	2,000	
Rental of leased plant (note (ii))	22,000	
Dividends paid	15,000	
Stock at 1 April 2005	37,800	
Trade debtors	53,200	
Turnover		278,400
Income from investment property		4,500
Equity shares of £1 each fully paid		150,000
Profit and loss reserve at 1 April 2005		112,500
Investment property revaluation reserve at 1 April 2005		7,000
8% (actual and effective) loan note (note (iii))		50,000
Accumulated depreciation at 1 April 2005 – buildings		60,000
– plant		26,000
Trade creditors		33,400
Deferred tax		12,500
Bank		5,400
	739,700	739,700

The following notes are relevant:

(i)   The land and buildings were purchased on 1 April 1990. The cost of the land was £70 million. No land and buildings have been purchased by Kala since that date. On 1 April 2005 Kala had its land and buildings professionally valued at £80 million and £175 million respectively. The directors wish to incorporate these values into the financial statements. The estimated life of the buildings was originally 50 years and the remaining life has not changed as a result of the valuation.

Later, the valuers informed Kala that investment properties of the type Kala owned had increased in value by 7% in the year to 31 March 2006.

Plant, other than leased plant (see below), is depreciated at 15% per annum using the reducing balance method. Depreciation of buildings and plant is charged to cost of sales.

(ii) On 1 April 2005 Kala entered into a lease for an item of plant which had an estimated life of five years. The lease period is also five years with annual rentals of £22 million payable in advance from 1 April 2005. The plant is expected to have a nil residual value at the end of its life. If purchased this plant would have a cost of £92 million and be depreciated on a straight-line basis. The lessor includes a finance cost of 10% per annum when calculating annual rentals. (Note: you are not required to calculate the present value of the minimum lease payments.)

(iii) The loan note was issued on 1 July 2005 with interest payable six monthly in arrears.

(iv) The provision for corporation tax for the year to 31 March 2006 has been estimated at £28.3 million. The deferred tax provision at 31 March 2006 is to be adjusted to a credit balance of £14.1 million.

(v)   Stock at 31 March 2006 was valued at £43.2 million.

Required, prepare for Kala:

(a) A profit and loss account for the year ended 31 March 2006.   (9 marks)

(b) A statement of the movement in share capital and reserves for the year ended 31 March 2006.   (5 marks)

(c) A balance sheet as at 31 March 2006.   (11 marks)

                                                                                        (25 marks)

Note: A statement of total recognised gains and losses is NOT required.

3   Reactive is a publicly listed company that assembles domestic electrical goods which it then sells to both wholesale and retail customers. Reactive's management were disappointed in the company's results for the year ended 31 March 2005. In an attempt to improve performance the following measures were taken early in the year ended 31 March 2006:

   –   a national advertising campaign was undertaken,
   –   rebates to all wholesale customers purchasing goods above set quantity levels were introduced,
   –   the assembly of certain lines ceased and was replaced by bought in completed products. This allowed Reactive to dispose of surplus plant.

Reactive's summarised financial statements for the year ended 31 March 2006 are set out below:

Profit and loss account	£million
Turnover (25% cash sales)	4,000
Cost of sales	(3,450)
Gross profit	550
Operating expenses	(370)
Operating profit	180
Profit on disposal of plant (note (i))	40
Finance costs	(20)
Profit before taxation	200
Taxation	(50)
Profit for the financial year	150

Balance Sheet	£million	£million
Tangible fixed assets		
Property		300
Plant and equipment (note (i))		250
		550
Current assets		
Stock	250	
Debtors	360	
Bank	nil	
	610	
Creditors: amounts falling due within one year		
Bank overdraft	10	
Trade creditors	430	
Taxation	40	
	(480)	130
Creditors: amounts falling due after more than one year		
8% loan note		(200)
		480
Capital and reserves		
Equity shares of 25 pence each		100
Profit and loss account reserve		380
		480

Below are ratios calculated for the year ended 31 March 2005.

Return on year end capital employed (profit before interest and tax over total assets less current liabilities)	28.1%
Net asset (equal to capital employed) turnover	4 times
Gross profit margin	17 %
Net profit (before tax) margin	6.3 %
Current ratio	1.6:1
Closing stock holding period	46 days
Debtors' collection period	45 days
Creditors' payment period	55 days
Dividend yield	3.75%
Dividend cover	2 times

Notes:

(i)   Reactive received £120 million from the sale of plant that had a carrying amount of £80 million at the date of its sale.

(ii) the market price of Reactive's shares throughout the year averaged £3.75 each.

(iii) there were no issues or redemption of shares or loans during the year.

(iv) dividends paid during the year ended 31 March 2006 amounted to £90 million, maintaining the same dividend paid in the year ended 31 March 2005.

Required:

(a) **Calculate ratios for the year ended 31 March 2006 (showing your workings) for Reactive, equivalent to those provided.** (10 marks)

(b) **Analyse the financial performance and position of Reactive for the year ended 31 March 2006 compared to the previous year.** (10 marks)

(c) **Explain in what ways your approach to performance appraisal would differ if you were asked to assess the performance of a not-for-profit organisation.** (5 marks)

(25 marks)

4   **(a)** The qualitative characteristics of relevance, reliability and comparability identified in the ASB's *Statement of principles for financial reporting* are some of the attributes that make financial information useful to the various users of financial statements.

Required:

Explain what is meant by relevance, reliability and comparability and how they make financial information useful. (9 marks)

(b) During the year ended 31 March 2006, Porto experienced the following transactions or events:

(i)   entered into a finance lease to rent an asset for substantially the whole of its useful economic life.

(ii) a decision was made by the Board to change the company's accounting policy from one of expensing the finance costs on building new retail outlets to one of capitalising such costs.

(iii) the company's profit and loss account prepared using historical costs showed a loss from operating its hotels, but the company is aware that that the increase in the value of its properties during the period far outweighed the operating loss.

Required:

Explain how you would treat the items in (i) to (iii) above in Porto's financial statements and indicate on which of the Statement's qualitative characteristics your treatment is based. (6 marks)

(15 marks)

5   SSAP 9 *Stocks and long-term contracts* deals with accounting for long-term contracts whose durations usually span at least two accounting periods.

Required:

(a) **Describe the issues of revenue and profit recognition relating to long-term contracts.**   (4 marks)

(b) Beetie is a construction company that prepares its financial statements to 31 March each year. During the year ended 31 March 2006 the company commenced two construction contracts that are expected to be completed in the accounting period ended 31 March 2007. The position of each contract at 31 March 2006 is as follows:

Contract	1	2
	£'000	£'000
Agreed contract price	5,500	1,200
Estimated total cost of contract at commencement	4,000	900
Estimated total cost at 31 March 2006	4,000	1250
Certified value of work completed at 31 March 2006	3,300	840
Contract billings invoiced and received at 31 March 2006	3,000	880
Contract costs incurred to 31 March 2006	3,900	720

The certified value of the work completed at 31 March 2006 is considered to be equal to the revenue earned in the year ended 31 March 2006. The percentage of completion is calculated as the value of the work completed to the agreed contract price.

Required:

Calculate the amounts which should appear in the profit and loss account and balance sheet of Beetie at 31 March 2006 in respect of the above contracts.   (6 marks)

(10 marks)

Answers

DO NOT TURN THIS PAGE UNTIL YOU HAVE
COMPLETED THE MOCK EXAM

A plan of attack

What's the worst thing you could be doing right now if this was the actual exam paper? Sharpening your pencil? Wondering how to celebrate the end of the exam in about 3 hours time? Panicking, flapping and generally getting in a right old state?

Well, they're all pretty bad, so turn back to the paper and let's sort out a **plan of attack**!

First things first

You have fifteen minutes of reading time. Spend this looking carefully through the questions and deciding the order in which you will attempt them. As a general rule you should attempt the questions that you find easiest first and leave the hardest until last.

This paper has five compulsory questions. Therefore, you do not have to spend your 15 minutes reading time working out which questions to answer. So you can use it to read the paper and get some idea of what you need to do. At this stage you can make notes on the question paper but not in the answer book. So scribble down anything you feel you might otherwise forget.

It's a good idea to just start with Question 1. Once you have the consolidation question done, you will feel more relaxed. Question 1 will have lots of information and you should read it a second time before you start. Get really clear about % shareholdings and dates on which they were acquired. In this question 1 you have an associate to deal with, so you know you have an additional working to do. Get the formats down and then proceed methodically with the workings.

Question 2 is a single company accounts preparation question. This is where the examiner can bring in leases, construction contracts, fixed/non-current asset complications and other issues he wants to examine. In this case you have a lease and some revaluations. Again, set the formats out and then tackle the workings. Make it very clear to the marker which workings belong to which question and cross-reference them.

Question 3 is on interpretation of accounts. You should not have any trouble with the ratios, but you must be able to *interpret* them. Read the answer carefully to see what this means.

Question 4 is a discussion question and you must ensure you are answering the question, not just writing down everything you know. In part (b), you have to be clear which characteristic relates to which issue.

Question 5 is a construction contract, which was straightforward if you knew what to do. This is a popular topic, so do not neglect it.

You've got spare time at the end of the exam.....?

If you have allocated your time properly then you **shouldn't have time on your hands** at the end of the exam. But if you find yourself with five or ten minutes to spare, check over your work to make sure that there are no silly arithmetical errors.

Forget about it!

And don't worry if you found the paper difficult. More than likely other candidates will too. If this were the real thing you would need to **forget** the exam the minute you leave the exam hall and **think about the next one**. Or, if it's the last one, **celebrate**!

Question 1

Top tips. Part (a) provides you with important information for part (b) so make sure you do that first and get clear what the shareholdings are and how you will treat them. Note also that the investments have been held for **six months**, so take care working out the pre-acquisition profits.

Easy marks. Most of the work in this question concerns the goodwill, the associate and the tangible fixed assets. You should be able to score easy marks on the goodwill, the fixed assets and the consolidated reserves.

Marking scheme

		Marks
(a)	1 mark per relevant point	5
(b)	Balance sheet:	
	goodwill	3½
	tangible fixed assets	2
	Investments – associate	3
	– other	1
	current assets	2
	creditors – 1 year	1
	8% loan notes	½
	10% loan notes	1
	equity shares	1
	profit and loss account	3
	minority interest	1½
		20
	Total for question	25

(a)   The acquisition of an 80% holding in Silverton can be assumed to give Pumice **control**. Silverton should therefore be treated as a **subsidiary** from the date of acquisition and its results consolidated from that date.

As Silverton is being treated as a subsidiary, the investment in loan notes is effectively an intercompany loan. This should be cancelled on consolidation, leaving the remaining £1m of Silverton's loan notes as a long-term liability in the consolidated balance sheet.

The shares in Amok represent a 40% holding, which can be presumed to give Pumice '**significant influence**', but not control. Amok should therefore be treated as an **associate** and its results brought into the consolidated financial statements using the equity method.

(b)   PUMICE GROUP
      CONSOLIDATED BALANCE SHEET AT 31 MARCH 2006

	£'000	£'000
Fixed assets		
Intangible: goodwill (W2)		3,600
Tangible fixed assets (W6)		30,300
Investment in associate (W3)		11,400
Investments – other (W7)		1,400
		46,700
Current assets (W8)	20,500	
Creditors; amounts falling due within one year (10,000 + 3,500 – 1,500 (W8))	(12,000)	
Net current assets		8,500
Total assets less current liabilities		55,200
Creditors: amounts falling due after more than one year:		
8% loan note	(4,000)	
10% loan note (2,000 – 1,000 (W7))	(1,000)	
		(5,000)
		50,200
Capital and reserves		
Share capital (parent)		10,000
Profit and loss account (W5)		37,640
		47,640
Minority interest (W4)		2,560
		50,200

Workings

1   *Group structure*

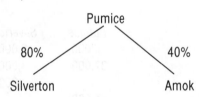

Pumice

80%   40%

Silverton   Amok

2   *Goodwill*

	£'000	£'000
Silverton:		
Cost of investment		13,600
Less: fair value of net assets and liabilities acquired:		
Share capital	3,000	
Pre-acquisition reserves ((8,000 – (2000 × 6/12))	7,000	
Fair value adjustments: land	400	
plant	1,600	
	12,000	
Group share 80%		(9,600)
Goodwill		4,000
Amortisation (4,000/5 × 6/12)		(400)
Carrying value		3,600

		£'000	£'000
Amok:			
Cost of investment (1.6 m × 6.25)			10,000
Less fair value of net assets acquired:			
Share capital		4,000	
Pre-acquisition reserves (20,000 − (8,000 × 6/12))		16,000	
		20,000	
Group share 40%			(8,000)
Goodwill			2,000
Amortisation ((2,000/5) × 6/12)			200

3 Associate

	£'000
Cost of investment (£6.25 × 1.6m)	10,000
Share of post-acquisition profit (8,000 × 6/12) × 40%	1,600
	11,600
Less goodwill amortisation (W2)	(200)
Carrying value	11,400

4 Minority interest

	£'000
Silverton – net assets at balance sheet date	11,000
Fair value adjustments (W2)	2,000
Depreciation adjustment (£1.6m/4 × 6/12)	(200)
	12,800
Minority share 20%	2,560

5 Consolidated reserves

	Pumice £'000	Silverton £'000	Amok £'000
Per balance sheet	37,000	8,000	20,000
Additional depreciation (W4)		(200)	
Unrealised profit ((6,000 − 4,000) /2)	(1,000)		
Pre-acquisition reserves (W2)	-	(7,000)	(16,000)
	36,000	800	4,000
Group share: 800 × 80%	640		
4,000 × 40%	1,600		
	38,240		
Goodwill amortisation: Silverton (W2)	(400)		
Amok (W2)	(200)		
	37,640		

6 Tangible fixed assets

	£'000
Pumice	20,000
Silverton	8,500
Fair value adjustments (W2)	2,000
Additional depreciation (W4)	(200)
	30,300

7 *Other investments*

	£'000
Pumice – per balance sheet	26,000
Investment in Silverton	(13,600)
Investment in Amok (W2)	(10,000)
Intercompany loan note	(1,000)
Other investments	1,400

8 *Current assets*

	£'000
Pumice	15,000
Silverton	8,000
Unrealised profit in stock ((6,000 – 4,000) / 2)	(1,000)
Intercompany debt	(1,500)
	20,500

Question 2

Top tips. The main issues in this question were the asset revaluations and the finance lease. Always check the *remaining* useful life of the revalued asset. With a finance lease you must note whether payments are made in advance or in arrears. In this case they are made in advance, so the amount payable within one year includes no interest relating to a future period.

Easy marks. You may have been confused by the finance lease but they were plenty of marks available for fixed assets and you could have scored a few more easy marks by dealing correctly with the tax.

Marking scheme

		Marks
(a)	Profit and loss account	
	Turnover	½
	Cost of sales	4½
	Operating expenses	½
	Investment income	½
	Finance costs	1 ½
	Taxation	1 ½
		9
(b)	Movement in share capital and reserves	
	Brought forward figures	1
	Profit for period	1
	Revaluation gains	2
	Dividends paid	1
		5
(c)	Balance sheet	
	Land and buildings	2
	Plant and equipment	2
	Investment property	1
	Stocks and trade debtors	1
	Trade creditors and overdraft	1
	Accrued interest	½
	Lease obligation: interest and capital one year	1
	capital over one year	1
	Corporation tax provision	½
	8% loan	½
	Deferred tax	½
		11
	Total for question	**25**

(a) KALA:
     PROFIT AND LOSS ACCOUNT FOR THE PERIOD ENDED 31 MARCH 2006

	£'000
Turnover	278,400
Cost of sales (W1)	(115,700)
Gross profit	162,700
Operating expenses	(15,500)
Operating profit	147,200
Investment income	4,500
Interest payable (W2)	(10,000)
Profit before tax	141,700
Taxation (W3)	(29,900)
Profit for the financial year	111,800

(b) KALA:
     STATEMENT OF MOVEMENT IN SHARE CAPITAL AND RESERVES FOR THE PERIOD ENDED 31 MARCH 2006

	Share capital £'000	Investment property RR £'000	Revaluation reserve £'000	Retained earnings £'000	Total £'000
At 1 April 2005	150,000	7,000		112,500	269,500
Revaluation surplus (W6)			45,000		45,000
Valuation gain (90,000 × 7%)		6,300			6,300
Profit for the period				111,800	111,800
Dividends paid	-	-	-	(15,000)	(15,000)
	150,000	13,300	45,000	209,300	417,600

(c) KALA:
     BALANCE SHEET AS AT 31 MARCH 2006

	£'000	£'000
Tangible fixed assets (W4)		434,100
Investment property		96,300
		530,400
Current assets		
Stock	43,200	
Trade debtors	53,200	
	96,400	
Creditors: amounts falling due within one year:		
Trade creditors	33,400	
Accrued loan interest (3,000 – 2,000)	1,000	
Bank overdraft	5,400	
Amount due under finance lease (W7)	22,000	
Corporation tax	28,300	
	90,100	
Net current assets		6,300
Total assets less current liabilities		536,700
Creditors: amounts falling due after more than one year:		
8% loan note	50,000	
Amount due under finance lease (W7)	55,000	
		(105,000)
Provision for liabilities		
Deferred tax		(14,100)
		417,600
Capital and reserves		
Equity shares £1		150,000
Revaluation reserve (W6)		45,000
Investment property revaluation reserve		13,300
Profit and loss account		209,300
		417,600

Workings

1   *Cost of sales*

	£'000
Opening stock	37,800
Purchases	78,200
Depreciation (W5)	42,900
Closing stock	(43,200)
	115,700

2   *Interest payable*

	£'000
Loan note (50,000 x 8% × 9/12)	3,000
Finance lease interest (W7)	7,000
	10,000

3   *Corporation tax*

	£'000
Provision for year	28,300
Transfer to deferred tax (14,100 – 12,500)	1,600
	29,900

4   *Tangible fixed assets*

	Land £'000	Buildings £'000	Plant £'000	Leased plant £'000	Total £'000
Cost	70,000	200,000	156,000	92,000	518,000
Accumulated depreciation		(60,000)	(26,000)		(86,000)
Revaluation (W6)	10,000	35,000			45,000
Current year depreciation (W5)		(5,000)	(19,500)	(18,400)	(42,900)
Carrying value	80,000	170,000	110,500	73,600	434,100

5   *Depreciation*

	£'000
Buildings	
Revalued amount / remaining useful life: (175,000/(50-15))	5,000
Plant: (156,000 – 26,000) × 15%	19,500
Leased plant: (92,000/5)	18,400
	42,900

6   *Revaluation reserve*

	£'000
Land (80m – 70m)	10,000
Buildings (175m – (200m–60m))	35,000
	45,000

7   *Finance lease*

	£'000
Purchase price	92,000
Instalment paid 1 April 05	(22,000)
Balance 1 April 05	70,000
Interest 10%	7,000
Balance 31 March 06	77,000
Due within one year	22,000
Due after one year	55,000
	77,000

[Note that the amount due within one year will be paid on 1 April 06 i.e. before the accrual of any further interest. Therefore we do not need to deduct any future interest from this amount.]

Question 3

Marking scheme

			Marks
(a)	one mark per ratio		10
(b)	1 mark per valid point	maximum	10
(c)	1 mark per valid point	maximum	5
		Total for question	25

(a)   ROCE = 220/680 × 100 = 32.3%

Net asset turnover = 4,000/680 = 5.9 times

Gross profit margin = 550/4,000 × 100 = 13.8%

Net profit margin = 200/4,000 × 100 = 5%

Current ratio = 610/480 = 1.3:1

Closing stock holding period = 250/3,450 × 365 = 26 days

Trade debtors collection period = 360/3,000* × 365 = 44 days

* credit sales

Trade creditors payment period = 430/3450 × 365 = 45 days

Dividend yield = 22.5/375* × 100 = 6%

* Dividend per share (90/400)/market price of share

Dividend cover = 150/90 = 1.67 times

(b)   **Analysis of the comparative financial performance and position of Reactive for the year ended 31 March 2006**

The first thing to notice about Reactive's results is that the ROCE has increased by 4.2 percentage points, from 28.1 to 32.3. On the face of it, this is impressive. However, we have to take into account the fact that the capital employed has been reduced by the plant disposal and the net profit has been increased by the profit on disposal. So the ROCE has been inflated by this transaction and we should look at what the ROCE would have been without the disposal. Taking out the effects of the disposal gives us the following ratios:

ROCE = 180/ (680 + 80) × 100 = 23.7%

Net asset turnover = 4,000/760 = 5.3 times

Net profit margin = 160/4,000 × 100 = 4%

Comparing these ratios to those for the period ended 31 March 2005 we can see that **ROCE has fallen**. This fall has been occasioned by a fall in the net profit margin. The asset turnover has improved on the previous year even after adding back the disposal.

The net profit margin can be analysed into two factors – the gross profit margin and the level of expenses. The **gross profit percentage is 3.2% down** on the previous year. This is probably due to the rebates offered to wholesale customers, which will have increased sales at the expense of profitability. The replacement of some production lines by bought in products will probably also have reduced profit margins. Sales may have been increased by the advertising campaign, but this has been additional expense charged against net profit. It looks as if management have sought to boost revenue by any available means. The plant disposal has served to mask the effect on profits.

Reactive's **liquidity has also declined** over the current year. The current ratio has gone down from 1.6 to 1.3. However, there has also been a sharp decline in the stockholding period, probably due to holding less raw material for production. It could be that the finished goods can be delivered direct to the wholesalers from the supplier. This will have served to reduce the current ratio. The debtors collection period has remained fairly constant but the creditors payment period has gone down by 10 days. It looks as if, in return for prompt delivery, the finished goods supplier demands prompt payment. This fall in the creditors period will have served to improve the current ratio. We do not have details of cash balances last year, but Reactive currently has no cash in the bank and a £10m overdraft. Without the £120m from the sale of plant the liquidity situation would obviously have been much worse.

The **dividend yield has increased** from 3.75% to 6%, which looks good as far as potential investors are concerned. But we are told that the dividend amount is the same as last year. As there have been no share issues, this means that the dividend per share is the same as last year. Therefore the increase in dividend yield can only have come about through a fall in the share price. The market is not that impressed by Reactive's results. At the same time the dividend cover has declined. So the same dividend has been paid on less profit (last year's dividend cover was 2.0, so profit must have been £180m). Management decided it was important to maintain the dividend, but this was not sufficient to hold the share price up.

To conclude, we can say that **Reactive's position and performance is down** on the previous year and any apparent improvement is due to the disposal of plant.

(c) A **not-for-profit organisation** needs funds to operate, just as a profit-making organisation does. It is also required to make good and sensible use of its assets and spend within its budget. To this degree, calculation of certain financial ratios and their comparison to the previous year is valid and would yield information about how well the organisation is run, and how well it manages its funds.

However, there are a number of differences between a profit-making and a not-for-profit organisation. A not-for-profit organisation does not have the basic purpose of increasing the wealth of its shareholders or of achieving a return on capital. Its success or failure is judged by the degree to which it achieves its objectives. These are laid down in a whole different set of parameters. A hospital has many different targets to meet – some of them apparently not that useful. One of its major targets will be to cut the length of its waiting lists for operations. Local government bodies may be judged on the basis of whether they have secured VFM (value for money) in spending local taxes. Schools are judged on their examination passes and their budgets may be affected by issues such as how many of their children are considered to have 'special needs'.

A charity will judge its success by the amount of work it has achieved in line with its mission statement, and by the level of funding and donations it has secured – without which nothing can be achieved.

It is worth pointing out that, just as a profit-making organisation may seek to enhance the picture given by its financial statements, not-for-profit organisations may also be driven in the same direction. It has been found in the UK that some hospitals have brought forward minor operations and delayed major ones in order to secure maximum impact on the waiting list and meet government targets. Some schools have a policy of only entering pupils for exams which they have a good chance of passing. This keeps up their pass rate and their position in the school league tables.

Question 4

Marking scheme

		Marks
(a)	3 marks each for relevance, reliability and comparability	9
(b)	2 marks for each transaction ((i) to (iii)) or event	6
	Total for question	**15**

(a) **Relevance**

The relevance of information must be considered in terms of the decision-making needs of users. It is relevant when it can influence their economic decisions or allow them to reassess past decisions and evaluations. Economic decisions often have a predictive quality – users may make financial decisions on the basis of what they expect to happen in the future. To some degree past performance gives information on expected future performance and this is enhanced by the provision of comparatives, so that users can see the direction in which the company is moving. The separate presentation of discontinued operations also shows how much profit or loss can be attributed to that part of the operation will be not be there in the future. This can also affect valuation of assets. One aspect of relevance is materiality. An item is material if its omission or misstatement could influence the economic decisions of users. Relevance would not be enhanced by the inclusion of immaterial items which may serve to obscure the important issues.

Reliability

Information can be considered to be reliable when it is free from error or bias and gives a true and fair view of what it is expected to represent. The profit and loss account must be a reliable statement of the results of the entity for the period in question and the balance sheet must fairly present its financial position at the end of the period. Financial statements in which provision had not been made for known liabilities or in which asset values had not been correctly stated could not be considered reliable. This also brings in the issue of substance over form. Transactions should be represented in accordance with their economic substance, rather than their legal form. This principle governs the treatment of finance leases, sale and leaseback transactions and consignment stock. If these types of transactions are not accounted for in accordance with their economic substance, then the financial statements are unreliable.

Comparability

Comparability operates in two ways. Users must be able to compare the financial statements of the entity with its own past performance and they must also be able to compare its results with those of other entities. This means that financial statements must be prepared on the same basis from one year to the next and that, where a change of accounting policy takes place, the results for the previous year must also be restated so that comparability is maintained. Comparability with other entities is made possible by use of appropriate accounting policies, disclosure of accounting policies and compliance with Financial Reporting Standards. Revisions to standards have to a large degree eliminated alternative treatments, so this has greatly enhanced comparability.

(b)   (i)   The 'substance' of a finance lease is that the lessee has acquired an asset using a loan from the lessor. Porto should capitalise the asset and depreciate it over its useful economic life (which is the same as the lease term). A finance lease liability should be set up for the same amount. The liability will be reduced by the lease payments, less the notional finance charge on the loan, which will be charged to the profit and loss account. This presents the transaction in accordance with its substance, which is a key aspect of reliability.

      (ii)   The Board has decided to switch to capitalisation of borrowing costs. This is a change of accounting policy and so requires retrospective adjustment. Borrowing costs expensed up to this point should be added to the carrying value of the retail outlets and credited to finance costs in the profit and loss account and to the profit and loss reserve. A similar adjustment must be made to the previous year's financial statements. The current year's financial statements and the corresponding amounts will then appear as though this policy had always been in force, thus ensuring comparability.

      (iii)   This issue has to do with relevance. It could be said that the use of historical cost accounting does not adequately reflect the value of assets in this case. This can be remedied by revaluing the properties. If this is done, all properties in the category will have to be revalued. This will probably give rise to a higher depreciation charge, so it will not improve the operating loss in the profit and loss account, but the excess can be credited back to reserves in the balance sheet.

Question 5

> **Top tips.** Construction contracts appeared regularly under the old syllabus and will probably feature regularly in F7. Make sure you know how to calculate the balance sheet amounts.
>
> **Easy marks.** Part (a) was 4 easy marks and you could get another 2 easy marks for getting the profit and loss amounts correct.

			Marks
(a)	one mark per valid point to	**maximum**	4
(b)	turnover (mark for each contract)		1
	profit/loss (mark for each contract)		1
	stocks		1
	debtors		1
	payment on account		1
	provision		1
			6
	Total for question		**10**

(a) Revenue recognition is an important issue in financial reporting and it is generally accepted that revenue is earned when goods have been accepted by the customer or services have been delivered. At that stage revenue is said to have been realised. However, if this were applied to long-term contracts, the effect would not necessarily be to give a true and fair view.

As a long-term contract can span several accounting periods, if no revenue were recognised until the end of the contract, this would certainly be prudent but would not be in accordance with the accruals concept. The financial statements would show all of the profit in the final period, when in fact some of it had been earned in prior periods. This is remedied by recognising attributable profit as the contract progresses, as long as ultimate profitability is expected. Any foreseeable loss is recognised immediately.

(b) PROFIT AND LOSS ACCOUNT

	Contract 1 £'000	Contract 2 £'000	Total £'000
Turnover	3,300	840	4,140
Cost of sales			
(Contract 1: 4,000 × 60%)	(2,400)		
(Contract 2: balancing figure)		(890)	(3,290)
Attributable profit/(loss)	900	(50)	850

BALANCE SHEET

	£'000
Current assets	
Stock: long-term contract balances	1,500
Debtors: amounts recoverable	300
Creditors: amounts due within one year	
Payments on account (880 – 840)	40
Provision for losses (890 – 720)	170

Workings

Contract 1

	£'000
Contract price	5,500
Costs to date	(3,900)
Costs to complete (4,000 – 3,900)	(100)
Estimated total profit	1,500
Profit to date: 1,500 x 3,300/5,500 =	900
Long term contract balance:	
Costs to date	3,900
Transferred to cost of sales	(2,400)
	1,500
Amount recoverable on contract:	
Turnover	3,300
Payments on account	(3,000)
	300

Contract 2

	£'000
Contract price	1,200
Costs to date	(720)
Costs to complete (1,250 – 720)	(530)
Expected total loss	(50)

ACCA
Examiner's answers

1 (a) As the investment in shares represents 80% of Silverton's equity shares it is likely to give Pumice control of that company. Control is the ability to direct the operating and financial policies of an entity. This would make Silverton a subsidiary of Pumice and require Pumice to prepare group financial statements which would require the consolidation of the results of Silverton from the date of acquisition (1 October 2005). Consolidated financial statements are prepared on the basis that the group is a single economic entity.

The investment of 50% (£1 million) of the 10% loan note in Silverton is effectively a loan from a parent to a subsidiary. On consolidation Pumice's asset of the loan (£1 million) is cancelled out with £1 million of Silverton's total loan note liability of £2 million. This would leave a net liability of £1 million in the consolidated balance sheet.

The investment in Amok of 1.6 million shares represents 40% of that company's equity shares. This is generally regarded as not being sufficient to give Pumice control of Amok, but is likely to give it significant influence over Amok's policy decisions (eg determining the level of dividends paid by Amok). Such investments are generally classified as associates and FRS 9 *Associates and joint ventures* requires the investment to be included in the consolidated financial statements using equity accounting.

(b) Consolidated balance sheet of Pumice at 31 March 2006

		£'000
Intangible fixed assets:		
Goodwill (4,000 – 400 (w (ii)))		3,600
Tangible fixed assets (w (i))		30,300
Investments – associate (w (iii))		11,400
– other ((26,000 – 13,600 – 10,000 – 1,000 intra-group loan note))		1,400
		46,700
Current assets (15,000 + 8,000 – 1,000 (w (iv)) – 1,500 current account)	20,500	
Creditors: amounts falling due within one year (10,000 + 3,500 – 1,500 current account)	(12,000)	
Net current assets		8,500
Total assets less current liabilities		55,200
Creditors: amounts falling due after more than one year		
8% Loan note	(4,000)	
10% Loan note (2,000 – 1,000 intra-group)	(1,000)	(5,000)
		50,200
Capital and reserves:		
Equity shares of £1 each		10,000
Reserves:		
Profit and loss account (w (v))		37,640
		47,640
Minority interest (w (vi))		2,560
		50,200

Workings in £'000

(i)	Tangible fixed assets		
	Pumice		20,000
	Silverton		8,500
	Fair value – land	400	
	– plant	1,600	2,000
	Additional depreciation (see below)		(200)
			30,300

The fair value adjustment to plant will create additional depreciation of £400,000 per annum (1,600/4 years) and in the post acquisition period of six months this will be £200,000.

(ii)	Goodwill in Silverton:		
	Investment at cost		13,600
	Less – equity shares of Silverton (3,000 x 80%)	(2,400)	
	– pre-acquisition reserves (7,000 x 80% (see below))	(5,600)	
	– fair value adjustments (2,000 (w (i)) x 80%)	(1,600)	(9,600)
	Goodwill on consolidation		4,000

Goodwill amortisation will be £4,000/5 years x 6/12 =		400
The pre-acquisition reserves are:		
At 31 March 2006		8,000
Post acquisition (2,000 x 6/12)		(1,000)
		7,000

(iii) Purchase of Amok

Cost of investment (1,600 x £6.25)			10,000
Less			
Net assets at 1 October 2005:			
Equity 31 March 2006	24,000		
Profit 1 October 2005 to 31 March 2006 (8,000 x 6/12)	(4,000)		
	20,000	x 40%	(8,000)
Goodwill			2,000
Carrying amount at 31 March 2006			
Cost			10,000
Share post acquisition profit (8,000 x 6/12 x 40%)			1,600
Less goodwill amortisation (2,000/5 years x 6/12)			(200)
Carrying amount			11,400

(iv) The unrealised profit (URP) in stock is calculated as:

Intra-group sales are £6 million of which Pumice made a profit of £2 million. Half of these are still in stock, thus there is an unrealised profit of £1 million.

(v) Consolidated reserves:

Pumice's reserves		37,000
Silverton's post acquisition (((2,000 x 6/12) - 200 depreciation) x 80%)		640
Amok's post acquisition profits (8,000 x 6/12 x 40%)		1,600
URP in stock (see (iv))		(1,000)
Goodwill amortisation (w (ii)) – Silverton	400	
(w (iii)) – Amok	200	(600)
		37,640

(vi) Minority interest

Equity shares of Silverton (3,000 x 20%)	600
Profit and loss reserve ((8,000 – 200 depreciation) x 20%)	1,560
Fair value adjustments (2,000 x 20%)	400
	2,560

2 (a) Kala – Profit and loss account – Year ended 31 March 2006

	£'000	£'000
Turnover		278,400
Cost of sales (w (i))		(115,700)
Gross profit		162,700
Operating expenses		(15,500)
Operating profit		147,200
Investment income – property rental		4,500
Finance costs – loan (w (ii))	(3,000)	
– lease (w (iii))	(7,000)	(10,000)
Profit on ordinary activities before tax		141,700
Taxation (28,300 + (14,100 – 12,500))		(29,900)
Profit for the financial year		111,800

(b) Kala – Statement of movement in share capital and reserves – Year ended 31 March 2006

	Equity shares £'000	Investment property resv £'000	Land and building revln reserve £'000	Profit and loss account £'000	Total £'000
At 1 April 2005	150,000	7,000	nil	112,500	269,500
Profit for period (see (a))				111,800	111,800
Revaluation (w (iv))		6,300	45,000		51,300
Equity dividends paid				(15,000)	(15,000)
At 31 March 2006	150,000	13,300	45,000	209,300	417,600

(c) Kala – Balance sheet as at 31 March 2006

	£'000	£'000
Tangible fixed assets		
Land and buildings (w (iv))	250,000	
Plant (w (iv))	184,100	434,100
Investment properties (90,000 + (90,000 x 7%))		96,300
		530,400
Current assets		
Stock	43,200	
Trade debtors	53,200	
	96,400	
Creditors: amounts falling due within one year		
Trade creditors	33,400	
Accrued loan interest (w (ii))	1,000	
Bank overdraft	5,400	
Lease obligation (w (iii)) – accrued interest	7,000	
– capital	15,000	
Corporation tax	28,300	
	(90,100)	
Net current assets		6,300
Total assets less current liabilities		536,700
Creditors: amounts falling due after more than one year		
8% loan note	(50,000)	
Lease obligation (w (iii))	(55,000)	(105,000)
Provisions for liabilities		
Deferred tax		(14,100)
		417,600
Capital and reserves (see (b) above):		
Equity shares of £1 each		150,000
Reserves:		
Revaluation reserves – land and buildings	45,000	
– Investment property	13,300	
Profit and loss account	209,300	267,600
		417,600

Workings in brackets in £'000

(i)   Cost of sales:

	£'000
Opening stock	37,800
Purchases	78,200
Depreciation (w (iv)) – buildings	5,000
– plant: owned	19,500
leased	18,400
Closing stock	(43,200)
	115,700

(ii) The loan has been in issue for nine months. The total finance cost for this period will be £3 million (50,000 x 8% x 9/12). Kala has paid six months interest of £2 million, thus accrued interest of £1 million should be provided for.

(iii) Finance lease:

	£'000
Net obligation at inception of lease (92,000 – 22,000)	70,000
Accrued interest 10% (current liability)	7,000
Total outstanding at 31 March 2006	77,000

The second payment in the year to 31 March 2007 (made on 1 April 2006) of £22 million will be £7 million for the accrued interest (at 31 March 2006) and £15 million paid of the capital outstanding. Thus the amount outstanding as an obligation over one year is £55 million (77,000 – 22,000).

(iv) Fixed assets/depreciation:
Land and buildings:
At the date of the revaluation the land and buildings have a carrying amount of £210 million (270,000 – 60,000). With a valuation of £255 million this gives a revaluation surplus (to reserves) of £45 million. The accumulated depreciation of £60 million represents 15 years at £4 million per annum (200,000/50 years) and means the remaining life at the date of the revaluation is 35 years. The amount of the revalued building is £175 million, thus depreciation for the year to 31 March 2006 will be £5 million (175,000/35 years). The carrying amount of the land and buildings at 31 March 2006 is £250 million (255,000 – 5,000).

Plant: owned
The carrying amount prior to the current year's depreciation is £130 million (156,000 – 26,000). Depreciation at 15% on the reducing balance basis gives an annual charge of £19.5 million. This gives a carrying amount at 31 March 2006 of £110.5 million (130,000 – 19,500).

Plant: leased
The fair value of the leased plant is £92 million. Depreciation on a straight-line basis over five years would give a depreciation charge of £18.4 million and a carrying amount of £73.6 million.

The carrying amount of all plant in the balance sheet at 31 March 2006 is therefore £184.1 million (110,500 + 73,600)

3 (a) Note: figures in the calculations are in £million

Return on year end capital employed	32.3 %	220/(550 + 130) x 100
Net assets turnover	5.9 times	4,000/680
Gross profit margin	13.8 %	(550/4,000) x 100
Net profit (before tax) margin	5.0 %	(200/4,000) x 100
Current ratio	1.3:1	610:480
Closing stock holding period	26 days	250/3,450 x 365
Debtors' collection period	44 days	360/(4,000 – 1,000) x 365
Creditors' payment period (based on cost of sales)	45 days	(430/3,450) x 365
Dividend yield	6.0%	(see below)
Dividend cover	1.67 times	150/90

The dividend per share is 22.5p (90,000/(100,000 x 4 i.e. 25p shares). This is a yield of 6.0% on a share price of £3.75.

(b) Analysis of the comparative financial performance and position of Reactive for the year ended 31 March 2006

Profitability
The measures taken by management appear to have been successful as the overall ROCE (considered as a primary measure of performance) has improved by 15% (32.3 -28.1)/28.1). Looking in more detail at the composition of the ROCE, the reason for the improved profitability is due to increased efficiency in the use of the company's assets (asset turnover), increasing from 4 to 5.9 times (an improvement of 48%). The improvement in the asset turnover has been offset by lower profit margins at both the gross and net level. On the surface, this performance appears to be due both to the company's strategy of offering rebates to wholesale customers if they achieve a set level of orders and also the beneficial impact on sales revenue of the advertising campaign. The rebate would explain the lower gross profit margin, and the cost of the advertising has reduced net profit margin (presumably management expected an increase in sales volume as a compensating factor). The decision to buy complete products rather than assemble them in house has enabled the disposal of some plant which has reduced the asset base. Thus possible increased sales and a lower asset base are the cause of the improvement in the asset turnover which in turn, as stated above, is responsible for the improvement in the ROCE.

The effect of the disposal needs careful consideration. The profit (before tax) includes a profit of £40 million from the disposal. As this is a 'one-off' profit, recalculating the ROCE without its inclusion gives a figure of only 23.7% (180m/(550m + 130m + 80m (the 80m is the carrying amount of plant)) and the fall in the net profit percentage (before tax) would be down even more to only 4.0% (160m/4,000m). On this basis the current year performance is worse than that of the previous year and the reported figures tend to flatter the company's real underlying performance.

BPP
LEARNING MEDIA

Liquidity
The company's liquidity position has deteriorated during the period. An acceptable current ratio of 1.6 has fallen to a worrying 1.3 (1.5 is usually considered as a safe minimum). With the debtors collection period at virtually a constant (45/44 days), the change in liquidity appears to be due to the levels of stock and trade creditors. These give a contradictory picture. The closing stock holding period has decreased markedly (from 46 to 26 days) indicating more efficient stock holding. This is perhaps due to short lead times when ordering bought in products. The change in this ratio has reduced the current ratio, however the creditors' payment period has decreased from 55 to 45 days which has increased the current ratio. This may be due to different terms offered by suppliers of bought in products.

Importantly, the effect of the plant disposal has generated a cash inflow of £120 million, and without this the company's liquidity would look far worse.

Investment ratios
The current year's dividend yield of 6.0% looks impressive when compared with that of the previous year's yield of 3.75%, but as the company has maintained the same dividend (and dividend per share as there is no change in share capital), the 'improvement' in the yield is due to a falling share price. Last year the share price must have been £6.00 to give a yield of 3.75% on a dividend per share of 22.5 pence. It is worth noting that maintaining the dividend at £90 million from profits of £150 million gives a cover of only 1.67 times whereas on the same dividend last year the cover was 2 times (meaning last year's profit (after tax) was £180 million).

Conclusion
Although superficially the company's profitability seems to have improved as a result of the directors' actions at the start of the current year, much, if not all, of the apparent improvement is due to the change in supply policy and the consequent beneficial effects of the disposal of plant. The company's liquidity is now below acceptable levels and would have been even worse had the disposal not occurred. It appears that investors have understood the underlying deterioration in performance as there has been a marked fall in the company's share price.

(c) It is generally assumed that the objective of stock market listed companies is to maximise the wealth of their shareholders. This in turn places an emphasis on profitability and other factors that influence a company's share price. It is true that some companies have other (secondary) aims such as only engaging in ethical activities (eg not producing armaments) or have strong environmental considerations. Clearly by definition not-for-profit organisations are not motivated by the need to produce profits for shareholders, but that does not mean that they should be inefficient. Many areas of assessment of profit oriented companies are perfectly valid for not-for-profit organisations: efficient stock holdings, tight budgetary constraints, use of key performance indicators, prevention of fraud etc.

There are a great variety of not-for-profit organisations; eg public sector health, education, policing and charities. It is difficult to be specific about how to assess the performance of a not-for-profit organisation without knowing what type of organisation it is. In general terms an assessment of performance must be made in the light of the stated objectives of the organisation. Thus for example in a public health service one could look at measures such as treatment waiting times, increasing life expectancy etc, and although such organisations don't have a profit motive requiring efficient operation, they should nonetheless be accountable for the resources they use. Techniques such as 'value for money' and the three Es (economy, efficiency and effectiveness) have been developed and can help to assess the performance of such organisations.

4 (a) Relevance
Information has the quality of relevance when it can influence users' economic decisions on a timely basis. It helps to evaluate past, present and future events by confirming, or perhaps correcting, past evaluations of economic events. There are many ways of interpreting and applying the concept of relevance, for example, only material information is considered relevant as, by definition, information is material only if its omission or misstatement could influence users. Other common aspects of relevance are the debate as to whether current value information is more relevant than that based on historical cost. An interesting emphasis placed on relevance within the Statement is that relevant information assists in the predictive ability of financial statements. That is not to say the financial statements should be predictive in the sense of forecasts, but that (past) information should be presented in a manner that assists users to assess an entity's ability to take advantage of opportunities and react to adverse situations. A good example of this is the separate presentation of discontinued operations in the profit and loss account. From this users will be better able to assess the parts of the entity that will produce future profits (the continuing operations) and users can judge the merits of the discontinuation ie has the entity sold a profitable part of the business (which would lead users to question why), or has the entity acted to curtail the adverse affect of a loss-making operation.

Reliability
The Statement states that for information to be useful it must be reliable. The quality of reliability is described as being free from material error (accurate) and representing faithfully that which it purports to portray (ie the financial statements are a faithful representation of the entities' underlying transactions). There can be occasions where the legal form of a transaction can be engineered to disguise the economic reality of the transaction. A cornerstone of faithful representation is that transactions must be accounted for according to their substance (ie commercial intent or economic reality) rather than their legal or contrived form. To be reliable information must be free from deliberate or systematic bias (ie it is neutral). Biased information attempts to influence users (to perhaps come to a predetermined decision) by the manner in which it is presented. It is recognised that financial statements cannot be absolutely accurate due to inevitable uncertainties surrounding their preparation. A typical example would be estimating the useful economic lives of fixed assets. This is addressed by the use of prudence which is the exercise of a degree of caution in matters of uncertainty. However, prudence cannot be used to deliberately understate profit

or create excessive provisions (this would break the neutrality principle). Reliable information must also be complete; omitted information (that should be reported) will obviously mislead users.

Comparability

Comparability is fundamental to assessing an entity's performance. Users will compare an entity's results over time and also with other similar entities. This is the principal reason why financial statements contain corresponding amounts for previous period(s). Comparability is enhanced by the use (and disclosure) of consistent accounting policies such that users can confirm that comparative information (for calculating trends) is comparable and the disclosure of accounting policies at least informs users if different entities use different policies. That said, comparability should not stand in the way of improved accounting practices (usually through new Standards); it is recognised that there are occasions where it is necessary to adopt new accounting policies if they enhance relevance and reliability.

(b)   (i)   This item involves the characteristic of reliability and specifically the use of substance over form. As the lease agreement is for substantially the whole of the asset's useful economic life, Porto will experience the same risks and rewards as if it owned the asset. Although the legal form of this transaction is a rental, its substance is the equivalent to acquiring the asset and raising a loan. Thus, in order for the financial statements to be reliable (and comparable to those where an asset is bought from the proceeds of a loan), the transaction should be shown as an asset on Porto's balance sheet with a corresponding liability for the future lease rental payments. The profit and loss account should be charged with depreciation on the asset and a finance charge on the 'loan'.

         (ii)   This item involves the characteristic of comparability. Changes in accounting policies should generally be avoided in order to preserve comparability. Presumably the directors have good reason to believe the new policy presents a more reliable and relevant view. In order to minimise the adverse effect a change in accounting policy has on comparability, the financial statements (including the corresponding amounts) should be prepared on the basis that the new policy had always been in place (retrospective application). Thus the assets (retail outlets) should include the previously expensed finance costs and profit and loss accounts will no longer show a finance cost (in relation to these assets whilst under construction). Any finance costs relating to periods prior to the policy change (ie for two or more years ago) should be adjusted for by increasing profits brought forward in the profit and loss reserve (equity).

         (iii)   This item involves the characteristic of relevance. This situation questions whether historical cost accounting is more relevant to users than current value information. Porto's current method of reporting these events using purely historical cost based information (ie showing an operating loss, but not reporting the increases in property values) is perfectly acceptable. However, the company could choose to revalue its hotel properties (which would subject it to other requirements). This option would still report an operating loss (probably an even larger loss than under historical cost if there are increased depreciation charges on the hotels), but the increases in value would also be reported (in equity) arguably giving a more complete picture of performance.

5   **(a)**   The correct timing of when revenue (and profit) should be recognised is an important aspect of a profit and loss account showing a true and fair view. Only realised profits should be included in the profit and loss account. For most types of supply and sale of goods it is generally accepted that a profit is realised when the goods have been manufactured (or obtained) by the supplier and satisfactorily delivered to the customer. The issue with long-term contracts is that the process of completing the project takes a relatively long time and, in particular, will spread across at least one accounting period-end. If such contracts are treated like most sales of goods, it would mean that revenue and profit would not be recognised until the contract is completed (the "completed contracts" basis). This is often described as following the prudence concept. The problem with this approach is that it may not show a true and fair view as all the profit on a contract is included in the period of completion, whereas in reality (a true and fair view), it is being earned, but not reported, throughout the duration of the contract. SSAP 9 remedies this by requiring the recognition of profit on uncompleted contracts in proportion to some measure of the percentage of completion applied to the estimated total contract profit. This is sometimes said to reflect the accruals concept, but it should only be applied where the outcome of the contract is reasonably foreseeable. In the event that a loss on a contract is foreseen, the whole of the loss must be recognised immediately, thereby ensuring the continuing application of prudence.

(b) **Beetie**

Profit and loss account	Contract 1 £'000	Contract 2 £'000	Total £'000
Turnover	3,300	840	4,140
Cost of sales (balancing figure)	(2,400)	(890)	(3,290)
Attributable profit/(loss) (see working)	900	(50)	850

Balance sheet

Stock: long-term contract balances

	Contract 1 £'000	Contract 2 £'000	Total £'000
Costs to date	3,900	720	4,620
Transferred to cost of sales	(2,400)	(720)	(3,120)
	1,500	nil	1,500

Debtors: amounts recoverable

	Contract 1 £'000	Contract 2 £'000	Total £'000
Turnover	3,300		3,300
Payments on account	(3,000)		(3,000)
	300		300

Creditors: amounts falling due within one year

	Contract 1 £'000	Contract 2 £'000	Total £'000
Payments on account (880 – 840)		40	40
Provisions			
Cost incurred and losses to date (890 – 720)		170	170

Workings in £'000:

Estimated total profit:

	Contract 1 £'000	Contract 2 £'000
Agreed contract price	5,500	1,200
Estimated contract cost	(4,000)	(1,250)
Estimated total profit/(loss)	1,500	(50)

Percentage complete:

Work certified at 31 March 2006	3,300
Contract price	5,500
Percentage complete at 31 March 2006 (3,300/5,500 x 100)	60%
Profit to 31 March 2006 (60% x 1,500)	900

At 31 March 2006 the increase in the expected total costs of contract 2 mean that a loss of £50,000 is expected on this contract. In these circumstances, regardless of the percentage completed, the whole of this loss should be recognised immediately.

Pilot Paper F7 (UK)
Financial Reporting (United Kingdom)

Marking Scheme

This marking scheme is given as a guide in the context of the suggested answers. Scope is given to markers to award marks for alternative approaches to a question, including relevant comment, and where well-reasoned conclusions are provided. This is particularly the case for written answers where there may be more than one acceptable solution.

1	**(a)**	1 mark per relevant point	**5**
	(b)	Balance sheet:	
		goodwill	3½
		tangible fixed assets	2½
		investments – associate	3
		– other	1
		current assets	2
		creditors – 1 year	1
		8% loan notes	½
		10% loan notes	1
		equity shares	1
		profit and loss account	3
		minority interest	1½
			20
		Total for question	**25**

2	**(a)**	Profit and loss account	
		turnover	½
		cost of sales	4½
		operating expenses	½
		investment income	½
		finance costs	1½
		taxation	1½
			9
	(b)	Movement in share capital and reserves	
		brought forward figures	1
		profit for period	1
		revaluation gains	2
		dividends paid	1
			5
	(c)	Balance sheet	
		land and buildings	2
		plant and equipment	2
		investment property	1
		stocks and trade debtors	1
		trade creditors and overdraft	1
		accrued interest	½
		lease obligation: interest and capital one year	1
		capital over one year	1
		corporation tax provision	½
		8% loan	½
		deferred tax	½
			11
		Total for question	**25**

3	**(a)**	one mark per ratio		10
	(b)	1 mark per valid point	maximum	10
	(c)	1 mark per valid point	maximum	5
			Total for question	25
4	**(a)**	3 marks each for relevance, reliability and comparability		9
	(b)	2 marks for each transaction ((i) to (iii)) or event		6
			Total for question	15
5	**(a)**	one mark per valid point to	maximum	4
	(b)	turnover (½ mark for each contract)		1
		profit/loss (½ mark for each contract)		1
		stocks		1
		debtors		1
		payment on account		1
		provision		1
				6
			Total for question	10

Part 2 Examination – Paper 2.5(GBR)
Financial Reporting (UK Stream)

June 2006 Answers

1   (a)   Hydan
Consolidated profit and loss account year ended 31 March 2006

	£'000	£'000
Turnover (98,000 + 35,200 – 30,000 intra-group sales)		103,200
Cost of sales (w (i))		(77,500)
Gross profit		25,700
Operating expenses (11,800 + 8,000 + 375 goodwill (w (ii)))		(20,175)
Interest receivable (350 – 200 intra-group (4,000 x 10% x 6/12))		150
Interest payable		(420)
Profit before tax		5,255
Taxation (4,200 – 1,000 tax relief)		(3,200)
Profit after tax		2,055
Minority interest (w (iv))		1,400
Profit for the financial year		3,455

Consolidated balance sheet as at 31 March 2006

	£'000	£'000
Intangible fixed assets:		
Goodwill (3,000 – 375 (w (ii)))		2,625
Tangible fixed assets (18,400 + 9,500 + 1,200 – 300 depreciation adjustment)		28,800
Investments (16,000 – 10,800 – 4,000 loan)		1,200
		32,625
Current assets (w (v))	24,000	
Creditors: amounts falling due within one year (w (v))	(14,300)	9,700
Total assets less current liabilities		42,325
Creditors: amounts falling due after more than one year		
7% bank loan		(6,000)
Minority interest (w (iv))		(3,800)
		32,525
Capital and reserves:		
Ordinary shares of £1 each		10,000
Reserves:		
Share premium	5,000	
Profit and loss account (w (iii))	17,525	22,525
		32,525

Workings in £'000

(i)   Cost of sales

Hydan	76,000
Systan	31,000
Intra-group sales	(30,000)
URP in stock	200
Additional depreciation re fair values	300
	77,500

(ii)   Goodwill/Cost of control in Systan:

Investment at cost (2,000 x 60% x £9)		10,800
Less – ordinary shares of Systan	2,000	
– share premium	500	
– pre-acquisition reserves (6,300 + 3,000 post acq loss)	9,300	
– fair value adjustment	1,200	
	13,000 x 60%	(7,800)
Goodwill on consolidation		3,000
Goodwill amortisation will be £3,000/4 x 6/12 =		375

(iii) Consolidated reserves:

Hydan's reserves		20,000
Systan's post acquisition losses (see below) (3,500 x 60%)		(2,100)
Goodwill amortisation (w (ii))		(375)
		17,525

The adjusted profits of Systan are:		
Per question		6,300
Adjustments — URP in stock (4,000 x 5%)	(200)	
– additional depreciation	(300)	(500)
		5,800

(iv) Minority interest in profit and loss account

Systan's post acquisition loss after tax	3,000
Adjustments from (w (iii))	500
Adjusted losses	3,500 x 40% = 1,400

Minority interest in balance sheet	
Ordinary shares and premium of Systan	2,500
Adjusted profits (w (iii))	5,800
Fair value adjustments	1,200
	9,500 x 40% = 3,800

(v) Current assets and creditors payable within one year

Current assets:	
Hydan	18,000
Systan	7,200
URP in stock	(200)
Intra-group balance	(1,000)
	24,000

Creditors payable within one year:	
Hydan	11,400
Systan	3,900
Intra-group balance	(1,000)
	14,300

(b) Although Systan's revenue has increased since its acquisition by Hydan, its operating performance appears to have deteriorated markedly. Its gross profit margin has fallen from 25% (6m/24m) in the six months prior to the acquisition to only 11·9% (4·2m/35·2m) in the post-acquisition period. The decline in gross profit is worsened by a huge increase in operating expenses in the post-acquisition period. These have gone from £1·2 million pre-acquisition to £8 million post-acquisition. Taking into account the effects of interest and tax a £3·6 million first half profit (pre-acquisition) has turned into a £3 million second half loss (post-acquisition). Whilst it is possible that some of the worsening performance may be due to market conditions, the major cause is probably due to the effects of the acquisition. As the question states Hydan has acquired a **controlling** interest in Systan and thus the two companies are related parties. Since the acquisition most of Systan's sales have been to Hydan. This is not surprising as Systan was acquired to secure supplies to Hydan. The terms under which the sales are made are now determined by the management of Hydan, whereas they were previously determined by the management of Systan. The question says sales to Hydan yield a consistent gross profit of only 5%. This is very low and much lower than the profit margin on sales to Hydan prior to the acquisition and also much lower than the few sales that were made to third parties in the post acquisition period. It may also be that Hydan has shifted the burden of some of the group operating expenses to Systan – this may explain the large increase in Systan's post acquisition operating expenses. The effect of these (transfer pricing) actions would move profits from Systan's books into those of Hydan. The implications of this are quite significant. Initially there may be a tendency to think the effect is not important as on consolidation both companies' results are added together, but other parties are affected by these actions. The most obvious is the significant (40%) minority interest, they are effectively having some of their share of Systan's profit and balance sheet value taken from them. It may also be that the management and staff of Systan may be losing out on profit related bonuses. Finally, any party using Systan's entity financial statements, for whatever purpose, would be basing any decisions they make on potentially misleading information.

2 **(a)** Darius profit and loss account for the year ended 31 March 2006

	£'000	£'000
Turnover (w (i))		221,800
Cost of sales (w (i))		(156,200)
Gross profit		65,600
Operating expenses		(22,400)
Investment income		1,200
Loss on investment property (w (ii))		(700)
Profit on ordinary activities before interest		43,700
Finance costs (5,000 – 3,200 ordinary dividend (w (v))		(1,800)
Profit before tax		41,900
Taxation (w (iii))		(6,400)
Profit for the financial year		35,500

(b) Statement of total recognised gains and losses for the year ended 31 March 2006

	£'000
Profit for the financial year	35,500
Unrealised surplus on land and building	21,000
Unrealised deficit on investment property	(1,800)
Total gains and losses recognised since the last annual report	54,700

(c) Darius balance sheet as at 31 March 2006

	£'000	£'000
Tangible fixed assets		
Land and buildings (63,000 – 3,200 (48,000/15 years))	59,800	
Plant and equipment (w (iv))	27,300	87,100
Investment property (w (ii))		13,500
		100,600
Current assets		
Stock (10,500 – 300 (w (i)))	10,200	
Trade debtors (13,500 + 1,500 JV)	15,000	
	25,200	
Creditors: amounts falling due within one year		
Trade creditors (11,800 + 2,500 JV)	14,300	
Bank overdraft	900	
Taxation	8,000	
	(23,200)	
Net current assets		2,000
Total assets less current liabilities		102,600
Creditors: amounts falling due after more than one year		
10% Redeemable preference shares of £1 each		(10,000)
Provisions for liabilities		
Deferred tax (w (iii))		(3,600)
		89,000
Capital and reserves:		
Ordinary shares of 25p each		20,000
Reserves:		
Revaluation reserve	21,000	
Profit and loss reserve (w (v))	48,000	69,000
		89,000

Workings in £'000

(i) Sales

Per question	213,800
Joint venture revenue	8,000
	221,800

Cost of sales:	
Per question	143,800
Closing stock adjustment (see below)	300
Joint venture costs	5,000
Depreciation – building (48,000/15 years)	3,200
– plant (w (iv))	3,900
	156,200

The damaged stocks will require expenditure of £450,000 to repair them and then have an expected selling price of £950,000. This gives a net realisable value of £500,000, as their cost was £800,000, a write down of £300,000 is required.

(ii) SSAP 19 *Accounting for investment properties* requires investment properties to be included in the balance sheet at their open market value with any surplus or deficit going to a revaluation reserve. However, the overall balance on the investment property revaluation reserve cannot be negative. Thus the fall in current period of £2·5 million (16m – 13·5m) will first be applied to the balance in the investment property revaluation reserve of £1·8m and the remaining £700,000 must be written off to the profit and loss account.

(iii) Taxation:

Provision for year	8,000
Deferred tax (see below)	(1,600)
	6,400

Accelerated capital allowances are £12 million. At a rate of 30% this would require a balance sheet provision for deferred tax of £3·6 million. The opening provision is £5·2 million, thus a credit of £1·6 million will be made in the profit and loss account.

(iv) **Plant and equipment**

	Plant
Per trial balance	36,000
Joint venture plant	12,000
	48,000
Accumulated depreciation 1 April 2005	(16,800)
Carrying amount prior to charge for year	31,200
Depreciation year ended 31 March 2006 at 12·5%	(3,900)
Carrying amount at 31 March 2006	27,300

(v) Profit and loss reserve

Balance b/f	15,700
Profit for period	35,500
Ordinary dividends paid (20,000 x 4 x 4p)	(3,200)
	48,000

Note: preference shares that are redeemable have the substance of debt and under FRS 25 *Financial instruments: disclosure and presentation* the preference dividend should be treated as a finance cost and the share capital itself should be treated as a creditor.

3 **(a)** The purpose of the Statement is to assist the various bodies and users that may be interested in the financial statements of an entity. It is there to assist the ASB (the Board) itself, preparers, auditors and users of financial statements and any other party interested in the work of the Board. More specifically:

- the primary purpose is to assist the Board by providing a coherent frame of reference to be used in the development of new and the review of existing standards
- this should ensure standards (and other pronouncements) are developed consistently by reducing the need to debate fundamental issues (such as whether an item is an asset or a liability) each time a standard is produced
- the Statement will help preparers to understand the Board's approach and thus enable them to apply accounting standards more effectively. Additionally the Statement should help preparers in dealing with new or emerging issues which are, as yet, not covered by an accounting standard
- the above is also true of the work of the auditor, in particular the Statement can assist the auditor in determining whether the financial statements conform to accounting standards. The Statement contributes to the development of the true and fair concept which is of prime importance to the auditor.

It is important to realise that the Statement is not itself an accounting standard and thus cannot override the requirements of a specific standard. Because of this the Statement does not contain requirements on how financial statements should be prepared. Indeed, the Board recognises that there may be occasions where a particular accounting standard is in conflict with the Statement. In these cases the requirements of the standard should prevail. The Board believes that such conflicts will diminish over time as the development of new and the revision of existing standards will be guided by the Statement and the Statement itself may be revised based on the experience of working with it.

(b) Definitions – assets:
The Statement defines assets as 'rights or other access to future economic benefits controlled by an entity as a result of past transactions or events'. The definition puts the emphasis on control rather than ownership. This is done so that the balance sheet reflects the substance of transactions rather than their legal form. This means that assets that are not legally owned by an entity, but over which the entity has the rights that are normally conveyed by ownership are recognised as assets of the entity. Common examples of this would be finance leased assets and other contractual rights such as aircraft landing rights. An important aspect of control of assets is that it allows the entity to restrict the access of others to them. The reference to past events prevents assets that may arise in future from being recognised early.

– liabilities:
The Statement defines liabilities as 'obligations of an entity to transfer economic benefits as a result of past transactions or events'. Many aspects of this definition are complementary (as a mirror image) to the definition of assets. However, the Statement stresses that the essential characteristic of a liability is that the entity has an obligation, which is interpreted as being unable to avoid the future outflow of resources to settle it. Such obligations are usually legally enforceable (by a binding contract or by statute), but obligations also arise where there is an expectation (by a third party) of an entity to assume responsibility for costs where there is no legal requirement to do so. Such obligations are referred to as constructive obligations (by FRS 12 *Provisions, contingent liabilities and contingent assets*). An example of this would be repairing or replacing faulty goods (beyond any warranty period) or incurring environmental costs (e.g. landscaping the site of a previous quarry) where there is no legal obligation to do so. Where entities do incur constructive obligations it is usually to maintain the goodwill and reputation of the entity. One area of difficulty is where entities cannot be sure whether an obligation exists or not, as it may depend upon a future uncertain event. These are more generally known as contingent liabilities.

Importance of the definitions of assets and liabilities:
The definitions of assets and liabilities are fundamental to the Statement. Apart from forming the obvious basis for the preparation of a balance sheet, they are also the two elements of the financial statements that are used to derive the other elements. Equity (ownership) interest is the residue of assets less liabilities. Gains and losses are changes in ownership interests, other than contributions from, and distributions to, the owners. In effect, a gain is an increase in an asset or a reduction of a liability whereas a loss is the reverse of this. Transactions with owners are excluded from the definitions of gains and losses. Gains and losses should be recognised when there is sufficient evidence of a new asset or liability (or an increase in an existing asset or liability) and they can be measured at a monetary amount with sufficient reliability.

Currently there is a great deal of concern over 'off balance sheet finance'. This is an aspect of what is commonly referred to as creative accounting. Many recent company failure scandals have been in part due to companies having often massive liabilities that have not been included on the balance sheet. Robust definitions, based on substance, of assets and liabilities in particular should ensure that only real assets are included on the balance sheet and all liabilities are also included. In contradiction to the above point, there have also been occasions where companies have included liabilities on their balance sheets where they do not meet the definition of liabilities in the Statement. Common examples of this are general provisions and accounting for future costs and losses (usually as part of the acquisition of a subsidiary). Companies have used these general provisions to smooth profits i.e. creating a provision when the company has a good year (in terms of profit) and releasing it to boost profits in a bad year. Providing for future costs and losses during an acquisition may effectively allow them to bypass the profit and loss account as they would become part of the goodwill figure.

(c) **(i)** Whilst it is acceptable to value the goodwill of £2·5 million of Trantor (the subsidiary) on the basis described in the question and include it in the consolidated balance sheet, the same treatment cannot be afforded to Peterlee's own goodwill. The calculation may indeed give a realistic value of £4 million for Peterlee's goodwill, and there may be no difference in nature between the goodwill of the two companies, but it must be realised that the goodwill of Peterlee is internal goodwill and accounting standards prohibit such goodwill appearing in the financial statements. The main basis of this conclusion is one of reliable measurement. The value of acquired (purchased) goodwill can be evidenced by the method described in the question (there are also other acceptable methods), but this method of valuation is not acceptable as a basis for recognising internal goodwill.

(ii) Accruing for future costs such as this landscaping on an annual basis may seem appropriate and was common practice until recently. However, it is no longer possible to account for this type of future cost in this manner, therefore the directors' suggestion is unacceptable. FRS 12 *Provisions, contingent liabilities and contingent assets* requires such costs to be accounted for in full as soon as they become unavoidable. The Standard says that the estimate of the future cost should be discounted to a present value (as in this example at £2 million). The accounting treatment is rather controversial; the cost should be included in the balance sheet as a provision (a credit entry/balance), but the debit is to the cost of the asset to give an initial carrying amount of £8 million. This has the effect of 'grossing up' the balance sheet by including the landscaping costs as both an asset and a liability. As the asset is depreciated on a systematic basis (£800,000 per annum assuming straight-line depreciation), the landscaping costs are charged to the profit and loss account over the life of the asset. As the discount is 'unwound' (and charged as a finance cost) this is added to the balance sheet provision such that, at the date when the liability is due to be settled, the provision is equal to the amount due (assuming estimates prove to be accurate).

(iii) The directors' suggestion that the convertible loan should be recorded as a liability of the full £5 million is incorrect. The reason why a similar loan without the option to convert to equity shares (such that it must be redeemed by cash only) carries a higher interest rate is because of the value of the equity option that is contained within the issue proceeds of the £5 million. If the company performs well over the period of the loan, the value of its equity shares should rise and thus it would (probably) be beneficial for the loan note holders to opt for the equity share alternative. FRS 25 *Financial instruments: disclosure and presentation* and FRS 26 *Financial instruments: measurement* require that the value of the option is to be treated as equity rather than debt. The calculation of value of the equity is as follows:

	£'000
Year 1 400 x 0·91	364
Year 2 400 x 0·83	332
Year 3 5,400 x 0·75	4,050
Present value of the cash flows	4,746
Proceeds of issue	(5,000)
Difference is value of equity	254

Initially the loan would be shown at £4,746,000.

The profit and loss account would show:

	£'000	£'000
Loan interest paid (£5m x 8%)	400	
Accrued finance costs (balance)	75	475 (i.e. £4·746m x 10%)

At 31 March 2006 the loan would have a carrying amount of £4,821,000 (£4,746,000 + £75,000)

4   (a)   Boston – Cash Flow Statement for the year ended 31 March 2006:

Reconciliation of operating profit to net cash inflow from operating activities

Note: figures in brackets are in £'000	£'000	£'000
Operating profit per question		75
Adjustments for:		
depreciation of fixed assets	35	
loss on sale of hotel	12	47
		122
increase in current assets (155 – 130)		(25)
decrease in other current liabilities (115 – 108)		(7)
Net cash flow from operating activities		90

Cash Flow Statement		
Net cash flow from operating activities (above)		90
Servicing of finance: interest paid		(10)
Taxation paid		(30)
Capital expenditure:		
purchase of fixed assets (see below)	(123)	
sale of fixed assets (40 – 12)	28	(95)
Cash outflow before financing		(45)
Financing:		
Issue of ordinary shares (20 + 20)	40	
Issue of loans (65 – 40)	25	65
Increase in cash (15 + 5)		20

Workings	£'000
Fixed assets – carrying amount	
Balance b/f	332
Disposal	(40)
Depreciation for year	(35)
Balance c/f	(380)
Cost of assets acquired	(123)

(b)   Report on the financial performance of Boston for the year ended 31 March 2006

To: The Board of Boston
From: A N Other
Date:

Profitability (note figures are rounded to 1 decimal place)
The most striking feature of the current year's performance is the deterioration in the ROCE, down from 25·6% to only 18·0%. This represents an overall fall in profitability of 30% ((25·6 – 18·0)/25·6 x 100). An examination of the other ratios provided shows that this is due to a decline in both profit margins and asset utilisation. A closer look at the profit margins shows that the decline in gross margin is relatively small (42·2% down to 41·4%), whereas the fall in the operating profit margin is down by 2·8%, this represents a 15·7% decline in profitability (i.e. 2·8% on 17·8%). This has been caused by increases in operating expenses of £12m and unallocated common costs of £10m. These increases represent more than half of the net profit for the period and further investigation into the cause of these increases should be made. The company is generating only £1·20 of sales per £1 of net balance sheet assets this year compared to a figure of £1·40 in the previous year. This decline in asset utilisation represents a fall of 14·3% ((1·4 – 1·2)/1·4 x 100).

Liquidity/solvency
From the limited information provided a poor current ratio of 0·9:1 in 2005 has improved to 1·3:1 in the current year. Despite the improvement, it is still below the accepted norm. At the same time gearing has increased from 12·8% to 15·6%. Information from the cash flow statement shows the company has raised £65 million in new capital (£40m in equity and £25m in loans). The disproportionate increase in the loans is the cause of the increase in gearing, however, at 15·6% this is still not a highly geared company. The increase in finance has been used mainly to purchase new fixed assets, but it has also improved liquidity, mainly by reversing an overdraft of £5 million to a bank balance in hand of £15 million.

A common feature of new investment is that there is often a delay between making the investment and benefiting from the returns. This may be the case with Boston, and it may be that in future years the increased investment will be rewarded with higher returns. Another aspect of the investment that may have caused the lower return on assets is that the investment is likely to have occurred part way through the year (maybe even near the year end). This means that the profit and loss account may not include returns for a full year, whereas in future years it will.

Segment issues
Segment information is intended to help the users to better assess the performance of an enterprise by looking at the detailed contribution made by the differing activities that comprise the enterprise as a whole. Referring to the segment ratios it appears that the carpeting segment is giving the greatest contribution to overall profitability achieving a 48·6% return on its segment assets, whereas the equivalent return for house building is 38·1% and for hotels it is only 16·7%. The main reason for the better return from carpeting is due to its higher segment net profit margin of 38·9% compared to hotels at 15·4% and house building at 28·6%. Carpeting's higher segment net profit is in turn a reflection of its underlying very high gross margin (66·7%). The segment net asset turnover of the hotels (1·1 times) is also very much lower than the other two segments (1·3 times). It seems that the hotel segment is also responsible for the group's fairly poor liquidity ratios (ignoring the bank balances) the segment current liabilities are 50% greater than its current assets (£60m compared to £40m); the opposite of this would be a more acceptable current ratio.

These figures are based on historical values. Most commentators argue that the use of fair values is more consistent and thus provides more reliable information on which to base assessments (they are less misleading than the use of historical values). If fair values are used all segments understandably show lower returns and poorer performance (as fair values are higher than historic values), but the figures for the hotels are proportionately much worse, falling by a half of the historical values (as the fair values of the hotel segment are exactly double the historical values). Fair value adjusted figures may even lead one to question the future of the hotel activities. However, before jumping to any conclusions an important issue should be considered. Although the reported profit of the hotels is poor, the market values of its segment assets have increased by a net £90 million. New net investment in hotel capital expenditure is £64 million (£104m – £40m disposal); this leaves an increase in value of £26 million. The majority of this appears to be from market value increases (this would be confirmed if the statement of total recognised gains and losses was available). Whilst this is not a realised profit, it is nevertheless a significant and valuable gain (equivalent to 65% of the group reported net profit).

Conclusion
Although the company's overall performance has deteriorated in the current year, it is clear that at least some areas of the business have had considerable new investment which may take some time to bear fruit. This applies to the hotel segment in particular and may explain its poor performance, which is also partly offset by the strong increase in the market value of its assets.

Yours A N other

Appendix

Further segment ratios	Carpeting	Hotels	House building
Return on net assets at fair values (35/97 x 100)	36·1%	8·3%	30·2%
Asset turnover on fair values (times) (90/97)	0·9	0·5	1·1

Note: workings have been shown for the figures for the carpeting segment only, the other segments' figures are based on equivalent calculations.

5　(a)　Profit and loss account for the year ended 31 March 2006

	Alfa £m	Beta £m	Ceta £m	Total £m
Turnover	8	2·0	4·8	14·8
Cost of sales	(7)	(3·5)	(4·0)	(14·5)
Profit/(loss)	1	(1·5)	0·8	0·3

Balance sheet as at 31 March 2006

		Alfa	Beta	Ceta	Total
Long-term contract balance	(12·5 – 11·5)	1·0	nil	nil	1·0
Amounts recoverable on contracts	(14 – 12·6)	1·4　(2 – 1·8)	0·2	4·8	6·4
Provision for losses charged to cost of sales			(1·5)		(1·5)

Workings (in £m):

Alfa	at 31 March 2005	at 31 March 2006	Year ended 31 March 2006
Work invoiced (5·4/90%)	6·0	(12·6/90%)　14·0	8
Cost of sales (balancing figure)	(4·5)	(11·5)	(7)
Profit (see below)	1·5	2·5	1
Percentage complete (6/20 x 100)	30%	(14/20 x 100)　70%	
Attributable profit (£5m x 30%)	1·5	((£5m x 70%) – £1m rectification)　2·5	

Prior to the rectification costs (which must be charged to the year in which they are incurred), the estimated profit on the contract is £5 million (£20m – £15m).

BPP
LEARNING MEDIA

Beta

Due to the increase in the estimated cost Beta is a loss-making contract and the whole of the loss must be provided for as soon as it is can be anticipated. The loss is expected to be £1·5 million (£7·5m – £6m). The sales value of the contract at 31 March 2006 is £2 million (£1·8/90%), thus the cost of sales must be recorded as £3·5 million. As costs to date are £2 million, this means a provision of £1·5 million is required.

Ceta

Based on the costs to date at 31 March 2006 of £4 million and the total estimated costs of £10 million, this contract is 40% complete. The estimated profit is £2 million (£12m – £10m); therefore the profit at 31 March 2006 is £0·8 million (£2m x 40%). This gives an imputed sales (and debtor) value of £4·8 million.

(b) **(i)**   Savoir – EPS year ended 31 March 2004:

The issue on 1 July 2003 at full market value needs to be weighted:

	40m x 3/12 =	10m
New shares	8m	
	48m x 9/12 =	36m
		46m

Without the bonus issue this would give an EPS of 30p (£13·8m/46m x 100).

The bonus issue of one for four would result in 12 million new shares giving a total number of ordinary shares of 60 million. The dilutive effect of the bonus issue would reduce the EPS to 24p (30p x 48m/60m).
The comparative EPS (for 2003) would be restated at 20p (25p x 48m/60m).

EPS year ended 31 March 2005:

The rights issue of two for five on 1 October 2004 is half way through the year. The theoretical ex rights value can be calculated as:

Holder of	100 shares worth £2·40 =	£240	
Subscribes for	40 shares at £1 each =	£40	
Now holds	140 worth (in theory)	£280	i.e. £2 each.

Weighting:

	60m x 6/12 x 2·40/2·00 =	36 million
Rights issue (2 for 5)	24m	
New total	84m x 6/12 =	42 million
Weighted average		78 million

EPS is therefore 25p (£19·5m/78m x 100).
The comparative (for 2004) would be restated at 20p (24p x 2·00/2·40).

(ii)   The basic EPS for the year ended 31 March 2006 is 30p (£25·2m/84m x 100).

Dilution

Convertible loan stock
On conversion loan interest of £1·2 million after tax would be saved (£20 million x 8% x (100% – 25%)) and a further 10 million shares would be issued (£20m/£100 x 50).

Directors' options
Options for 12 million shares at £1·50 each would yield proceeds of £18 million. At the average market price of £2·50 per share this would purchase 7·2 million shares (£18m/£2·50). Therefore the 'bonus' element of the options is 4·8 million shares (12m – 7·2m).

Using the above figures the diluted EPS for the year ended 31 March 2006 is 26·7p (£25·2m + £1·2m)/(84m + 10m + 4·8m)).

Part 2 Examination – Paper 2.5(GBR)
Financial Reporting (UK Stream)

December 2006 Answers

1 (a) Cost of control in Sunlee:

	£'000	£'000
Consideration		
Shares (20,000 x 80% x 3/5 x £5)		48,000
Less		
Equity shares	20,000	
Pre acq reserves	18,000	
Fair value adjustments (4,000 + 3,000 + 5,000)	12,000	
	50,000 x 80%	(40,000)
Goodwill at date of acquisition		8,000

(b) Carrying amount of Amber 30 September 2006:

	£'000	£'000
Net assets other than goodwill ((50,000 – 20,000) x 40%)		12,000
Goodwill (see below)		9,500
Carrying amount at 30 September 2006		21,500
Goodwill		
Cost of investment		
Cash (6,000 x £4)		24,000
Less		
Net assets at 1 July 2005:		
Equity 1 October 2005	50,000	
Losses to date of acquisition (20,000 x 9/12)	(15,000)	
	35,000 x 40%	(14,000)
Goodwill		10,000
Amortisation (see (c) below)		(500)
Goodwill at 30 September 2006		9,500

(c) Hosterling Group
Consolidated profit and loss account for the year ended 30 September 2006

	£'000	£'000
Turnover (105,000 + 62,000 – 18,000 intra group)		149,000
Cost of sales (see working)		(89,000)
Gross profit		60,000
Distribution costs (4,000 + 2,000)		(6,000)
Administrative expenses (7,500 + 7,000)		(14,500)
Goodwill amortisation (see below)		(1,600)
Group operating profit		37,900
Share of loss from associate (24,000 x 3/12 x 40%)	(2,400)	
Amortisation associate's goodwill (see below)	(500)	(2,900)
		35,000
Finance costs (1,200 + 900)		(2,100)
Profit before tax		32,900
Taxation – Group (8,700 + 2,600)	(11,300)	
– Associate (4,000 x 3/12 x 40%)	400	(10,900)
Profit after tax		22,000
Minority Interest ((13,000 – 1,000 depreciation adjustment) x 20%)		(2,400)
Profit for the financial year		19,600

Note: the dividend from Sunlee is eliminated on consolidation.
Goodwill amortisation for year ended 30 September 2006 is:
 Sunlee – £1·6 million (8m/5 years)
 Amber – £500,000 (10m/5 years x 3/12).

Working	£'000
Cost of sales	
Hosterling	68,000
Sunlee	36,500
Intra group purchases	(18,000)
Additional depreciation of plant (5,000/5years)	1,000
Unrealised profit in stock (7,500 x 25%/125%)	1,500
	89,000

2 (a) Tadeon – Profit and loss account – Year to 30 September 2006

	£'000	£'000
Turnover		277,800
Cost of sales (w (i))		(144,000)
Gross profit		133,800
Operating expenses (40,000 + 1,200 (w (ii)))		(41,200)
Investment income		2,000
Finance costs – finance lease (w (ii))	(1,500)	
– loan (w (iii))	(2,750)	(4,250)
Profit before tax		90,350
Tax (38,000 – 1,200)) (w (iv))		(36,800)
Profit for the period		53,550

(b) Tadeon – Balance Sheet as at 30 September 2006

	£'000	£'000
Fixed assets		
Tangible fixed assets (w (v))		299,000
Investments at amortised cost		42,000
		341,000
Current assets		
Stock	33,300	
Trade debtors	53,500	
	86,800	
Creditors: amounts falling due within one year		
Trade creditors	18,700	
Accrued lease finance costs (w (ii))	1,500	
Finance lease obligation (w (ii))	4,500	
Bank overdraft	1,900	
Corporation tax payable (w (iv))	38,000	
	(64,600)	
Net current assets		22,200
Creditors: amounts falling due after more than one year		
2% Loan note (w (iii))	51,750	
Finance lease obligation (w (ii))	10,500	(62,250)
Provisions for liabilities		
Deferred tax (w (iv))		(14,800)
		286,150
Share capital and reserves:		
Equity shares of 20 pence fully paid (w (vi))		200,000
Reserves		
Share premium (w (vi))	28,000	
Revaluation reserve (w (v))	16,000	
Profit and loss account (w (vii))	42,150	86,150
		286,150

Workings (note workings figures in brackets are in £'000)

(i)	Cost of sales:	£'000
	Per trial balance	118,000
	Depreciation (12,000 + 5,000 + 9,000) (w (v))	26,000
		144,000

(ii) Vehicle rentals/finance lease:
The total amount of vehicle rentals is £6·2 million of which £1·2 million are operating lease rentals and £5 million is identified as finance lease rentals. The operating rentals have been included in operating expenses.

	£'000
Finance lease	
Fair value of vehicles	20,000
First rental payment – 1 October 2005	(5,000)
Capital outstanding to 30 September 2006	15,000
Accrued interest 10% (current liability)	1,500
Total outstanding 30 September 2006	16,500

In the year to 30 September 2007 (i.e. on 1 October 2006) the second rental payment of £6 million will be made, of this £1·5 million is for the accrued interest for the previous year, thus £4·5 million will be a capital repayment. The remaining £10·5 million (16,500 – (4,500 + 1,500)) will be shown as a creditor payable after more than one year.

(iii) Although the loan has a nominal (coupon) rate of only 2%, amortisation of the large premium on redemption, gives an effective interest rate of 5·5% (from question). This means the finance charge to the profit and loss account will be a total of £2·75 million (50,000 x 5·5%). As the actual interest paid is £1 million an accrual of £1·75 million is required. This amount is added to the carrying amount of the loan in the balance sheet.

(iv) Tax and deferred tax

The profit and loss account charge is made up as follows:	£'000
Current year's provision	38,000
Deferred tax (see below)	(1,200)
	36,800

There are £74 million of deductible temporary differences at 30 September 2006. With a corporation tax rate of 20%, this would require a deferred tax liability of £14·8 million (74,000 x 20%). The tax on the sale of the leasehold property will be £4 million (£20m x 20%). This forms a part of the deferred tax liability at 30 September 2006. Therefore £4 million must be transferred to deferred tax and debited to the property revaluation reserve. The effect of deferred tax on the profit and loss account is therefore a credit of £1·2 million (14,800 – 4,000 – 12,000 b/f).

(v) Fixed assets/depreciation:
Non-leased plant
This has a carrying amount of £96 million (181,000 – 85,000) prior to depreciation of £12 million at $12\frac{1}{2}\%$ reducing balance to give a carrying amount of £84 million at 30 September 2006.

The leased vehicles will be included in fixed assets at their fair value of £20 million and depreciated by £5 million (four years straight-line) for the year ended 30 September 2006 giving a carrying amount of £15 million at that date.

The 25 year leasehold property is being depreciated at £9 million per annum (225,000/25 years). Prior to its revaluation on 30 September 2006 there would be a further year's depreciation charge of £9 million giving a carrying amount of £180 million (225,000 – (36,000 + 9,000)) prior to its revaluation to £200 million. Thus £20 million would be transferred to a revaluation reserve. The question says the revaluation gives rise to £20 million of deductible temporary differences, at a tax rate of 20%, this would give a credit to deferred tax of £4 million which is debited to the revaluation reserve to give a net balance of £16 million. Summarising:

	cost/valuation £'000	accumulated depreciation £'000	carrying amount £'000
25 year leasehold property	200,000	nil	200,000
Non-leased plant	181,000	97,000	84,000
Leased vehicles	20,000	5,000	15,000
	401,000	102,000	299,000

(vi) Suspense account

The called up share capital of £150 million in the trial balance represents 750 million shares (150m/0·2) which have a market value at 1 October 2005 of £600 million (750m x 80 pence). A yield of 5% on this amount would require a £30 million dividend to be paid.

A fully subscribed rights issue of one new share for every three shares held at a price of 32p each would lead to an issue of 250 million (150m/0·2 x 1/3). This would yield a gross amount of £80 million, and after issue costs of £2 million, would give a net receipt of £78 million. This should be accounted for as £50 million (250m x 20p) to equity share capital and the balance of £28 million to share premium.

The receipt from the share issue of £78 million less the payment of dividends of £30 million reconciles the suspense account balance of £48 million.

(vii)

Profit and loss account	£'000
At 1 October 2005	18,600
Year to 30 September 2006	53,550
less dividends paid (w (vi))	(30,000)
	42,150

3 **(a)** Most forms of off balance sheet financing have the effect of what is, in substance, debt finance either not appearing on the balance sheet at all or being netted off against related assets such that it is not classified as debt. Common examples would be structuring a lease such that it fell to be treated as an operating lease when it has the characteristics of a finance lease, complex financial instruments classified as equity when they may have, at least in part, the substance of debt and 'controlled' entities having large borrowings (used to benefit the group as a whole), that are not consolidated because the financial structure avoids the entities meeting the definition of a subsidiary.

The main problem of off balance sheet finance is that it results in financial statements that do not faithfully represent the transactions and events that have taken place. This may mean that they show a 'true' view (in a legal sense), but not a 'fair' view. Reflecting the substance of transactions is an important qualitative characteristic of useful information (as described in the *Statement of principles for financial reporting* and FRS 5 *Reporting the substance of transactions*). Failure to reflect the commercial substance of transactions will mean that the financial statements lack reliability. A lack of reliability may mean that any decisions made on the basis of the information contained in financial statements are likely to be incorrect or, at best, sub-optimal.

The level of debt on a balance sheet is a direct contributor to the calculation of an entity's balance sheet gearing, which is considered as one of the most important financial ratios. It should be understood that, to a point, the use of debt financing is perfectly acceptable. Where balance sheet gearing is considered low, borrowing is relatively inexpensive, often tax efficient and can lead to higher returns to shareholders. However, when the level of borrowings becomes high, it increases risk in many ways. Off balance sheet financing may lead to a breach of loan covenants (a serious situation) if such debt were to be recognised on the balance sheet in accordance with its substance.

High gearing is a particular issue to equity investors. Equity (ordinary shares) is sometimes described as residual return capital. This description identifies the dangers (to equity holders) when an entity has high gearing. The dividend that the equity shareholders might expect is often based on the level of reported profits. The finance cost of debt acts as a reduction of the profits available for dividends. As the level of debt increases, higher interest rates are also usually payable to reflect the additional risk borne by the lender, thus the higher the debt the greater the finance charges and the lower the profit. Many off balance sheet finance schemes also disguise or hide the true finance cost which makes it difficult for equity investors to assess the amount of profits that will be needed to finance the debt and consequently how much profit will be available to equity investors. Furthermore, if the market believes or suspects an entity is involved in 'creative accounting' (and off balance sheet finance is a common example of this) it may adversely affect the entity's share price.

An entity's level of gearing will also influence any decision to provide further debt finance (loans) to the entity. Lenders will consider the nature and value of the assets that an entity owns which may be provided as security for the borrowings. The presence of existing debt will generally increase the risk of default of interest and capital repayments (on further borrowings) and existing lenders may have a prior charge on assets available as security. In simple terms if an entity has high borrowings, additional borrowing is more risky and consequently more expensive. A prospective lender to an entity that already has high borrowings, but which do not appear on the balance sheet is likely to make the wrong decision. If the correct level of borrowings were apparent, either the lender would not make the loan at all (too high a lending risk) or, if it did make the loan, it would be on substantially different terms (e.g. charge a higher interest rate) so as to reflect the real risk of the loan.

Some forms of off balance sheet financing may specifically mislead suppliers that offer credit. It is a natural precaution that a prospective supplier will consider the balance sheet strength and liquidity ratios of the prospective customer. The existence of consignment stock may be particularly relevant to trade suppliers. Sometimes consignment stock, and its related current liabilities, are not recorded on the balance sheet as the wording of the purchase agreement may be such that the legal ownership of the goods remains with the supplier until specified events occur (often the onward sale of the goods). This means that other suppliers cannot accurately assess an entity's trade creditors and consequently the average creditor payment period, both of which are important determinants in deciding whether to grant credit.

(b) (i) Debt factoring is a common method of companies releasing the liquidity of their trade debtors. The accounting issue that needs to be decided is whether the trade debtors have been sold, or whether the income from the finance house for their 'sale' should be treated as a short term loan. The main substance issue with this type of transaction is to identify which party bears the risks (i.e. of slow and non-payment by the customer) relating to the asset. If the risk lies with the finance house (Omar), the trade debtors should be removed from the balance sheet (derecognised in accordance with FRS 5 and FRS 26). In this case it is clear that Angelino still bears the risk relating to slow and non-payment. The residual payment by Omar depends on how quickly the debtors are collected; the longer it takes, the less the residual payment (this imputes a finance cost). Any balance uncollected by Omar after six months will be refunded by Angelino which reflects the non-payment risk.

Thus the correct accounting treatment for this transaction is that the cash received from Omar (80% of the selected debtors) should be treated as a current liability (a short term loan). A 'linked' presentation is not appropriate as Omar may be repaid from Angelino's other assets (say if the level of bad debts were very high). The difference between the gross trade debtors and the amount ultimately received from Omar (plus any amounts directly from the trade debtors themselves) should be charged to the profit and loss account. The classification of the charge is likely to be a mixture of administrative expenses (for Omar collecting debtors), finance expenses (reflecting the time taken to collect the debtors) and bad debt charges.

(ii) This is an example of a sale and leaseback of a property. Such transactions are part of normal commercial activity, often being used as a way to improve cash flow and liquidity. However, if an asset is sold at an amount that is different to its fair value there is likely to be an underlying reason for this. In this case it appears (based on the opinion of the auditor) that Finaid has paid Angelino £2 million more than the building is worth. No (unconnected) company would do this knowingly without there being some form of 'compensating' transaction. This sale is 'linked' to the five year rental agreement. The question indicates the rent too is not at a fair value, being £500,000 per annum (£1,300,000 – £800,000) above what a commercial rent for a similar building would be.

It now becomes clear that the excess purchase consideration of £2 million is an 'in substance' loan (rather than sales proceeds – the legal form) which is being repaid through the excess (£500,000 per annum) of the rentals. Although this is a sale and leaseback transaction, as the building is freehold and has an estimated remaining life (20 years) that is much longer than the 5 year leaseback period, the lease is not a finance lease and the building should be treated as sold and thus derecognised.

The correct treatment for this item is that the sale of the building should be recorded at its fair value of £10 million, thus the profit on disposal would be £2·5 million (£10 million – £7·5 million). The 'excess' of £2 million (£12 million – £10 million) should be treated as a loan (long-term liability). The rental payment of £1·3 million should be split into three elements; £800,000 building rental cost, £200,000 finance cost (10% of £2 million) and the remaining £300,000 is a capital repayment of the loan.

(iii) The treatment of consignment stock depends on the substance of the arrangements between the manufacturer and the dealer (Angelino). The main issue is to determine if and at what point in time the cars are 'sold'. The substance is determined by analysing which parties bear the risks (e.g. slow moving/obsolete stock, finance costs) and receive the benefits (e.g. use of stock, potential for higher sales, protection from price increases) associated with the transaction.

Supplies from Monza
Angelino has, and has actually exercised, the right to return the cars without penalty (or been required by Monza to transfer them to another dealer), which would indicate that it has not 'bought' the cars. There are no finance costs incurred by Angelino, however Angelino would suffer from any price increases that occurred during the three month holding/display period. These factors seem to indicate that the substance of this arrangement is the same as its legal form i.e. Monza should include the cars in its balance sheet as stock and therefore Angelino will not record a purchase transaction until it becomes obliged to pay for the cars (three months after delivery or until sold to customers if sooner).

Supplies from Capri
Although this arrangement seems similar to the above, there are several important differences. Angelino is bearing the finance costs of 1% per month (calling it a display charge is a distraction). The option to return the cars should be ignored because it is not likely to be exercised due to commercial penalties (payment of transport costs and loss of deposit). Finally the purchase price is fixed at the date of delivery rather than at the end of six months. These factors strongly indicate that Angelino bears the risks and rewards associated with ownership and should recognise the stock and the associated liability in its financial statements at the date of delivery.

4 (a) Cash Flow Statement of Minster for the Year ended 30 September 2006:
Reconciliation of operating profit to net cash inflow from operating activities

	£'000	£'000
Operating profit		162
Adjustments for:		
Depreciation of tangible fixed assets	255	
Amortisation of software (180 - 135)	45	300
		462
Working capital adjustments		
Decrease in stock (510 – 480)	30	
Decrease in debtors (380 – 270)	110	
Increase in amounts due from long-term contracts (80 – 55)	(25)	
Decrease in trade creditors (555 – 350)	(205)	(90)
Net cash inflow from operating activities		372

Cash Flow Statement for Minster year ended 30 September 2006

		£'000
Net cash inflow from operating activities		372
Returns on investments and servicing of finance (note 1)		(23)
Taxation (w (ii))		(54)
Capital expenditure (note 1)		(600)
Equity dividends paid (500 x 4 x 5 pence)		(100)
Cash outflow before use of liquid resources and financing		(405)
Financing (note 1)		385
Decrease in cash (35 – (40 – 25))		(20)

Note 1
Returns on investment and servicing of finance

	£'000	£'000
Investment income received (20 – 15 gain on investments)	5	
Finance costs paid (40 – 12 re unwinding of environmental provision)	(28)	(23)
Capital expenditure		
Purchase of – tangible fixed assets (w (i))	(410)	
– software	(180)	
– investments (150 – (15 + 125))	(10)	(600)
Financing		
Issue of equity shares (w (iii))	265	
Issue of 9% loan note	120	385

Workings (in £'000)

			£'000
(i)	Tangible fixed assets:		
		carrying amount b/f	940
		non-cash environmental provision	150
		revaluation	35
		depreciation for period	(255)
		carrying amount c/f	(1,280)
		difference is cash acquisitions	(410)
(ii)	Taxation:		
		tax provision b/f	(50)
		deferred tax b/f	(25)
		profit and loss account charge	(57)
		provision c/f	60
		deferred tax c/f	18
		difference is cash paid	(54)

BPP
LEARNING MEDIA

	£'000
(iii) Equity shares	
balance b/f	(300)
bonus issue (1 for 4)	(75)
balance c/f	500
difference is cash issue	125
Share premium	
balance b/f	(85)
bonus issue (1 for 4)	75
balance c/f	150
difference is cash issue	140

Therefore the total proceeds of cash issue of shares are £265,000 (125 + 140).

(b) Report on the financial position of Minster for the year ended 30 September 2006

To:
From:
Date:

Operating cash flows:
Minster shows healthy cash inflows of £372,000 from operating activities. This is considered by many commentators as a very important figure as it is often used as the basis for estimating the company's future maintainable cash flows. Subject to (inevitable) annual expected variations and allowing for any changes in the company's structure this figure is more likely to be repeated in the future than most other figures in the cash flow statements which are often 'one-off' cash flows such as raising loans or purchasing fixed assets. The operating cash inflow compares well with the underlying operating profit of £162,000. This is mainly due to depreciation charges of £300,000 being added back to the profit as they are a non-cash expense. The operating cash inflow of £372,000 together with the reduction in net working capital of £90,000 is more than sufficient to cover the company's taxation payments of £54,000, finance payments of £28,000 and the dividend of £100,000 and leaves an amount to contribute to the funding of the increase in fixed assets. It is important that these short term costs are funded from operating cash flows; it would be of serious concern if, for example, interest or tax payments were having to be funded by loan capital or the sale of fixed assets.

There are a number of points of concern. The dividend of £100,000 gives a dividend cover of less than one (85/100 = 0·85) which means the company has distributed previous year's profits. This is not a tenable situation in the long-term. The size of the dividend has also contributed to the lower cash balances (see below). There is less investment in both stock levels and trade debtors. This may be the result of more efficient stock control and better collection of debtors, but it may also indicate that trading volumes may be falling. Also of note is a large reduction in trade creditor balances of £205,000. This too may be indicative of lower trading (i.e. less stock purchased on credit) or pressure from suppliers to pay earlier. Without more detailed information it is difficult to come to a conclusion in this matter.

Capital expenditure:
The cash flow statement shows considerable investment in fixed assets, in particular £410,000 in tangible fixed assets. These acquisitions represent an increase of 44% of the carrying amount of the tangible fixed assets as at the beginning of the year. As there are no disposals, the increase in investment must represent an increase in capacity rather than the replacement of old assets. Assuming that this investment has been made wisely, this should bode well for the future (most analysts would prefer to see increased investment rather than contraction in operating assets). An unusual feature of the required treatment of environmental provisions is that the investment in fixed assets as portrayed by the cash flow statement appears less than if balance sheet figures are used. The balance sheet at 30 September 2006 includes £150,000 of fixed assets (the discounted cost of the environmental provision), which does not appear in the cash flow figures as it is not a cash 'cost'. A further consequence is that the 'unwinding' of the discounting of the provision causes a financing expense in the profit and loss account which is not matched in the cash flow statement as the unwinding is not a cash flow. Many commentators have criticised the required treatment of environmental provisions because they cause financing expenses which are not (immediate) cash costs and no 'loans' have been taken out. Viewed in this light, it may be that the information in the cash flow statement is more useful than that in the profit and loss account and balance sheet.

Financing:
The increase in total capital expenditure of £600,000 has been largely funded by an issue of shares at £265,000 and raising a 9% £120,000 loan note. This indicates that the company's shareholders appear reasonably pleased with the company's past performance (or they would not be very willing to purchase further shares). The interest rate of the loan at 9% seems quite high, and virtually equal to the company's overall return on capital employed of 9·1% (162/(1,660 + 120)). Provided current profit levels are maintained, it should not reduce overall returns to shareholders.

Cash position:
The overall effect of the year's cash flows has worsened the company's cash position by an increased net cash liability of £20,000. Although the company's overdraft has reduced by £15,000, the cash at bank of £35,000 at the beginning of the year has now gone. In comparison to the cash generation ability of the company and considering its large investment in fixed assets, this £20,000 is a relatively small amount and should be relieved by operating cash inflows in the near future.

Summary

The above analysis shows that Minster has invested substantially in new fixed assets suggesting expansion. To finance this, the company appears to have no difficulty in attracting further long-term funding. At the same time there are indications of reduced stock, trade debtors and creditors which may suggest the opposite i.e. contraction. It may be that the new investment is a change in the nature of the company's activities (e.g. mining) which has different working capital characteristics. The company has good operating cash flow generation and the slight deterioration in short term net cash balance should only be temporary.

Yours ....

5 (a) (i) FRS 3 Reporting financial performance defines discontinued operations as those that are sold or terminated and satisfy all of the following conditions:

(i) the sale or termination is completed within the year or up to a maximum of three months after the year end

(ii) the activities have ceased permanently

(iii) the discontinuation has a material effect on the nature and focus of the operations and represents a material reduction in operating facilities either by withdrawing from a particular market (whether class of business or geographical) or from continuing operations.

(iv) the assets, liabilities, operating results and activities are clearly distinguishable, physically, operationally and for financial reporting purposes.

The intention of this requirement is to improve the usefulness of the financial statements by improving the predictive value of the (historical) profit and loss account. Clearly the results from discontinued operations should have little impact on future operating results. Thus users would focus on the continuing activities in any assessment of future income and profit. Part of FRS 3's requirements in this area is that new business should be separately disclosed as a sub analysis of continuing operations. Possibly the reason for this is that the comparative figures would not include any amounts for these new activities (this would enable more reliable trend analysis).

The above definition is, at first appearance, rather rigorous and perhaps complex. It is suggested that a precise definition of a discontinued operation is required to avoid 'misleading' reporting. The presumption that analysts and other users will focus on continuing operations, and therefore tend to disregard the results of discontinuing operations may lead some directors to wish to classify loss making operations as discontinued (where they would attract less attention) when they are not. Conversely directors may prefer operations that have been profitable, but are about to be sold, to be included in continuing operations. Taking this to an extreme, all profit making operations would be shown in continuing operations and loss making operations would be shown as discontinuing regardless of which were continuing or discontinuing. The ASB regards such practice as unacceptable, hence the rigorous definition. It should be noted that some company directors have complained that operations that have genuinely been sold or terminated do not meet all the requirements of the definition of a discontinued operation in FRS 3 (in particular relating to part (iv) of the definition above). Consequently they have to be reported in continuing operations which they believe is misleading and contravenes the purpose of the Standard.

(ii) The timing of the board meeting and consequent notifications is within the post balance sheet three month period allowed by FRS 3. The notification to staff, suppliers and the press seems to indicate that the directors are 'demonstrably committed to the termination' and, although the business had not yet been closed down, once it has it will clearly have 'ceased permanently'. From the financial and other information given in the question it appears that the travel agencies are 'clearly distinguishable'. Probably the main issue is with part (iii) of the above definition. The company is still operating in the holiday business; therefore there is no material reduction in a class of business or geographical location. However, there does appear to be a change in the 'nature and focus of the business'. The selling of holidays through the Internet compared with through high-street travel agencies requires very different assets, staff knowledge and training and has a different cost structure. Therefore it would seem the announced closure of the travel agencies would appear to meet the definition of a discontinued operation.

(iii) Partway Profit and loss account for the year ended:

	31 October 2006		31 October 2005	
Turnover	£'000	£'000	£'000	£'000
Continuing operations	23,000		22,000	
Acquisitions	2,000		nil	
	25,000		22,000	
Discontinued operations	14,000	39,000	18,000	40,000
Cost of sales		(36,000)		(32,000)
Gross profit		3,000		8,000
Net operating expenses		(2,600)		(2,000)
Operating profit/(loss)				
Continuing operations	4,000		4,500	
Acquisitions	400		nil	
	4,400		4,500	
Discontinued operations	(4,000)		1,500	
Profit before tax		400		6,000

Note: other presentations are acceptable.

(b) (i) Comparability is one of the principal qualitative characteristics of useful financial information. It is a vital attribute when assessing the performance of an entity over time (trend analysis) and to some extent with other similar entities. For information to be comparable it should be based on the consistent treatment of transactions and events. In effect a change in an accounting policy breaks the principle of consistency and should generally be avoided. That said, FRS 18 *Accounting polices* says that consistency is not an end in itself and there are circumstances where it becomes necessary to change an accounting policy. These are mainly where it is required by a new or revised accounting standard, UITF Abstract or applicable legislation or where the change would result in financial statements giving a fairer presentation (true and fair view) of the entity's results and financial position.

It is important to note that the application of a different accounting policy to transactions or events that are substantially different to existing transactions or events or to transactions or events that an entity had not previously experienced does NOT represent a change in an accounting policy. It is also necessary to distinguish between a change in an accounting policy and a change in an estimation technique.

In an attempt to limit the problem of reduced comparability caused by a change in an accounting policy, FRS 18 (and FRS 3 *Reporting financial performance*) say the general principle is that the financial statements should be prepared as if the new accounting policy had always been in place. This is known as retrospective application. The main effect of this is that both current and comparative financial statements should be restated by applying the new policy to them and adjusting the opening balance of equity in the comparative statements. Any change in accounting policy required by a specific Standard or UITF Abstract should be dealt with under the transitional provisions (if any) of that Standard or Abstract (normally these apply the general rule of retrospective application).

(ii) This issue is one of the timing of when revenue should be recognised in the profit and loss account. This can be a complex issue which involves identifying the transfer of significant risks, reliable measurement, the probability of receiving economic benefits, relevant accounting standards and legislation and generally accepted practice. Applying the general guidance in FRS 5 *Reporting the substance of transactions* (including application note G), the previous policy, applied before cancellation insurance was made a condition of booking, seemed appropriate. At the time the holiday is taken it can no longer be cancelled, all monies would have been received and the flights and accommodation have been provided. There may be some compensation costs involved if there are problems with the holiday, but this is akin to product warranties on normal sales of goods which may be immaterial or provided for based on previous experience of such costs. Payments in advance of the 'delivery' of goods would not normally be a trigger to recognise a sale of goods, they are simply a prepayment. Interpreting this for Partway's transaction would seem to confirm the appropriateness of its previous policy.

The directors of Partway wish to change the timing of recognition of sales because of the change in circumstances relating to the compulsory cancellation insurance. The directors are apparently arguing that the new 'transactions and events' are substantially different to previous transactions therefore the old policy should not apply. Even if this does justify revising the timing of the recognition of sales, it is not a change of accounting policy because of the reasons outlined in (i) above.

An issue to consider is whether compulsory cancellation insurance represents a substantial change to the risks that Partway experiences. An analysis of past experience of losses caused by uninsured cancellations may help to assess this, but even if the past losses were material (and in future they will not be), it is unlikely that this would override the general guidance and accepted accounting policy relating to payments made in advance of delivery. It seems the main motivation for the proposed change is to improve the profit for the year ended 31 October 2006 so that it compares more favourably with that of the previous year.

To summarise, it is unlikely that the imposition of compulsory cancellation insurance justifies recognising sales at the date of booking when a deposit is received, and, even if it did, it would not be a change in accounting policy. This means that comparatives would not be restated (which is something that would actually suit the suspected objectives of the directors).

Review Form & Free Prize Draw – Paper F7 Financial Reporting (UK) (6/07)

All original review forms from the entire BPP range, completed with genuine comments, will be entered into one of two draws on 31 July 2007 and 31 January 2008. The names on the first four forms picked out on each occasion will be sent a cheque for £50.

Name: _____   Address: _____

_____

_____

How have you used this Kit?
(Tick one box only)

☐ Home study (book only)

☐ On a course: college _____

☐ With 'correspondence' package

☐ Other _____

Why did you decide to purchase this Kit?
(Tick one box only)

☐ Have used the complementary Study text

☐ Have used other BPP products in the past

☐ Recommendation by friend/colleague

☐ Recommendation by a lecturer at college

☐ Saw advertising

☐ Other _____

During the past six months do you recall seeing/receiving any of the following?
(Tick as many boxes as are relevant)

☐ Our advertisement in *Student Accountant*

☐ Our advertisement in *Pass*

☐ Our advertisement in *PQ*

☐ Our brochure with a letter through the post

☐ Our website www.bpp.com

Which (if any) aspects of our advertising do you find useful?
(Tick as many boxes as are relevant)

☐ Prices and publication dates of new editions

☐ Information on product content

☐ Facility to order books off-the-page

☐ None of the above

Which BPP products have you used?

Text	☐	Success CD	☐	Learn Online	☐
Kit	☑	i-Learn	☐	Home Study Package	☐
Passcard	☐	i-Pass	☐	Home Study PLUS	☐

Your ratings, comments and suggestions would be appreciated on the following areas.

	Very useful	Useful	Not useful
Passing ACCA exams	☐	☐	☐
Passing F7	☐	☐	☐
Planning your question practice	☐	☐	☐
Questions	☐	☐	☐
Top Tips etc in answers	☐	☐	☐
Content and structure of answers	☐	☐	☐
'Plan of attack' in mock exams	☐	☐	☐
Mock exam answers	☐	☐	☐

Overall opinion of this Kit   Excellent ☐   Good ☐   Adequate ☐   Poor ☐

Do you intend to continue using BPP products?   Yes ☐   No ☐

The BPP author of this edition can be e-mailed at: marymaclean@bpp.com

Please return this form to: Nick Weller, ACCA Publishing Manager, BPP Learning Media Ltd, FREEPOST, London, W12 8BR

Review Form & Free Prize Draw (continued)

TELL US WHAT YOU THINK

Please note any further comments and suggestions/errors below.

Free Prize Draw Rules

1 Closing date for 31 July 2007 draw is 30 June 2007. Closing date for 31 January 2008 draw is 31 December 2007.

2 Restricted to entries with UK and Eire addresses only. BPP employees, their families and business associates are excluded.

3 No purchase necessary. Entry forms are available upon request from BPP Learning Media Ltd. No more than one entry per title, per person. Draw restricted to persons aged 16 and over.

4 Winners will be notified by post and receive their cheques not later than 6 weeks after the relevant draw date.

5 The decision of the promoter in all matters is final and binding. No correspondence will be entered into.